THE BIG DECEPTION

How Psychotherapy and Counseling Really Work

DAVID W. SHAVE

ROBERT E. KRIEGER PUBLISHING COMPANY
MALABAR, FLORIDA
1989

Original Edition 1989

Printed and Published by
ROBERT E. KRIEGER PUBLISHING CO., INC.
KRIEGER DRIVE
MALABAR, FLORIDA 32950

Copyright © 1989 by Robert E. Krieger Publishing Co., Inc.

All rights reserved. No part of this book may be reproduced in any form or
by any means, electronic or mechanical, including information storage and re-
trieval systems without permission in writing from the publisher.
No liability is assumed with respect to the use of the information contained herein.
Printed in the United States of America.

Library of Congress Cataloging-in-Publication Data

Shave, David W., 1931-
    The big deception : how psychotherapy and counseling really work /
by David W. Shave.
    p. cm.
    ISBN 0-89464-339-8 (alk. paper)
    1. Psychotherapy. 2. Counseling. I. Title.
RC480.5.S4449 1989
616.89'14—dc19   88-39726
                                                   CIP

10 9 8 7 6 5 4 3 2

CONTENTS

THE BIG DECEPTION
How Psychotherapy and Counseling Really Work

Foreword

My interest in communication theory began with Little, Brown and Company publishing my THE LANGUAGE OF THE TRANSFER- ENCE twenty years ago. Concepts introduced in this book were contin- ued and expanded when the Robert E. Krieger Publishing Company brought out in 1974 THE THERAPEUTIC LISTENER and the Warren Green Company published COMMUNICATION BREAKDOWN in 1975. PSYCHODYNAMICS OF THE EMOTIONALLY UNCOM- FORTABLE published by the Warren H. Green Publishing Company in 1979 carried these concepts much further. This present book which I hope is more organized, more easily understood and better presented evolves from these previous books. They provide the basis for this book. They all contain the primordial ideas that emerge here as more devel- oped concepts. With permission from the publishers, some case examples and vignettes have been taken or adapted from these earlier publications. Chapters Four and Seventeen for instance contain many favorite ex- amples of mine that I have published earlier. I am particularly indebted to the Warren H. Green Publishing Company and to the Robert E. Krieger Publishing Company for the use of these excerpts. The reader may want to refer to these earlier works to see for himself the evolu- tionary process involved. These past books from which this present one culminates attest to a continued fascination with communication theory. While attempting to advance the knowledge of unconscious psychodyn- amics in communication, what becomes strangely apparent that both providers and consumers of psychotherapy and counseling should rec- ognize is a big deception. This book attempts to uncover that deception.

Introduction

Although psychotherapy is over 100 years old, how it works has remained a mystery to the majority of psychiatrists and psychologists, and whether it works at all is an unanswered question to the rest. The muddled and contradictory theories for the origin and resolution of emotional uncomfortableness have led to confusion among not only its practitioners, but the public as well. Those who advocate a particular school or model of psychotherapy have constructed a "Tower of Babel," so that there is dissension, bickering, and an inability to agree or even communicate with one another. This "tower" has prevented the psychotherapists from presenting to the public one plausible and basic theory for the efficacy of psychotherapy. Many professionals from outside the field feel that psychotherapy is only squandering money from duped people, from a hoodwinked government, and from "conned" insurance companies. Illustrious men of science have gone on record as skeptical of the efficacy of any form of psychotherapy. Even eminent psychiatrists have questioned the scientific basis of psychotherapy and many now see little reason for its existence. Why shouldn't they, when psychotherapy has been facetiously defined as two people talking to each other and therapists likened to leeches? Insurance companies have always been reluctant to fund psychotherapy as they do other treatments and have seriously questioned psychotherapy as an acceptable treatment modality in medicine.

The credibility of psychotherapy and the entire field of counseling has always been challenged because the evidence for its necessity has seemed so confused and so scientifically unsound. It seems that when we have multiple treatments for a problem, we don't know what we're doing. The various forms of psychotherapy and counseling can make anyone wonder if the psychotherapists and counselors really know what they're doing. In a recent study of community mental health centers, it was found that in some of these centers psychotherapy and counseling weren't being given by a psychiatrist, or a psychologist, or a social worker, or even by a nurse, but by former mental patients! It is little wonder that insurance companies have questioned the efficacy and funding of psychotherapy and counseling if so little expertise is necessary. That question of funding has now made it most imperative to determine what psychotherapy or counseling is, how it actually works, what skills are involved, and whether it is really worth the money invested. Psychotherapy and counseling is a two billion dollar a year business in the United States and well over ten percent of the U.S. population can be considered emotionally uncomfortable and in need of some type of help. The benefit of the "talk therapies" has indeed become a pressing national concern, not only to those who fund such therapies, but also to the professionals involved, to those people in the therapies, and to others who are contemplating treatment for their emotional uncomfortableness.

The psychotherapists and counselors haven't progressed very far at all in answering basic questions since Anton Mesmer tried to present the healing power of magnets in 1784, before being ousted from France by the French Academy of Medicine and Science. Like the psychotherapists and counselors of today, he couldn't come up with an acceptable scientific basis for his many cures. Unless a treatment is based on scientific principles, it runs the risk of being removed. Yet, those who practice psychotherapy and counseling know full well that talking can heal, or can harm, and that for it to be therapeutic for the more emotionally uncomfortable person, professional involvement is required. These professionals have seen a multitude of people who were very emotionally uncomfortable become more comfortable. They know too, that without psychotherapy or counseling these people might have been hypochondriacal, and might have joined the millions who seek a resolution of their emotional uncomfortableness in medical and surgical treatments.

The cost of hypochondriasis for the U.S. population in needless and repetitious diagnostic testing, prolonged hospital stays, expensive medical and surgical consultations and treatments is an undetermined billion dollar figure each year. Hypochondriasis manifests itself with imagined and exaggerated illnesses and conditions, and with excessive worrying, overconcern, and preoccupation with health and sickness. The vast majority of it is unrecognized by either the sufferer or the physicians involved. What physicians do recognize as hypochondriasis is only the tip of the iceberg of its true extent. There have been no studies, or call for such studies, to clearly define hypochondriasis, to understand how to recognize or treat it, or to learn how costly it really is to the patients themselves, the government, or insurance companies. When over eighty percent of people who contact a physician, do so primarily for an underlying emotional reason, it is unlikely that the medical profession itself will be of much help in determining the extent and cost of hypochondriasis without some outside prodding.

Where psychiatry once stood alone, unchallenged in its domain, the psychologists, the social workers, and the counselors of a multiplicity of orientations have aggressively staked out territories, with the quacks and charlatans making inroads into areas disputed by the professionals. During the past two decades, there has been a subtle antipsychiatry movement brought on by a number of causes. Psychoanalysis, which once provided accepted explanations, has become mired in an outdated theoretical rut, unacceptable to too many. The fourth largest medical specialty, psychiatry, and particularly community psychiatry, has been unable to define its role, while psychologists, social workers, and counselors have clearly defined theirs to themselves and to the public. The recent explosion, in the past two decades, of a hierarchy of professional subspecialties, as well as cults, fads, and even quackery, in the resolution of emotional uncomfortableness, has complicated psychiatry's endeavor to delineate its role. The multiplicity of widely varying theories of etiology, as well as widely varying proposed treatments, cannot but intensify the confusion, not only among professionals and practitioners, but in the lay public as well.

Someone who is emotionally uncomfortable for whatever reason may purposefully involve himself in some other form of psychotherapy; he may choose one of the many forms of counseling, cults, fads, or outright quackery, and still resolve that emotional uncomfortableness. The concept of "mental illness," as opposed to "normalcy," or of a "sick person" versus a "sick society," has been so ill-defined, and so open to question, even by the psychiatrists themselves, that most individuals can easily exclude themselves from any psychiatric categorization, and seek help elsewhere.

The vacuum of an undefined specialty, like psychiatry, that treats undefined problems, has become filled with narrowly defined specialists of other professions, whose appropriate role and function are more readily seen by the public. They offer specific therapies for specific problems in reality and they do so without an onus that these therapies or the therapists deal with the "crazy," the "deranged," the "unbalanced," the "insane," and the "mentally ill." They simply offer a more acceptable alternative to psychiatric treatment, without the risk of being labeled. People who don't think they are so "bad off" that they need to see a psychiatrist prefer not to waste their time, or the doctor's, with "psychiatric treatment." The specific therapies, for specific problems in reality, are as numerous as those problems in reality. One has only to determine the specific cause in his reality, for the origin of his emotional uncomfortableness, and then seek out the specific therapist or counselor who treats that problem. With a virtual smorgasbord of therapies available that deal with specific problems of reality, one has only to decide what therapy fits best with his determined problem. Like the trend in medicine today to go directly to the medical specialist who treats a specific medical problem, the emotionally uncomfortable person decides, *himself*, what his problem is, and what therapies may work best for him.

Man is an intellectual being who perceives, evaluates and concludes, with intellectual functioning that is logic-oriented. He looks for cause-and-effect-oriented explanations for the origin of his uncomfortableness. If he thinks he knows what is making him emotionally uncomfortable, then he will logically select some type of corrective action he thinks will remedy that problem. If one concludes he has a problem with an inferiority complex, logically he may seek a clinical psychologist's help to learn to overcome his feelings of inadequacy. If one has a specific phobia, she can join a therapy group that specifically deals with that phobia. If one views his emotional uncomfortableness as stemming from a problem with his marriage, he logically may consult a marriage counselor. If one feels that her emotional uncomfortableness is originating in a sexual problem, she may seek the help of a sex counselor. One has only to use his intellect, his reasoning powers, and his logic to decide what his problem is, and then find the specific and often "certified" counselor for that problem. It isn't fitting with "good reality thinking" to look for an illogical explanation, or an illogical resolution, for any uncomfortableness.

The specificity of reality-oriented therapies that logically address themselves to the specific problems of reality has resulted in a profusion of techniques and associated theories. Although these often contradict, and often vary in degree of scientific basis, they all seem to have the potential of working well for some people, but never for all. What might work for one person at one time, may not work at all for the same person at another time. What sustains these therapies is their success in making those who were emotionally uncomfortable more comfortable. What may appear to be quackery, unfounded in a scientific base, ironically may be more beneficial for some people than a form of therapy, unquestionably not quackery, but well-founded on a scientific basis. In this regard, it is interesting to note that the biggest complaint of modern medicine is that in its shift to the scientific, it has lost its art. That art of medicine never rested on any scientific basis, neither does the therapy of the quack or the charlatan, nor the power of the priest, the minister, the rabbi, or the witch doctor to make the emotionally uncomfortable comfortable. They all can work wonders for some, and they all have their staunch adherents and defenders, who will gladly give testimonials for the efficacy of that therapy. When a person *knows* he's been emotionally uncomfortable and *knows* he's become comfortable from involvement in a certain therapy, how can anyone logically dispute the benefit of that therapy?

What makes the problem of determining efficacy even more complex is the added fact that many people who are emotionally uncomfortable become emotionally comfortable *without* any form of psychotherapy, counseling, medical treatment, faith, cultism, or quackery. Problems in the family, or in the marriage, disappear; excessive alcohol intake diminishes; depression lifts; phobias, panic attacks and fears go away; sexual problems are resolved; and people with inferiority, guilt or rejection complexes feel more adequate and more acceptable. Those people who, either at work or at home, were so critical, condemning and fault-finding, and were so difficult if not impossible with whom to get along seem to become nicer with no treatment. Some people, too, seem to remain emotionally comfortable all their lives and don't ever seem to show much emotional uncomfortableness in any of its varied forms and degrees, as others do. How this happens doesn't appear to have any delineated scientific basis either, yet there are many who could give testimonial to the efficacy of "no therapy."

It is only logical that when one can perceive no reason for his uncomfortableness, or his undesirable behavior, in his outer reality, or that environment around him, he concludes that it *must* be arising from his inner reality—that inter-relationship of biochemistry, anatomy, physiology, and neurology within the soma which is so subject to genetic defect, disease, and dysfunction. With this logical conclusion, one can suspect such things as cyclic body biorhythms, or perhaps brain dyssynchrony. It is only logical to consider abnormal variations of blood sugar, thyroxin, aldosterone, estrogen, progesterone, or glucocorticoids or perhaps undetected vitamin insufficiencies that might be producing minute neuro-physiological changes, with profound emotional effects. One who is well-read in the latest scientific advances may logically feel that his uncomfortableness originates in some synaptic dysfunction, altered neuro-endocrinology, limbic lobe irregularities, or elevated platelet monamine oxidase activity.

Psychiatry has come to support this reasoning. With a need for psychiatry to define its role, in the face of burgeoning and threatening specialty therapies for outer reality problems, it has retreated to organic medicine, attempting to insure an undisputed territory of its own. Some now feel in psychiatry's recent discovery of the brain the mind was lost. The shift in psychiatry is away from Freud, and back to Kraepelin, for an explanation of emotional uncomfortableness. Biochemical theories of imbalance, readily accepted, readily funded, and unquestioned, are now in vogue, and are replacing the old psychoanalytic theories of the mind. Such organicity is so "in" that one might well wonder from the recent trend in human behavior research whether psychiatry isn't just an unexplored aspect of neurology. This organic emphasis in psychiatry makes it fashionable for children with behavior problems to be diagnosed as "minimal brain dysfunctional," and for adults with behavior problems as "biochemically unbalanced," when nothing in the outer reality seems to be the cause. When nothing seems different in a person's outer reality, an inner biochemical etiology is logically concluded for the "endogenous depressions" or the "endogenous anxiety attacks." With these diagnoses, neither the person himself, nor his emotionally significant others, need to be blamed.

Dr. Alan A. Stone, Professor of Law and Psychiatry at Harvard University, and a past president of the American Psychiatric Association, urged, in his address to the annual meeting of that association in 1969, that all psychiatrists should become "diligent eclectics" and should guard against the tendency to exalt one model, "school" or theory of practice over another. But to practice eclectically demands an eclectic theory—one that is basic, inclusive, and unifying. If psychotherapy and counseling do work, even if only for a few, there must be some basic eclectic theory to explain it all. It must embody a fundamental formulation of how anyone becomes emotionally uncomfortable, how that emotional uncomfortableness can be resolved through all the possible means, and how emotional comfortableness can be maintained. It must underlie all known theories that have been presented for the origin and resolution of emotional uncomfortableness, clarifying them as myopic dogma, and demonstrating that they have a subtle common denominator beneath their mystique and superficial cloaking. Yet, it must not propose a specific mode of treatment, but only a general theory that can explain any effective technique—scientific, unscientific, or religious—for making those who are emotionally uncomfortable comfortable. It has to be a bio-psycho-social theory, with immense implications and ramifications that will permit an explanation of a profusion of techniques that work for some, and not others. It has become obvious that a biological, or a psychological, or a behavioral, or a social model is inadequate to explain, by itself, all emotional comfortableness and all emotional uncomfortableness. One must conclude that a bio-psycho-social model is more appropriately inclusive and more representative of true actuality, than any individual model. A bio-psycho-social model implies an eclectic theory that encompasses not only all aspects of the biological, the psychological, and the social, but also includes all the aspects and capabilities of the religions, and even quackery, in changing emotional uncomfortableness to comfortableness.

There is no more pressing need in the study of emotional uncomfortableness, in all its varied forms, than to develop such a basic and inclusive dynamic theory. There is no such theory, in any literature, that explains just how the therapeutic effect is made, whether it is in psychotherapy, or counseling, or a form of medical treatment or quackery. The development of a basic eclectic theory for the origin of man's emotional uncomfortableness and its resolution is long overdue, particularly as many psychiatrists, psychologists and counselors, regardless of their formal training, practice eclectically anyway, and have done so for a number of years. In this book, we shall proceed in this necessary endeavor. Without this basic theory that can explain how "talk therapies" work, we can't even begin to solve the problem of appropriate funding.

Cassirer called man "animal symbolicum," and termed this symbolic system as the third and decisive link between the receptor and effector systems that other animals share. This symbolic system is an evolutionary acquisition that comes with higher brain function, and transforms and separates the whole of human life from other forms of life. It makes a world of perceived hard facts secondary, and it can even influence or direct the perception of those facts. But Cassirer might have called man "animal emotionalicum," for that symbolic system is unavoidably an *emotional* one. Man lives in the midst of an inner world of hopes and fears, fantasies and dreams, and emotional misperceptions, misevaluations, and misjudgments. His very thinking and cognitive processes, both conscious and unconscious, are all influenced by this symbolic system, which we can term his *emotional unreality*, composed of an entangled web of personal human experience. Man, the intellectual and logical, is always contradicted by man, the emotional and illogical.

We shall see, in our attempt to determine how psychotherapy and counseling work, that a person doesn't really know what makes him emotionally uncomfortable, and that he doesn't really know what makes him emotionally comfortable, either. He may often *think* he does. There are too often illogical reasons for his degree of comfortableness, which involve his emotional unreality, and not those deceptive logical reasons attributed to his outer and inner reality. In this book we will be forced to make a case against reality. When it doesn't make sense to have so many different theories of etiology and so many different treatments for the emotionally uncomfortable, we must turn to something beyond the obvious or the logical—to something illogical and subtle, which will fit with that emotional unreality that underlies man's inner and outer realities. We must look to that emotional symbolic system, beneath conscious awareness and beyond the world of logic, for our answers. We shall recognize a logic within the illogic, and a scientific basis within the unscientific. Above all, we shall see the deceptions that the intellectual human mind can make.

It will be no simple task to explain how psychotherapy or counseling works, or for that matter, to explain how quackery works either. But to present a scientific understanding of it all is the purpose of this book. We shall see in this endeavor that there is a great complexity of psychodynamics involved when any two people talk to each other. Within this complexity of communication, we will capture an understanding of an elusive entity never before even known to exist. We shall see this entity as a common root to all the varied and contrasting forms of emotional uncomfortableness that deceptively appear in reality to be unrelated. We shall see that this strange entity, which is continually changing in size and shape, has the power to distort one's very perceptions of reality, to subvert intellectual thinking, to determine success and failure, and to produce in man both good and evil. It enhances that special skill of the practicing psychotherapist or counselor to transform emotional uncomfortableness to comfortableness, to know well this awesome entity and to be able to recognize it hiding in its varied forms behind reality.

This book is written specifically for the practicing psychotherapist or counselor, to show the deception that man's conscious mind may make as to the specific causes of his emotional problems and the specific solutions to those problems. This book will reveal the deception that professionals unwittingly practice in accepting reality-oriented explanations for emotional uncomfortableness. Behind these deceptions of etiology and remedy, we will solve the secret of how psychotherapy or counseling really works, understanding better what it is and what it does.

CHAPTER 1
Man's Basic Emotional Need

We are often wisely admonished not to get emotional. We know that when emotional, we can do some pretty foolish things that we may sorely regret later. Although there is a distinct advantage to being cool, calm, and collected, we're just not always that way. In fact, it is interesting to note that we all began life from an act of emotion. Emotions are simply unavoidable in human life. They are important, more so than we would like to acknowledge. And although we would like to credit our intellect with the most basic cause of our behavior, unfortunately, this is not usually the case. It's our emotions that are subtly, and sometimes not so subtly, determining what we do or don't do, what we think and even how we perceive reality. Throughout our lives, we must contend with, suffer, or enjoy the emotional aspects of others. To understand this emotional side of human life, let's start back at the unique stage as a fetus inside the womb.

Before birth, we never experienced hunger pangs or the discomforts associated with waste removal, because these two most basic requirements of biological life are constantly being met through the umbilical cord. The unborn human is totally dependent, but also totally protected. It is cradled in amniotic fluid, effectively cushioned and free of even temperature changes. Perhaps not surprisingly, then, when the newborn leaves this blissful environment and the umbilical cord is severed, he emerges with a cry. No longer is he one with his mother, but now must exist as a separate entity unto himself. Beyond the obvious physical significance of birth in the baby's experience of his environment, there is perhaps an emotional significance—an ominous sign of things to come—in that even the first experience with reality causes a cry.

Now the baby's physiological needs, once continually met inside the womb, must be met through the mothering process. In addition to a need for nourishment, the problem of waste removal shows itself for the first time; diapers must be changed to keep the baby dry and comfortable. There is a need for emotional nourishment as well: a need for human closeness—to be touched and held. One researcher, working with monkeys, has shown that there is a definite need for this emotional mothering in primates, a need for closeness, for being held, cooed to, and rocked. He has demonstrated that monkeys that are given satisfaction of all their physiological needs, while none of the emotional needs are met, don't grow up to be emotionally comfortable monkeys. They are timid and fearful. They don't get along well with other monkeys. Their behavior is different from that of the other monkeys who have been given the emotional closeness of a mothering monkey. Even more so than a monkey, the human infant requires this emotional nourishment.

The infant obviously must depend on others for the meeting of her need for physiological and emotional nourishment. The neonate spends most of her time in contented sleep, oblivious to reality. When she is awakened by her physiological or emotional needs, they are quickly met and the infant goes back to blissful sleep. A pattern then develops in which the infant is awakened by some irritating aspect of reality. Whether it's wetness, coldness, frightening noises, hunger, the sundry discomforts of the cradle, or even a finicky gastro-intestinal system gearing up to work on its own, perhaps varying combinations of them all and more, reality from the beginning of life is essentially an irritating intrusion on blissful sleep. It produces a need for human closeness and caring when the baby is awakened by reality. Upon waking, her needs are met by the mothering process and she then falls back to sleep, where she doesn't have to put up with reality. The psychoanalysts theorize that this feeling of need and its consequent gratification, so closely experienced by the newborn, fosters a feeling of omnipotence and centrality arising from all the attention, care, and love that she receives in early life.

This period of earliest infancy is also a unique time in that the infant is aware only of her needs and that these needs are met as soon as they are experienced. Sleep brings a relief from reality. Never again will the infant be as much the center of attention and as well protected from the vicissitudes of reality as she is in early infancy. Her world, as she perceives it, seems solely to revolve around her. Those analysts theorize that the infant, while awake, has the feeling that she is the most important thing in all the universe.

As the infant grows older, she spends less time in sleep and perceives more of reality. She will experience delays between the time she is awakened by her needs, and the time they are met through the mothering process. She may be frustrated because she is more conscious of her need for nourishment, as well as the problems of waste removal; these needs are not always immediately met by the mothering person or people. Through discomfort, the infant perceives more of reality. She learns that she is not the center of the universe; she may not even be the center of the family. As she becomes more aware of reality, she also recognizes her insignificance in the universe. It becomes more evident that the experience of the need doesn't always bring forth immediate gratification. The feelings of omnipotence and centrality then *must* subside into the unconscious mind because the need to be constantly protected from any irritations, cared for, loved, and to be the center of attention does not fit well with reality.

The part of the mothering process that meets these needs is called, by the psychoanalysts, the "good breast" because the needs are closely associated with the feeding process. The "good breast" provides us with emotional nourishment; it meets our need to be protected, cared for, wanted, needed, and loved. It fosters the feeling of omnipotence and centrality. Because of its affinity with the feeding process, where the mouth is so significant and where dependency is so obvious, the psychoanalysts call this emotional nourishment the *oral dependency need*. The frustrating aspect of the mothering process is the "bad breast." It entails that which doesn't meet the oral dependency need. It thwarts omnipotence and centrality. The "bad breast" is perceived during delays in need gratification, and involves a perceived frustration of that oral dependency need.

The analysts, in trying to understand human emotions, go on to make the sexual need the most important need of man. And here is where we will differ with them. Freud lived in the Victorian age, when sexuality was suppressed. Because of this, it developed an unwarranted, exaggerated importance. Most of his old theories, involving castration fears, penis envy, and incestuous desires to cohabit with one's mother or father are now seen by many to be antiquated or even ridiculous. In such a sexually liberal age as the present one, where just about anything sexual is tolerated, there is little reason to keep anything of this nature unconscious. When it comes to understanding human emotions, and what eventually makes a person happy in life, sex has always been overemphasized. Unfortunately, I've seen many suicide notes in my years, but I've yet to see a single one that states or even implies: "I'm committing suicide because I didn't get enough sex." Too often, one sees instead suicide notes where the person writes that he feels unwanted, uncared for, or unloved.

The sexual need is reality-oriented. It's a concern of the conscious mind. In contrast, the oral need—the need to be cared for, to be needed—tends to subside along with the need for omnipotence and centrality into the unconscious, into an emotional unreality. That need to be always "first and foremost," that need to experience only good luck, that need to be always "right," and that need to avoid discomfort, irritation, pain, or stress has to be unconscious. It's incompatible with reality-oriented conscious functioning. So a person's oral dependency need becomes unconscious and becomes more a part of the emotional unreality. We can see evidence of this unconscious need for a single exclusive totally gratifying relationship and a need for omnipotence and centrality in the promises of many of man's religious beliefs. As each person goes through the reality of life's hardships, she often carries a longing to reconstitute the circumstances of earliest infancy, when she was unaware of anything other than her own emotional need and its total satisfaction before sleep. But this desire must be put into a realm that supersedes or goes beyond reality. No other desire even approaches the magnitude of this emotional one. It is of this desire that every religion is made; the promise of an eventual blissful state similar to that experienced in earliest infancy with the "good breast." By this I mean the promise of a complete fulfillment of all that the oral dependency need demands in some nebulous life hereafter. In the promised hereafter, we are told there will be little of recognized reality; there will only be the pure and unadulterated need and the "good breast" which totally and exclusively meets the need.

This oral dependency need, which gets pushed into the unconscious and into one's emotional unreality, remains the most basic and most important need of man. One only has to ponder how important the need to feel wanted, needed, cared for, and loved is to anyone. Some people erroneously think "sex makes the world go 'round." Although the oral dependency need can become sexualized, all that's really behind the animalistic act of sex is the oral dependency need—the need to be wanted, needed, admired, adored, loved, and made exclusively the center of attention. Actually, it's the oral dependency need, the importance of being important, that seems to make the world go 'round. In the unconscious we're still first and foremost, even if we consciously tell ourselves that we can't possibly be, and therefore shouldn't always expect to be first or central or always most important to others, or always free of irritation, pain, bad luck, and misfortune.

If we look around we will see symbols of the importance of the oral dependency need. The importance of being the center of attention is conveyed in church spires and tall monuments. Where analysts may see these as phallic symbols, in their preoccupation with the penis, they are really symbols of the importance of the oral dependency need. Flagpoles, large cars, and the imposing domes of public buildings symbolize the oral dependency need on the most basic level. Rather than being sexual symbols, they represent concretized reflections of the importance and significance of the "good breast," and all that it conveys emotionally with regard to omnipotence and centrality. If the symbol does have a sexual implication or significance, it does so only superficially to the more basic oral dependency need. For instance, even if a man were to brag about the size of his penis, or his sexual prowess, or his many sexual conquests, he is really saying, "Look how great I am." Beneath the superficial sexual presentation or symbolism lies the oral dependency need.

If we look deeply enough, we will see the oral implication of many aspects of life. Look at the word "nurse" as an example. The meaning of the verb is to suckle at the breast. This is the origin of the noun. A nurse is someone who takes care of a person and gives a person his or her attention, making that person comfortable. Even in songs and hymns, we can see reflections of the oral dependency need. Popular songs often speak of the need to be wanted and loved. Many hymns reflect God's caring and man's need for His nurturing which represents the desire for oral dependency need gratification with a religious orientation. Peel off the reasons for any of man's behavior, like the layers of an onion, and we'll eventually get down to the oral dependency need at the very core as man's one true motivation. It can be covered by lots of different layers—financial, religious, marital, etc.—but underneath them all is the oral dependency need.

It is an inescapable need that we all share. Its fulfillment is necessary for an emotionally comfortable existence in life. If we can better understand this unavoidable need, perhaps we can also better understand ourselves and others. But the need isn't always so easily seen. In the earliest period of life, human beings are totally dependent on other people that the oral dependency need is obvious. As we mature, the need becomes much less obvious. It becomes hidden in reality concerns and involvements, and becomes more spread out. The same amount of need still exists, even though it's hidden and diffused. It surfaces once again in its concentrated form during old age, when we must again rely on other people for care. The elderly person must be fed, bathed, and have other physiological needs, such as waste removal, attended to by others. Restricted by physical disabilities, the oral dependency need may show itself with a longing for visitors or family members who are often busy with their own lives. Although the oral dependency need is more obvious near the beginning and end of life, it remains, in our emotional unreality, throughout our entire lives.

We can see this oral dependency need not only with human beings and other primates, but even with other animals. For example, if the owner of two dogs pats one of them, the other dog may become jealous and may growl or bark in an attempt to make itself the center of attention. This perhaps is evidence of the oral dependency need in creatures other than the primates.

The need to be protected, wanted, needed, cared for, looked up to, central, and omnipotent is found in almost all known religions. For instance, gods and goddesses in Greek and Roman mythology were often bickering and fighting about who was central, most important or omnipotent in certain areas of life. Even in the Judeo-Christian tradition, the Divine shares with us characteristics of that oral dependency need. In the Old Testament of the Bible, again and again, man is admonished: "Thou shalt have no other gods before me." Repeatedly this is emphasized, and the greatest cause of God's anger, we are told, is when that commandment is broken. With an apparent concentration in the meeting of His oral dependency need in His people He admits to jealousy. For example, Exodus 20 says: Thou shalt not bow down thyself to them, nor serve them; for I, the Lord thy God, am a jealous God . . . " In the New Testament, when Jesus is asked, "What is the most important commandment?", he replies, "To love the Lord thy God with all thy heart and with all thy soul."

This most important need of man, the oral dependency need, is gratified—to a degree—at first through the mothering process. Some infants have more of their oral dependency needs met early in life than others because of circumstances in their reality. Those infants, who receive more emotional nourishment from the mothering person or persons, for whatever reasons, are more comfortable about venturing into relationships with others than are those infants who have a large unmet oral dependency need. The child who has had more oral dependency need gratification begins then to diffuse this need, relying more and more on many other people to meet it. In these relationships, the oral dependency need is met through subtle emotional involvements and their associated communication. It involves an interaction with others, particularly talking and listening to others.

Most stockbrokers would tell us to avoid unnecessary risk by diversifying our investments, and that by this means we can prevent financial ruin. One can see similar advantages in diversifying our emotional investments, in this process of diffusion. In this way, if for any reason we perceive that we're taking a loss in an emotional investment, or not meeting our oral dependency need in one relationship, we can draw gratification from the other invested relationships and thereby prevent emotional ruin.

Man's oral dependency need can be likened to his biologic need for water. Physically, we can't live without water; emotionally, life is much more difficult without people, experiences, and situations that meet our oral dependency needs. We supply our bodies with the water from many different sources. All of the foods we eat contain water; a tomato, for instance, is ninety percent water. Of course, anything we drink has water in it, and under the cover of varying flavors the water tastes better, offering more interesting and diverse ways to quench thirst. Just as water is necessary for the satisfaction of thirst in biological life, and is readily available in a variety of sources, so the gratification of the oral dependency need is necessary in emotional life, and should also be drawn from a variety of sources. Restated more directly, oral dependency need gratification is as much an absolute necessity to emotional life as water is to biological life. As an emotionally comfortable person goes through life, his oral dependency needs are subtly met through these familial, social, business, professional, recreational, and religious involvements. This variety provides different flavors and tastes to the gratification of the oral dependency need; it makes life "appetizing." People who are emotionally uncomfortable have had less of their oral dependency needs met. Consequently, they may try to avoid or deny their emotional need. Their past attempts may have left a bad taste in their mouths and rather than duplicate these experiences, they may seem to prefer to try to go without.

Just as physical problems arise if we deny ourselves water, severe emotional problems may arise if our oral dependency need continues to go unmet. If we are deprived of emotional water, we become like the dehydrated person in the desert who finally finds water, and needs it so badly that she doesn't care that it may be contaminated. Furthermore, her ability to recognize contaminated water has decreased by her previous deprivation. The more thirsty she is, the less discriminating she is. If she hasn't had water for three days, and she finds an oasis with poisoned or polluted water, she might conclude that it is the tastiest water she ever had in her life. Similarly, the person who has a large unmet oral dependency need develops an intense emotional thirst. She will often try to quench that thirst, or gratify that need, from one source of emotional water, through one relationship, and make a similar erroneous conclusion. When a person has gone through enough personal disappointments, misfortune and bad luck or one relationship let-down after another, and then tried to do without those relationships, anyone can look good. Others might see this "anyone" as thoroughly contaminated, but she will tend to see him, like that first view of the oasis, as greater than he really is. Being involved with such contaminated people, like drinking polluted water, can quickly make a person sick.

Having tasted here and there, a good judge of water enjoys its different flavors. That ability to judge well comes from the diversity in tasting. Similarly, people who are emotionally comfortable enjoy their relationships; they, too, have "tasted" here and there. They have developed a zest for life. They take their emotional nourishment from many different people, in different experiences and situations. They seem to know good water when they see it, and readily recognize polluted water. Other people have a history of drinking polluted water and not recognizing it until it has made them sick. These are the people who then may decide that any water is bad for them. They have perceived frustrations of their oral dependency need in their attempts to gratify it, and they then try to deny their oral dependency need, which only causes them more problems. The more we meet our need for water, the more physically comfortable we tend to be. Likewise, the more we gratify our oral dependency need, the more emotionally comfortable we tend to be; the more we do it *diffusely*, the more discerning we are.

We can now define emotional maturity as a diffusion of the oral dependency need. The more emotionally mature a person is, the more the meeting of her oral dependency need is spread out among many people, experiences, and situations; the more it is being met in a wide sphere of relationships. The emotionally immature person is too dependent on too few and even, at times, may be exclusively dependent on one person. Another sign of emotional immaturity is a tendency to want to deny the need. This tendency toward denial comes about when one who is too dependent on too few, and too frequently experiencing frustration, blames the oral dependency need itself. The emotionally mature, or emotionally comfortable, person doesn't have this desire to deny the oral dependency need and will venture into other relationships. This person seems to enjoy "feeding" from many sources so that his oral dependency need appears less concentrated. It may appear, because it is so diffused, that he doesn't even have a need. If his need becomes frustrated in one relationship, he can draw gratification from his wide array of other relationships. If the emotionally mature person is hurt in a relationship, the hurt will not be as deep or as intense as that of the emotionally immature person, whose needs are being met in one relationship or in too few relationships. The emotionally immature person, who is meeting his need through one or a few people, can be deeply emotionally hurt and gives these too emotionally significant people the power to manipulate him. He is so emotionally dependent on them that they have control over him, and have a potential to hurt or let down, whereas the emotionally mature person cannot be so easily manipulated by a few, nor so easily hurt or let down, because he has diffused his dependency.

Think of this diffusion toward emotional maturity as an inverted pyramid. At the apex of the pyramid is the time of infancy. As we mature into adulthood, we add blocks by diffusing our oral dependency need gratification, so that the inverted pyramid becomes more massive. If for any reason, the diffusion is lost, the pyramid becomes smaller and we regress toward immaturity and may end up back at the infancy point. We have become too dependent on too few and our oral dependency need is once again easy to see. From another perspective, one may envision oral dependency need gratification in earliest infancy as likened to a hawser, a thick unit of rope. As the person emotionally matures, the strands that make up this hawser become more spread out. It is still the same hawser, the same amount of emotional need, although it now doesn't appear massive at all. The same amount of oral dependency need is present in the adult as was present in the infant, but what was once an obvious need, singular in appearance, becomes thread-like strands as it broadens, eventually becoming, for the emotionally mature person, lost in his reality involvements.

The diffusion of the oral dependency need does not mean that one relationship cannot be special with regard to oral dependency need gratification. But as a statue needs a wide plinth, the special relationship should have a wide base of other relationships to support it. These other relationships help meet the oral dependency need so that fewer demands are made on that special relationship at the top. It remains a comfortable relationship because there's less of that need or that demand for the special other to "show me that you care," a desire that can become desperate at times. The plinth of many other relationships is needed to elevate and hold that special relationship steady. If not so firmly supported, the relationship will not remain special for very long, and like the statue, will most likely fall.

If we are too dependent on too few to meet our oral dependency need, then all of our oral dependency need may not be adequately met. In order to be emotionally comfortable and to stay that way, we must have a high degree of our need being consistently met. That secret of happiness and inner peace is not concentrated in any one thing, one person, one experience, or one situation in reality, but spread out and diffused in the emotional unreality. The root of genuine happiness or contentment is in that emotional unreality hidden within the unconscious where we feel that we should be important, central, omnipotent, etc., regardless of what we know to be logical or true in reality. The more our oral dependency need is met this way, the more these feelings are enhanced. The real reason for emotional comfortableness is oral dependency need gratification, below the level of reality, which we find in the subtle emotional involvements and the associated communication of our relationships.

We can find some of the most emotionally uncomfortable people in state hospitals. These people seem characterized by having few, if any, friends, and they usually show a disinclination to make friends. They appear too dependent on too few and to have kept the meeting of their oral dependency need concentrated. Or they appear to be denying their basic need, wanting no emotional involvement with anyone. Because they don't readily make friends, doctors often lock the bedroom doors in the morning after patients have come out so that the patients can't get back into their rooms. In this way, they are forced to become involved with other people. Association with others eventually makes them more comfortable and can keep them comfortable. They participate in group therapy, occupational therapy, and recreational therapy, and these therapies are simply organized involvements with other people. When not in these therapies, they begin to talk to other patients. The important thing is that they relate emotionally to other people. The more people, the better, they provide what is necessary to get and keep emotional comfortableness. But this contact is also the hardest thing for some people to initiate. It is certainly the hardest thing for patients who end up in a psychiatric hospital to do. We can speculate it was their inability to involve themselves with enough others that got them so emotionally uncomfortable in the first place.

In the following, we can see an example of finding the polluted oasis and not recognizing it, one result of not meeting the oral dependency need from a great many sources:

All my life I've been searching for the perfect mate. I've had so many disappointments in love that when I found Eugene it was like he was the answer to all my prayers. It was easy to fall in love with him as he was the most loving person I had ever met. I never knew a love like his. He was so kind and considerate of me. He couldn't do enough to please me, and acted as though he worshipped me. He'd do anything to be with me and I couldn't believe that I had somehow met someone as wonderful as he was. He constantly showed to me that he felt the same way about me as I did about him. We had both gone through so much in our past lives that we seemed so happy that we had found each other. He had had it rough in life and so had I. We both had so much in common a deep need for love. He insisted that I renounce my family, give up all my friends, and even change my job to be with him. And I gladly did this, as I was so unhappy before and so depressed with the life I was leading. I wanted him and no one else. He wanted only me and was jealous if I wasn't with him. He told me I was his only reason for living, and he was mine. We were so happy. But when we moved to another city leaving everyone behind he began to change into a hideous Mr. Hyde. He says I'm not the same person he married either and maybe I'm not. Our love for each other is equalled now only by our hate for each other.

These people lost whatever diffusion of their oral dependency need they had. The supportive plinths for a special relationship were removed.

They both became too dependent on too few and regressed from emotional maturity to being emotionally immature with a single person their predominant source of oral dependency need satisfaction. Like that small infant we saw earlier, they demanded to be emotionally nurtured and to be the center of the other's attention, but when reality appeared frustrating and not so nurturing, the relationship began to fall apart. Diffusion decreases the demands on any one relationship and ensures a more consistent nurturing process. There is less a focus on one person, fewer demands to be the constant center of that other's attention, and less of a need to be omnipotent in that relationship.

The emotionally comfortable or mature person meets her oral dependency need subtly, through spontaneous communication. When she talks and someone else listens, the situation duplicates the time in early infancy during which she was the center of attention, because she is the focus of the listener's attention. The act of listening to somebody else talk brings about a subtle emotional phenomenon. The listener is meeting the other person's oral dependency need, no matter what the other is talking about. This happens in the communication of all relationships. If we perceive that someone else is listening to us, we can meet our oral dependency need, which aids in overcoming any emotional uncomfortableness we might have. The speaker is utilizing her mouth in the same way that she did when she first met the need for nourishment. We meet the oral dependency need through a subtle, emotionally nourishing process which includes our talking and becoming emotionally involved with someone else as this other person listens. The content of the communication is reality-oriented, but it is the unconscious emotional process of communication that is so important to the oral dependency need, so the content is actually inconsequential.

Veterans who have come back from the Vietnam War have often required psychological help. But a lot of veterans, it was determined, did not want any psychological or psychiatric treatment. They only wanted the chance to talk and listen. The VA set up what they call "rap centers" where an emotionally uncomfortable veteran can go and "rap." The veteran can talk about what he feels is important and somebody will listen. Comfortable people do this all the time to maintain that comfortableness. People who are more uncomfortable, however, have a greater unmet oral dependency need because of perceived frustrations in their lives and a greater need, therefore, to "rap," and to have someone listen.

I have found out how important listening is in my practice. I've learned I don't really need the psychiatric, psychological, or analytical theories I was taught in training. Really, all I have to do is listen to change people from being emotionally uncomfortable to being comfortable. Certainly,

I have to ask questions, too, and I do have to make comments which convey an interest in what the other person is talking about. But I encourage the other person to do most of the talking. Whatever the subject might be, it still meets the person's oral dependency needs when she perceives that I listen with genuine interest, and I do find that people talk about very interesting things. Talking and listening tend to make people comfortable regardless of their reality situation, and to blunt the perceived reality frustration.

I had the pleasure of sitting next to the wife of the mayor of a nearby town at a dinner a few years ago and when she asked what I did for a living, I told her that I was essentially a listener. She told me that her husband was also a very good listener and had a great reputation for listening. She told me of an incident that happened while her husband was in office. A woman came to him describing all types of frustrations that she was having with rats. The woman said that the rats were everywhere. They were in her basement. They ate her dog food. They killed her cat. They strewed her garbage around. She tried everything to get rid of them and nothing helped. She was telling the details of all this to the mayor when he finally interrupted and asked, "My God, where is it in the city that you live?" She said, "Well, I don't live in the city." Then he said, "Well, why did you come here to tell me all about this?" And she said, "Because I knew you'd listen." Somehow she felt better in relating her troubles to someone she knew would listen. We all have these "rats of reality" that need to be talked out if we are to remain emotionally comfortable. Somehow, when we talk about our own "rats" to someone that we perceive is listening, we don't perceive the "rats" as being as bad, or as frustrating, as we did originally. And they do become more easily eliminated.

To demonstrate again how important listening is, I'd like to share an observation of mine during my psychiatric residency at the outpatient clinic of a large psychiatric hospital in Iowa. Many people felt that they had a psychiatric problem and would telephone to try to see a doctor on the psychiatric staff. Because of the large number of outpatients, a new patient had to wait a couple of weeks before he got to see a psychiatrist. During that time, he was scheduled to talk with a social worker and give a social history. A social history includes all the details of the emotional problems and much background information. But because the social workers were also inundated with work, the social worker would have to ask the person to come back several times to continue the social history. Sometimes he'd have to come back four or five times. These social histories were very extensive and detailed as a good social history should be. I soon became impressed with the number of patients who originally had severe emotional problems, some of them on the verge of considering suicide or divorce, who, by the time they completed the social history, didn't want to see the psychiatrist. They were feeling better, their problems were much less severe, and they wanted to keep on telling the social history. The social worker had made them more comfortable by listening. Yet there had been no treatment attempt whatsoever by the social worker.

I am reminded of the old horse and buggy doctor who didn't know much about the science of medicine but knew plenty about the art of caring about his patients. He made house calls, which conveyed his concern for the centrality of the patient, as opposed to today's typical situation where the patient must sit in an emergency room waiting hours to see an unknown doctor. The old doctor usually knew the whole family and was a very good listener. This ability to listen well with genuine interest and caring is essentially the very core of that art of medicine. It met the oral dependency needs of his patients and many of his patients felt a lot better after he made the call. This is the kind of doctor we miss today, when many doctors who know so much about the science of medicine seem to know nothing of the art. They make us feel like case numbers. The essence of a good bedside manner is in the listening, in the caring and in making the patient feel he is the center of attention. The modern doctor may have tremendous knowledge about the medical facts of diseases, but if he isn't a good listener and doesn't have a good bedside manner, we may not feel better and we could feel worse. A doctor who lacks the time in his too busy schedule to listen long enough to meet his patients' oral dependency needs will have a more difficult job getting them to feel better. Sometimes it seems as if too many doctors have become more disease-oriented or interested in other things than they are personally concerned with their patients. Any person that is uncomfortably sick has a need for someone to listen. That uncomfortableness from whatever reason creates more of a need for oral dependency gratification. Listening provides this.

Oral dependency need gratification that brings about emotional comfortableness is an emotional, not an intellectual process. It has to be experienced emotionally. If it were an intellectual process we could read one chapter of a psychology book every night and we would feel better after we finished the book, but in reality we wouldn't be emotionally better at all. We would be emotionally better off if we were to discuss each chapter of the psychology book with two or three people or even a group. But we could read any book on any subject and it would produce the same therapeutic benefit if we talked to other people about it. People buy more psychology books on how to resolve emotional uncomfortableness by intellectualizing; the desired emphasis is on an intellectually-oriented "do-it-yourself" solution rather than an emotionally-oriented one that must involve other people. We can be very knowledgeable, even about the psychology of emotional uncomfortableness, and still be emotionally uncomfortable ourselves because emotional uncomfortableness is always resolved in an emotional process. When we are not involved enough with people, we run the risk of becoming emotionally uncomfortable. One can successfully run a state psychiatric hospital and still commit suicide, as one psychiatrist whom I knew did. One can be a well-recognized authority and author of many books on the psychology of interpersonal relationships and still end up a patient in a psychiatric hospital. Or one can be a well-known and successful marriage counselor who is most intellectually knowledgeable about what makes a good marriage but whose own marriage ends in divorce.

Parents often take popular classes on parenting that are entitled "How to handle your child" or "How to be a better parent." Good parents are those people who emotionally meet their children's oral dependency need to allow them to emotionally mature. These classes imply that good parents behave on an intellectual, not an emotional level. But it's less an intellectual process than it is an emotional one that adequately satisfies a child's oral dependency need. To meet a child's oral dependency need consistently, the parent must be emotionally involved in many relationships. A parent may know, intellectually all the "how-tos," and "dos" and "don'ts" of being a good parent and not actually be a good parent. Yet a parent, who has had no classes in parenting and may never have read anything about the parenting process, but has many relationships in which her oral dependency need is difffusely met, may be an excellent parent without any of this intellectual knowledge. So one doesn't learn to become a good parent as much as one emotionally becomes a good parent. It's a deception to believe otherwise.

Although man's greatest desire is to have his oral dependency need met, doing so is quite individualistic, and uniquely focused for each person. This is why the promise of the hereafter, that reunion with the "good breast," cannot be made too specific to reality in any religion and still appeal to many people. For instance, an Arctic Circle Eskimo's vision of heaven might approach an equitorial Zulu's vision of hell. Oral dependency need gratification, like the vision of the "good breast," translates poorly into reality. So the idea of heaven is never spelled out too concretely in reality terms because the satisfaction of the oral dependency need exists on a very personal and emotional level, not a reality-oriented one.

What satisfies one individual in the meeting of his oral dependency need in reality may frustrate another person. For example, one of the five star generals of the Second World War was George Marshall, Chief of Staff of the Army, who took offense when anyone called him "George." He wanted to be called "General." Even when President Roosevelt once called him "George," he took offense. Another five star general, Douglas MacArthur, took similar offense when anyone called him "Douglas" or "Doug." Even his wife didn't call him "Doug;" she called him "General." He was always "General MacArthur" and he wanted it that way. H. H. Arnold, who also became a five star general and has been called the "father of the American Air Force," took great pleasure in people calling him "Hap." Similarly, another five star general of the Second World War, Eisenhower, was known to everyone as "Ike." As we can see from this example, an act can be perceived by the one person as a meeting of his oral dependency need while the same act can be perceived by another person as frustrating it. For instance, suppose you offer a piece of cake to a person. One person may think this act indicates you care for her and a little of her oral dependency need is met. Another person, however, might see the act of offering him a piece of cake as a frustration or a rejection of his oral dependency need because he may think, "She doesn't really care about me because she's trying to get me to gain weight. She feels I'm repulsive and she wants me to look even more so!" Or, suppose you offer a candy bar to the same first person. This person might unconsciously think, "The candy bar is sweet, therefore, she thinks I'm sweet." This would be a meeting of her oral dependency need. The second person might think, "The candy bar has nuts in it, she thinks I'm nuts!" He perceives a rejection of his oral dependency need. So the meeting of the oral dependency need becomes in reality unique to each individual. People don't always like the same flavor of ice cream; that's why there are so many flavors. We know there are "different strokes for different folks" and it is not unusual to see so many contrasts in people. I had a sixteen year old high school student brought to me when she became unable to go to school. She confided to me that she had developed a dreaded fear of passing gas in her classes. Though her family physician had prescribed various medications, she still refused to go to school. This was at the very same high school attended by another student who had been brought to me by his mother after complaints were made by the school about his behavior, one act of which was to pass gas loudly in his classes in an attempt to be the center of attention.

What can make one person happy in reality, can make another person unhappy, creating a basic complexity in understanding people that needs to be explored a little further. In doing so, we shall see that man's emotional comfortableness is always dependent on others and that to maintain comfortableness, he must continually maintain a symbolic umbilical cord in his relationships to meet his oral dependency need.

In the next chapter, we'll see that there are times in anyone's life when he has a much greater oral dependency need that presses to be gratified.

CHAPTER 2
Gratifying and Frustrating the Basic Emotional Need

Having identified man's most basic emotional need, let's look now at the ways in which it's met, the results of having it met, and just what happens when it's not met. Oral dependency need gratification, as it did in our infancy, tends to give the feeling that "everything is all right." This feeling can enable us effectively to handle discomfort, frustration, stress, pain and disappointments in life. These are always perceived under the influence of the degree of oral dependency need gratification. It is difficult to appreciate another person's frustration, stress, and pain because one cannot measure a person's unconscious levels of perceived gratification of his oral dependency need. When the oral dependency need is not being adequately met, frustration, stress, pain and those often unavoidable disappointments in life will be more intensely experienced. On the other hand, when the oral dependency need is unconsciously perceived as being more fully met, any frustration, stress, and pain in reality will seem less intense. What should become evident, then, is that the level of gratification of the oral dependency need is most crucial in determining the effect of experienced disappointment, stress, and pain on a person. Someone with a high degree of unconsciously perceived oral dependency need gratification may experience a measurably high amount of discomfort, stress, or pain with little untoward effect. Someone else with a low degree of unconsciously perceived oral dependency need gratification may experience a measurably trivial amount of discomfort, stress, or pain with a massive untoward effect. Along with being unable to measure a person's perceived oral dependency need satisfaction, one is usually unable to measure the reality of actual stress or pain. Disappointments, stress, and pain are always "in the eye of the beholder." This isn't to say that a person doesn't have stress or pain when someone else can see little if any basis for such in his reality. It does say, however, that the level of unconsciously perceived oral dependency need gratification is a determining factor for the degree of experienced disappointment, stress, or pain.

Since in anyone's reality, there will always be a varying degree of unavoidable disappointment, stress, and pain to handle, there will always be a varying urgency to fill this void in oral dependency need gratification from his relationship sphere. One's emotional involvement in his relationship sphere is of prime importance in countering whatever disappointments, stress or pain reality may present. This involvement, carried on within a network of friends and acquaintances—discussing likes and expressing dislikes, enjoyably chitchatting and sharing the particulars of day-to-day life—can keep a person emotionally comfortable and better able to handle the "downs" in life.

When one does not have his oral dependency need adequately met, he feels emotionally uncomfortable. He may think the uncomfortableness stems wholly from a physical problem or is the by-product of a particular stressful situation in his life. But the underlying cause of the emotional uncomfortableness is often simply a failure to meet the oral dependency need to the necessary level to be emotionally comfortable. For example, one man—let's call him Bob—came to see me with feelings of loneliness and unhappiness. His case shows how oral dependency need frustration heightens the experience of stress, while oral dependency need gratification lessens it in even the most extreme circumstances. Bob began by explaining that he felt the people he worked with didn't like him; he was always feeling sick and experiencing stress. As he put it, his job was "a pain." It wasn't a comfortable job for him because he experienced too much anxiety and too much pressure. When I asked him if he'd ever had a job in the past he'd really liked, he told me that while he was in the army in Vietnam he had enjoyed his work. He enjoyed his fellow workers, didn't feel much stress or pressure, and rarely went on sick-call. But with this job he was often right in the middle of combat. The reality of his situation in Vietnam was that people were actually trying night and day to kill him. Yet he didn't feel as much stress or "pressure" then as he did in his civilian job. When I asked Bob why he had been more comfortable in Vietnam, he said "We felt like we were all in the same boat."

That "We're all in the same boat" feeling comes from oral dependency need gratification. The army had forced Bob into a situation where he was having more of his oral dependency need met. Quite surprisingly, many people will often describe their years of military service as their most comfortable in much the same way Bob did. In civilian life Bob was not emotionally involved with as many people since he had a tendency not to want to be involved. Consequently he became too dependent on his wife. Because he was no longer getting as much of his oral dependency need met, he perceived more stress, even though in reality-oriented terms, his job was obviously much less stressful and certainly less life-threatening than his job in Vietnam.

I remember another case in which a man told me that his wife had constantly accused him of having an affair. She was extremely jealous and very possessive. She was emotionally overly dependent on him and he on her. But she didn't have many friends, or the emotional involvements of a work situation that he did. She was, therefore, more dependent, and, in trying to protect the source of her need gratification, had become more jealous and more possessive, causing her to make accusations of unfaithfulness. Each time he came home late, even though he had worked hard at the office, she would accuse him of being out with another woman. He couldn't handle this stress and would angrily deny any unfaithfulness. They then would get into a fight. This didn't meet either one's oral dependency need.

Finally, this man did get involved with another woman, and had a sexual affair for six months. However, during those six months, he was also having more of his oral dependency need met in this new relationship. Because of his greater oral dependency need gratification, he was better able to handle stress when he came home late. When his wife would begin to make angry accusations, instead of getting upset, he could be more emotionally supportive. He accepted her anger and irritation without getting angry. This met more of her oral dependency need and made a better relationship. She calmed down, and he said that for those six months she didn't accuse him of having an affair even when he came home late after he'd just had a sexual encounter. Her suspicions of his having an affair stopped while he was having the affair. He would come home late, reassure her of his love, give her emotional support, and could accept any of her anger without getting angry himself. The marriage went better than it ever had before.

After six months, however, his affair ended when the other woman moved away. Again the marriage got worse. His wife reverted to being suspicious and accusing him of having an affair, and he went back to feeling stressed and fighting with her. Again they were too dependent on each other. I'm not recommending extramarital affairs to improve marriage relationships. What I'm trying to illustrate is that oral dependency need gratification improves ability to put up with stress and reduces irritability. In fact, it's the only thing that will work when you get right down to it.

Since we meet much of our oral dependency need through emotionally gratifying relationships, we are better able to get through the rough times in life when we are surrounded by friends. In fact, these "rough times" may not appear rough at all. Frustration, stress, and pain are not perceived as so overwhelming when friends are around. For example, one World War II army officer told me that a soldier isolated in a foxhole at night could be expected to shoot off all his ammunition by midnight and would be an ineffective "nervous wreck" the rest of the night. He would perceive tremendous stress, fear every little noise, and be panic-stricken by the silence. But in a foxhole with four or five of his buddies, he tended to have the feeling that everything would be all right. He didn't perceive the same degree of stress. He wasn't fearful of every little noise, and the silence didn't bother him. Surrounded by his buddies, he had the feeling that he could more easily handle anything, and he was a much more effective soldier.

Sometimes, people end up in isolated "foxholes" of life, hunkered down in the midst of their battles, cut off from the support of others. In feeling so alone, they experience a high degree of stress and function ineffectively. What they need to do is get some good buddies in that foxhole with them so they can have more of that feeling that everything will be all right. Gaining that feeling, they become more effective in handling life's battles.

Consider another example. If a person going through an operation has many good friends or close relatives around to meet her oral dependency need during this time of severe discomfort and frustration, she will perceive less stress and pain. If a person has been in the hospital, she knows that during visiting hours when family members and good friends are available to talk to, her situation may not seem quite as bad as it does during the rest of the day.

Just as oral dependency need gratification helps keep us more comfortable in times of frustration, stress, and pain, it leads to the expectation of more oral dependency need gratification. In other words, it fosters optimism. That "everything is all right" feeling that comes from the perception of oral dependency need gratification, first experienced in earliest infancy, leads to the feeling that "everything is *going* to be all right." It is the basis for the feeling in a man who has had one heart attack that somehow he will successfully avoid another. It's the emotional basis for a person being able to live with seemingly no worries in an area long overdue for an earthquake or a natural calamity. It is also the basis for the feeling in a man about to enter combat that somehow, with good luck and fortune he will successfully come through it all unscathed.

Oral dependency need gratification affects our expectations for the future, and also our perceptions of the past, in a positive manner. When we perceive oral dependency need gratification, we seem to forget past worries and frustrations that we may have actually experienced. If we are reminded of these by someone else, we either overlook them or feel that these worries and frustrations were insignificant, and we do this "discounting" to the same degree that our perceived oral dependency need gratification level has risen.

Time seems to heal hurts, disappointments and pain. When we lose someone because this person dies, moves away, or simply rejects us, it can leave an emotional void in our lives. A void can be created by sickness, bad luck, misfortune, or unavoidable disappointments. Time can heal this void and this oral dependency need frustration by allowing us to draw more from our oral dependency need gratifying relationships. Gradually, the new relationships or parts thereof fill lost ones. Nonperson oriented frustrations are compensated by drawing more gratification from the interpersonal relationship sphere. The more involved we are with more people, the more potential sources we have for ongoing oral dependency need gratification.

Drugs and alcohol temporarily dissolve the unmet oral dependency need, giving the same feeling as oral dependency need gratification. But this effect is not lasting, nor is it the same as true oral dependency need gratification. These substances decrease the feelings of loneliness, emptiness, and the need for others that comes from an unmet oral dependency need from whatever causes. Just about every culture, past or present, has brewed at least one form of alcohol. Perhaps it's because people of every culture have experienced the frustrations of the oral dependency need.

Drugs such as marijuana, cocaine, and heroin can make a person forget those frustrations; they temporarily remove the "mental" pain of accumulated bad luck, failed relationships, and the feeling of always coming last in the priorities of others. This temporary lessening of pain, this boost to the perception that "things are going to be all right" gives the person a sense that more of the oral dependency need is being met. He also feels that these needs are being met without needing people in the way he may have felt he needed them before. When his frustrations have been viewed as people-oriented, this feeling of not needing people is a good feeling. This is only a temporary perception on the part of the drug or alcohol user, however. It's an artificial "high."

The more we have our oral dependency need gratified, the more we feel good. We tend to enjoy life; we may even have a zest for life; we're not lonely because we're emotionally feeding from so many different people, experiences, and situations. It's a natural high. We tend not to be so easily frustrated by people. Taking drugs or not taking drugs depends very little on teaching or learning efforts. The basic reason that alcohol and drugs are so popular throughout the population is that they seem to diminish the unmet oral dependency need. Alcohol enables the bum alone on the street to live with himself, or the person too dependent on too few and experiencing marital frustrations not to need his wife. The feelings of frustration in the interpersonal relationship sphere seem to decrease with alcohol and drugs. Since this feeling of gratification is both false and temporary, his disregard for other people and their oral dependency needs may create more emotional problems and lead to more need frustration for him.

People who are too dependent on too few, like the wife of the man who had an affair, tend to worry about the source of their oral dependency need gratification. They are afraid to lose those few persons on whom they rely to meet their oral dependency needs. This worry can be see between boyfriend and girlfriend, husband and wife, two homosexuals, parent and child, or any other relationship you might think of. One person may be very jealous of another person if the other is involved emotionally in other relationships. A parent may worry excessively about a child's health if she is too dependent on that child to meet her own emotional need. These people feel that they have to watch out for their few sources of oral dependency need gratification. Although it is true that many unfortunate things that can happen to us in our daily lives, someone who has many emotionally gratifying relationships will not have to worry as much about a sole source to meet his oral dependency need. If we have many people with whom to meet our oral dependency need and we lose one, we will not be so devastated by the loss. People who are too dependent on too few, who tend to worry more about losing their sources of oral dependency need gratification, are understandably much more devastated by such losses.

The opposite of oral dependency need gratification, of course, is oral dependency need frustration. We must learn reality at the price of oral dependency need gratification: the oral dependency need must be frustrated. We have seen that reality frustrates us right from the beginning of life. Life offers us a continuing array of put-downs and misfortunes. We all must bear some degree of disappointment in our relationships. Most of us can't live as a king or queen, and even if we could, we'd have to face illness, accidents, old age and the loss of loved ones. Reality ensures frustration of the oral dependency need.

Everyone has experienced a certain amount of bad luck. Some of us more than others. Luck is often a deciding factor in our lives. Many people who have reached financial success say that just being in the right place at the right moment played a big part in their success. Even living or dying can be a matter of luck. Ask any combat veteran how important luck can be. One veteran told me that once when he was in a glider on a combat mission, he was asked by another soldier to change seats with him. After an initial thought of "Why the hell should I?" he switched. The unlucky soldier who changed places with this man was, only moments later, instantly killed by a piece of shrapnel.

Some people seem to be plagued with bad luck, while others have good luck. One major airline I know doesn't hire pilots if they have had bad luck. It isn't any fault of these pilots, but they're just not hired. I heard one commercial pilot say that he had been flying for twenty-five years and had never had the bad luck of even a flat tire on his aircraft. He went on to tell that while he was a bomber pilot in World War II, he went through many a hair-raising raid over Germany. Then, one day, he was ill and couldn't fly. It was on that day that the plane he would have flown never came back. That's how luck works, and when we perceive that we're lucky, it meets our oral dependency need; but when we're unlucky, it frustrates our oral dependency need.

Any experiences of inferiority, inadequacy, unacceptableness, guilt, or failure frustrate the oral dependency need. Losses in the ability to experience pleasure of any type are also a frustration of one's oral dependency need. The loss in the ability to control oneself or others is likewise a frustration. The experiencing of a loss in freedom from control by others, being regimented by others, or being shown as inferior, inadequate, unacceptable, unclean, a failure, guilty, wrong, incomplete, or having impending trouble are frustrations. Experiencing an inability to deny aspects of reality that counter the feelings of omnipotence or centrality can frustrate the oral dependency need. The appearance, or the sudden uncovering of things previously denied, such as guilt-laden experiences or situations, are further frustrations of the oral dependency need.

One woman who came to see me angrily told me, "My husband seems to love his dog more than he loves me. When he comes through the door at night, the first thing he does, before he even says 'hello' to me, is pat that damn dog. I'd be so happy if I had just half the attention he gives the dog." She had perceived a frustration of her oral dependency need because she felt that she was not first and foremost, coming second to the dog. Another woman told me essentially the same thing saying she felt unwanted, only her story was about tomato plants. She said the first thing her husband did when he came home from work was get the hose out and water "his damn tomato plants—like they were more important than me." More than dogs and tomato plants are frustrating in life. Fatigue, disappointment, pain, body dysfunction, illness, accidents, hardship, and the cold, hard facts of reality can also frustrate our oral dependency need and may do so on a regular basis. Like these two women, we can unconsciously lump them together and deceptively blame things like dogs and tomato plants.

Reality continually reminds us that our days are numbered here on earth, and that no one can live forever. We're all too frequently disappointed in what we want from life in regard to our goals, ambitions, and desires; we're unavoidably disappointed in our interpersonal relationship sphere. Since we live in reality it behooves us to know reality well. Just that knowing frustrates the oral dependency need. Frustration is necessary to live comfortably. For instance, in order to build up immunities, we must suffer through certain childhood diseases, which are frustrations of our oral dependency need. Some of this frustration in life is necessary to avoid greater frustration later. We learn reality best through frustration. A child can only know, for instance, that fire burns by being burned. Of course, this is a frustration of his oral dependency need; however, in experiencing a minor burn, we hope he will avoid the greater pain of more serious burns later that would cause even greater frustrations of his oral dependency need. In other words some oral dependency need frustration is necessary to prevent greater frustration later. So this frustration is not only unavoidable it's *necessary* in order to live in reality. If one is fortunate, one can learn the lessons for living in reality by experiencing just a little of the unpleasantness, the discomforts, and the pain in order to avoid a greater amount of the same. Yet that very process of learning to live in reality and recognizing reality concerns is an inescapable put-down to the oral dependency need and the desire for omnipotence and centrality.

It is becoming obvious that we tend to rationalize our feelings and perceptions. We look for reasons to explain why we feel the way we do. However, the feeling of being considered important by yourself and others comes more from the meeting of the oral dependency need rather than from any "fact" of reality. One can say, if he's feeling important, "I'm important because _____," and just fill in the blank that's appropriate for his situation in reality; anything that's logical or makes sense will do. Somebody else though may be in the same reality situation as you, and if he doesn't feel important, may give other logical reasons for feeling unimportant. Even though one has the same reality situation, one doesn't necessarily feel important or unimportant. In fact, one may even want to commit suicide. Sometimes a person who we would logically conclude should think highly of himself because of his reality situation, surprises us and those who know him by committing suicide. Then there are those others who, because of their miserable situations in life, we would logically conclude would think little of themselves, and who we might think would want to consider suicide, but apparently don't. Some of these people may surprise us in that they're enjoying life. The reality situation then has very little to do with the feeling of importance. What really makes one feel important is the degree of oral dependency need gratification he has. This need is met unconsciously in the emotional unreality. Unconsciously, a rationalization is made, using "facts" of reality to reflect that emotional unreality. A deception is therefore created because the rationalization implies that one feels important or unimportant because of those presented "facts" of reality. It isn't the reality of patting a dog or the watering of tomato plants. It's the emotional unreality, rather than the reality, that is directly determining those feelings.

A man told me that when he was nineteen he joined the army and in that first year of military service wished that he could be a colonel. Being a colonel, he rationalized, would surely meet his oral dependency need. Well, he is a colonel today, but his hair is mostly gone and what's left is gray and now he tells me that whenever he sees a nineteen year old soldier, he wishes that he could be nineteen again and "to hell with being a colonel." He'd trade if he could. Turning back the years to nineteen, he feels, would surely now meet his oral dependency need. The feeling of importance comes from what is within, and is then rationalized by being put into reality terms. It is not unlike a little child who, while shopping with his mother, constantly exclaims, "Give me this; give me that!" Usually, when you buy it and give it to him, he is still not happy. People use deceptive rationalizations to explain their unmet oral dependency need in much the same way; they often feel, "I need this to feel happy," or "This is what makes me unhappy." If whatever it is tends to be reality-oriented, then it tends to be misunderstood as the true origin. There is no one person, experience, or situation, other than having your oral dependency need met, that we can present to others and say "this is going to make you happy"—no such universal answer exists in reality. Happiness or unhappiness, emotional comfortableness or uncomfortableness, is a direct reflection of the emotional unreality.

I had an interesting case like that of the little child in the store. A college student saw me for a course of therapy at several different times, which is possible when you've had almost a quarter of a century of psychiatric experience in one place, as I have. Each time he came to me, he was uncomfortable with himself. Each time he presented a similar reality rationalization as his explanation for his emotional uncomfortableness. The first time he told me he felt unhappy because he didn't have a bachelor's degree. If he had a bachelor's degree, he rationalized, he would feel good about himself. He was very down on himself, but as I listened during the course of therapy to the details of his explanation, he eventually became more emotionally comfortable and after a few months, discontinued. I didn't see him again until several years later, when he again came to see me feeling very unhappy. This time he presented his rationalization for his emotional uncomfortableness by saying, "I would feel better about myself if I had a master's degree. If I only had my master's degree, I could be happy because a lot of people have their bachelor's degrees these days. It's the master's degree that really counts." Once again, he was feeling so unimportant he couldn't make himself study. I listened to the details of this explanation and everything associated with it. After two or three months, he discontinued therapy after he became more emotionally comfortable when his oral dependency need was more adequately met. I didn't see him for three more years, when he again came to see me, and you guessed it! This time, his explanation was that he needed a Ph.D. degree to make him feel good about himself. A master's degree, he rationalized, was not enough to make a person happy and feel important. I haven't seen him since, but if he comes back, he'll have some other reality-oriented rationalization.

People who are experiencing a great amount of oral dependency need frustration often feel that others don't understand them. This is rationalized as, "You don't know what it was like to _____." I have heard people tell me, "You don't know what it was like to grow up in the Depression," or, "You don't know what it was like to have grown up with six brothers and sisters," or "You don't know what it's like to have grown up as an only child." Listening to as many reasons for uncomfortableness as I have, you hear sharply contrasting ones where it becomes very evident that something else is involved, something other than what the person is so logically presenting as the cause for the uncomfortableness. For example, recently there has been much concern, as more mothers enter the work force, about the emotional problems that the mother's absence could cause in her "latch-key kid." Yet, I've heard several people say over the years that their emotional problems came from having their mothers at home all the time. I've also heard people say, "You don't know what it was like to have a father who was always away on business trips" and then "You don't know what it was like to have a father who did his work at home and was always there." In other words, these people are saying, "You couldn't possibly understand what it is like to have your oral dependency need so frustrated," but it's easy to see that the reasons they give for their emotional uncomfortableness are rationalizations set deceptively in reality.

Sometimes the unmet oral dependency need will be unrationalized; a person will say, "There's something missing in my life but I don't know what it is," "There's a void," or "I seem to be looking for something I can't find." Sometimes they'll ask, "Why do I feel so empty?" Contrasting themselves with emotionally comfortable people whom they know, they'll say, "I seem to lack something that others seem to have; I'm different from others." The unconscious hasn't come up with a rationalization yet. This unrationalized state often precedes a rationalization that may develop later. The later-developed rationalization attempts to explain the previous void: "What I lacked was _____," or "My problem was _____." It's as if whatever fills the blank was the answer to the emotional problem.

Oral dependency need frustration, no matter what its origin—perhaps physiologic dysfunction, illness, a failed relationship, being fired from a job, or just bad luck—results in anger. Since we all must experience need frustration, because we all must contend with reality, we all experience some degree of anger. It's an unavoidable part of living in reality.

Likewise, everyone has a need to release anger. The frustrations may seem insignificant, but when anger is allowed to build up without being released a little at a time, small frustrations can create an unconsciously perceived mountain of accumulated anger. Many molehills, stacked side by side and upon one another, can add up to something mountainous.

Those who accumulate anger allow it to pile up like straws on a camel's back. Like the last straw that breaks the camel's back, one more apparently insignificant frustration may cause all of the anger to come crashing down at once. The very fact that this anger is expressed so explosively, despite its seemingly insignificant precipitating event, attests to the existence of the underlying accumulated "mountain." To give an example, I'd like to cite an article I read in a local newspaper a year or so ago. A twenty-three year old man had a slight auto accident; someone bumped into the fender of his car, an event that was, by anyone's standards, a rather minor accident. It didn't seem minor to this man, however, probably because he had been accumulating anger from one disappointment after another. The man denting his fender was the "last straw" for this person, because he took a pistol out from under the seat, shot, and killed the man. His anger had built up to an explosive level, and he took it all out on one person. If he hadn't accumulated so much anger, we could theorize that the same event would not have precipitated the same reaction. Similarly, I read in another newspaper that a man stabbed another person to death on a city bus because this other person, after being asked not to smoke, said "I'll smoke if I want to" and lit a cigarette. Here, too, the lighting of the cigarette was the straw that broke the camel's back. Hardly a week goes by, that one doesn't read of similar examples of mountainous anger being expressed over things of molehill significance.

Another illustration can be seen in an event that happened to a woman who came to see me a few years ago. She said that her husband had a terrible temper and at times would act as though he were absolutely crazy. When I asked for an example, she told me about a time when they were both stretched out on a blanket on a crowded beach. She said something that she felt was innocuous but about which he was apparently very sensitive. All of a sudden he angrily jumped up, calling her every vile name he could think of in front of everyone else on the beach. He yanked the blanket so that she rolled off and then balled it up, ran to the water's edge, and threw it into the ocean. Then he ran back, grabbed the radio, and threw that into the ocean. She told me she was mortified. He felt terribly guilty the next day, and neither of them could understand his reaction. Most of the time, she said, he seemed so nice and easygoing. He was rather shy, had no close friends, and was overly dependent on her. He didn't want her to have any friends either. Rather than seeing his problem as accumulated anger, she wondered if his reaction was caused by hypoglycemia, epilepsy, or perhaps a brain tumor. She was looking for a logical explanation, but we suspect that his reaction was emotional in origin: a release of anger caused by unconsciously perceived oral dependency need frustration that had accumulated because he was too dependent on too few.

Sometimes the rationalization given seems to imply a reference to an accumulation of "reasons" to express anger. This is shown in what a ten year old boy, brought to me as a behavior problem, told me about his nine year old sister Mary Beth. "I hit Mary Beth with a water balloon and really got her good! But my mother jumped on me and made me go to my room and that made me mad. I was just paying her back for all the little things that she has been doing all along, like picking on me and putting me down. I just paid her back all at once, but my mother doesn't seem to understand that I'm paying Mary Beth back."[1]

Just as oral dependency need gratification gives us emotional nourishment, anger, caused by oral dependency need frustration, is our emotional waste product. There is a continual need to get rid of it so that it doesn't build up. Anger in our unconscious emotional life can be likened to urea in our biologic life. When the kidneys break down, and we are unable to rid ourselves of urea, it builds up and causes severe physical problems. When we can't rid ourselves of emotional waste, it too causes severe problems—emotional as well as physical—if we keep that anger inside. Ask any medical doctor what this kind of anger that we push down can do to the gastrointestinal tract or heart.

We need to express our anger and it's best if we can get rid of it without hurting anyone. This is important to remember because for someone who has undergone great frustrations of his oral dependency need, for whatever reasons, it is not enough simply to give love; the accumulated anger from those perceived put-downs must be expressed as well. Comfortable people do not feel guilty about expressing anger because they can spread it around. Just as they have diffused the gratification of their oral dependency need, they can diffuse their anger expression. The emotionally maturing person can get rid of anger in his or her expanding world of relationships. If we are emotionally involved with many people, we don't have to risk "dumping" all our anger on one person. We can drop a little here, a little there, and it won't even be noticed. You would be surprised how some people can indirectly slip a little anger in where it's not even seen.

If one is too dependent on too few, he is faced with a dilemma. He needs to get rid of anger, but he can't spread it around because he is only involved with a few people. Like the baby who doesn't want to endanger his supply of milk by biting the breast, he doesn't want to jeopardize the relationship that gives him oral dependency need gratification by expressing anger to the other person. So he tends to repress this anger and accumulate it. Additionally, because people who are too dependent on too few need a relationship so badly, they don't often see the oral dependency need frustrating aspect of the relationship which might be so obvious to someone else. If they are to avoid risking their only oral dependency need gratifying relationship, they have to see that relationship as rosy or certainly better than it is. They unconsciously perceive frustrations, some of which may be referable to those on whom they're too dependent, which they consciously tend to deny. This fosters the accumulation process. A little anger from a molehill of frustration here and a little anger from a molehill of frustration there can build to a mountain of accumulated anger. The exact origin of any accumulated anger is most difficult if not impossible to determine. The person who is not so dependent on too few and therefore doesn't have the tendency to accumulate anger may, in contrast, experience mountainous frustrations of his oral dependency need and have less of a problem with accumulated anger.

Often a person who is too dependent on too few will have an outburst of anger after he has been drinking. As we have said, alcohol temporarily reduces the unmet oral dependency need. It lowers the feeling that one must worry about jeopardizing further dependency need gratification. For this reason, the person may more readily express anger after a few drinks. With a seemingly low level of unmet oral dependency need, there is no unconscious concern about expressing anger. The alcoholic, however, is usually too dependent on too few and can ill afford to express such anger. He or she has too much anger built up, and it will tend to come out too directly on too few people. The feeling that the unmet oral dependency need has been lowered allows the person to express his or her anger, but it is too directly expressed to the same people on whom the person will be dependent later for more oral dependency need gratification. A husband may break up the furniture and beat his wife while his relatives, and later even the alcoholic himself, search for a reason for the intense expressions of anger. They fail to see that rather than the alcohol, it is the being too dependent on too few that is the basic problem. They falsely conclude, "Alcohol seems to do something to him—if he just didn't drink there'd be no problem."

We all, unconsciously, rationalize our accumulated anger; I am sure you have heard yourself say, "I'm angry because _____." Like the blank in "I'm important because _____," this blank can be filled in with re- ality-oriented explanations on which the unconscious focuses this anger. But the accumulated anger was there first, in the emotional unreality, with a reality reason for it being later given.

Often, when people who are too dependent on too few and allow a lot of anger to build up lose control, they direct their violent anger outbursts toward those few who gratify their oral dependency need. They may later deeply regret this and feel very guilty about it. Spouse abuse, child abuse, and pet abuse are a few examples of the way in which people accumulate a great amount of anger and then take out their anger on the very things that meet their most important need. When one is in an exclusive relationship, that is, one in which all the oral dependency need gratification that should be drawn from a full relationship sphere is instead focused on one person, that one other person is going to have all of his love. But because of this situation the other person is at a very high risk to catch all of his anger, too.

Let me tell you about a woman who came to see me a few years ago after an isolating snowstorm. She and her husband had been snowed in for four days and couldn't get out. She later confided to me, "If I hadn't gotten out of that house when I did, I would have gone for my husband's jugular vein!" She was implying that need to express anger. The need was building up and she was feeling that she was ready to kill him for any or no reality reason. If those people, experiences, and situations one usually turns to in expressing the little bits of anger accrued from just having to live in reality aren't available, the anger builds up and one can end up "dumping" it all on one other person. One develops a need to "dump" it first and then unconsciously thinks of a rationalization while "dumping" it. If this woman had been snowed in all by herself, she might have gotten "cabin fever," which involves feelings of depression and loneliness when the anger is kept in. There are people like this woman who normally don't want to be by themselves or exclusively with another person. Sometimes because of circumstances in their lives they can get "snowed in" and thus become too dependent on too few. But, let the snow melt, and they're busily emotionally involved with other people again.

Unlike these people are the ones who want an exclusive relationship; they demand it. They snow themselves in with an exclusive other, or else with too few, and suffer the consequences. They may even resent the intrusion of others into their exclusive relationship. They often say, "If we could only be together on a deserted island by ourselves, we'd be happy. Why can't others leave us alone?" If they were alone on some deserted island, one might well wonder if it wouldn't be too long before they'd start "dumping" anger on each other, perhaps arguing about where the coconuts should be stored. They'd find some reality-oriented reason to express their built-up anger to each other. By spreading the anger around, one avoids the burdensome demands of an exclusive relationship, the potential of a massive frustration of one's oral dependency need, the need to "dump" accumulated anger on a single person, and the potentially quite harmful need to repress it.

By diffusing the oral dependency need, we avoid the concentrated love and concentrated anger problems. If we are emotionally involved in many relationships, we can express indirectly little bits of anger at a time. We don't have to hold back on anger expression causing a build-up of anger that eventually must be "dumped". There is no one person on whom we have to "dump" our anger when things don't go well in life. To spread our anger around is what I say friends are for. Note, too, that because oral dependency is a two-way street, when we are diffusely involved, we're much less likely to be "dumped" on by someone else. So, we not only avoid being manipulated or having "games" played with us, but we also avoid being "dumped" on, or as many of my patients tell me "being shit on."

Direct anger is the type that can cause a lot of hurt feelings. It is characteristic of those who are too dependent on too few. If I'm angry at you, I yell at you. You might yell back at me, which can turn our anger into a massive fight. If I can express the anger indirectly, by talking about something else I dislike, I'm more likely to stay emotionally comfortable and so are you. I may not even know that I am expressing my anger, but unconsciously, I am doing so. In this way, I can get rid of my anger without jeopardizing our relationship. Indirect anger expression will only work, however, if I have many relationships throughout which I can meet some of my oral dependency need and I can spread my anger. Life for me becomes less noticeably emotional, more "even-keeled" and my relationships are more stable.

In the next chapter, we will see the ways in which we can diffuse our oral dependency need and our anger. We will learn about the dynamics of some of our unconscious thinking and of indirect anger expression.

1. Adapted from: PSYCHODYNAMICS OF THE EMOTIONALLY UN-COMFORTABLE, Warren H. Green Publishing Company, St. Louis, MO 1979

CHAPTER 3
Anger: How It Develops and How We Get Rid of It

Often we express the anger produced by oral dependency need frustration in a relationship that had nothing, in reality, to do with the accrual of the anger. In reality, it doesn't always make sense, but the process that allows us to do this is unconscious, a part of the emotional unreality. As an example of this process, consider a man named Bill Green.

Bill Green had a bad day at the office. His boss, frustrated that the business was not going well, took some of those frustrations out on Bill. Also, Bill didn't accomplish all that his boss wanted him to accomplish that day, so he felt additional pressure and stress from those expectations, too. In turn, he went home and took his frustrations out on his wife. He got very angry at her, and she saw this as just another example of his losing control and showing his temper. What has really happened is that the boss had a frustration of his unconscious omnipotence and centrality—his oral dependency need—when the business didn't go the way that he felt it should have gone; this frustration produced anger, and this "taking out frustration on somebody else" became an expression of anger toward Bill. Bill's inability to accomplish all that he wanted to accomplish, feeling stressed and frustrated in his work, is an added oral dependency need frustration on Bill's part. Then when he goes home he transfers this build-up of anger onto his wife, they have an argument, and Bill shows his temper. This procedure is an unconscious phenomenon called *transference*.

In order to understand what is involved in transference, we have to look more closely at Bill Green's situation. The boss is frustrated by his business difficulties. He is able to get rid of his anger on Bill because he has somehow equated Bill with the frustrating business. The business problems and Bill are two entirely different things in reality, but in the unconscious of the boss, they have been equated, perhaps by the unconsciously perceived characteristic that both are "frustrating" to him. Unconsciously equating these two entirely different things in reality, the boss is able to take the anger accrued from the frustration of his oral dependency need in the business and unload it on Bill. Then Bill comes home and duplicates this phenomenon. When he comes home, he unconsciously perceives that his wife doesn't treat him right in something that she does or doesn't do. For instance, she could have been preparing dinner when he might have expected her to come running over with open arms and give him a kiss. So we can theorize then that these two entirely different people—his boss at work and his wife at home—are somehow equated so that he can take the anger accrued at work and unload it on his wife. Bill's perception of them both "not treating me right," like the characteristic that Bill's boss perceives in the business and in Bill of being "frustrating," can equate the two situations in the unconscious.

If we look at these situations and this type of equating, we can see that very different people, experiences, and situations have potential of being equated in the unconscious by the part-oriented equating. This part-equating is based on a perceived characteristic, aspect, or trait. We can see from our examples that the unconscious can equate two entirely different people, experiences, or situations in reality, on the basis of any unconsciously perceived characteristic. It could be "not loving," "not treating right," or being "frustrating." For instance, a person may get sick, and because of the sickness has a frustration of his oral dependency need; but he then takes this resulting anger out on his best friend. There is something about the situation of being sick and his friend that is equated so that he can unload some of his anger.

A characteristic seen in one person, experience, or situation can be seen in another person, experience, or situation regardless of true reality, and this characteristic is then used to equate. For example, Bill Green's wife was preparing his dinner. She was doing something for him, but he perceived, unconsciously, that she was "not treating him right." The determination of the equating characteristic is all in the eye of the beholder. Through this transference, which involves equating unconsciously perceived characteristics, we can take the anger accrued from past involvements that have been unconsciously perceived as oral dependency need frustrating and transfer this anger to people, experiences, and situations in the here-and-now.

We can see from Bill's case the importance of the diffusion of which we spoke in Chapter Two. Bill cannot express anger to his boss without threatening their relationship. But if Bill continually takes out all the frustration that he accrues at work on his wife, he will jeopardize that relationship. If Bill had seen a friend after work, he could have expressed some of that anger to the friend instead of dumping it all on his wife. For example, Bill may have shared a locker at work with his friend and suddenly noticed that his friend's belongings took more than half the space. He may have unconsciously perceived that this friend was "not treating him right," and gotten rid of some anger by telling his friend, sharply, to "put less stuff in the locker." Then, when he went home, he would have less anger to express to his wife. Bill's boss also needed to diffuse his expression of anger. If he continues to dump all of his anger on Bill, Bill may decide to quit his job. Like Bill, the boss needs to spread his anger around so that it is less intense.

Both Bill and his boss use rationalizations to present, deceptively, the origins of their anger. If anyone asked him, Bill might say that he was angry at his wife because she "didn't even greet me at the door." Bill's boss would say that he was angry at Bill, maybe because "Bill took too many coffee breaks today." But the anger is already there and needs to come out. And it comes out under a rationalization that tends to be logical, reality-oriented, and to make sense. The unconscious presents the rationalization to the other person and to the angered person's conscious as a result of being angry when, the reader should recognize, the anger had built up from previous frustrations of the oral dependency need. It may have a multiplicity of unconsciously perceived origins and usually does. It's *accumulated* anger. It's there prior to the rationalization. The rationalization is secondary, creating a deception in regard to that about which we consciously become angry; things that we consciously feel angry about aren't really the causes of our anger. Those people who have the greatest amount of anger which is expressed in some rationalization are those who have the most accumulated anger from various oral dependency need frustrations.

The accumulated anger can be expressed in rationalizations that are socially acceptable, as in a cause to stamp out sin and corruption, for example, whatever that might be to the person who is giving the rationalization. But those who have the most anger against sin, corruption, vice, injustice, etc., are often those who have had the greatest tendency to build up anger from oral dependency need frustration. They are usually in situations where they are too dependent on too few, which fosters the accumulation of anger. The people who are not too dependent on too few and who have a situation in life in which they're having more of their oral dependency needs met have less accumulated anger with which to contend. If they have any (and we know that they must have *some* anger because they can't have *all* their oral dependency needs met), their anger is so spread out that they never have that much accumulated anger to express in concentrated form; we will not find them on the forefront of the battles against crime, sin, corruption, injustice, or whatever. It is those people who are too dependent on too few, who are accumulating more anger, who can then express their anger within some rationalization supported by others. But those who are even more inclined to be too dependent on too few may be more characterized by temper outbursts and may have even less control in channeling their anger into social endeavors or other interpersonal areas.

As we have said, we all accrue some anger when we experience oral dependency need frustration; it is an inevitable part of living in reality. We have really simplified this process because the oral dependency need is usually frustrated on a part-oriented basis in our involvements with people, experiences, and situations so that the frustration and anger build-up is entirely unconscious. We all, at some time, may become angry with a person to whom we cannot directly express this anger, because the situation is inappropriate, or we don't want to jeopardize the relationship. But through the part-equating of transference, we can get rid of this anger, by transferring it to someone whom we have unconsciously equated, in part, with that which has frustrated us. We are often unaware of the true reason for our anger because of its part-oriented origin and because the unconscious deceptively creates a rationalization based on whole persons, or whole experiences, or whole situations to explain the anger to the conscious. The diffusion of anger is based on the phenomenon of transference. It's that unconscious part-oriented equating that allows the diffusion process, in regard to accumulated anger, to take place. Only through the transference can we spread our anger around.

The diffusion of oral dependency need gratification in one's relationship sphere is done in precisely the same manner. The perceived characteristics would be, for example, "making me feel like I belong," "making me enjoy life," "making me feel important," or "liking to be with me." All these different unconsciously perceived characteristics can be used to equate, on a part-oriented basis, people, experiences, and situations that in reality may be entirely different and unrelated. The unconscious perceives a characteristic, or a part, that equates the two things so that a continuation of satisfaction of the oral dependency need can be had, thereby allowing a diffusion. That unconscious part-equating of transference is the very mechanism that allows the diffusion of the oral dependency need among different people in a variety of situations. The oral dependency need gratifying parts of people, experiences, and situations long gone from reality are unconsciously equated with parts of people, experiences, and situations in the person's present. We are beginning to see that our unconscious functioning is all done in parts. We meet our oral dependency need in or by parts, we are frustrated in or by parts, and we equate in or by parts. And one unconsciously perceived part of a person, experience, or situation in the past, present, or here-and-now, may be seen as frustrating while another part may be seen as gratifying the oral dependency need.

Those people who, for whatever reason, have more of a buildup of an unmet oral dependency need tend to turn to one person, experience, or situation in an attempt to draw more oral dependency need gratification from that one. This is similar to what we saw in regard to a high amount of built-up anger with Bill—there's a tendency to take it out on one. People who are emotionally comfortable tend to diffuse their oral dependency need and, in fact, as more of their oral dependency need is perceived as met, the more they tend to do it. Because they get emotionally involved with more people, the oral dependency need appears less intense. It is less noticeable than the oral dependency need in the emotionally immature person. The small child who has more of her oral dependency needs met makes friends more easily, and involves herself with other people because she feels more secure and has a good self-image; she feels loved. She is comfortable in venturing out, as opposed to the small child who doesn't have his oral dependency needs met, who tends to stay close to his oral dependency need gratifying person or persons because he has been frustrated before.

This transference based on part-equating is possible because the unconscious has an infinite number of characteristics that can do its equating, and it doesn't have to make the equating fit reality. The two very different people, experiences, or situations may even be equated when parts of them are unconsciously perceived as sharing only a lack of a certain characteristic. For example, two people may be equated because neither of them is "abusive," "rejecting," "threatening," or perhaps "unloving." Once I had a woman tell me in therapy "I always feel so much alone . . . like I have nothing in common with anybody else. I went to this informal gathering last week and was just standing there feeling so much out of place when a woman came up to me and said, 'I'm a mother and a wife. Do we have something in common?' I said very quickly 'No, we don't. I'm not either one of them!' But a young fellow was standing nearby and upon hearing this came over, saying: 'I guess *we* have something in common . . . I'm *not* a mother or a wife *either*!' We both laughed and then got to talking."[1] Any two people, experiences, or situations can be readily equated by the unconscious. The basis for this unconscious part-equating is limitless.

The ability to diffuse oral dependency need gratification through transference allows us to fill the void that is left when we lose people, experiences, or situations that gratified our oral dependency need. We all lose people, experiences, and situations in reality for different reasons.

People get mad at us, or they move away; we change jobs, or we finish college and go on to something else. The longer we live, the more people we will lose to death. We can't replace the people; however, transference allows us to continue to draw a meeting of the oral dependency need from unconsciously perceived parts of new people, experiences, and situations.

The child who ventures out and diffuses her oral dependency need gratification is unconsciously equating, *in part*, the other people who are gratifying her oral dependency need with the person or people who first and later gratified it. This transference is not the same as that which the psychoanalysts present as transference. The psychoanalysts say that we tend to relate to someone else, especially in the psychoanalytic situation, as we did to our mothers or fathers. They imply an orientation to the *whole*, that is, a whole person or a whole situation. That is quite different from the transference being discussed here. Our transference isn't based on equating whole people, experiences, or situations, but on equating parts from unconsciously perceived similar characteristics. This part-equating does not take place in just some therapy or counseling situation either, but in all of our relationships and in all of our different experiences and situations. It is an unavoidable, naturally occurring, unconscious phenomenon.

Now that we have seen how transference works with regard to the diffusion of both anger and oral dependency need gratification, let us turn to a more complex process. We saw that both Bill Green and his boss had expressed anger directly through the unconscious transference process. Through the transference we can also express anger indirectly, which always causes fewer relationship problems. And there is a greater tendency to express anger indirectly the more we have diffused our oral dependency need gratification, in other words, the more emotionally mature we are. We can see indirect anger expression in the case of a patient of mine whom we'll call Mary Smith.

Mary was a successful chemist who had won many awards for her work several years before this incident. In high school, Mary had had a chemistry teacher who had told her that she had no aptitude for chemistry. But Mary liked chemistry and decided to study it in college. Now that she was a successful chemist, she decided to go back to her hometown and show that chemistry teacher how wrong he had been about her aptitude. So she packed up her awards and went home for a visit. Mary's anger, however, was not really at the chemistry teacher for making her feel unimportant in that school class. She had been ill a few weeks before, and during the past week, the man she had been dating had stopped calling. She wanted to take her frustrations out on her old chemistry teacher who had frustrated her centrality and omnipotence ten years earlier. She had unconsciously equated the teacher, in part, with her present situation. When Mary arrived at her old high school, she learned that the teacher had died several years earlier. She called Jane, an old high school friend, and suggested that they dine together. At dinner, Mary told Jane about the reason for her visit. She was quite emotional when she told Jane how she'd planned to "show that old fool exactly what kind of aptitude I have," and Jane listened in agreement. After dinner, Mary felt much better; she no longer felt as though she needed to tell the teacher off. If anyone had told Mary that this was because she had unconsciously equated Jane, in part, with the chemistry teacher, and that the reason she'd come home was that she equated the chemistry teacher, in part, with being ill and her friend who hadn't called her, she'd have thought that they were crazy. But Mary expressed her anger about her present situation, indirectly, by telling Jane about her anger toward the old chemistry teacher. What Mary did was to use the here-and-now of Jane and herself to reduce the emotional problems of her present situation of having too much accumulated anger. She was able to "make right" the injustice, remembered from years ago, that was contained in her rationalization.

The conscious mind uses Aristotelian logic. In reality, "A" is "A" and cannot be "B"; something can be "A" or "B," not "A" and "B" at the same time, nor anything in between. Aristotelian logic is oriented toward time. It distinguishes a difference between what's past and what's present. But the unconscious uses primary process thinking not based on logic. In the emotional unreality, with primary process thinking, there is no orientation to time and therefore no distinction made between the past, the present, and the here-and-now. In the unconscious, yesterday is today and no water goes over the dam. Things, persons, experiences, events, and situations from the past, present, and here-and-now are contained in the reservoir of the unconscious mind. In the unconscious, "A" can be "B"; "A" can be both "A" and "B" at the same time; and something can be part "A" and part "B." The unconscious can perceive a characteristic or the lack thereof shared by "A" and "B" and then equate the two. The working of the unconscious mind is based on this illogical equating. The part-equating is done by the unconscious, with no regard for the element of time, as we see in Mary's case. The person that Mary's unconscious equated, in part, with her present situation was from ten years earlier; then Jane was equated in part with a person from the past and a situation in the present. This is an equating across time—past and present and finally between speaker and listener in the here-and-now.

Mary was able to express her anger to Jane indirectly, and draw oral dependency need gratification about Jane because Jane supported Mary's feelings about her chemistry teacher. Suppose two people have built up anger from different frustrations of their oral dependency need. One of them says, "I hate Colonel Khadafi. He's a threat to the whole world. Someone should do the bastard in." The other says, "I agree. I can't stand him either!" Transference allows the listeners to unconsciously equate Khadafi, in part, with their own oral dependency need frustrating persons, experiences, or situations. But they do not have to express their anger directly to Colonel Khadafi, because they can also unconsciously equate each other, in part, with the oral dependency need frustrations and Colonel Khadafi. They are each able to support and accept the other's anger because it is subtle; it is on the unconscious level, and it is being expressed indirectly.

Indirect or subtle anger expression is similar to indirect or subtle drawing of oral dependency need gratification. Both are on an unconscious part-oriented basis. Indirect anger tends to be less intense because of the diffusion process. It can be expressed as dislikes. Therefore, what we talk about to someone else with regard to what we dislike, or, with a little more anger behind it, what we despise, or even what we hate, is actually an unloading of the anger that has built up from the unconsciously perceived frustrations of our oral dependency need. It's expressed anger that's not oral dependency need threatening. In like manner, what we tell someone else we like, or with a little more concentrated meeting of the oral dependency need, what we enjoy or even what we love, is a reflection of the oral dependency need gratification being received from that relationship. It is really a piece of the "good breast" that is being unconsciously perceived in our involvements with people, experiences, and situations that we say we like, enjoy, or love. When we talk about something or someone that we like, we are saying that we equate our listener, in part, with this oral dependency need gratifying aspect of that someone or something. When the listener agrees, he confirms the reciprocation of the oral dependency need gratification. So when we say, "I like _____" to someone, we are really saying, "I like you," and when they say, "I do, too," they are really saying, "I like you, too." Substitute "dislike" for "like," and anger expression is supported.

It is not surprising then, that people with similar likes and dislikes often become friends. They mutually support each other's oral dependency need gratification as well as their anger expression. However, this is all done on an unconscious, indirect basis in the more comfortable relationships. One has less of a potential for getting into emotional difficulties if one meets his oral dependency need and gets rid of his anger on an unconsciously perceived "part-person," "part-experience," or "part-situation" basis, rather than directly. A whole person orientation that directly meets the oral dependency need or that directly receives anger has a greater potential for creating problems.

To see how diffusion plays a part in accepting the anger expressed by someone else and in the confirmation of mutual oral dependency need gratification, let's go back to Bill Green whom we saw coming home to his wife after he had an uncomfortable amount of his oral dependency needs frustrated in his work situation. If his wife had been out, emotionally involved with other people when Bill was at work, she would probably have a lot more of her oral dependency needs met. Therefore, she'd be more emotionally comfortable and more able, because of having met more of her own oral dependency needs, to tolerate any stress and frustration and even more able to tolerate a direct expression of anger toward her. Maybe she had been working during the day in a job she enjoyed that brought her into contact with people who met her oral dependency need when they listened to her and accepted her indirectly expressed anger. Maybe she'd been involved in church or charity work, or perhaps she had been visiting with some of her friends. But that emotional involvement with others tends to meet her oral dependency need and allows her to get rid of anger. When Bill comes home "mad," or with a real need to unload anger, as well as a need to meet some of his unmet oral needs, his wife can more easily handle him. His dilemma of wanting to feed off the "good breast" while wanting to bite the "bad breast" at the same time—both of which are too much embodied in his wife—is more easily resolved. She doesn't have a lot of accumulated unmet oral dependency needs and doesn't have a lot of accumulated anger. She's more emotionally comfortable. He finds something wrong with what she's doing or not doing, saying or not saying, and he gets directly angry with her. But she says, "Bill, I can tell you've had a hard day at the office; why don't you sit down here and tell me about it." Maybe she gives him a kiss and a hug because she's aware that he wants some attention, some caring, and a little love. She may not know it as a need for more oral dependency need gratification, but we do. Bill's wife, since she doesn't have a lot of unmet oral dependency needs herself, doesn't expect him to kiss and hug her. She doesn't have as much of a need for this because she's had more of her oral dependency need met in her involvement with others. So whether she gets a kiss and big hug in return is not so crucially important to her. She can comfortably give Bill the attention and caring he needs. Because she does this, Bill doesn't continue to find fault with her but begins to tell her about his day at work. Bill's direct anger expression wasn't taken personally. And her ability not to take directly expressed anger personally comes from her emotional comfortableness. Bill now tells his wife about his feeling that his boss treated him unfairly. He gets his anger out indirectly by telling his wife about his boss. As his wife listens to him and supports him emotionally, all his anger comes out. She's able to listen better because more of her oral dependency needs are met during the day. She doesn't have the pressure to talk that a higher unmet oral dependency need gives. Bill, who has more of a need for oral dependency need gratification, needs to talk. So he talks and she listens. He gets more comfortable, sleeps soundly that night and is ready for work the next day. In the morning, he relates comfortably to his boss.

Contrast this with a situation where Bill's wife isn't involved enough with other people. Maybe she's been home cleaning out closets and trying to keep the house in order the way she thinks he expects her to. Suppose she doesn't like to "waste time" chatting, gossiping, or just "running off at the mouth." Maybe she's the type who wants to accomplish a lot of work so she doesn't find the time—nor would she enjoy it if she did—to be with people. Because she hasn't had people listening to her, she doesn't have enough of her oral dependency need met to be really comfortable herself. She hasn't had the opportunity to spread around a little anger indirectly in her conversations with others. So when Bill comes home and begins to express anger directly to her, she gives it right back. He's too emotionally significant to her, and she's too dependent on too few to overlook directly expressed anger. It hurts too much and can devastate her. She expects him to give her a kiss and a hug because "I've been working hard and putting up with a lot right here at home—I haven't had it easy, so don't yell at me." She needs oral dependency need gratification from Bill, and she doesn't want, nor can she handle, Bill's anger toward her. This desire to have her oral dependency need met and desire to avoid having any anger expressed is not what Bill needs if he's to become emotionally comfortable. He requires a meeting of his unmet oral dependency need and some unloading of his anger to someone who will accept it. What he gets from his wife now is more frustration of his oral dependency need and no chance to get rid of anger. She wants to talk, and she wants him to listen. But he wants to talk, and he wants her to listen. Neither does much listening to the other, and neither does much accepting of the other's anger. What anger he "dumps" on her, she "dumps" right back. A fight ensues where each blames the other for his or her emotional uncomfortableness. If they don't continue to fight, frustrating the meeting of each other's oral dependency needs and thwarting each other's attempts to get rid of anger, then they give each other the "silent treatment," which doesn't help either. Bill goes to bed but can't sleep until he gets up and has a few drinks. His wife gets a migraine headache, and she can't sleep either. The next day Bill calls in sick and doesn't go to work.

What the reader should see is that emotional involvement with others is the key to a comfortable home life for Bill. This emotional involvement with others can be under any reality orientation. Bill's involvement with others might be under the guise of a baseball orientation. He could express his anger, for instance, over certain players who aren't playing as well as he thinks they should. The person listening to Bill talk accepts this anger. The listener is, in part, the baseball player—equated by the phenomenon of transference in Bill's unconscious. The anger gets out. The players Bill likes, and tells his listener he likes, are equated through that same transference. His listener is, in part, the baseball players whom he likes. It is an unconscious confirmation of the perceived gratification of his oral dependency need from that listener listening to him talk about baseball. His wife's involvement might be under a reality orientation of church work, charity work, bowling, or perhaps a work situation. It's an *emotional* process of becoming comfortable. It's an unconscious process and not a conscious one.

Now we can see the deception in trying to follow reality-oriented advice as to how to have a good relationship with your spouse. "Greet him at the door with a smile." The irony is that if Bill's wife stayed home, read every marriage book there was on how to make a better marriage, and memorized perfectly the "dos" and "don'ts," she wouldn't do as well in her marriage as the wife who never read a single marriage book chapter or even one page of a chapter but enjoyed people and was emotionally involved with others, meeting her oral dependency needs and getting rid of her anger. The person who knows the "dos" and "don'ts" can't hide the feelings. They're bound to show through whatever front a person is attempting to put on. It's a deception to think that we *learn* to be emotionally comfortable. It's a deception too to think we learn to control our tempers. It may appear that way when the "need" to express anger has decreased. It's an emotional process and not a learning process at all. But how often have we heard "He has to learn to control his temper"?

As an example of indirect, mutually supported anger expression, and the indirect confirmation of reciprocal oral dependency need gratification, consider the dialogue of two teachers, Joan and Nancy, who meet in the hallway of their school. They engage in spontaneous communication while monitoring the changing of classes. Remember that whoever is talking is meeting her oral dependency need from the listener. Note that each speaker refers to an unconsciously perceived and equated aspect of the listener; there is mutual support for this unconscious part-person orientation that provides a mutual meeting of the oral dependency need. The favorably described "Barbara" is a reference to the unconsciously favorably perceived aspects of each person by the other, that is oral dependency need gratifying. The references to both the "Smith boy" and "Mrs. Franklin" represent mutually accepted and supported anger expression by, and to, each other.

Joan:	What's new?
Nancy:	Just got through straightening out that Smith boy. I've been wanting to do that for a long time. I can't stand him.
Joan:	Good for you! He's the perfect brat! I can't stand him either! I hope you gave him what he deserves!
Nancy:	Well, I went up one side of him and down the other. He's had no respect for authority, so I decided I'd lay the law down to him. I would have liked to put him against the nearest wall and shot him.
Joan:	That would be too good for him. (Both laugh) Where are you going this weekend?
Nancy:	Barbara and I are going shopping in Washington. We went a month ago and had such a nice time, we thought we'd try it again. She's so much fun to be with (smiles and puts her hand on Joan's arm) I really enjoy myself with her.
Joan:	She is nice (smiles back). I went to last year's teachers' convention with her and we had a ball.
Nancy:	I got stuck the whole week with that old Mrs. Franklin. All she talked about was how hard she works and how easy the other teachers have it!
Joan:	She's full of you know what!
Nancy:	She really is! Say, why don't the two of us go together this year?
Joan:	Let's! Sounds like fun! Talk with you more about it at lunch!
Nancy:	See you then.

The above example shows both forms of oral dependency need gratification involved in spontaneous communication: one is where someone talks to another who listens, making the speaker the center of attention; and the other is where there is indirect anger expression which is not only accepted but even supported. When one expresses anger and perceives acceptance of this anger expression, it meets the oral dependency need. It does so by fostering the omnipotence embodied in the oral dependency need. If we're emotionally comfortable, we do each of these diffusely in a wide sphere of emotional involvements, all of which are subtle. The meeting of our oral dependency need then, if we are emotionally mature, is predominately unconsciously done through the phenomenon of transference. This is also true for the expression of the anger that comes from unconsciously perceived frustrations of the oral dependency need. Both are done on a part-oriented basis and both below the level of awareness.

In the next chapter, we will look more closely at the unconscious process of part-equating. Through a closer examination of the language used in transference, we will be able to see more clearly how it is spontaneous communication that, like the umbilical cord, both emotionally nourishes us and emotionally eliminates our waste on a continuing basis.

1. COMMUNICATION BREAKDOWN Warren H. Green Publishing Co St. Louis MO 1975

CHAPTER 4
How the Unconscious Continually Affects Our Communication

It is becoming apparent that the unconscious works without our knowing it. As an example of the unconscious in action, suppose that a family is having a guest for dinner, and decides to play an after dinner game. Before the guest arrives, the family has decided to answer questions that he might ask with: "yes," "yes," "no," "yes," "yes," "no," etc. After dinner the host tells the guest that he's going to play a game, and explains that the guest is to go out of the room and then the family will think up a story. The guest's job is to ask questions of each member at the table to see how quickly he can reconstruct the story that he thinks the members at the table have made up. He is told he will go around the table, as many times as is necessary, asking one question of each member, racing the clock to find out the story. He will be the first to guess a story and register his time and then another person will take a try at guessing the group's next story. After he goes out of the room, wait a few minutes, then when he comes back, let him ask his question. With his questions and the family's pre-arranged stock answers, he'll make up a story from his unconscious without knowing he's doing it. Remarkable stories are made up under these circumstances because the person will do it with no inhibitions whatsoever; he thinks it's the *family's* story, so it may even get a little sexy. He's actually projecting, unconsciously, what's on his mind. Of course, the embarrassed guest will never come back to dinner again. This game suggests that what comes to mind during a conversation is unconsciously determined and things talked about may convey hidden meanings without the speaker realizing what is taking place.

The unconscious works similarly in spontaneous communication and in dreams. Let's take a look at the dream first. The dream has a *manifest content* and a *latent content*. The manifest content is what is "seen" by the dreamer. It tends to be oriented to the dreamer's reality—past or present people, experiences, or situations in his life. But the manifest content is only superficial, for the latent content of the dream lies beneath it. The latent content is oriented to the dreamer's emotional unreality, and is based on primary process thinking. The unconscious forms the manifest

46

content as a way to present the latent content. For instance, a person may have a dream about a little boy fishing beside a small stream in Colorado. The dreamer has had some associations with streams in Colorado, so it is easy for his unconscious to "set the stage" for the manifest content of this dream. Everything seems perfect in his dream, but there is a sense of foreboding. Suddenly a grizzly bear appears, sees him fishing, and charges toward him. One could go on to make up more of the manifest content of the dream, but in the latent content, the little boy is the dreamer, in part, and the bear is some person or some situation in his life that is suddenly coming upon him as a most pronounced danger. We see, therefore, that the manifest content may be presented in a drama that doesn't seem like it has anything to do with the dreamer, but it actually does. The unconsciously created manifest content is like a play, acted out to convey the dreamer's different emotional conflicts, through symbols, metaphors, and analogies. The surface meaning is only a vehicle for something that is much more important.

Spontaneous communication also has a manifest and latent content. The language that we use in communication is usually oriented to something in our reality situation. But the reality-oriented topic of conversation is only the manifest content, a vehicle for underlying latent content, which is oriented to our emotional unreality. Primary process thinking equates some unconsciously perceived aspect of the listener, or some unconsciously perceived aspect of the self with what is being talked about in the manifest content. This part-equating is expressed in the latent content of communication. The language of spontaneous communication is a mechanism enabling the process of transference to work. This transference language allows anger *at* our listener to be expressed and oral dependency needs to be met *by* the listener, indirectly and unconsciously, in the latent content, while the manifest content may seem to have nothing to do with the listener.

The manifest content, in both the dream and in spontaneous communication, is secondary in formation and importance to the emotional problems and conflicts of the latent content. The latent content is formed first. Then the manifest content is developed to manifest the problem or content in all its different ways and to present hoped-for resolutions. In dreams, this unconscious functioning is called *dream work*. The unconscious perceives the emotional problems of the person, perceives various ways to present these problems, and perceives various resolutions. Then it sets the problem and its resolution into a drama, which makes up the secondarily formed manifest content. As in the dream the manifest content of transference language is secondarily formed. The latent content is primary in both origin and importance. We can call the unconscious process that forms the manifest content of communication from an existing latent content *language work.*

Freud once called the dream the "Royal Road to the Unconscious." But if you were ever impressed by the unconscious functioning in dream work, you should be even more so with language work, since it involves at least one other person and requires a greater rapidity and complexity than dream work. In language work there is a constant unconscious monitoring of the other person's manifest content, a constant monitoring of any nonverbal behavior, and a constant evaluating of the information received. Then the latent content is changed or adjusted, and a manifest content is created with amazing rapidity. The unconscious functioning in its awesome language work deals with present part-person, part-experience, and part-situation equating that is far more complex than the seemingly more simple perception of reality by the conscious mind.

But a deception is created. The secondarily formed manifest content appears as though it's spontaneous. "Thoughtless" small talk and the ease of chitchatting hides all the language work that actually determines not only what is said but also how it's said in the manifest content. One has all of reality from which to choose a manifest content to hide the latent content. Consider what occurs in recalling a dream. "Dream recall" and the dream's manifest content are not the same at all. When a dream is told to someone else, it becomes the manifest content of communication, under the influence of the transference. Though most haven't, some dream researchers have actually recognized the transference language of dream recall. They've said that they can see references to the listener—in these cases, the dream researcher—in the recall of the dream that the person is presenting. The true manifest content of a dream is usually hidden. Though one may attempt to remember it, in telling it to another person the process becomes influenced and distorted because of the operating transference factor within that relationship. We can now say that Freud was only partly right in calling the dream the "Royal Road to the Unconscious," for the true "Royal Road" is spontaneous communication. It certainly lends itself to far more interesting analysis than the dream, but because it is an unconscious process it would be denied by the speaker. The analysis of transference language is far more inclusive and incorporates any manifest content including that oriented to a dream.

The transference language of spontaneous communication is similar to the dream in purpose. The dreaming process is believed to be not only a way of presenting the emotional problems of the dreamer, but also an attempt to resolve them. In the bear dream, what is being presented is that there is unmet danger, that action must be taken, and that unless the right action is taken, there could be a monumental disaster. Spontaneous communication is also a way of attempting to resolve emotional problems by getting rid of anger and meeting the oral dependency need.

It has been said that we all dream every ninety minutes while we are asleep. This can be determined by electroencephalographic monitoring. When the sleeping person is monitored, one can see when the sleeper is dreaming because the electroencephalogram will easily detect his eye muscles moving his eyes as the sleeper begins to watch the dream. For instance, if in our dream about the bear, the bear comes out of the woods on the little boy's extreme left, the sleeper's eyes will turn to the extreme left to see the bear. Dream researchers feel that dreaming is universal and that when people are deprived of these dream periods by being awakened every time the electroencephalogram shows rapid eye movements indicating that a dream is beginning to take place, they tend to become more emotionally uncomfortable. They tend to be less able to handle the stress and frustration of their everyday life. Thus, dream researchers speculate that the dreaming process is conflict resolving—it tends to resolve the emotional conflicts that we know basically involve the problems of getting our oral dependency needs met, remaining central and omnipotent in our emotional worlds, and getting rid of anger.

Just as we all dream, we all use transference language in an attempt to meet the oral dependency need and to get rid of anger. The necessity to dream regularly is analogous to the necessity to engage in spontaneous communication, to chitchat or gossip, regularly. When people are isolated, either physically or because of their inability to perceive oral dependency need gratification (something we'll examine later), they tend to become emotionally uncomfortable. So the deprivation of spontaneous communication, like dream deprivation, causes similar emotional problems.

It may seem hard to believe that when one spontaneously talks to someone else about likes and dislikes, he is unconsciously talking about that someone else. Or that when someone talks about another person or something that is close to herself, she is unconsciously talking about herself. It can become rather obvious in a psychotherapy or counseling situation, the reason being that the person who comes in for psychotherapy or counseling is usually one who has become too dependent on too few, and has a high unmet oral dependency need. As we have said, those people with a high unmet oral dependency need are often searching for an intense meeting of that need; thus, they tend to form a more intense or concentrated transference with someone who will listen. As a result their transference language is more readily seen. When talking to a therapist, a client appears to say, through indirect transference language, "This is my emotional problem and I am transferring it into our relationship so that you and I can work it out together." Transference is much harder to pick up in the everyday conversation of more emotionally comfortable people, but it is still there. It can happen as spontaneously as striking up a conversation with someone while you're on vacation. I'm sure you've done this before, while waiting in line for a train, at an amusement park, in an airplane, or going through customs while on a trip. You just meet someone standing near you by striking up a conversation. It becomes more emotionally involved when this spontaneous communication involves friends. Believe it or not, this type of spontaneity in our daily communication can keep us emotionally comfortable and return us to comfortableness after we've become emotionally uncomfortable for whatever reason. Daily spontaneous communication is as necessary as dreaming to maintain emotional comfortableness and, like dream deprivation, deprivation of spontaneous communication can produce emotional uncomfortableness.

Communication, then, involves much more than the transfer of information. We have seen that the unconscious equates parts of people, experiences, and situations, and uses this illogical part-equating in the communicative process. Using the language of transference, people can gain oral dependency need gratification and express their anger indirectly. It is because of this transference process that any one relationship reflects, to a degree, all of an individual's other relationships, both past and present. Even the therapeutic relationship reflects, and is influenced by, a person's other past and present relationships. This interweaving transference factor, binding all of an individual's relationships, is based on part-equating—that illogical process which cannot be measured. The manifest content of transference language is really metaphorical, conveying what is being perceived about the relationship. Since all relationships, even the most casual, are transference relationships, the transference process is always operable to a degree in communication, and transference language is present to the same degree. Under the reality-oriented guise of being rational, intellectual, and logical, there is an irrational, illogical, and emotionally oriented part-person, part-experience, and part-situation interrelating that is always operating in spontaneous communication. This then gives the relationship an emotional conflict resolving potential. Where the purpose of conscious communication is the transfer of information, unconscious communication has a purpose of utilizing the relationship in the here-and-now to resolve emotional problems past and present.

Manifest content can be factual, scientific, and unquestionably correct, but whatever a person spontaneously brings up in communication has

something, emotionally, to do with the unconsciously perceived transference situation. The motivation for whatever is spontaneously mentioned or brought up comes from the latent transference interaction
between speaker and listener. Spontaneous communication is continually
conveying a metaphorical manifest content that has something to do
with the unconscious perceptions of the individual and his relationship
with the listener. Even when a person spontaneously volunteers information about his past, what he brings up is metaphorically appropriate
for the unconsciously perceived situation within his relationship to the
listener at that very moment. This creates an interesting set of dynamics
in the communicative process of someone who is emotionally uncomfortable. Whatever the person is upset about in the present is a reflection
of her emotional problems in the distant past. In other words, her past
emotional conflicts or problems are reflected into her present emotional
difficulties. Whatever she is talking about is metaphorical for what she
unconsciously equates and perceives, in part, in the here-and-now situation between the listener and herself. The past and present are brought
together and made one within the immediate transference relationship.

In order to see the functioning of this transference language, let's look
at some examples taken from therapy situations, where the language is
more obvious. In the following excerpt, it is obvious that this woman
identifies some aspect of herself with her dog "Lady." People often talk
about themselves by talking about something with which they unconsciously identify; the subject becomes a projection of an aspect or a part
of that person. For example, this woman who lived on an island denied
that she had any emotional problems. She said that everything was "just
fine"; her childhood had been "just fine," and she knew of no problems
she'd had with her family or with other people. I had the feeling, as you
will too, that she was talking about herself when she chatted on about
her situation to me as follows:

I live out on the island with Lady. We don't get many visitors as it's rather
inaccessible [and she is too] except when the tide's up and you can get a boat
over the bars. I like to talk to people that have an interest in dogs. You can
always find me anywhere you find Lady and vice versa. We're always together.
She was a stray and I don't know how she ended up on the island. I wish she
could tell how, but of course she can't. I know she had been treated terribly. She
was probably beaten and underfed, if not outright starved. People can be so
cruel to dumb animals like that. There ought to be a law against such neglect.
[I replied, "Yes, there should be."] You can tell that she's been hurt in the past.
She's very meek and painfully shy, and so terrified of people. Unless she's gotten
to know you, she'll hide under the house with her tail between her legs. [She
laughs and I smile.] You won't see her at all as she's so timid and passive. She's
afraid even now and will stay in the background even around people she knows.

[I add, "She's had it pretty rough."] Yes, she has. And I bet she would tell you about it if only she could. It's made her so she's not like other dogs. She's never running around playfully or barking or making a lot of noise like most dogs. And she's petrified of thunderstorms. [She laughs.] I'm that way, too. I guess she's a lot like me.[1]

In another case, a patient who had an emotional inability to talk about her own problems, except in terms of persistent and unrelieved gastro-intestinal distress, had a pet guinea pig named Jake. Her therapist learned that she kept the pet in a box in her kitchen. In the busy, patient-filled clinic this woman seemed particularly gratified when each time the therapist saw her he spontaneously asked how Jake was doing. "He hates to stay in that box all cooped up!" she would reply at first; then added so appropriately, "Jake is having a terrible time. He never seems to get enough to eat." She would volunteer, as she would not other information, how "He squeaks with excitement whenever he hears that refrigerator door open!" She herself was invariably one of the first patients through the clinic door on the day of her appointment, always well in advance of her scheduled time, eager to take in the emotional nourishment her therapeutic relationship gave her. As a boy, the therapist himself had had a guinea pig, and could knowingly sustain and support her manifest content centering around Jake's problems and needs. Jake was soon doing "fine," and the patient herself began to verbalize her problems in a more personally oriented manifest content that brought about even more emotional comfortableness. Through talking about Jake and having the therapist listen, the woman began to meet her own oral dependency need.

One depressed patient's "psychotherapy" consisted entirely of talking about his interest in gardening. Though the therapist himself never raised a single successful vegetable garden, the client seemed to receive much emotional gratification from these "talks" about gardening. His wife told the nurse, "He seems to enjoy these talks with the doctor so much. He looks forward to coming here, and he's been more active as a result of it all." He took renewed interest in his gardening, and became socially active, relating to others with a gardening interest. During these talks, he indirectly ventilated his anger and subtly met his oral dependency needs. He became less and less depressed and grew more confident. Psychological problems were never discussed at any time in the manifest content. He laughingly accepted a return appointment with the therapist one time when offered with, "Well, let me catch you when the onions are up just to see how that garden is coming along."

The manifest content of transference language allows a distance from the various ambivalent and often conflicting or contradicting aspects of ourselves or our listeners. We don't tell the listener directly how we feel; our feelings wouldn't make sense in reality if we had a lot of ambivalent or mixed feelings. We can always deny that we were talking about ourselves or our listener. We can avoid what is characteristic of any love-hate relationship where there is too much love and anger directly expressed to the same person. Transference language allows us to do it indirectly with distance and safety. A person who says, for example, "My husband wants to know if I should get out more" wants to know *herself*, but she presents it in regard to reality as her husband wanting to know. She may then go on to present different aspects of her own conflicting ambivalence saying, "I don't think I need to get out more, but my husband does." She is implying that she feels, but only in part, that she needs to get out more, unconsciously equating some aspect of herself with her husband. Logically, this woman cannot say directly that she does and doesn't think she needs to get out more. She's wondering if she should get out more and, at the same time, implies that her listener, she feels, thinks she should get out more by asking the listener if he thinks she should get out more. When her ambivalence is presented directly, it doesn't make sense. But through transference and unconscious part-equating, she is able to present her own ambivalence in a way that makes sense and fits with reality. And through this process, the ambivalence is reduced. If it were directly expressed the ambivalence could easily be intensified.

In the following example, it should be obvious that Carol is talking indirectly about her therapist, expressing her anger at him through talking about her brother and Rosalyn. Carol was an executive secretary with a long history of relationships that had turned sour and, after becoming depressed, she sought professional help. She had been seeing her psychotherapist twice a week for several months during which time she became much more expressive of her feelings and much less depressed. In the session previous to this one, the therapist told Carol that he wouldn't be available for therapy the following week because he'd be out of town. He told her ahead of time that he would be away, so she could express her anger and work out the dilemma of his absence, which occurs because she has been meeting so much of her oral dependency need in the therapy situation. Even though, in reality, she knows that her therapist must leave at times, in her unconscious, she still wants to be central. His leaving frustrates her centrality, so she becomes angry. Because he told her of his absence ahead of time, Carol is able to express her anger.

When Carol talks of Rosalyn, Rosalyn is she, in part. She shows a little of her own self-image when she talks about Rosalyn. She says Rosalyn's "nothing but an old tramp," associating a sinful connotation with the meeting of the oral dependency need; it becomes sexualized. She implies that Dick, who is the therapist, in part, is getting his need met whenever he wants, and she expresses anger over this. When she tells the therapist, "I shouldn't care about Rosalyn, but I do," she means "I shouldn't care about myself, but I do."

This session, which occurred after the therapist had told Carol that he'd be away the next week, went as follows:

I've been very upset since I saw you last. It's that damn Dick. I think at times my brother purposefully does things just to upset me. Apparently he's going away for a few weeks and he's leaving Rosalyn behind. Now that makes me madder than hell! I don't think it's fair for him to go off and leave her. What he needs is a good slap in the face to knock a little sense into him. Who in the hell does he think he is, anyway, using people the way he does? [Therapist shrugs.] I've known all along that Dick is a taker and a taker only. I'm ashamed to be related to a person with such a despicable attitude as his. [Sneers at therapist.] God, does he make me mad! I know Rosalyn is nothing but an old tramp anybody could lay if they were that hard up, but he's the one that brought her home. He's the one that felt sorry for her and took her in. Dick was playing that good Samaritan role to help her out. Hell, help her out! All he was doing was laying her and now I guess he's tired of her. I wasn't supposed to know about all this, but I found out that Dick and Rosalyn have been closer than some people think. [Therapist: "Oh?"] Just the other day I came downstairs and saw two pillows on the couch, so I asked Dick, 'Did you and Rosalyn sleep down here last night?' He said, 'Oh, we were just talking together. That's all.' I know damn well it was otherwise. His idea of talking together involves her getting laid! What gets me is that Dick acts so saintly, and he has such a self-righteous attitude. He's supposed to be helping her. Now he tells me he's leaving her and that she can fend for herself for all he apparently cares. I can't prevent him from leaving. He says it's necessary for him to go. For all I know he won't be back. That's been done to me plenty of times before. So I end up an emotional pawn in this damn rotten situation that he's making. It was the very same thing I went through in my recent marriage and maybe that's why I'm so upset now. I can see the same thing happening to Rosalyn that happened to me with Bradford. [Bradford is her ex-husband but also the therapist, in part, with different connotations than "Dick" or "Mother".] I trusted Bradford. I tried to have faith in him, but that's just it. I would have been spared all the emotional turmoil I went through if I had been involved in some affair with somebody else or if I turned to alcohol like my father did. I guess I'm not the type of girl to do either one. Maybe I'd be better off if I did. I probably wouldn't be sitting here in this chair all upset if I had done either one. I'm always getting hurt. When will it ever end? [She cries softly for several minutes.] What is it about me that all I can see is someone leaving someone else? It's so damn depressing. I ought not to care about Rosalyn, but I do. Can you tell me why a person does a thing like Dick is doing to Rosalyn?

Doesn't he have any conception of morality or decency? [Therapist shrugs.] Maybe we're supposed to get rid of Rosalyn before he gets back. You know, dump her out like old garbage. I'm so mad at him now that I hope to hell he never does come back. [Thoughtful pause.] If he wants to shack up with her, okay, that's his business, but he ought to take her with him—not dump her. I guess he's gotten tired of her and he's off to find some other person who's down and out that he can pull his 'good Samaritan' act on. If he really cared for her, he'd be taking her with him. [Pauses and then smiles warmly at the therapist.] Well, maybe it helps a little for me to spout off to you about that damn brother of mine. [Therapist says, "Dick does need straightening out. But I doubt you've seen the last of him. He'll be back."] Oh, I suppose so. [Pause.] Oh! I just now remembered something. Before I go, let me get this straight. You won't be here next week? [Therapist: "Right."] Well, I hope you have a nice trip or vacation, or whatever it is. I feel you certainly deserve one with all you have to put up with from me.[2]

It should be noted that Carol didn't have to talk about Dick and Rosalyn in therapy; what the person spontaneously brings up is unconsciously determined. It is only the vehicle for the latent communication. She could have talked about something else in manifest content, but it would have conveyed latently the very same thing. If her session had been longer, she would probably have presented the same emotional conflict, hidden under different manifest contents, several times.

Another client began her session by telling the therapist, "Good morning, you look very nice today. Is that a new suit? [Therapist smiles.] I haven't seen it before. [Pause.] Well, what I want to know today is if there's any hope for my marriage." Later in the session, she began talking about her husband. "All he's interested in is his own self. He reminds me of a fat pig. He went out the other day and bought himself a new sports coat and a turtle-neck sweater. Didn't buy me a damn thing! Then he thinks he looks great with it on! Just great! [Sneers.] Well, I want you to know he's nothing but a big fat pig in a new sports coat to me!"[2] This woman has equated the therapist and his "new suit" with her husband and his "new sports coat." The therapist is the husband, in part. Through transference language she can get her anger out so that when she goes home her need to tell her husband that he is a "fat pig" is diminished because her anger is less. In addition, it is interesting to note that part of her anger comes from her perception that he didn't buy her a "damn thing"; in other words, he doesn't meet her oral dependency need and she feels it is his fault.

These examples are a little more obvious than what we would see in everyday spontaneous communication. It is clear that Carol is talking not only about the situation with her brother, but also about the situation with her therapist. In the second example, it is clear that the client part-equates her husband and the therapist. Transference language should be veiled and indirect to keep communication going. The emotionally uncomfortable person who tends to be too dependent on too few has a more intense transference and therefore a more evident transference language. In a nontherapeutic relationship, blatant anger, even though indirect, might end the relationship. If transference language becomes unveiled and obvious, others will "read" it, which, in turn, may cause the listener to become angry. If either of these women had some friends, she would have diffused her anger, and have kept it more hidden.

Sometimes the physical gestures of a speaker make the transference language rather obvious. The following example involves a young man who saw a doctor who is a friend of mine in the hospital after the man's wife had been admitted late at night following a suicidal gesture. This man and his wife were caught up in a love-hate relationship and as a result, he had a high unmet oral dependency need and anger. When he talked to my friend while standing in the hospital hallway, he formed an intense transference right away because of that great amount of un-met oral dependency need and unexpressed anger. He began to tell my friend about the argument he and his wife had just prior to her manipu-lative suicidal attempt and excitedly said, "She got right up in my face, yelling at me that I was no damn good!" He got up close to this doctor to act this out yelling himself. He continued to push his face in my friend's and then went on, "She then started to poke me in the chest with her damn finger." Then he started doing it to the doctor. At this point my friend decided he really didn't need this, so he interrupted the man and said, "You should have given her a shove and told her to shut up!" He told me that he then gave the man "a hell of a shove" that sent him back about two feet; that did make him shut up. It probably wasn't very therapeutic for the man, but the doctor who was tired of this obvious emotional re-enactment got his point across.

The gestures can be a lot less obvious than this and still make the transference language quite evident. One woman told me, "I hate Albert . . . I despise him. [Sneers directly at therapist.] I can't stand to even look at his face. [Averts her face.] I hate to spend any time with him except right now I've got to put up with him but as soon as I get independent, I'm leaving the bastard!" This woman had transferred her anger onto the therapist. As long as she doesn't say things like this to Albert, they probably will continue their relationship. A therapist or counselor can accept her indirect anger, as anyone can, without giving anger back or getting angry. Albert would probably not be as accepting of anger di-rectly expressed to him.

The reason that people come in for therapy is that they have a great

deal of unmet oral dependency need; they have a great deal of accumulated unexpressed anger which causes them to form an intense transference in therapy. Sometimes, however, even in a therapeutic
relationship, the transference language can slip by if the therapist becomes too involved in the manifest content of the spontaneous communication, as happened in the following example. A depressed person
who was beginning to express her anger to me complained that her
husband wasn't doing enough to provide for her and the children. She
told me, "He doesn't give me enough money to buy the kinds of food
that children ought to have when they're growing—they're tired of eating baloney all the time." I spontaneously supported her anger expression by remarking, "He can certainly do a lot more than he's doing now."
She then remarked, "I think I've charged all the groceries at the store
that I dare to," and I spontaneously replied, "Well, let your husband
take care of the bill. The grocer isn't starving; let him wait."[2] Unfortunately, it wasn't until later that I remembered this session and picked
up on both her and my own transference language, when I discovered
that she hadn't paid for her past few sessions.

It should be evident by now that we speak in metaphor. The unconscious creates these metaphors so that we can gratify our oral dependency
need and get rid of our anger, in ways that, in comfortable communication, will not be noticed by others or by the conscious mind. We use
metaphors to allow ourselves distance in expressing our ambivalent feelings. By keeping the feelings unconscious and their expression indirect,
metaphors protect us from direct rejection and the resulting frustration.

To give you an example of the advantages of metaphor, a shy thirteen-
year-old girl with a big inferiority complex came to see me when she
had difficulty in going to school. She came in one week bringing a Cab-
bage Patch doll whom she had named Heather. I have a jar of gum drops
on my desk, and since she was getting over her shyness and feelings of
inferiority, she said, "Heather would like a gum drop." She's not quite
comfortable enough, yet, to take a rejection so she doesn't ask for it
herself. She says, instead, that "Heather would like a gum drop." Heather
is metaphorical for herself but it would be Heather who would take the
rejection if I said "no." The metaphor allows a comfortable distance and
protects against a total personal rejection. I said, "Sure, Heather can
have a gum drop." As I was getting out a yellow gum drop, she said,
"Heather prefers a black one." So I said, "Sure, Heather can have a black
one." But then she quickly followed this with, "Heather wants two, one
for her and one for a friend." The metaphor allows this girl to express
her feelings and desire for a gum drop without risking rejection and
more oral dependency need gratification.

In this example, it is obvious that Heather is metaphorically the girl. People often use other people for things that they identify with themselves, or with which they're closely associated, as metaphors for themselves. Other examples would be Lady, the dog, who was metaphorical for her owner, or Jake, the guinea pig. Carol's brother, Dick, is metaphorically the therapist, both of whom are leaving for a few weeks, and the husband with the new sports jacket is metaphorically the therapist in his new suit. In some cases, hunger is a metaphor for the need for emotional nourishment and food is metaphorically oral dependency need gratification. For instance, "Heather wanted a gum drop," the woman's husband wouldn't give her money for the grocer and "Jake . . . never seems to get enough to eat." Through the metaphors of the manifest content, the speaker can convey contrasting and often contradictory feelings about his oral dependency need and about his anger, which may involve wanting and not wanting the oral dependency need met, and wanting and not wanting to express anger. The more emotionally uncomfortable a person becomes, the more ambivalent the person tends to be. This mixture of contrasting feelings is best kept in the emotional unreality, since it may fit poorly in that person's reality. Each one of us lives in two very different worlds: the world of reality, and the world of emotional unreality. These two worlds are marvelously related through spontaneous communication.

In reality, communication deals with the transfer of information between two or more people. But the latent content, through transference language, concerns itself with resolving emotional uncomfortableness. One is crucial to reality; the other is crucial to the emotional unreality. Both are interrelated and each can effect the other. Talking and listening bring them together. If we can get a person to talk, under any manifest content whatsoever, and we listen to that person, we can subtly meet his oral dependency needs. We also subtly accept his anger, which he expresses indirectly; thus, he will become more comfortable and less ambivalent or mixed up in his feelings. When we talk spontaneously, our listener does the same for us. That's the way transference language works; it's all done under a guise of reality. We maintain our emotional comfortableness predominantly through this means. We meet our oral dependency need, and we get rid of our anger unconsciously, all below the level of reality. Since this process is unconscious, and works through the transference language, the manifest content or subject matter of communication is unimportant.

I had as a patient a little boy who wouldn't go to school; all he talked about to me was softball. Softball was his manifest content, and talking about it helped him resolve his emotional uncomfortableness. His father, however, didn't understand. The boy spontaneously related his father's views during an early therapy session, saving "He asked me what we talked about last time and when I told him it was softball, he hit the ceiling! 'What a waste! If you want to talk about softball, you can talk to me and save forty five dollars a week!" [2] The father couldn't see how talking about softball could resolve the reasons why the boy would not go to school. An unconscious and guilt-laden aspect of the boy obviously didn't either. But the boy could convey, metaphorically, the difficulties he was having with those who were emotionally significant to him, including the therapist himself, by talking about softball. A resolution of his emotional problems was obtained which might not have occurred if those emotional problems had been approached directly. These emotional problems are often too ambivalent to make sense in reality anyway.

Understanding the unconscious language work and the transference language of even the simplest conversations opens an entirely new dimension in communication and psychodynamics for the therapist or counselor. It forms the very foundation for the professional listener's skill in resolving emotional problems. In the next chapter, we'll see what some of these unconscious emotional problems are.

1. Adapted from: THE THERAPEUTIC LISTENER, Robert E. Krieger Publishing Company, Melbourne, FL 1974
2. Adapted from: COMMUNICATION BREAKDOWN, Warren H. Green Publishing Company, St. Louis, MO 1975

CHAPTER 5
How One Becomes Emotionally Independent

Being independent is unquestionably advantageous in life. In being independent, an individual is more free to do what he wants and is not at someone else's beck and call. He doesn't worry about how others feel about him. He's more free to say what he wants without fear of recrimination. Being independent means he doesn't rely on someone else to make him happy or give him a reason for living. When a person is independent, he tends to be able to avoid the unhappiness in life that may come from the relationship sphere. He can do this by not giving someone that power to make him not only the happiest person in the world, but also to make him the unhappiest as well. That very person who at one time may be his reason for living, may be at another time his reason for dying. An independent person, avoids the tendency to have emotions determine behavior. It's easier to let intellect determine behavior, perceptions of the world, and life in general.

Being truly independent is a most enviable position in life. Some people are genuinely independent. They have become this way by sufficiently meeting their oral dependency need. They started out in early life avoiding bad luck and getting a good share of their oral dependency need met. Consequently, they felt secure enough to venture out emotionally, continuing to meet that oral dependency need in their widening sphere of relationships. They went from being dependent on one or a few people to being dependent on many people, experiences, and situations to meet that same amount of oral dependency need. They're not dependent on one person, experience, or situation; but they are diffusely dependent, which makes them genuinely independent.

To visualize this process of becoming emotionally mature or genuinely independent, picture a round circle sitting on a line. The area in the circle is the oral dependency need, and everything above the line represents reality and the conscious. That which is below the line represents the emotional unreality and the unconscious. For the infant or small child, the meeting of her oral dependency need is in that circle above the line. It is met with whole persons. As this person emotionally matures, the circle begins to sink below the line and begins to elongate. And as this emotional maturity progresses, more and more of the area previously concentrated above the line drops below the line where it is less readily seen, if it is seen at all. The need is still being met, but now more diffusely and less consciously. Parts of people, experiences, and situations are being used to meet the need rather than whole people, whole experiences, or whole situations. The more of the circle that is above the line, however, the greater the concentration of the dependency need and the more vulnerable the person is to frustrations from whole people, or whole experiences, or whole situations. It is from a recognition of this that the rationalizations come for the fear of getting to be dependent on somebody else. Yet we can see that unless one becomes dependent on someone else who consistently satisfies the oral dependency need, so she can venture out as we saw that the infant did in the earlier chapters, she cannot go on with the diffusion process in the meeting of her oral dependency need. She becomes trapped in a whole person meeting of her need. In an emotionally mature or genuinely independent person, there may remain a small area above the line which may represent a special or a recognizably emotionally significant person, experience, or situation, but most of the meeting of her oral dependency need is below the line, unconscious and diffuse, and oriented to parts rather than wholes. So this emotionally mature person has become truly independent by diffusely gratifying her dependency need, and that is the only way to attain true independence.

This genuinely independent person characteristically enjoys other people. The independent person seems to be able to overlook, or not to notice, or not to be bothered by aspects of people, experiences, and situations that are negative or imperfect. This person can literally "feed" emotionally from the positive, the nice, or perfect aspects or parts of these people, experiences, and situations. Because she seems to do this so well, she doesn't strive to be independent by avoiding the meeting of the oral dependency need. Although the person is truly independent, she doesn't seem to value independence; being independent isn't a goal in her life, it isn't a position to be attained or maintained, and it's never an issue either emotionally or intellectually. The truly independent person never prides herself on being independent but she is.

Now contrast this emotionally mature and genuinely independent person with one who wasn't as fortunate for whatever reason or reasons in having his oral dependency need so well met in early life. This second person seems less able, later in life, to diffuse his oral dependency need and attain emotional maturity. He may show a reluctance to venture out emotionally and "feed" from many. Note that although the circumstances of oral dependency need frustration may have been other than person related (i.e. injuries, sickness, bad luck, etc.), the result is still an insecurity and a tendency to cling to one or too few people, experiences, or situations. The person tends to be more dependent on whole persons, whole experiences, and whole situations for the meeting of his oral dependency need. In the visualized circle and line, this person has more of the circle above that line between conscious reality and the unconscious emotional unreality. With this emotionally immature person, we may see contrasting desires—wanting the oral dependency need met and not wanting it met, wanting to be alone and not wanting to be alone, wanting to be independent and "grown up," and not wanting to be independent and "grown up," and finally, wanting to be as dependent as a baby on some other person, and not wanting to be dependent or like a baby.

One can often easily recognize, then, the emotionally immature person. He will be overly dependent on another person, or upon too few others, while at the same time, making an issue of independence. These are the individuals you hear emphasizing "Don't depend on others," "Stand on your own two feet," "Don't get close to others or you'll get hurt," and "Familiarity breeds contempt." To be able to stand alone, not needing others, seems to be the prized emotional goal for this person. And he has past experiences to create rationalizations for this built-in tendency to want to deny his unavoidable oral dependency need. Wanting to be independent, not wanting to emotionally "feed" from others, and denying the oral dependency need makes this person more vulnerable to a whole person or whole experience or whole situation exclusive attempt at meeting the oral dependency need. This person has a pseudo-independence and is more subject to having one or more of the various forms of emotional uncomfortableness, when forced to repress anger. Even when extremely happy, when he believes he's found the perfect source on a whole person basis for the meeting of his oral dependency need, he continues to have a great potential for emotional uncomfortableness. That source of great happiness can become too easily that person's source of great unhappiness. So what we see in the person who has not diffused the meeting of his oral dependency need, is emotional immaturity, an ever-present potential for unhappiness, a tendency to have one or more of the various forms of emotional uncomfortableness, and a past history of often grief-filled, terminated, or deteriorated relationships.

A combat veteran who had required multiple psychiatric hospitalizations shows this tendency to be over-involved emotionally with another person. Circumstances of fate terminated too disastrously the meeting of his oral dependency need. If he didn't angrily run berserk, he became fearful and phobic, or depressed and suicidal.

> I went to Vietnam with my good and only buddy Charlie. I had joined the army when my marriage broke up. I never was one of those people with a lot of friends, usually it was just one other person or none at all. That's when I met Charlie. He and I were so close that I really took it hard when he was killed one day on patrol. I became a madman, ran berserk shooting up the camp and had to be hospitalized for a week. I didn't feel better until I befriended another person that reminded me of Charlie. We got to be good friends, and even though his name wasn't Charlie, I got to calling him Charlie and he accepted this. It was just a nickname to him, but to me it was like relating to the original Charlie. Without a Charlie, you can't go through what I did in that living hell. We were closer than any other two people in the whole battalion. He and I were always together just like that first Charlie. Then one day, he too was shot and killed. I was depressed and had to be hospitalized after I tried to commit suicide. Again, I didn't feel better until I found another Charlie. That Charlie got it stepping on a mine. That's how my tour of duty went. One Charlie after the other, and in between, depression, running berserk, living nightmares, phobias, and the psycho ward. It got so that I could count the number of weeks ahead of time before I knew that I'd be losing one Charlie and would have to find another. I finally reached the conclusion that I didn't want any more Charlies because I knew what would happen. I didn't want to see anyone and wouldn't even talk to anyone. I kept to myself all the time. It was after that that I had a complete nervous breakdown and was discharged from the army.

Like this veteran, some people in civilian life seem caught up in living hells of their relationship sphere. They turn to one "Charlie," and when they perceive that the other is using them, or that the other has grown tired of them, the relationship deteriorates. It can be terminated as rapidly as if the person had been shot and killed when they suddenly perceive the other has changed from a caring good buddy to something else. They too can conclude it's better not to have a "Charlie" and they try to do without. But it's experiencing that deprivation, "the lows," that then causes the need for a high. Unlike the person who has diffused his dependency need, who doesn't deny his need, who doesn't experience the lows or the deep valleys of oral dependency need frustration, and who then doesn't need a high, the emotionally immature person has a repetitive tendency to be too involved with too few. Consequently she becomes too vulnerable to circumstances of fate or the whims of others for a consistent meeting of her oral dependency need.

The past history of grief-ridden relationships stands in marked contrast to those of the genuinely independent person. Such a person tends to have more gratifying relationships that are not characterized by being associated with either grief, deterioration, or such disastrous terminations. These relationships that meet the oral dependency need on a part-oriented basis are *accumulated*. They tend to be ongoing; they are maintained and not left behind. This process of adding still more emotionally gratifying relationships in one's day to day involvements to those that one has already accumulated is part of that diffusion process. It's part of becoming emotionally mature.

The emotionally immature person shows a tendency to go from one emotionally intense relationship that may initially appear "wonderful" or "heavenly" to another similar one. The first relationship deteriorates to be oral dependency need frustrating, with no part of it being perceived as oral dependency need gratifying. It goes from being perceived as "heavenly," a major source of happiness, to "hellish," or a major source of unhappiness and grief. After an attempt to deny the oral dependency need, the person again becomes caught up in a whole person, experience, or situation in the meeting of his oral dependency need. The previous relationship isn't retained as an emotional source for meeting the oral dependency need. If anything, it's a target for expressed anger. So this emotionally immature person doesn't accumulate gratifying relationships to promote the diffusion process and that will make his relationships less and less emotionally intense. He's unable to draw a meeting of the oral dependency need from many people. He seems to demand a single source and then becomes caught up in the pitfalls of this type of involvement. He often refers to other relationships as "acquaintances" or "not real friends." He leaves behind a trail of failed relationships made up of whole oriented targets for his expressed anger. Characteristically he wants to put as much distance between himself and these targets for expressed anger, leaving them out of his emotional life.

This "need" to be independent that is so characteristic of the emotionally immature person may be individualistically rationalized, as "my father died when I was only ten years old, so I had no other choice but to be independent and self-reliant," or "My parents were both very independent people so I learned from them not to get close to others" or, "My need to be independent comes from a long line of disappointments I've had when I've depended on others, so that I learned to be a very independent person." This same "need" to be independent, indicative of past oral dependency need frustrations manifests itself with a reluctance to be involved emotionally with others—as: "I don't want others butting into my personal affairs"; "You have to be careful what you say to people in this town"; "I don't like getting close to others as it only results in trouble." Rationalizations are often given as factual reasons for not becoming emotionally involved with others, such as, "I've always had too much to do and too little time to do it in, to be just sitting around with people wasting my time," or, "I've never been a person who enjoyed gossiping. In fact, I'd probably feel guilty if I did that." Some may rationalize this tendency not to diffuse their emotional involvements with, "I just don't see where talking about a problem ever solved anything. I'm a doer not a talker. I'm a person who has always taken pride in accomplishing something, and in doing a good job. I've always had projects that I work on. I guess I take my enjoyment from things like that, not from running my mouth with others."

To illustrate how strongly this "need" to be independent is felt by some and how important it is to them, let me tell you about a family I know. The husband is a self-made millionaire and nationally-known business success and who directs his financial empire with an iron hand. I know him to demand perfection, as only he can define it, from everyone who works for him. He's hardworking and drives himself and others toward goals he sets. He prefers hard work. He appears self-confident, aggressive, and quick to see things that aren't right in his business. But I also know he's not easy to live with. He's been married several times and his past wives describe him as "heartless," "thoughtless," "inconsiderate," "uncaring," and sometimes "cruel." They describe him as easily angered, having a very low threshold for any stress or frustration, and often showing a most vile temper. He comes across in his marriages as an uncompromising stickler for routine, continually clock-conscious, always under pressure, and constantly criticizing and finding fault. They also say he's impossible to please. But what he prides himself on the most, above everything else is his "independence." To him this is the most valued characteristic of his personality.

One doesn't have to look too closely, however, to see that it is a facade of independence. He's not emotionally mature and hasn't diffused the meeting of his oral dependency need. He often becomes overly dependent on a new wife or another woman, and upon the deterioration of this relationship, goes on to another, again becoming overly dependent. Past relationships are used for anger expression, if at all, but usually the emotional door is slammed shut and he has nothing to do with them again. From his earliest life, when his father died and his mother abandoned him to an unloving and uncaring aunt, he has always been hurt when he has gotten too emotionally dependent on too few. Logically, he assumes the solution to this past pattern of grief-filled relationships is to be independent by denying the oral dependency need.

Not to need others for anything is his goal in life. Gathering and hoarding money is, for him, an apparent attempt to be "self-sufficient and not need others." He told me he preferred to buy his love if he really needed it, but somehow he would still become entrapped in an emotionally intense relationship that would rapidly deteriorate as far as mutually meeting oral dependency needs. The mother of his sixteen-year-old son, tearfully told me how the father had insisted that the boy attend a survival school "to learn to be independent." He was sent to another state for two weeks, "to learn to be independent," and spent three days alone on an island where he was supposed to live off the land. His mother told me he sat and cried for the whole three days. At the end of the summer, the father insisted he be sent to a military school for boys, again "to learn to be independent"—to learn not to need others, to be self-sufficient and to be emotionally strong. The boy's mother was told by the father not to visit her son and that no other relatives or friends were allowed to visit him. Because the father was such a financial success, his wisdom about all matters was respected, even by his ex-wives. When the boy became depressed at the military school, failed his classes, and was unable to make friends, his mother was blamed for raising "an emotional cripple"; because of her he must have inherited inferior genes. The father felt that his son surely didn't take after him. When the boy began to show suicidal tendencies, he was finally transferred to a private residential psychiatric facility where he still lives.

We've already seen the pitfalls of trying to deny the oral dependency need and likened denial to trying to go without any water after finding water that was contaminated. We saw that one simply becomes more thirsty and an even poorer judge of water. So people who are emotionally immature, who extol the advantages of being independent, and who try so diligently to become independent seem characterized by frequently choosing the wrong type of person to meet their oral dependency need. Their relationships are often love-hate relationships, which consistently fail to meet the oral dependency need that allows a feeling of emotional security so that they can venture into the diffusion process. They seem to seek out one relationship after another, to meet the high unmet oral need, which for one reason or another doesn't satisfy. Sometimes it becomes evident that the person who is sought out also has an intense unmet oral need which may appear as a great love to give. The problems associated with this "great love to give," often involving a hidden need to express anger, may guarantee that oral dependency needs won't be consistently met.

Such relationships seem to set a pattern that will tend to keep the person emotionally immature. They tend also to ensure that the person will keep making an issue of, and keep trying to gain, independence.

What the person really needs is a low-key, less intense but consistently gratifying relationship to promote the diffusion process. The ambivalent or love-hate relationships the person seems to get involved keep him emotionally immature. Although wanting to be "independent," the person still requires an intense meeting of his oral dependency need. He becomes vulnerable to being emotionally involved with those who have the most love to give, and as we already know, are the very ones with the potential to give the most hate as well. That desire for intense love, which the emotionally mature person saw only very early in his life and then lost as he diffused his sources, may continually trap the emotionally immature person into degrees of love-hate relationships and a tendency to manifest the different forms of emotional uncomfortableness when he has to keep his anger inside.

These people who consciously seek independence by denying their oral dependency need often make an analogy of not wanting "crutches" in life, implying the goal of wanting to stand alone. When a person uses the analogy of crutches, it's a dead giveaway to his emotional immaturity, his pseudo-independence, and his being too dependent on too few. The person will always be glad to tell you about the problems and grief of being too dependent on too few and he can do so with convincing examples from his own experience. But that independence he seeks is one associated with isolation and loneliness, as opposed to the genuine independence of the emotionally mature person, which isn't isolating or lonely at all. In fact, it's the very opposite. It's the emotionally immature person who will, characteristically, complain of isolation and loneliness, not the emotionally mature person. Not wanting crutches in life, desiring to be able to "stand alone," and not needing others are the hallmarks of the person who has a false independence.

One hears this analogy of not wanting crutches so many times in people who have come to psychotherapists and counselors with various forms of emotional uncomfortableness. "Make me so I don't need others," one hears in those who are emotionally immature. Emotionally uncomfortable people often have a problem with alcohol. These people, when told to get involved in A.A., often make statements like, "I want to do this myself—I want to prove to myself and others that I can lick this problem alone." Getting help from A.A. is a sign of weakness to them. "A.A. is just a crutch and I want to show myself I don't need a crutch." This person, more than likely, continues to be too dependent on too few and continues to drink excessively. Others, too dependent on too few, who are not manifesting an alcohol problem but instead some other form of emotional uncomfortableness, when told to get involved in a church of their choosing, frequently will give rationalizations for their resistance and their "need" to be independent, like, "Church is just a bunch of hypocrites and I don't want to associate with people who think they're 'holier than thou'." One can always find a rationalization for being independent and not relying on others.

It's well known that no man can stand alone for long. Many still seem compelled to try. What we're proposing instead is a utilization of as many supports as possible. The person is better shored up this way and less likely to fall. Furthermore the person who does go it alone the longest, who doesn't seem to use crutches, and who doesn't want anything to do with others, can always be found in the back wards of a state psychiatric hospital. This psychotic person who isn't in contact with reality and lives within his own dream world is the epitome of the erroneous goal sought by the emotionally immature person. This psychotic person won't involve himself with others and wants nothing to do with dependence, or anything associated with or symbolizing it. He characteristically won't take medication; it must be hidden in his orange juice if he takes it at all. Given pills, he'll "cheek" them, and spit them out later. The greatest problem in the pharmacologic treatment of psychiatrically hospitalized patients is getting them to take their medications.

We see this same resistance to taking pills, because they symbolize dependence, to a lesser degree in the pseudo-independent person. They often make statements like, "I'm the type of person who hates to take pills—I mean I won't even take an aspirin if I can help it!" They admit to a fear of anything addicting. This fear of addiction is symbolic of the fear of dependence. And dependence *is* addicting. But by diffusing the need gratifying sources, it becomes less abusive. In fact, if diffused enough, it loses all aspects of being even potentially abusive. When it's not diffused dependence on others or chemical dependencies, which are symbolic substitutes for this dependence on others, are most likely to involve abuse.

The person who is attempting to deny his dependency need is the very one most likely to end up too dependent on too few. The teetotaler who fears to take a drop of alcohol is often the person who has the most potential to abuse it. The person who fears the most addicting medications is often the very person who will later abuse addictive medications for one rationalization or another. These people fear dependence, yet they are the people who get overly dependent on too few. They often appear as either alcoholics or teetotalers. They can't seem to drink in moderation. But neither can they seem to get emotionally involved with others in moderation. They overdo it. They get too involved. Like many alcoholics, they swing from drinking too much alcohol to not drinking at all and then back to drinking too much. They often appear overly dependent on someone emotionally, or else pseudo-independent and professing to not need others. There's nothing in between. They vacillate, like the alcoholic who's not in A.A., between the two extremes. Pseudo-independence, or being overly dependent on one other person or on too few, are the only positions they seem to be able to take. Like the alcoholic who can't drink in moderation, they can't meet their oral dependency need with moderation. They seem to abuse emotional dependency and are abused by it. Like the solution for the alcoholic, being forced into A.A., these people who are too dependent on too few often have to be forced into emotional involvements with others in order to diffuse their emotional sources and to decrease the tendency to repress anger, which we shall see is intimately related to the different forms of all human emotional uncomfortableness.

After many years in the practice of psychiatry, I can readily see certain patterns in a person's life that tend to make the person prone to the emotional problems about which he or she has come to me for help. Whether it is depression; anxiety; phobias, incapacitating feelings of inferiority, pain, or stress; being too worried about physical health to an almost incapacitating degree; or some focus of unbearable self-unacceptance, certain familiar patterns in the person's past life become evident. Whether it's been marital problems, a feeling of being rejected, victimized, harassed, or other severe problems in relationships, certain problems create a feeling of deja vu—that one has heard and seen it all before. The names of the patients are different, and the places and people of whom they talk are different, but the patterns and characteristics are the same. The subtle patterns one sees so often are a conscious striving to be independent and a characteristic fear of dependence.

There is another frequently occurring characteristic in people who come on their own to see me in my outpatient psychiatric practice. They seem to have attained a level of recognizable success in life. If not financially successful, they are successful in some other endeavor. Or they're married to a successful person. They may even be manifesting an aspect of success by being the teenager or young adult of a successful family. I recognize that I only see people in my outpatient practice who can afford me. But in the past years I've worked in mental health clinics where indigents may go for help with emotional problems. I continue to do charity work at the local hospital, and again I often see evidence of this conscious striving to be independent and this characteristic fear of dependence. Whether financially well off, whether successful in life in any endeavor or situation, or down-and-out and a "dreg of society," these people share a tendency to want consciously to be independent, to not need others, and to try to avoid personal involvements.

In looking at those in my outpatient practice, I repeatedly see people who are now incapacitated to a degree by a form of emotional uncomfortableness, but who previously functioned at a high level and were fairly successful in some reality endeavor. They were able to function admirably before, but are now incapacitated. This period of inability to function well seems to stand in contrast to their past performance. These people will tell me, as one person recently did, "I just can't understand this change in myself. I've always been on top. I'm the person that led the company in sales last year. I'm the one who won the 'most valuable citizen award' two years ago. I've been Sunday School superintendent at my church for over five years. I've always prided myself on being a leader, on being strong and self-reliant. But what has happened to me? I'm drinking too much, I'm smoking too much, and all I seem to be able to do is either sit and stare at TV all day or fight with my wife, and I know I shouldn't do that with all that she has to put up with from me. I'm so irritable even the littlest thing upsets me and I fly off the handle. I worry about things I didn't worry about before, and I feel I have to do things I didn't know I had to do. It all overwhelms me. Where life was fun before, it's now a hassle that really isn't worth it. I've been having this thought of getting out a shotgun and just blowing my head off. I think the whole family would be better off. What's wrong with me anyway? Why have I changed? Nothing's changed in my life that I know of."

This person can't attribute his emotional uncomfortableness to any person, experience, or situation that might have frustrated his oral dependency need and its omnipotence or centrality. He will tell us that nothing is different in his life. There's been no psychological trauma or bad luck. But what often becomes apparent upon more careful analysis, is that this person seems to have become too dependent on too few. Perhaps he's lost a friend or confidante, moved to a new area, changed jobs; for whatever reason, he ends up too dependent on too few. This condition may initially be difficult to see. For instance, one woman told me, "I don't know why all I want to do is sit and cry—I have no reason to whatsoever. My husband is the most wonderful person in the world. He'd do anything for me. He makes more money in a year than my father made in his entire lifetime. I've never had it so good in my life. He'd give me anything and yet I'm not happy. I wake up each morning and I start to cry. I just don't understand it. I could understand this if it happened six months ago when I was getting a divorce from that son-of-a-bitch that I was married to. But my husband took me away from all that and now I live in a beautiful home and I could have a full-time maid if I wanted, but all I want to do is cry. I'm not able to go anywhere or see anyone." What her new husband did was to take her from targets for her expressed anger. He took her from what few friends she had, and she became too dependent on too few. The origin of the resulting emotional uncomfortableness is difficult to understand and it seems to defy a logical explanation in that there is apparently no great frustration of her oral dependency need. But frustrations of the oral dependency need, we already know, are unavoidable, and small though they may be, the resulting anger can accumulate. Where the person is too dependent on too few and is less able to express this anger, the accumulation continues to grow and emotional uncomfortableness of one form or another results. This woman, as nice as her life is now, is still exposed to oral dependency need frustrations. These are all on an unconscious level. Now, too dependent on too few, she accumulates repressed anger. This woman shows the tendency not to get emotionally involved enough with others, so she is unable to rid herself of that accumulated anger.

Whatever form emotional uncomfortableness takes seems to get worse as one accumulates more repressed anger. We shall see in the following chapters how forms of uncomfortable, incapacitating, and even life-threatening emotional distress are so intimately associated with the repression of anger. Rather than the amount of oral dependency need frustration causing the emotional problem, it will become apparent that the accumulation of repressed anger is the determining factor. That tendency to want to be independent and that inclination to be too dependent on too few will be seen as the basic dynamic issue in the creation of emotional uncomfortableness. How much early oral dependency need frustration, which determines the degree one feels a need to be independent, or how little a person is forced by his life's work or by circumstances and fate to be involved with others can create profound changes in one's emotional life. We shall see just what happens when anger is repressed in the next chapter.

CHAPTER 6
The Concept of Unconscious Guilt

Frustration of the oral dependency need produces anger and we all experience anger that must, at times, be repressed. When someone is unable to express anger and instead represses it, this anger takes on a new form. For lack of a better term, we will call this new form *unconscious guilt*. The term "unconscious guilt" was first mentioned by Freud in 1894, when he used it to explain an unconscious feeling of guilt that he tied in with a castration wish; guilt is sexualized in Freudian theory. Our theory uses the term unconscious guilt to mean not only guilt but a whole mass of feelings that repressed anger becomes. Unconscious guilt includes feelings of guilt but it also includes feelings of inferiority, inadequacy, unacceptableness, incompleteness, uncleanliness, being wrong, and a sense of impending doom. We will call these related feelings that compose unconscious guilt the *primary feelings*. No one of these feelings is any more important than any of the others, and all of them are present to make up unconscious guilt.

Others have caught a glimpse of the unconscious guilt but have described it in different ways in the psychiatric literature. Perhaps Wilhelm Reich, one of Freud's followers, saw it when he described something he knew was deep within the unconscious of people he analyzed as "dammed up, stagnant, sexual energy," which he felt created a "bad entity." He felt that sexual gratification was the solution for it, but the solution he proposed is actually oral dependency need gratification with a sexual orientation. The Victorian-age Freudians, for instance, thought that a spinster schoolteacher, one who did not get married or sexually involved, had displaced the meeting of her sexual need into teaching. We would say the teacher was meeting her oral dependency need through teaching. The oral dependency need can be met sexually; it can be met through teaching school; it can be met through many occupations. Becoming a teacher is not a displacement of sexual needs; it's just one way to meet the oral dependency need and maintain emotional comfortableness.

Although Reich sexualized the unconscious guilt, he was right in seeing it as coming from something "dammed up and stagnant," something which we know to be repressed anger rather than sexual energy. This anger does create a "bad entity." Often the feelings associated with unconscious guilt are seen as contaminants because they imply dirtiness, repulsiveness, and ugliness. When there is enough of this unconscious guilt, it is often equated with the filthiest of garbage or excrement. While trying to get this concept across at a workshop on communication I was recently presenting, one of the participants asked, "Can unconscious guilt be likened to a load of shit?" The answer is no if there is a relatively small amount of the unconscious guilt. The more there is of this unconscious guilt, though, the more it does take on those attributes, and it can surpass anything we know of in reality in its repulsiveness.

Just as oral dependency need gratification and expressed anger are rationalized, unconscious guilt is reflected in rationalizations that are reality oriented and make sense. But underneath the rationalization are all these feelings. For example, a man may say, "I feel inferior because I'm so short." Saying that he feels inferior because he's short in stature is something that his listeners can understand. It makes sense. He could list all of the inconveniences and disadvantages of being short, in reality. The deception is that he thinks the feeling of inferiority stems from the fact that he's short. He thinks that the fact he uses as a rationalization comes first. Yet there are other men who are just as short or even shorter and don't feel inferior, and many tall men who do feel inferior. The primary feelings are already there, in the unconscious, and the rationalization is presented to the conscious and to other people to explain those feelings. The rationalization originates in the current situation of the person using it. But we can usually find another person in the same situation without the same feelings of inferiority or inadequacy. Logically, if what is presented in the rationalization is really the origin of the feelings, this other person should feel the same way, too.

Another example of a logical rationalization of the primary feelings associated with the unconscious guilt can be seen in the man who says, "I feel inadequate because I'm financially poor." He might say, "I feel uncomfortable around other people because I'm financially inadequate." Yet there are many who are financially poor and do not feel inadequate or uncomfortable around other people and others who feel inadequate or uncomfortable around people yet are wealthy. Any of the primary feelings can be rationalized in much the same way. I may say that I feel guilty because I did something that some people feel is wrong and immoral. My unconscious presents this reality oriented reason for my feeling of guilt to my conscious mind and to others. It may make sense, but the same act of commission or omission can be done by someone else, and this person may feel little or no guilt. On the other hand, there are people who seem like saints, who have a worse sense of guilt than my own. The feelings, whether they are presented as feelings of inferiority, inadequacy, guilt, unacceptableness, incompleteness, uncleanliness, or failure, are there first; then the rationalization is made; the unconscious guilt created from repressed anger is there first. We deceive ourselves and we deceive others about the origin of our feelings because the feelings are always presented as coming directly from reality when they're actually coming from the emotional unreality.

All of the primary feelings are there, even though the rationalization may present only one or a few of them, perhaps presenting one as preceding the others or as being more important than the others. Suppose I am a college student. I have flunked out of school this semester. I'm telling you about it, and I say "I feel like a failure. I've failed at my studies, and it really upsets me to be such a failure. I've become an inferior student and I feel inadequate because my brother graduated from college. I feel guilty, too, because I used a lot of my parents' money to pay for school. And I know there's going to be trouble ahead because I have no job and no education." It seems as if feeling like a failure is most important and preceded the feelings of inferiority, inadequacy, guilt, and impending trouble; we catch glimpses of all the primary feelings, but they seem to be of less importance than the feeling of being a failure in this rationalization. Again, this is a deception. All of the feelings are there because they're all associated with the underlying unconscious guilt, and all are of equal importance; it's only in the rationalization, which is secondarily created, that one may take precedence over the others.

In the following example, the feeling of guilt seems predominant, but it is easy to see that all of the feelings are there; they eventually come out in the rationalization. A married man came to see me to talk about feelings which were actually arising from his unconscious guilt. His unconscious guilt developed from repressed anger. He said that he had been to see a prostitute. He went on, "I feel so guilty about cheating on my wife. I'm a terrible husband. And the kids. I feel pretty bad about being such an inadequate father. I'm worried I have a venereal disease, too, and may give it to my wife. I've been to several doctors who say I'm fine, but I'm still worried about it. I'm continually washing myself as I feel so unclean." The feeling that is emphasized in this rationalization is guilt, but as the man talks, all of the primary feelings become evident: guilt, inferiority, unacceptableness, inadequacy, fear of impending trouble, etc.

We can also see from this example, and the others that have been presented, that the rationalization has the orientation of each individual's reality. The unconscious focuses the rationalization on the most appropriate aspect of the person's reality. It's an unconscious function of the ego to create the rationalization to present to the conscious mind and to others. The man who went to see the prostitute does not condone either prostitution or marital infidelity, so his commission of both of these acts becomes the reality focus for the rationalization of his unconscious guilt and his feelings. The young man who flunked out of school had made college an important part of his life, so it naturally becomes the reality focus of his rationalization when his unconscious guilt increases. Likewise, with an increase in her unconscious guilt, a person from a very religious family may concentrate on the fact that she has not been to church for a few Sundays and give this reality-oriented reason for her primary feelings.

For example, consider the young woman from a religious family who went to church every Sunday when she was living with her parents. Recently, however, she began living on her own and hasn't been as faithful in her church attendance. The only primary feeling that she expresses in her rationalization is a sense of guilt about not attending church. But she is not feeling only guilt. As her story unfolds, it is apparent that she has implied feelings of inadequacy, inferiority, unacceptableness, shame, worthlessness, failure, and a sense that something terrible will happen. All of these feelings were present before her unconscious came up with the rationalization. The rationalization is focused on one feeling that makes the most sense, according to the reality of the person. But the "one issue" rationalization conveys not only the rationalized feeling but the other underlying primary feelings as well. The rationalization developed tends to fit the amount of unconscious guilt accumulated. That amount of unconscious guilt determines the intensity of the feeling being used in the rationalization.

It is also possible for the unconscious to come up with such a complex rationalization that the primary feeling that is being emphasized is not specifically mentioned at all. Social workers, psychologists, or analysts may hear such a rationalization and then describe "underlying feelings of inferiority" or "underlying feelings of guilt" or an "underlying feeling of impending doom." But what they heard was a rationalization that implied one of those primary feelings. They see only the tip of the iceberg of unconscious guilt, only a small portion of the mass of primary feelings that make up the unconscious guilt, which lies below the surface of the rationalization.

The construction of rationalizations to give reality oriented explanations for unconscious guilt shows the immensity of the functioning of the unconscious. Not only is the unconscious coming up with metaphorical language through which to indirectly express anger and meet the oral dependency need, monitoring and adjusting to the metaphors in the communication of others, but it's also rationalizing unconscious guilt. To do so, the unconscious, which is aware of the primary feelings, must choose a reality orientation that makes sense to the individual and can explain all or one of the feelings to his conscious mind and to other people. It must keep track of the individual's reality, and his emotional unreality as well, in order to make the rationalization.

The unconscious must also present a rationalization that can encompass the quantity of unconscious guilt that is present. The less unconscious guilt, the easier it is for the unconscious to find a logical rationalization for it. It's harder to come up with a rationalization that makes sense for more unconscious guilt; sometimes unconscious guilt builds up, and it's not rationalized. The person will say something like, "I've begun to feel unacceptable around others, but I don't know why," or "I feel inadequate about my work, but I'm not sure why I do," or "I have this feeling of foreboding, but I don't know why." Sometimes the person will admit to a feeling that he has something nebulously bad that others don't have, and that it makes him feel different from others. The unconscious guilt has built up quickly, and there's nothing that the unconscious has found to present to the conscious and to other people to "explain" that feeling of inadequacy, inferiority, unacceptableness, or guilt. The implication is that there are degrees of feeling inferior, inadequate, or guilty, which reflect the amount of accrued unconscious guilt. Sometimes, when one can't come up with a rationalization that fits his degree of unconscious guilt and is appropriate to his reality situation, the unconscious guilt will remain unrationalized for a time. If one waits long enough, the unconscious will usually come up with some rationalization. Because of the high degree of unconscious guilt, however, it may construct one that strains logic and doesn't fit too well with reality. One may then appear to others to have an "unrealistic" rationalization and may even appear "crazy" or "schizophrenic" because of such a rationalization. The rationalization developed always reflects the amount of underlying unconscious guilt. So the rationalization that may seem unrealistic in regard to reality is actually realistic in regard to that person's emotional unreality.

People may use synonyms to express their primary feelings. They may say "I'm a freak," "I'm perverted," "I'm such a nerd," or "I'm a bimbo," when they mean "I feel unacceptable;" they may say "I'm a loser" or "I'm a nobody," meaning "I'm a failure" or "I feel inferior." They could say, "I'm nothing but a fake and a phony" to mean "I feel inadequate;" or "I'm a big zero," meaning "I'm worthless." I've even heard people say, "I'm not just a zero; I'm a minus sign because I detract." "I'm full of shit" is another common phrase. The list of synonyms for primary feelings could go on and on. Just about any word or expression you can think of that describes negative self-reflective feelings would belong on such a list. Each of the vernacular terms encompasses all of the primary feelings, although it may seem to stress one or only a few of them. For instance, "I'm such a nerd" emphasizes unacceptableness, but includes feelings of inferiority, shame, worthlessness, guilt, and the sense of impending trouble.

There are two types of unconscious guilt. The first of these is *personality core guilt*. When the personality is forming, during the early part of life, the personality core guilt is being set. The personality core guilt does not change in quantity. It can't be lowered after the personality is formed, and it stays at the same level throughout the rest of the person's life. It is equal to a *core unmet oral dependency need*, which also does not change in quantity. This core unmet need is a reflection of the oral dependency need frustration experienced in early life and the amount of repressed anger accrued during this time of personality formation.

We all have different experiences as far as having our oral dependency needs met early in life; it varies, even in the same families. Some children just seem to have better luck than others, and therefore, have more of their oral dependency needs met. A child who has bad luck, or is frequently ill may tend to develop a high personality core guilt. We had no control over when we were born, but the time at which we arrived into the family may have determined how much of our oral dependency need was met. For example, a child may be born while the father is at war or when one of the parents is just starting a career. In either case, the other parent has more demands on him, and the child will get less of his oral dependency need met. A child who is born into a family that maintains close ties with many relatives who meet the oral dependency need will get more oral dependency need gratification than will a child who seldom sees aunts, uncles, or grandparents, or a child whose relatives are fault-finding, criticizing, and punitive. A child with many siblings may or may not tend to get more of her need met. Some children may have a low core unmet need, and hence, develop a low personality core guilt. This is only true if relatives meet the child's oral dependency need, and the child has good luck and avoids the many misfortunes of early life.

There is no one set of circumstances in reality which guarantees high or low personality core guilt. The meeting and frustrating of the oral dependency need is perceived unconsciously, below the level of reality, on a part-person, part-experience or part-situation basis; because the amount of anger accumulated or expressed is so unconsciously determined, we can't pinpoint any one common factor in reality which leads to high, or low, personality core guilt. Children with more oral dependency need gratification may still accumulate anger to repress. Others with less oral dependency need gratification may have better circumstances to get rid of anger. Some children, however, do develop a high personality core guilt. These are the ones who have had more accumulated anger from a frustration of their oral dependency needs, for whatever reasons in the reality of their early emotional life, and have had limited opportunity to express it comfortably. If the child's oral dependency need is not being met consistently, for whatever reasons, and the accumulated anger is repressed, the child will develop a high personality core guilt. He or she will also have an equal amount of core unmet need which can't be lowered after the personality is formed and stays at the same level throughout the rest of his or her life. We shall see how the traits and characteristics of the personality will reflect both this personality core guilt and the core unmet oral need.

The second type of unconscious guilt comes from anger that is accrued after the formation of the personality. Daily perceived frustrations of the oral dependency need produce anger which sometimes must be repressed. This repressed anger becomes *added unconscious guilt*. It follows that those people with a high personality core guilt, who have a greater core unmet need and are less able to diffuse their oral dependency need gratification and anger expression, will tend to accrue added unconscious guilt more easily. Unlike personality core guilt, the amount of added unconscious guilt fluctuates in size like a balloon. When oral dependency need gratification is high and anger accrual is low, the balloon is small. But when one perceives oral dependency need frustration and accrues repressed anger, the balloon gets bigger. One must keep in mind the two processes involved: Oral dependency need frustration or gratification, and anger accumulation or expression—and how each can affect the amount of added unconscious guilt. In other words, one could have a relatively low level of oral dependency need frustration, but lacking opportunity for anger expression, end up with more added unconscious guilt than someone else with a higher level of oral dependency need frustration and a good opportunity for anger expression. The added unconscious guilt is added to the personality core guilt to make the total unconscious guilt.

In order to understand the dynamics of added unconscious guilt, picture a cube with six sides. We can label one side "perceived oral dependency need frustration;" another side, "unmet oral dependency need;" another, "repressed anger;" another, "added unconscious guilt;" another, "potential anger expression;" and the last, "potential oral dependency need gratification." All six entities are equal in quantity to one another.

Added unconscious guilt is most easily accrued by those people with high personality core guilt. These people find it more difficult to meet their oral dependency needs. They tend to be emotionally immature; they don't venture out emotionally, getting involved with a lot of people, experiences, and situations, because of their quantitatively greater feelings of inferiority, inadequacy, guilt, etc. With a very high amount of personality core guilt, these people often prefer to be by themselves, and because they are usually too dependent on too few, they must repress their anger, which in turn becomes added unconscious guilt. The high core unmet need causes a fear of the oral dependency need which leads some people to adopt an independent facade. "Loners" and people who have an "independent façade" tend to appear aloof. They seem to set an emotional distance between themselves and others because of the negative primary feelings of their high personality core guilt and because of that core unmet oral need that demands the distance. This emotional distance becomes characteristic of each personality and depends on the amount of personality core guilt and its equal amount of core unmet oral dependency need. The people with high personality core guilt may be characterized by liking to read or study, or work by themselves.

People with high personality core guilt develop traits or characteristics that attempt to compensate for the primary feelings of their personality core guilt. The feelings may be seen as contaminants: as dirty, messy, disorganized, imperfect, ugly, etc. Unconsciously then, the person tries to correct these "bad" feelings by being neat, organized, hardworking, perfect, etc. She may seem obsessed with cleaning up, correcting, or perfecting something in reality that, for her, symbolizes the added unconscious guilt. These same compensatory traits have a certain survival benefit, too. They give the person an ability to cope with reality situations in which she does not perceive oral dependency need gratification. These defenses against, or compensations for, unconscious guilt help the person with high personality core guilt to cope with reality situations that she perceives to be oral dependency need frustrating and in which she accrues added unconscious guilt.

The survival benefit in unconscious guilt should be readily recognizable. The added unconscious guilt that develops from deprivation in reality situations intensifies the defenses of the personality. Theoretically, the individual becomes more adaptable and more able to cope with his reality where oral dependency need gratification is being withheld by the circumstances of that reality. This does not contradict the fact that one is better able to withstand the stresses of reality by gaining more oral dependency need gratification. It means instead, that when oral dependency need gratification is not being perceived to a comfortable degree these compensatory defenses provide the individual with increased coping or survival capability.

A person with high personality core guilt may be unusually neat or organized. When he straightens the living room or his desk at work, he is symbolically putting the unconscious guilt in its place. Often, these people with high personality core guilt tend to be perfectionists; they want everything to be done perfectly. They're really trying to make themselves perfect, i.e., free from imperfection or those feelings of inferiority, inadequacy, unacceptableness, guilt, incompleteness, and impending trouble. They tend to be efficient, punctual, and hard-working. These people prefer hard work to immediate pleasures; they tend to put off pleasure until some later time. These are the people who work through their lunch hours, and would rather grab a sandwich and get back to work than take an hour to go to a restaurant and chat with some co-workers. Their perfectionism in regard to time makes them always punctual or even early. People with high personality core guilt are also apt to be worriers because they have more of that sense of impending trouble. This person may be the one in the office who works during lunch and does near-perfect work, yet worries about the work or even about the security of the job. If that which symbolizes the unconscious guilt is focused specifically in reality, a person may appear obsessed. If this involves work, this person may then appear obsessed with his particular work. The greater the amount of personality core guilt, the more one has of these traits (loving hard work, neatness, control, punctuality, organization, perfectionism, and the tendency to be obsessed), while the less personality core guilt one has, the less one has of these same traits.

Sometimes these traits may be evident only in parts of the person's life. For instance, this person who works hard at the office and keeps her desk meticulously organized may go home and throw clothes on the floor and let dirty dishes pile up in the kitchen sink. Someone else may be very hard-working and organized at both the office and home. The more personality core guilt one has, the more it tends to be reflectively spread throughout different aspects of one's life.

Personality core guilt is unconscious; we are not aware of these feelings of inferiority, inadequacy, incompleteness, unacceptableness, guilt, etc. We are also unaware that our traits of punctuality, organization, perfectionism, and the love of hard work are attempts at compensating for these core primary feelings. If we ask an office worker why he works so hard and why he's so organized, he'll say, perhaps, that he's being paid to work hard or that his boss depends on him to have certain things finished by the end of each day. Ask, for example, a very meticulous master sargeant in the army why he is so, and he'll say, "You have to be that way in the service." He doesn't see that there are plenty of people in the service who are *not* the same way. It is a rationalization for his personality traits. Likewise, a person who strives for perfection may remark, "I was always taught to do my best," or "My father always expected perfection from me."

Since personality core guilt and the associated primary feelings are unconscious, the rationalizations for conscious feelings of inferiority, and inadequacy are actually rationalizations for the feelings associated with added unconscious guilt. The added unconscious guilt creates primary feelings of its own that one begins to be aware of. If one is conscious of the primary feelings, they are coming from added unconscious guilt. The primary feelings of the personality core guilt are handled by the personality in its compensatory traits. In other words, one could have a high personality core guilt and if he or she didn't have any added unconscious guilt (which would, of course, be unlikely), he or she wouldn't be aware of any feelings of inferiority or inadequacy. If we were to ask a comfortable person with high personality core guilt if he or she felt inadequate, ordinarily the answer would be "no." He is unaware of the feeling, but one might see evidence that he has developed some characteristics to compensate for it. But when this person's oral dependency need is frustrated and he represses anger, accruing some added unconscious guilt, he may then say, "I feel inadequate because _____," filling in the blank with some reality-oriented reason.

These people with high personality core guilt experience oral dependency need frustration when their compensatory traits do not function or are prevented from functioning well. When someone interferes with the operation of their compensatory traits, they become angry. They may turn the anger on an emotionally significant person who has been unconsciously equated, in the transference, with the increase in added unconscious guilt. Trying to maintain the operation of these defenses may make it difficult to maintain comfortable relationships. High personality core guilt may cause problems in the few relationships that these people may have. For instance, I saw a woman with a high personality core guilt and apparently some increased added unconscious guilt who told me that she had been trying recently to get her teen-aged children to pick up their clothes and to do the dishes after they had dirtied them. But she couldn't get them to do anything. I reasoned that she couldn't get them to do anything was because she herself had always done it so well. She said she had tried letting the dishes pile up in the sink and leaving their clothes lying on the floor, but it bothered her so much that she was the one who ended up picking up the clothes and doing the dishes. It didn't bother the children, but it did her. They either had less personality core guilt or their defenses didn't manifest themselves in wanting clothes picked up or dishes washed. This poor woman would wax the kitchen floor so that it would be spotless, but they'd walk right across it with dirty feet, which would, of course, upset her. Like this woman who couldn't keep all the clothes picked up and the kitchen floor waxed, when one can't symbolically clean up, or contain, or dispose of, or organize, or perfect his added unconscious guilt, he experiences a frustration of his oral dependency need, which may lead to still more added unconscious guilt.

An increase in added unconscious guilt always intensifies the compensatory traits. When the woman in the above example becomes frustrated by her children leaving clothes on the floor and dishes in the sink, she develops anger. Because her only close relationships are with her husband and children, she may repress this anger, which becomes added unconscious guilt. Because her total unconscious guilt is now greater, her defenses intensify; she becomes even more concerned with keeping her home spotlessly clean. She builds up even more added unconscious guilt when her attempt to keep the kitchen floor waxed is frustrated. Then she may decide to clean the entire house from top to bottom. If she can do this cleaning without being frustrated, then she might take care of her added unconscious guilt.

When we can successfully handle our added unconscious guilt through intensified defenses, it's a way of meeting our oral dependency need. For instance, when we're able to dispose of, throw out, organize, clean, perfect, control, overcome a challenge, or prevent a failure or disaster, it's oral dependency need gratifying. When we're able to channel successfully our emotional unreality into our reality, we feel good about it because we've cleaned up our added unconscious guilt, covered it, organized it, or put it in its place; we've also met some of our oral dependency need. People with high personality core guilt have a built-in desire to do this. This may show itself as an affinity for work. They love to straighten things out, to bring order out of chaos, to perfect, and to beautify. So they may be noted for their ability to accomplish things. All these qualities have a reference to the underlying unconscious guilt. People with a high personality core guilt can stay emotionally comfortable when they are effectively handling their added unconscious guilt through their traits and defenses. By lowering their added unconscious guilt, they meet some of their oral dependency needs. Although the personality core guilt and core unmet need remain high, they are able to lower the added unconscious guilt coming from everyday oral dependency need frustrations by translating this into some reality endeavor. As an example, consider a woman whose family has been throwing things into a closet for several weeks, instead of neatly folding and hanging up their clothes and placing their shoes in a line against the back wall of the closet, as she usually does. For the past few weeks, her added unconscious guilt has been low. Today, she breaks her favorite prized vase while dusting, a chore which she loves. Breaking the vase is a bit of bad luck and a frustration of her oral dependency need, creating anger. She represses the anger and her added unconscious guilt increases. She may handle her increased added unconscious guilt by cleaning out the closet. She takes satisfaction in organizing the closet. She is symbolically putting the added unconscious guilt, those primary feelings, back into place, and by doing so, she meets her oral dependency need. We can speculate that other people with high personality core guilt, a large amount of these compensatory traits, and a tendency to accrue added unconscious guilt, which will intensify those traits, will also feel an increased "need" to control, organize, perfect, beautify, etc. They may appear more obsessed. When they translate this into their reality which might be the business world, or perhaps the arts or perhaps science, it may lead them toward success.

However, if the added unconscious guilt gets too high, and the person's compensatory traits can't handle the amount of added unconscious guilt accrued, the person will become even more frustrated and uncomfortable. Since those with high personality core guilt don't like to chitchat or gossip with others, and they are typically too dependent on too few, they may, at times, become the people whose defenses cannot handle an overwhelming increase in unconscious guilt. If the frustration that can't be handled manifests itself in directly expressed anger, it causes problems for both the person whose defenses are not working and for the others in his few relationships. Thus, people with high personality core guilt may find it difficult to meet the oral dependency needs of others. This can be a particular problem if the anger resulting from the overload of frustration is directed toward a child. The anger may frustrate the child's oral dependency need at the time the child's personality core guilt is being set. Perhaps the child is seen as hampering or blocking the operation of the defenses and may then be turned on with expressions of anger by the parent. Consider, for example, the mother who compensates for her unconscious guilt by keeping her house very neat. If she has been experiencing more stress than she usually does, she may feel a need to clean the house more meticulously, to keep everything in its place, down to the last knickknack. After she's cleaned and straightened, she goes into the dining room to find that her small child has left some of his toys on the floor. She turns on the child with an exaggerated expression of anger, and the child perceives a frustration of his own oral dependency need. Someone with less unconscious guilt probably would merely have instructed the child to put his toys away.

People with high personality core guilt may keep a wide "buffer zone" between themselves and others because of their own core primary feelings: they feel inferior, inadequate, worthless, guilty, etc. This emotional distance from other people tends to keep them too dependent on too few. They want to keep other people, who somehow symbolize the meeting of the oral dependency need, away: people who enjoy immediate pleasures; people who are not so concerned with being neat, punctual, or perfect. Sometimes these people want to place a distance between themselves and anything or anyone that is not perceived as perfect. They are often intolerant of people, experiences, or situations that they consider inferior, unacceptable, inadequate, worthless, incomplete, leading to failure, etc. They compensate for these feelings in themselves and they do not tolerate these characteristics in other people, making it particularly difficult for them to make friends with, and often even to relate to others. The higher the personality core guilt, the wider the "buffer zone" and the more intolerant one is of that which is perceived as symbolic of unconscious guilt.

Their intolerance of imperfection and their attempt to avoid people, experiences, or situations that would gratify the oral dependency need make it even harder for people with high personality core guilt to diffuse their need and their anger expression. Their lack of diffusion ensures that they will continue to easily accrue unconscious guilt. The more added unconscious guilt they accrue, the more intensely they must try to compensate for their primary feelings, with the traits they've developed as a result of their personality core guilt. When the compensatory traits are frustrated and anger is created, they must either repress the anger, building up even more unconscious guilt, or turn it on the few people to whom they're close.

Anyone's unconscious must always deal with this nebulous entity called unconscious guilt. In the next chapter, we'll take an even closer look at unconscious guilt and will discover the determining role it plays in success and failure.

CHAPTER 7
Understanding the Dynamics of Success and Failure

It is often difficult to recognize the qualities necessary to reach an outstanding level of success before someone does so. For instance, an instructor at Sandhurst, Britain's equivalent of West Point, said of one student, "He doesn't have the qualities we like to see in a Sandhurst graduate." Yet this student went on to become the well-known field marshal of World War II, Bernard Montgomery, the greatest British general since the Duke of Wellington. We do know it takes an ability to work exceedingly hard and long. Benjamin Franklin, who recognized this, once described success as ten percent genius and ninety percent sweat. Ask any high school teacher about recognizing students who will go on to be outstandingly successful, and he or she will often say that frequently it's not the students with the highest intelligence. There seems to be something else involved. Once, I had the pleasure of meeting and talking with one of the leading authorities on intelligence testing, a man who has written considerably on the subject. He told me that if he had the chance to be reborn, given the choice between having high intelligence and only a little of this "something else," or less intelligence and a great deal of this "something else," he would "unhesitatingly opt for the latter," for he knew this would ensure success.

We know that the "something else" seems built into the personality of some people. It has been shown that high intelligence is not necessarily the important factor in reaching an outstanding level of success. It certainly helps to have high intelligence, as it helps to have good luck, but this is not the deciding factor. This "something else" that seems to drive relentlessly or push a person appears to be the crucial factor in giving him or her that ability to work hard and long toward some form of success in reality. This "something else" is *required* to give that extraordinary capacity for hard work that is so necessary to attain an outstanding level of success. As with intelligence, some people seem to have a lot more of this "something else" than other people.

We know that at the very center of the personality lies the personality core guilt, and we can suspect that that "something else," or that drive to great success, is intimately associated with those core primary feelings. We might further suspect that the people who reach these outstanding levels of success have very high personality core guilt. Those compensatory traits of punctuality, the love of hard work, the desire for neatness and organization, that compensatory demand for perfection and quest for excellence as well as that ability to be obsessed can lead to reality success. More often than not, the outstanding level of success is in contrast to the person's early life when the odds seemed so much against him or her. Frequently, for instance, the one who becomes the multimillionaire is the very person who was born into poverty. His attempts to compensate for the primary feelings are translated into attempts to overcome obstacles in reality situations. He seems to be unconsciously trying to prove, by striving for success, that he is not what the core primary feelings unconsciously tell him he is: most inferior, inadequate, unacceptable, or incomplete. Comments by General "Hap" Arnold, whom we've previously mentioned, and General Curtis LeMay, one of the great Air Force generals of World War II, perfectly illustrate this point. General Arnold, apparently experiencing the feelings of inadequacy and incompleteness despite his past successes, often wrote to his wife, "I hope I am big enough to handle it." General LeMay was more explicit. He said, "Not once, during any switch of command, during any advancement in responsibility, have I ever considered that I was completely equipped for the new job at hand. Always I felt not fully qualified: needed more training, needed more information than I owned, more experience, more wisdom." Yet neither general ever let these doubts become known to his followers. On a similar note, I recently saw an interview with an internationally acclaimed musician. She said that reaching the top in her profession was easier than gaining longevity there. She'd been able to stay at the top, she said, because she never felt satisified with the way she performed. She could always see room for improvement. We should know now what is implied in the saying, "No man that became a success in life ever really thought he was."

These people also have a correspondingly high core unmet need, besides the drive to overcome or compensate for the primary feelings, that creates a "need" to find the limelight—to be central, to be the foremost, to have the most, to be the very best, and above all to be recognized. The highly successful business person may have tried to satisfy this "need" by creating a great business. How this person desires to be recognized becomes, of course, very individualistic. For instance, some may go "many extra miles" at work in order to win occupational awards or lead various community projects that receive recognition in the local press. They work long and hard to find the limelight, which so impresses others. The limelight may not even be on this earth. A person with a high core unmet need may strive not toward business success but toward religious success and look for rewards in the life hereafter. The push or drive that leads to success comes not only from the primary feelings of the personality core guilt, but also from the equal amount of core unmet oral dependency need that puts off immediate pleasure and translates itself into distant goals associated with that limelight of public acclaim, or perhaps special Divine recognition.

The compensatory drive or push and that "need" to be in the limelight are translated into specific reality situations and endeavors. Whether we are dealing with medicine, law, business, literature, the sciences, the theater, music, the military, or sports, we are observing the same tremendous drive. But its manifestation and orientation are different once it is translated into different reality situations. Outstanding levels of success require this push; they often require an all-consuming drive. For instance, one cannot become an Olympic gold medalist unless one has this type of drive. The person who wins the gold medal, or even competes in the Olympic Games, must give top priority to this drive to succeed. This person must be willing to spend an incredible amount of time, work, and sweat, and to forego many pleasures to succeed, to win the gold. To "win the gold" in any reality endeavor requires a love of hard work, and the willingness to put off pleasure, and even to endure hardships. The person must be obsessed with the goal. We tend to admire those people in the past who have had this all-consuming drive. If you read the biographies of Lewis and Clark, you will see that they endured unbelievable hardships to succeed—to reach the Pacific. Reaching the highest level in any reality endeavor, not just in athletics or exploration, takes exactly the same type of inward push. George Eastman is an example of this drive in business. He built the Kodak Company and amassed a fortune of over 150 million dollars. Anyone who reaches outstanding success in *any* endeavor must have this great push or drive, which comes from a very high personality core guilt and core unmet need. This needed push or drive, we know, comes from those same compensatory traits in anyone, but in those who have reached an outstanding level of success, these traits are more intense.

People who have very high personality core guilt are characteristically, as we know, very perfectionistic. *They* determine what is perfect. Because of this trait, they may not be easy to get along with. Also, the drive or push takes such priority that all else, including other people, may be relegated to insignificance. They may seem completely obsessed with the reality focus of the drive that may lead to outstanding success. So these people often grate against other people. They don't particularly care that they don't get along with others since they don't enjoy gossiping, chitchatting, or the pleasantries of others anyway.

Typically, the person with the perfectionism which comes from higher personality core guilt wants things done her way. She feels that only she knows what perfection is and how something can be done perfectly. She often comes across as dogmatic, uncompromising, and demanding, and in certain situations, this behavior can lead to great success. However, it doesn't help her to get along with other people. This is not her goal, unless perhaps her goal is political success. But even in that reality endeavor one can see the same drive, the same ability to be obsessed, and the same demand for perfection, translated instead into getting others to like her. These people who reach the great levels of success may seem a little odd or strange. We may talk about the eccentricities of a millionaire, for example. Oddities in behavior and thinking, and intolerance of imperfect people, things, experiences, or situations are characteristic of people with high personality core guilt and, as we've noted here, often of those who have reached outstanding success.

As an example of how the compensatory traits translate themselves into a reality situation, consider the young woman who plays the piano. She wants to be an outstanding concert pianist. So she can't just practice a couple of hours a day whenever she feels like it. She must be driven to succeed and that drive must come from within. It must be built into her personality from her earliest life. The direction that a person takes to achieve the outstanding success is often programmed. Perhaps when this woman was younger, her parents took her to many concerts, or perhaps she had a favorite aunt who gave her her first piano lessons and encouraged her to play seriously. Often, a person will have an emotionally significant other who directs his or her drive. It may help to have someone else push, as it may help to be highly intelligent, but the real push must come from within. This pianist is inwardly driven and becomes obsessed with musical perfection. She has a very high personality core guilt, which gives her a tendency to forego immediate pleasure and to love hard work. While other children are outside playing and having fun, she is inside, practicing the piano, trying to perfect her performance. While other teenagers are out on dates and at parties and school dances, she is at home practicing and perfecting. She seems to love practicing for hours every day. She plays each piece over and over, eliminating errors until she plays it perfectly. She decides what perfection is and is dissatisfied with anything less. She is on the road to outstanding success.

The same love of hard work, that demand for perfection, and that ability to be obsessed can be seen in the writer, who revises each line of poetry, each chapter of the novel, until he or she decides that it is perfect.

One well-known author rewrote each chapter of his books at least twenty times before being satisfied enough to send it to his publisher. In other situations, the perfection could show itself in an orientation toward time and punctuality. When Field Marshal Montgomery was asked how he became so successful, he replied, "I owe all my success in life to being fifteen minutes ahead of time." Such punctuality and concern with accomplishing things within a certain time would help a person reach success in the military, both on the battlefield and off. These people are all striving to reach the top; they are on a quest for excellence and they are obsessed with how this focuses itself in their reality. They want to tread in areas of acclaim, fame, or glory where no one else has stepped. In exploration, research, or whatever their focus in reality, they want to go where no one else has been; they want to do things that no one else has done, or to do things better than anyone else has ever done them.

They want to be widely known and honored for years to come. They want people to remember their accomplishments throughout the years and to remember just who accomplished these great things. I read about a man who remembered one of his schoolmates saying, "If I could find a Colossus of Rhodes and tear it down so that a hundred years later people would remember my name, I would do it." This schoolmate later did just that. Well over one hundred years later, we still remember the name of John Wilkes Booth because of the Colossus he tore down. The ancient Egyptian pharoah, Ramses II, who led Egypt so well during one of its greatest periods, made a statue to himself, with an inscription that reads, "If any man thinks that he is greater than Ramses II, let him make a statue that is greater than this." Man made nothing to surpass the size of this statue until the construction of Grand Cooley Dam. It is interesting to note that several years ago one of Ramses' toes began to deteriorate. The Egyptian government flew his mummy from the Cairo Museum to Paris to be examined by specialists there. When his body was brought down from the plane, French troops were drawn up on either side and presented arms to this political-military ruler of over three thousand years ago. This desire to be the center of attention, to be recognized, to be known and remembered for years hence, comes from the core unmet need, that need to be the center of attention.

When these people accrue added unconscious guilt, which we know they do easily because of their high personality core guilt, their compensatory traits become more intense, and this intensification often helps to keep them successful. When the pianist perceives oral dependency need frustration and represses the resulting anger, accruing added unconscious guilt, she feels a greater need to be perfect and may practice for six hours each day, rather than four. She must be "more perfect";

her standards of perfection become more exacting, more defined, and more difficult to achieve. She moves on to more challenging compositions and she becomes more obsessed. It is in like manner that any outstanding success is obtained. Because her added unconscious guilt has intensified her compensatory traits, she improves as a pianist. She may become the best in the world. As another example, imagine a highly successful business man who accrues added unconscious guilt. With the increase in his primary feelings, he feels more as though something is going to go wrong in his business. So he works harder and longer, worries more and checks and double checks many times to make sure that everything is being done perfectly. He anticipates all possible problems and in doing so prevents them by correcting whatever might cause a problem. By worrying about things that need to be worried about—those "what if"s of possible business problems—this man prevents the occurrence of anything that could take him from his level of success. Intensified defenses against those core primary feelings, we can see, help both the businessman and the piano player reach and maintain great success. The same is true of anyone who will reach the highest level of success in any reality endeavor.

Let's look at the graph at the end of this chapter and say that Line X represents the amount of unconscious guilt necessary for great reality success in some endeavor. Person A has low personality core guilt, and if he were to reach outstanding success, he would have to accrue a large amount of added unconscious guilt to reach that line. It is unlikely that Person A will become an outstanding success, because with a low amount of personality core guilt a high amount of added unconscious guilt isn't sustained. This person doesn't have much of that push or drive for success. He doesn't have a lot of core primary feelings that need to be compensated. Person B, however, has higher personality core guilt, and with a smaller amount of added unconscious guilt, she will be driven more to compensate her core primary feelings which may lead to reality success. But at times of lowered added unconscious guilt, this person may completely lose the drive or push toward great success. Person C is driven to succeed in reality by his personality core guilt alone. His drive doesn't cease; it's constant. With luck and just the right set of reality circumstances, he can become famous in his field. From this graph then we can see the relationship between personality core guilt and that drive that is so necessary for reality success.

With an increase in added unconscious guilt the defenses may be intensified to the point of excess where they no longer fit with the demands of a particular reality success. For example, consider again the successful businessman who worried about his business and by doing so insured the continuation of his success because of that very attention to detail. If his added unconscious guilt increases too much, his worrying may become excessive. But note that it is the reality of what is necessary for that particular success, that will decide what is "excessive." This may vary from time to time due to the circumstances necessary to maintain that level of success. Our successful businessman may begin to worry about things that wouldn't logically happen, and his worrying may spread to other areas of his life. After he's left for work in the morning, he may for instance have to go home two or three times to make sure that he turned off all the appliances and locked all doors and windows. He may even have to return at lunchtime just to make sure. Perhaps when he gets home from work in the evening, he can't relax because he's too worried about his business. His trait of worrying, which previously was an asset, helping him to achieve great success, has now become a liability because it has intensifed to the point of excess.

Anyone's assets can become liabilities if they are sufficiently intensified by an increase in added unconscious guilt. One man told me about his wife who was a meticulous housewife. Apparently at certain times, when her added unconscious guilt was greater and her traits of neatness and organization were intensified, she would have the bed made by the time he got back from going to the bathroom early in the morning even though he preferred to sleep later. She just couldn't stand to see a messed up bed, even for a few minutes. Another man who saw me worked at a nearby power plant. His job was to monitor gauges, and he was very good at it. He liked to check and control things, which we know was a defense against his unconscious guilt. We must theorize he was checking, symbolically, that the guilt was in its proper place. When his increased added unconscious guilt made this trait excessive, he would check the outside faucets at home to make sure they had been turned off. He'd check them when he got home and again before he went to bed. He'd worry that if they were dripping, the water pump would run all night and burn itself out (that feeling of impending trouble). He didn't trust himself or what he had done (that feeling of inadequacy or failure). His worry got worse as his added unconscious guilt increased. After he had gotten into bed, he'd think, "Did I *really* shut those off?" Then he'd get up and check them all over again. He'd go back to bed and think, "Did I really turn them the right way?" He told me that he did this twenty-two times in one night and that he couldn't sleep because of all the worrying. But he was complaining about one of his previous assets, intensified to the point of becoming a liability.

A trait that is an asset in one reality situation may prove to be a liability in another. There are times in a person's reality where it is advantageous to feel worry-free and secure, and other times where it is definitely advantageous to feel worried, insecure and uncertain. One will tend to take corrective action in reality in an attempt to alleviate the feeling of insecurity, and uncertainty, and in doing so may prevent an adverse situation or experience. There are situations in reality where one shouldn't have that feeling of "everything is going to be all right" or that "no need to worry" feeling, because things are *not* going to be all right and the person *should* worry. Having the feeling that they are may cause a person to take unwarranted risks that could lead to a harmful or an adverse situation or experience. One should see that in some reality situations, it might be highly advantageous to have a feeling "that every-thing *isn't* going to be all right," or the "need" to worry, that might then cause the person to take the necessary steps to alleviate or prevent what he fears in reality could possibly happen, and to avoid taking the risks he might have taken with less added unconscious guilt and more per-ceived oral dependency need gratification.

I knew a man who used to run a large nationally known business. He was a hard worker and a worrier. He made the company grow because he worked hard at it and worried about all the things that needed wor-rying about. He translated his need to work hard and to worry into his work reality which produced success. He was emotionally comfortable because he handled his added unconscious guilt through the business. Then he had a heart attack, and had to retire. No longer did he have the forced involvement with others that his work provided. As a person with high personality core guilt, he didn't enjoy the company of others. When he left work to spend his retirement with his wife, his opportunities for expressing anger decreased. He had no social involvements, no close friends, no hobbies, and his added unconscious guilt quickly built up. His wife brought him in to see me after she found him sitting by the furnace one night, worried "sick" that it might blow up. The trait that was an asset in his business had become a liability at home.

If the total unconscious guilt becomes too much for the defenses to handle, then the defenses may break down completely. Suppose our pianist accrues a large amount of added unconscious guilt, which com-bines with her already high personality core guilt to make her total unconscious guilt too much for her to manage with her perfectionism, hard work, and foregoing of pleasures, including that of chitchatting with others. As this added unconscious guilt increases, she works harder and longer; her standards of perfection become higher and higher, until finally, they become too high. She cannot possibly attain the level of perfection that she has now set for herself with *any* amount of work, so she gives up. She can't bring herself to go near the piano. Likewise, the millionaire who loves to go to the office, working hard and long in his business, may drive himself harder as his added unconscious guilt increases. What little chitchatting he did before, he now has no time for. When his unconscious guilt reaches a certain level, he can't go near the office. He acts as though he's given up. He can't even make himself read the *Wall Street Journal*, something he enjoyed when his added unconscious guilt was much lower. He'll tell you, as one typically does at this point, that he's not himself. His personality's defenses are overwhelmed by the greatly increased unconscious guilt, and his entire system of defenses breaks down. As another example, consider the college student with perfectionistic traits and that all-consuming drive for academic success. She characteristically receives the top grades in many of her classes, making sure and worrying that all her work is done on time and that every paper is neatly and perfectly typed. As her added unconscious guilt increases, she begins to worry more about a coming test. When it increases even more, she can't study for her test or write her papers, and she doesn't take the test. She has given up. Her added unconscious guilt now is too much for her compensatory traits to handle. She, too, complains she isn't herself.

When the defenses against the primary feelings break down completely, the person just seems to give up. Previously appearing strong, energetic, hardworking, goal-directed and controlled, the person now appears weak, listless, foundering and out of control. Lewis, of Lewis and Clark fame, a person who could withstand great hardships, translated this need to work and overcome challenges into an incredible trek to the Pacific. After he reached the Pacific, he became famous. But rather than enjoy his fame, he seemed to change; he wasn't himself. Eventually, he shot himself. You would think that someone like George Eastman, who amassed that 150 million dollar fortune, would have wanted to relax and enjoy his success. But he, too, gave up and killed himself. Marilyn Monroe was one of the most beautiful and admired women of her time. But she had a very unhappy personal life; she frequently saw psychiatrists and eventually may have killed herself as well. Ernest Hemingway committed suicide after reaching outstanding success. One can easily recall many other similar people who had reached the heights of success in their chosen fields. One would think that such success would bring with it a sense of satisfaction, a desire to enjoy the limelight. But there is a remarkably high incidence of suicide in all fields of endeavor among people who have reached the top level of success. If not suicide, there is striking evidence of emotional grief and suffering, which seems so incongruent with the level of success attained.

Giving up doesn't necessarily mean that the person commits suicide.

Where the person was once meticulously dressed and concerned with neatness and organization, he may become sloppy and disorganized in habits and dress. She may seem to stop trying where she was once hard-working. Or he may seek to escape the abusively high unmet need and the primary feelings through excesses of alcohol or through drugs. There are many people who attained success, but then seemed to give up for a while, appearing as "losers" in life, only to become successful again. We might theorize that this pattern reflects different levels of unconscious guilt. Consider a building contractor I saw who earned, through long hours and a great preoccupation with perfection and detail, a solid reputation; he saw one admirable project after another through to successful completion. Seemingly without warning, he gave up. No longer was he the driving force behind his company's success. His company went bankrupt and he stayed at home, not himself. It was not too long, however, before he regained his former traits. He became a developer of industrial parks and multimillion dollar projects. This new endeavor was once again marked by the same meticulous eye for perfection and detail that had distinguished him before. He worried about things that needed worrying about. He perfected things that needed perfecting. He was obsessed with developing. He drove himself and others as was necessary to accomplish what he did. He was back on top; however, he was not to stay there for long. He again seemed to give up and wasn't himself. His career continued to follow a "boom or bust" pattern—financial success one day, financial ruin the next.

So many of the people who have achieved what we think should make them pleased with themselves and emotionally comfortable in life are, ironically, extremely uncomfortable. Too many of the successful, like our developer, seem to have periods where they appear to have given up. If they can lower their added unconscious guilt, even a little, they go back to work, once more driving themselves toward success—accumulating, beautifying, perfecting, organizing and above all driving themselves to work long and hard. The contrast then, is that these people are either on the go, or they've given up. There may appear to be only a fine line between the two. When these people are given certain drugs, they slow down a bit. They're not so driven, and they don't reach such outstanding success either. They also don't get to the point of giving up. The drugs seem to help lower the unmet oral dependency need, and lower their added unconscious guilt. Their traits then are less intensified, and they are less driven to work, to worry, and to be perfect. I knew a house painter who was a perfectionistic in his work and had an excellent reputation. However, I also knew he often drank excessively. I asked a friend of his, "How can Bobby drink so much and paint at such heights?"

His friend answered, "He drinks just enough to get up the ladder each day but not quite enough to fall off." A lot of people use alcohol and drugs in a similar way to dissolve excessive added unconscious guilt so that they can keep going. It is not unusual to see the abuse of alcohol and drugs by those in the limelight of public acclaim and who, like Bobby, use it to keep going. Many of those most successful in life, without drugs and alcohol, would reach a point like our pianist, millionaire, and student, where they wouldn't be able to go near their work, and would complain that they were not themselves. Without the alcohol and drugs they wouldn't be so far up the ladder of success, working so spectacularly.

Although high personality core guilt is a prerequisite for success in reality, a person with too much may never achieve any reality success. He or she unconsciously feels so much inferiority, inadequacy, unacceptableness, incompleteness, guilt, uncleanness, or impending trouble because of having such a high personality core guilt, that he or she cannot handle it through the compensatory traits that would bring success in any reality endeavor. This person always seems as if he or she has given up because the personality core guilt, which does not change in quantity, is so great. In fact, his or her core unmet oral need, which also does not change in quantity, is so great that the person may invent some delusion in which the need to be central, or the need for the limelight, can be met. "I'm Napoleon," "I'm President Reagan," "I'm Jesus Christ" are a few examples of delusions I've come across. These people may try to live within the delusions that the unconscious mind has created to compensate for the unmet oral dependency need. Or, they may exhibit manifestations of the primary feelings of the unconscious guilt saying something like, "I have a terrible odor and I can't be around people because the smell that emits from me would kill anyone who might get too close." These people have enough unconscious guilt in the personality core to make them outstanding failures in life. They never do become outstanding successes.

To contrast these people with those who need some added unconscious guilt to make them break down, consider the soldier who has been in combat for many days on the front lines, where every hour he gets a frustration of his unconscious omnipotence and centrality as people try to kill him. Eventually, he may break down and become delusional. This reaction is similar to those people who end up feeling so alone in those foxholes of life, facing daily battles. Eventually, they too may break down. In the military, these breakdowns, where the soldier can become delusional, are known as "three-day schizophrenias." The soldier appears to be "schizophrenic." There is no way of differentiating between the schizophrenia one sees in a state psychiatric hospital and this "three-day schizophrenia," except that when these soldiers are taken off the front lines, taken away from the massive frustrations of combat, put in the hospital, and given some care and attention, they pull out of their "schizophrenia" within a matter of days. If we can lower their added unconscious guilt, they become themselves again. The men who may more quickly develop these "three-day schizophrenias" are often top-notch soldiers, but if they are kept on the front for too long, we may theorize that a great accrual of added unconscious guilt has caused them to become delusional. If the added unconscious guilt can be lowered, then they are return to their normal level of functioning. Rest them up for a few days in a hospital, and they're very quickly chitchatting and "rapping" with others in neighboring beds. These people had a great increase in their added unconscious guilt which has now been lowered. If someone has a high enough personality core guilt, this alone can cause him or her to be delusional. If schizophrenic, his drugs help him to live with his schizophrenia. It doesn't go away.

Referring again to the graph at the end of this chapter, let's now view Line X as the "delusional" line. Person A has a "three-day schizophrenia." To produce so much added unconscious guilt for this person would require some massive oral dependency need frustration and an isolating situation where resulting anger must be repressed. His added unconscious guilt is easily lowered because he has low personality core guilt, which means that he has no aversion to becoming involved with others and meeting the oral dependency need. Person B already has high personality core guilt, so she is closer to the line and more prone to become delusional. For her, it takes only a little added unconscious guilt, which she may easily accumulate, to reach the line. Person C has a personality core guilt which exceeds the line. His personality core guilt cannot be lowered, so Person C will keep his high level of unconscious guilt. He is delusional and will remain delusional. But for the people like Persons A and B whose added unconscious guilt has pushed them up to the delusional level, the added unconscious guilt can be lowered to a point where they can function adequately.

An example of someone who reached the delusional level because of an increase in added unconscious guilt is the college professor I saw who told his wife and children to drive to Boston; he planned to join them in a few days. His family was killed in an automobile accident on the way, which was a massive frustration of his oral dependency need. His increase in added unconscious guilt pushed him to the delusional level, and be believed that he had murdered his family; he went about calling himself a "murderer" and seeking appropriate punishment. However, after a few days in the hospital, where some of his needs were met, his added unconscious guilt decreased, and he began acting like himself again. He no longer was delusional, even though he was, of course, still grieving for his family.

Contrast this man to Person C, a man with such a high personality core guilt that its level reaches past the line at which he becomes delusional. He may be schizophrenic and will remain schizophrenic regardless of treatment; his personality core guilt cannot be lowered. No amount of psychiatric treatment will get him over this schizophrenia, though he can be made more comfortable with such treatment. He may say, with treatment, "I still hear voices but I just don't pay any attention to them any longer." When his guilt was at a much higher level, he couldn't disregard the voices.

We are told that there is a tendency for schizophrenia to run in families. But we know that outstanding success also seems to run in families. We often see a family in which, for instance, the grandfather was a highly successful businessman, then the father was very successful, and now the son exhibits the same drive to work hard and long to succeed in the business. Parents with high personality core guilt tend to produce children with high personality core guilt. Highly successful parents with this high personality core guilt often find it difficult to find the time to meet the oral dependency needs of their children, or to tolerate a child's imperfections during the time when the child's personality core guilt is forming. The children develop personality core guilt which may lead to great reality success. But if the personality core guilt is too high, they may end up delusional or as though they've given up. One sibling in a family may be outstandingly successful in some reality endeavor. Perhaps this person runs a multimillion dollar company as does one person I know. He appears self-reliant, driven, independent, and strong. His brother, however, has been in and out of psychiatric hospitals with a diagnosis of schizophrenia and can't even care for himself. The latter, we might theorize, got too much personality core guilt, which keeps him at the delusional level. I'm acquainted with a well-known judge in a nearby state who apparently has just the right amount of personality core guilt to drive him to substantial judicial success. However, his sister ended up with too much personality core guilt; she is "mentally ill" and is kept hidden by the family. I saw a young man in the psychiatric hospital where I trained who was brought there because he was delusional. While talking to him, I was impressed with his level of intelligence. He told me that his father was the president of a nationally-known company. His mother had a Ph.D. from a prestigious school and was involved with a nearby university and with the community. One might theorize that this young man ended up with too much personality core guilt.

Many highly successful people may not make good parents or even good spouses. Their traits of perfectionism, their love of hard work, their aversion to "wasting time" in chitchatting, and their aversion to immediate oral dependency need gratification often keep these people from meeting the oral dependency needs of children or spouses. For instance, Captain John Smith, the early American explorer, was never home for long. Neither were the early circuit riders whose names are still familiar in the Protestant faith. To be highly successful in any endeavor one can't stay at home meeting oral dependency needs. Admiral Byrd, that world famous admiral of the thirties, named one-fourth of the continent of Antarctica after his wife. If we pick up a map of the South Pole even today we'll see the large area called "Marieland." But his wife divorced him. Perhaps it was because he was never home either— always out on some ice floe. He was outstandingly successful as an explorer, but apparently, as a husband, some might feel he was a failure. When we talk to their spouses or relatives, we find that many of these highly successful people are characteristically "out on ice floes" as far as their personal lives are concerned. They're simply not at home; the particular reality success they're working toward or have reached demands their time. I've had many a spouse tell me that even when they *are* at home they're still "out on an ice floe," totally involved in the demands of their reality success. Spend pleasant time with your spouse and children, chat leisurely with old friends, stop and smell the roses, and you won't be outstandingly successful. You'll just be more emotionally comfortable.

One woman who had been diagnosed by another psychiatrist as schizophrenic came to see me. Her mother was outstandingly successful in the community and a "pillar of the church," admired by all who knew her, but hardly ever home, when she was, she constantly criticized. She told me, however, that her father was always home. He raised her, but he was usually upstairs writing a book and when he wasn't, he too was finding fault and criticizing. She said he was particularly good at that. Neither parent did much as far as meeting her oral dependency need. Yet her father was a well-known writer. An irony is becoming apparent: one doesn't have to have a mother or father who is an alcoholic, or drug-addicted, or "mentally ill" to have his or her oral dependency need frustrated in early life, to later become an emotional wreck; he or she can have extremely successful parents who are widely recognized and greatly admired and get the very same results. People with high personality core guilt tend to frustrate too easily their own children's oral dependency needs, whether they drink or don't drink. Some I know frustrate more when they don't drink a little. They either aren't home, or if they are, they're caught up in the demands of their success. Even when they're not they are frustrating others in the family with their standards of perfection, their demands for "independence," their affinity toward work, and their aversion to immediate pleasures. Yet if they frustrate just enough of their children's oral dependency needs early in life, their children too may end up with a high enough personality core guilt to be outstandingly successful but not so high that they become "mentally ill."

Another problem that is closely related to high unconscious guilt is alcoholism. When someone accrues too much added unconscious guilt, which those with high personality core guilt tend to do, he or she may have a tendency to abuse alcohol. With high personality core guilt, then, we may see not only the push for success and mental illness, but also the excessive use of alcohol. The person may seem to have a "need" to dissolve that high level of unconscious guilt and unmet oral dependency need in alcohol. If we refer again to the graph, Line X could now be viewed as the "need" to drink line. For a person who is prone to alcohol abuse, when his or her unconscious guilt reaches the "need" to drink line, he or she will tend to abuse alcohol. Person A must accrue a large amount of added unconscious guilt in order to reach this line. Since Person A has a low personality core guilt, a sustained high level of unconscious guilt would be unlikely. This person has little problem with alcohol. But Person B needs only a little more unconscious guilt because of her already high personality core guilt to reach this line. When Person B accrues added unconscious guilt, she may tend to abuse alcohol, but if she can lower the added unconscious guilt, she no longer feels this "need" to drink. Person C's "need" to drink line runs through the personality core guilt, which cannot be lowered, so he will always feel the "need" to drink.

A person like Person B may be told that she was born with a genetic biochemical aberration that includes an inability to handle alcohol and therefore needs to get into A.A. This would involve her with other people and force a reduction in that emotional distance that she keeps from other people, thereby lowering the unmet oral dependency need and the added unconscious guilt. Person B in A.A. may stop drinking if she stays active. A.A. works particularly well for people like Person B. It forces them to relate to other people, which they find difficult to do on their own, because of the high personality core guilt. This association enables them to meet the oral dependency need and lower the added unconscious guilt on a part-person, part-experience, part-situation basis. Person A appears to be able to easily "control" his drinking, because Person A has an affinity for other people. Person A's high added unconscious guilt level is only transitory. Person A doesn't have to be forced into participating with others. He naturally does so. Person A isn't involved in a marriage relationship where one is too dependent on too few. The spouse is emotionally active with many and isn't demanding an exclusive "it's just you and me against the world and why can't others leave us alone" relationship. Person B, in contrast, may have a spouse or parent who continues to make demands that Person B gratify her oral dependency need on a whole basis. This other person, who wants to maintain an exclusive relationship with Person B, may not want Person B going to A.A. and associating with others. A.A. does seem to recognize this problem and encourages the exclusive other to join Al Anon, which helps both people to be less dependent on too few. Person C, however, will not participate in A.A. and will continue to drink. He can't lower his unconscious guilt below the "need" to drink line.

The compensatory traits of high personality core guilt and alcohol abuse often go hand in hand. I was called to the emergency room one night when I was in training, where the nurse told me there was an alcoholic truck driver to treat. She had seen him many times before and warned me that he was hostile, couldn't say anything nice about anybody, and was always complaining. Before I saw him, his wife talked to me, and she told me that he was always finding fault, criticizing, and getting angry. He was a perfectionist, she said, but he decided what was perfect and what wasn't. She said that even if she did do something perfectly, he'd still manage to find fault with it; he'd want her to do it in even less time. Then I talked to him, and he was exactly the way they had described him. But I could see traits in him that could have led to success in the right reality situation. Being married to his wife, who demanded an exclusive relationship, and driving long hours in a truck alone, as he did, wasn't that reality. His drinking only made his reality worse. But he confided in me that his brother was a nationally-known military officer of the highest rank. I had the feeling that this man, who was an outstanding commander, had traits similar to those of his brother. I later saw another relative who knew the military commander well and confirmed that he had those same traits. He was a perfectionist, too, but instead of fault finding and expressing anger to his wife, he could express anger to those ranking below him to achieve that perfection he desired. He demanded that maneuvers be done perfectly and when they were, he wanted them done in less time. That put stars on his shoulders. I understand that he drank too, but not excessively. High personality core guilt often runs in families, and these two brothers had similar compensatory traits. The brother who was the military commander did not feel a need to dissolve his unconscious guilt with alcohol because he could express anger and meet his needs through his career. In the type of work he did, he had to be closely involved with other people. They could meet some of his oral dependency need on a part basis, and he could get rid of his anger on a part, or even a whole person basis. The truck driving brother was overly dependent on his wife and his unconscious guilt usually exceeded the "need" to drink line. But note that the truck driver's alcoholism was less linked to genetics or biochemical abnormalities in the body's ability to handle alcohol than linked to his high personality core guilt and his situation in life. A deception should now be apparent in believing otherwise.

If the compensatory traits of high personality core guilt and alcoholism often go together, it follows that alcoholism and success often become a combination. I remember reading in a well-known medical newspaper of an interview with a famous eighty-year old doctor and medical editor who gave as a reason for his success his long hours of work. He said that every medical student should plan on working at least eighty hours a week as he did. Unless a person planned on dedicating over eighty hours a week to work, this famous doctor felt they shouldn't be allowed to enter medical school. I thought later that it's no wonder so many doctors become alcoholics. An article in a recent journal of psychiatry stated that the addiction rate of physicians is ten times that of the general population. In this article, the authors also note that the addiction rate is similar for high-salaried business executives. Perhaps a little later, these researchers will discover that in any field of endeavor the outstandingly successful people, who often put in eighty hours a week because they must in order to succeed, share a similar need to drink excessively. It shouldn't surprise anyone if their addiction rates turn out to equal that of physicians. Alcohol dissolves the unmet oral dependency need. It dissolves the added unconscious guilt, if only temporarily, as do certain drugs. The irony is that the road to outstanding success may also be the very same road to addiction or to the nearest psychiatric hospital.

It's not the alcohol that ruins careers as much as a sustained level of too much unconscious guilt. This sustained high level of guilt can show itself in a wide variety of ways. It can show itself as delusional states, mental illnesses, drug abuse, or alcoholism. Certainly a person can't run a business if he's given up on life or become delusional, yet it's surprising how many people maintain high levels of success while slipping into alcoholic binges or mental illness and back out again. I know of many successful businessmen and professionals who will go away secretly, to get "detoxed," or to "rest up" in a private psychiatric hospital. The come back after a month or so and are soon running their businesses and professions again in a most admirable way. They can't seem to take off for leisure time, because they are types who find it difficult to take vacations and when on vacations, don't take them well.

Highly successful people are often completely unable or may find it difficult to meet the oral dependency needs of others. They all too often have children who have severe emotional problems, who are addicted to alcohol or drugs, or who are in and out of psychiatric institutions for whatever reasons. In my twenty-five years of practice, I have seen alcohol abuse, severe emotional problems, and visits to psychiatrists all kept secret in many of the very "best" families. My findings could be verified by almost any other psychiatrist in private outpatient practice. The facts will never become public or part of any psychiatric research because of the necessity for confidentiality. Not only are these highly successful people unable to meet the needs of their family members, but an intimate look at their own lives will often show that there are personal histories of emotional grief. Their lives often include many unhappy marriages, severe spouse and child abuse, alcoholism and drug addiction. Their personal lives don't support the perception that outstanding success brings happiness.

We know that real contentment and satisfaction in life come from having our oral dependency needs adequately met, preferably from the very beginning. The irony in all this should be becoming apparent. Having those traits that are associated with high personality core guilt, and outstanding success are not particularly conducive to meeting the oral dependency needs of someone else, whether that be a spouse, a child, or an employee. One's intolerance of imperfection may be too easily translated into the reality of these relationships and may not be in the best emotional interests of the other person. If that person is a child, not meeting her needs may be in her best interests in so far as later making her outstandingly successful in reality. But it very likely may not help her to be content later in life or to be satisfied with herself and others. Outstandingly successful people are not necessarily good parents; it is people with low personality core guilt and low added unconscious guilt who are much more likely to be. But we don't make statues to the good mother or the good father who has sufficiently met the oral dependency needs of the children. We never have, and we probably never will. We make statues to those who have high personality core guilt and who, as such, symbolize past frustrated and denied oral dependency needs, those who have persevered through deprivation, pain and suffering, those who have demanded perfection of themselves and others, and those who have worked relentlessly foregoing all immediate pleasures. We admire the exceptional reality success that they have attained. It is when we look to the other aspects of their lives that we often see the failures. They too frequently fail to meet the oral dependency needs of those close to them, and often they fail to find the contentment or satisfaction that they themselves desire. Those with low personality core guilt, who have low potential for becoming either outstanding successes or outstanding failures, are just emotionally comfortable people who do very well at meeting oral dependency needs, both their own and others'. Their biographies will probably never be written, and they won't be remembered years hence. One may very well wonder if they aren't better off not having the desire to be great successes in life than those that are.

Individuals With An Equal Amount of <u>Total</u> Unconscious Guilt

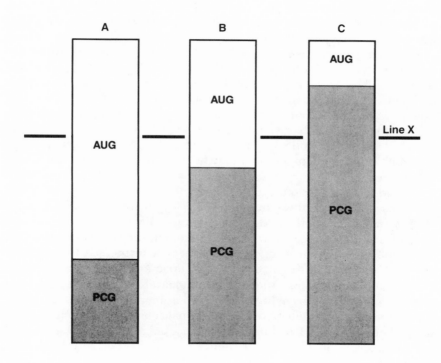

AUG = Added Unconscious Guilt
PCG = Personality Core Guilt

CHAPTER 8
The Deception in Perception

We perceive and interpret our reality—that is the world and all the people, experiences, and situations with which we are involved, as well as the reality of ourselves—with mental functioning that is affected by our emotional unreality, most particularly by the added unconscious guilt. It is in this perception of reality that deception is the greatest. We make it deceptive in that we accept this perception as true reality and present it to ourselves and others as such. We perceive a distortion and believe it to be objective reality.

To recognize the deception, let's look more closely at the added unconscious guilt. This form of unconscious guilt, in its varying amounts, is continually creating a degree of distortion in regard to our perception of reality. As the added unconscious guilt increases, there is proportionately more distortion. As it shrinks, there is less distortion in regard to actual reality. We deceive ourselves in failing to recognize the distortion. We simply continue to perceive reality, depending on our perceptive abilities, in a manner which may be very different from the actual or true reality.

The added unconscious guilt comes in three forms or positions, and we'll look at each of these in detail. The first of these positions is the *self-felt position*. When the added unconscious guilt is in this position, the primary feelings are seen as referable to oneself; they appear to emanate from one's perception of oneself. The person in the self-felt position perceives himself as inferior, inadequate, unacceptable, wrong, guilty, a failure, and headed for trouble. A rationalization is made from this perception. What we have previously seen in regard to rationalizing the added unconscious guilt have been rationalizations in the self-felt position. For example, "I feel inferior because _____," "I feel guilty because _____," or The primary feelings can also be paraphrased or expressed in the vernacular, such as "I'm a jerk," or "I feel like garbage and I stink." I've seen many people who used, "I'm just no good" to represent their self-felt added unconscious guilt. This phrase could be more specific, such as, "I'm no good at school," or "I'm no good in bed." Rationalizations for these feelings would follow: "I'm no good because I can't _____"; or "I'm a jerk for [doing] _____".

A very capable woman once said to me, "I feel unacceptable because of my hair. When my hair isn't just right, I don't feel right. I feel unacceptable to other people." In talking to this woman, I found out that she'd always been oriented toward the appearance of her hair. She had a high personality core guilt and was an efficient executive secretary with perfectionistic traits. She had her hair done often, and she spent a lot of time working with it. After she had used a new shampoo and changed beauticians, she was unhappy about the way her hair looked. This was because her added unconscious guilt had increased, and she used her hair as a reality focus for it. She spent more time looking in the mirror, trying to "fix" what she saw there. She withdrew; she didn't want to be around other people because she felt so unacceptable, so inferior, and so inadequate. She felt guilty for "ruining" her hair by trying a different shampoo and a different beautician. This woman is in the self-felt position, using her hair as a rationalization for the intensified primary feelings, which all seem to be oriented toward her hair.

The rationalization can concentrate on any part of a person's reality. It may be, "I feel inferior because I'm uneducated," "I feel unacceptable because I don't make very much money," or "I feel worthless and guilty because I don't have enough Christian love." It could even have a specific sexual orientation; for instance, a man could say, "I feel inadequate because my penis is too small." A person has his entire reality from which to draw in order to explain the level of inferiority, inadequacy, etc., that he is experiencing.

In the self-felt position, the primary feelings and the rationalization are made referable to the person, himself, or to any thing, any person, any experience, or any situation associated or identified with the person. For example, if I am a parent whose added unconscious guilt is in the self-felt position, I may say, "There's something physically wrong with my child. I don't want him going to school; I just *know* there's something wrong with him. So I'm going to keep him at home." I keep him at home for several days, and the school calls to tell me that I must either bring in a slip from a medical doctor or send the boy back to school. Although I've taken him to two different doctors who have found nothing wrong with him, I still feel that there's something physically wrong. I might tell you, "I am his mother, and I know him best, better than any doctor; I'm going to keep him at home." In this example, a person who is identified with the person presenting the rationalization becomes the focus of the rationalized increased added unconscious guilt.

I can also use experiences from my past as a rationalization for my feelings of guilt, inferiority, and worthlessness. Perhaps I am a Vietnam War veteran. I may say, "I feel unacceptable because I fought in the

Vietnam War. I know it was a very unpopular war. Lots of college kids and other people my age protested against it. I feel guilty and ashamed for fighting in it. If I had served in the Second World War, it would have been different. I'd be proud, and I'd feel like a hero. It was a popular war, and we won it. But I served in the Vietnam War, and I feel inferior because I was in such a losing war." In this example, the rationalization for present feelings is focused on a past experience.

Another example of someone who uses a past experience to rationalize feelings of added unconscious guilt in the self-felt position is that of the woman who had an abortion some years ago. She accrues added unconscious guilt in the present and she says, "I feel guilty because I had an abortion five years ago." This sounds reasonable; it makes sense. But it's a deception. First, she felt guilty, ashamed, inadequate, inferior, etc., from recently increased added unconscious guilt, then her unconscious seized the fact that she'd had an abortion to use as a rationalization. This deception is presented to other people, including psychiatrists, and they accept it. Then the psychiatrists can state that they have had many cases where women have not gotten over having abortions years before. What we're presenting is that the guilt these women feel, years later in the here-and-now, is the feeling emphasized in the rationalization only because it makes the most sense. Actually, all of the primary feelings are present, and they are all there before the rationalization of the abortion is created. We can theorize that when her added unconscious guilt had decreased in the past, she didn't feel guilty and might not have even thought of the abortion. It is only when the added unconscious guilt increases enough that the abortion rationalization is used. The deception therefore of a woman "never having gotten over her past abortion" should be apparent. We can also theorize that if she hadn't had the abortion, she would have found another rationalization that may have emphasized a different primary feeling when her self-felt added unconscious guilt increased.

As another example of utilizing a past experience to rationalize the primary feelings intensified from increased added unconscious guilt in the present, consider what a forty-year-old woman who just recently began feeling unacceptable and inadequate told me. "I think it all goes back to the time I was raped at the age of thirteen. After that I felt somehow unclean—you know, as though there was something somehow wrong with me. I thought that was in the past and had been forgotten for all these years but now I see I need to work it through." Some thirty years after the Korean War a veteran told me, "Those experiences are coming back to me. I can't sleep at night because of dreams and flashbacks about the battles I had been in. They're causing me to be so uncomfortable now I can't even function. I'm glad the Veterans' Administration has finally recognized this condition called the post-traumatic stress syndrome." The deception is that the experience of wartime service of years ago is utilized by the unconscious to "explain" the emotional uncomfortableness in the *present*. It is the rise in the added unconscious guilt in the *present* that is the basic problem—not what may appear so logical.

The added unconscious guilt may increase so quickly that the unconscious doesn't have a rationalization. If the person's added unconscious guilt is in the self-felt position, he or she might say, for instance, "I feel inferior but I don't know why." If you wait long enough, the person will usually come up with some rationalization. The following example shows further how the feeling comes before the rationalization. I saw a man who was overweight and who focused his added unconscious guilt on being fat. His rationalization was that he felt inferior and unacceptable because he was so fat. He felt guilty whenever he ate anything sweet or fattening. He felt as if something bad was going to happen to him because being fat wasn't healthy. So he decided to do something about it, and he lost the extra weight. Then his added unconscious guilt increased again, and he came in to see me saying, "I feel fat again, but I'm not fat." He's implying that he feels inferior, inadequate, unacceptable, incomplete, guilty, or headed for trouble. But in reality he's not overweight anymore. That "fat feeling" to him was metaphorical for all the primary feelings.

The way in which the added unconscious guilt focuses itself is always interesting. Sometimes you would think that a person should focus his rationalization on a particular thing—for instance, fat in people who are overweight. "Thin is in," yet some people who are grossly overweight do not focus their added unconscious guilt on being fat at all. They say, instead, that they feel inferior, unacceptable, and guilty due to some other aspect of their reality if their added unconscious guilt is increased in the self-felt position. How the added unconscious guilt is focused in reality becomes very individualistic.

The more the added unconscious guilt increases, the more intense the primary feelings become, and the more there is of the feeling that something must be done about whatever is being pinpointed as the origin of the feelings. For instance, a man may use his nose as the reality focus for his added unconscious guilt. He feels inferior, and unacceptable and says that this is because of his misshapen nose; the shape of his nose makes him feel self-conscious and shy. As his added unconscious guilt increases, he becomes more "painfully aware" of his misshapen nose. He doesn't want to be around other people because of his nose. With more added unconscious guilt, he makes an appointment with a plastic surgeon. He may say, "I've put this off long enough, and now I'm going to do something about it." But because of the plastic surgeon's backlog of patients, the appointment isn't for another month. In the meantime his level of added unconscious guilt decreases. Now he no longer feels such an urgent need to fix his nose. But he gives a reality reason for putting it off: "I can't go to the plastic surgeon because I have to take a business trip that week." It's as though reality has caused him to put off having something done about his nose rather than his decreased added unconscious guilt. But if his added unconscious guilt increases again, those reality reasons will no longer seem so important. Regardless of the business trip, he'll find a way to see the plastic surgeon.

As this man's added unconscious guilt increases, his feelings, concerning his nose, become more intense. He goes from, "I *feel* unacceptable; I *feel* ugly" to "I *am* unacceptable; I *am* ugly." The change from "I feel _____" to "I am _____" is significant because "I feel _____" implies that "I could be wrong; I see myself as _____, but there is a possibility that in reality, I'm not." But "I *am* _____" implies that the primary feelings, the added unconscious guilt, has become a perceived fact of reality.

When the added unconscious guilt increases, the primary feelings may tend to spread out. The reality focus of the rationalization may become broader. In the above example, as the man's added unconscious guilt increased, he concentrated more intensely on his misshapen nose as his reality focus. But instead of wanting to have something done about his nose when his added unconscious guilt increases, his reality focus may spread out. He may go from "My nose is misshapen, and it makes me feel unacceptable" to "I feel unacceptable because my nose is misshapen, my hair is thinning, I'm overweight, and my work isn't right," and so forth. Eventually, he could bring in other aspects of his life, such as his home and his financial status, until finally, he says, "Everything about me is unacceptable, inferior, wrong, etc."

The added unconscious guilt can increase until it reaches the delusional level, as we saw in Chapter Seven. The rationalization becomes delusional because it must reflect the increase in the quantity of added unconscious guilt. The more added unconscious guilt that is present, the more reality becomes distorted. Consider again, for instance, the woman who felt unacceptable because her hair wasn't "just right." As her added unconscious guilt in the self-felt position increased, she felt more and more that something was wrong with her hair until finally, she believed that she could smell her hair rotting. Because she used that new shampoo, she believed her hair was decaying, and she could actually smell it at times when her added unconscious guilt was at its highest. As her added unconscious guilt decreased, the smell would be less noticeable.

Someone's added unconscious guilt could reach the delusional level and be reflected through the use of some substitute for the primary feelings in reference to himself. One of my patients came in one day with a blood blister and said, half-jokingly, "Oh my God! I have AIDS." AIDS, in this case represents the primary feelings. With enough added unconscious guilt, this man may have himself tested for the AIDS virus, and even if he's told he doesn't have it, he may still think, "I have AIDS. I shouldn't be around other people," and he may withdraw from others, feeling he's infectious.

Once, during my residency, I was called in the middle of the night to see a new admission. I came in to find a policeman on each arm of a woman who was wearing an old army gas mask that no amount of coaxing could persuade her to remove. At the time I didn't think about the position of her added unconscious guilt, but in retrospect, I can see that if her added unconscious guilt was in the self-felt position, she would have been wearing the mask because she felt that she emitted a terrible, poisonous odor.

Another person whose added unconscious guilt was in the self-felt position and had increased to the delusional level was a college student who came to see me. She was a very attractive young woman who had suffered from bulimia. Bulimia is a common problem among adolescent and college-age girls who try to lose weight by making themselves throw up what they eat. This woman told me, "Looking back, it seems unbelievable. I could stand in front of the mirror, nude, and still see that ugly fat. I couldn't stop doing what I was doing because I kept seeing that ugly, disgusting fat. I know now it wasn't there because I only weighed eighty pounds!" This young woman was not only attractive but intelligent and perfectionistic as well. Getting an "A" was not enough for her; she had to get the highest marks in the class. Summa cum laude was not good enough, she had to be valedictorian. Her high personality core guilt gave her this drive for perfection and also made it easy for her to accumulate enough added unconscious guilt to reach the delusional level.

With enough added unconscious guilt, one can pick something in reality and twist it around to make sense to him, as a rationalization. However, it may not make sense to others. For instance, about ten years ago, a house in a nearby town burned down. A small child was killed in the fire, which was suspected to be the result of arson. Several days later a man, apparently sent by his wife, came to see me. He said, "You know,

I have a feeling that I'm the person who lit that fire." This seemed rather strange as he had a good job in a well-known company and was generally well-respected. His feelings were coming from his increased self-felt added unconscious guilt. He worked very hard and long and had few friends and few pleasures. He had a feeling that he was the one who lit the fire. When he told his wife, she said, "You're crazy! My God, go see a psychiatrist!" When he came in, he told me that she had tried to reassure him, "I sleep with you every night. How could you have lit the fire that night?" He said to me, "Well, sometimes I get up and go to the bathroom and get back into bed without her ever knowing that I've gone. I could have sneaked out of the house, gone down there and lit that fire, and then gone back to bed; she never would have known it." This man's added unconscious guilt has greatly increased. He feels intensely inferior, inadequate, unacceptable, wrong, guilty, a failure, and headed for trouble. He explains these feelings to himself and others using the fatal fire that he's heard about on the news. His rationalization, though, makes sense only to him; his wife thinks he's crazy. With a little more added unconscious guilt instead of saying, "I have a feeling that I'm the person who lit that fire," he may say, "I *am* the arsonist. I started that fire, and I murdered that child."

However, the man's feeling that he started a fire is similar to the "three-day schizophrenia" of combat. If his added unconscious guilt is lowered, he won't feel as though he lit the fire. The same is true of the woman whose hair wasn't "just right," the man with the misshapen nose, the girl with bulimia, or the man who had that "fat feeling." When their added unconscious guilt is high, their rationalization may approach or reach the delusional level and reality is strained to give "reasons" for the feelings of ugliness, repulsiveness, inferiority, guilt, etc. And if other people can't see it, those with the delusion invariably say, "You don't understand." If the woman's husband and co-workers say, "But I *like* your hair that way. With most of the newer styles, you don't want every hair in place," she'll say, "You don't understand. My hair must be neatly arranged. I just don't feel right with my hair this way." Or tell the eighty-pound college girl, "You're getting too thin. You should really stop losing weight. You're starting to look as if you just escaped from Auschwitz." She'll reply, "You don't understand. There's fat on my body, and I'm ugly." If their rationalizations don't make sense to other people, they believe the other people "just don't understand." Yet, if the added unconscious guilt is lowered, they can see reality more clearly. The first woman will see that her hair doesn't look bad, and the second will see that she has lost too much weight.

If the added unconscious guilt remains high, the person may make the emotional unreality *become* reality. For instance, a man in the self-felt position feels, "There's something wrong with my work," so he takes more time doing his work because he wants to make sure it's done perfectly. Consequently, he doesn't get all his work finished during the day and takes a lot of papers home at night. This same thing happens every day for several weeks; soon he has so much work piled up that he can't finish it all, and he stops going in to the office. Now there actually *is* something wrong with his work; he has made reality fit his emotional unreality.

Added unconscious guilt in the self-felt position can be lowered in several similar ways. One of these ways is through very hard work. The person feels as though she should work harder. If she works hard enough, she can assuage the unconscious guilt. The sweat and the push that we saw with high personality core guilt, intensified by the added unconscious guilt, can lower the added unconscious guilt. Depriving oneself of anything pleasurable can lower the added unconscious guilt. With a lower amount of self-felt added unconscious guilt, the person may allow herself only a little pleasure, but when the added unconscious guilt increases, she foregoes even that and works even harder. Where before she might have spent one evening a week doing something pleasurable or relaxing, now she doesn't allow herself any pleasure at all. It can also be lowered through forms of self-sacrifice. Because the person feels so inferior, and so inadequate, he feels the need to "pay a price." It's as though the unconscious says, "If I suffer, I will atone for my feelings of inferiority, guilt, and worthlessness." The person can suffer in different ways: through financial deprivation—by giving more to charity or to the church; or through various forms of other self-sacrifice. When one reaches the delusional level, one can suffer by physically sacrificing part of the self, that is, cutting off something. It is not uncommon for schizophrenics to cut off their penises, symbols of sexual pleasure. There have also been cases where females have cut off their breasts. The Dutch artist Van Gogh cut off his ear.

This type of self-sacrifice also involves enduring pain, which helps to lower the added unconscious guilt. In certain religious practices, we can see the same concept in operation though usually not to the same degree. In the caves of ancient man handprints can be found on the walls, placed there, scholars believe, during ceremonies which had a religious significance. These prints show that one finger has been cut off. The man sacrificed and went through this pain to atone for the primary feelings. In Christianity, giving up something pleasurable for Lent is an example of the same principle of atonement for the primary feelings of inferiority, inadequacy, and guilt. Many American Indian religions required the enduring of some kind of pain in order to purify oneself. As an example, one Indian tribe required a young man to hang himself with pins, by a piece of his own skin, for purification. Some Christians must literally wear sackcloth and ashes to become purified, while other religions may call for the person to walk over hot coals. The endured pain lowers the self-felt added unconscious guilt to such a level that the person feels "purified."

Self-sacrifice that induces pain, like castration, or even plastic surgery, often requires hospitalization. For instance, while the man who was going to "give up" part of his nose is hospitalized, he may endure painful examinations or laboratory testing and this can lower his added unconscious guilt. When the man has his plastic surgery and gets some of his needs met in the hospital, he feels more comfortable when he is discharged. He's more comfortable because his added unconscious guilt has been lowered, but he attributes it to having finally done something about his nose. If the person does something about the rationalization that involves self-sacrifice or hard work, then it is the self-sacrifice and hard work that lowers the added unconscious guilt. It is these factors which make the person more comfortable, not changing the fact that he gave as a rationalization for the uncomfortableness.

During the Middle Ages in Europe, the mentally ill were often "treated" by being beaten. A mentally ill person was thought to be "possessed by the devil," so the administered punishment was to "beat the devil out of him." One might speculate that one reason this treatment lasted for hundreds of years was that it improved some patients' conditions. If so, it would be because the beatings decreased added unconscious guilt in the self-felt position and the person became less delusional or not delusional at all.

Alcohol and certain drugs can also temporarily lower the self-felt added unconscious guilt. We have mentioned that alcohol and drugs seem to lower the unmet oral dependency need, and whenever the unmet need is lowered, the added unconscious guilt is lowered by the same amount. An example is the man who feels inferior, inadequate, and unacceptable. He goes to a dinner-dance with his wife, but she can't get him to leave the table and dance. He's not going to get out in the middle of the dance floor because he feels so inferior and inadequate. After he's had enough alcohol, he may not only dance in the middle of the floor, but he may climb on top of the table and dance. The alcohol decreases the feelings of inferiority, inadequacy, and unacceptability, as do certain drugs. Some people feel so unacceptable, so worthless, and so guilty, that they don't want to go out among people. However, after they take certain drugs, either street drugs or drugs given them by a physician, these feelings decrease, and they're ready to be around people again. Many people seem to need alcohol or drugs to do this.

The second form of added unconscious guilt is the *misperceived position*. In this position, the primary feelings are made referable to how someone else feels, or to how others feel, about the individual. The person in the misperceived position feels that, "He feels I'm inferior, inadequate, unacceptable, wrong, guilty, and headed for trouble." A rationalization is given, such as, "She feels I'm inferior because _____," or "He thinks I'm unacceptable because _____," Paraphrasing or using the vernacular, the primary feelings in the misperceived position would be expressed as, "He thinks I'm a loser," "She thinks I'm a jerk," or "She feels I'm ugly and repulsive"; and rationalizations like, "She thinks I'm no good because _____" would follow. The feelings of the misperceived position can be presented in a variety of ways, but they are always presented as coming from someone else. It may be stated in any of the following ways, and many more, as long as the primary feelings are attributed to someone else or others:

"You think I'm a loser."
"They're insinuating that I'm worthless."
"She says I'm inferior."
"According to them, I don't matter."
"He acts as though I'm repulsive."
"He looked at me like I was crazy."
"They're trying to show me up as an idiot."
"He's accusing me of being a problem."
"She makes me feel that I'm no good."
"He talks to me like I'm irresponsible."

One feeling may be emphasized because it makes the most sense according to the person's reality situation. The woman who had always been oriented toward her hair would use her hair as a rationalization for her feelings because this aspect of her reality would make the most sense as a "reason" for her increased added unconscious guilt. The feeling that she emphasizes is unacceptability because that, too, makes sense in her reality situation. From the misperceived position, her rationalization would be "The other secretaries in the office don't accept me because of my hair." Although her rationalization emphasizes unacceptability, all the other primary feelings are present within the context of the rationalization. She believes that the other secretaries find her unacceptable because of her hair but also implied are the other primary feelings, including, "The other secretaries think I'm headed for trouble because of my hair." These are all rationalizations for primary feelings in the misperceived position.

Any aspect of reality can become a rationalization as long as it logically fits the person's situation. "He thinks I'm inferior because I'm uneducated," "They don't accept me because I don't make lots of money," "The other women at church feel that I'm guilty for not having enough Christian love" are examples of rationalizations using different aspects of reality. The rationalization can be drawn from anywhere within the entirety of the person's reality, and it must equal the amount of added unconscious guilt.

In the misperceived position, the primary feelings and the rationalization may be made referable to how someone else feels about a person, experience, or situation that is associated or identified with the individual. For example, if I am a parent whose added unconscious guilt is in the misperceived position, I may say, "The other kids at school don't accept my son," or "The teachers at my son's school feel that he's an inadequate student." A person who is identified with the person presenting the rationalization becomes the reality focus of the added unconscious guilt.

I may use past experiences to rationalize my feelings that someone else feels I'm inferior, inadequate, unacceptable, wrong, guilty, a failure and headed for trouble. If I am a Vietnam War veteran, I may say, "Some people don't accept me because I fought in the Vietnam War. It was an unpopular war, and people think I'm inferior because I didn't protest it, the way a lot of other people did. If I had served in World War II, things would be different; people would look up to me. But since I served in Vietnam, people feel that I'm guilty and wrong." The experience of service in Vietnam is used here as a rationalization for the increased misperceived added unconscious guilt in the present.

Likewise, suppose that a woman had an abortion five years ago. Her added unconscious guilt in the misperceived position increases so that she uses the past experience as a rationalization for her primary feelings arising in the present. She then says, "He feels I'm guilty because I had an abortion. He can't leave that in the past. He won't let me forget it in little things he says and does, even though it's been over five years." When her added unconscious guilt increases, she feels more intensely that he thinks she's guilty. If she hadn't had the abortion, she'd still believe that he considers her inferior, inadequate, unacceptable, or guilty, but she'd use some other reality-oriented rationalization to explain why.

Sometimes the added unconscious guilt is unrationalized. The person would then say, if her added unconscious guilt is in the misperceived position, "I don't know why he feels I'm inferior," or "I don't know why she doesn't accept me." Usually, if you wait long enough, she will come up with something, using some aspect of her reality. She could use physical appearance: "They don't accept me because of my nose." She could use social and financial status: "They see that I'm inadequate because I'm not in their class. They don't accept me because I don't have a high-paying job."

As the added unconscious guilt increases, the feeling may become more intense. Someone may go from "I feel that he believes I'm worthless and guilty" to "I *know* that he feels I'm worthless and guilty." Or the feeling may spread out, going from "He feels my work is unclean and inadequate" to "*Everyone* sees my work is unclean and inadequate." Instead of "My daughter doesn't care about me," the feeling could spread out with an increase in misperceived added unconscious guilt to become "*No one* cares about me."

The added unconscious guilt can increase until it reaches the delusional level. In the misperceived position, the rationalization, the reality "reason" why "they feel I'm inferior" must equal the amount of added unconscious guilt. Consider the woman who thought that the other secretaries found her hair unacceptable. With an increase in added unconscious guilt, she may believe that other people can smell the rotting odor from her hair. She may even tell her husband, "The people at the office can smell my hair rotting," and ask, "Can't you smell it?" His answer will make no difference because she believes that other people can smell her hair, and she will continue to believe so until her added unconscious guilt decreases. Using AIDS as a symbol for the primary feelings, if the man with the blood blister were in the misperceived position, he would have said, "Oh my God! You probably think I have AIDS!" and with more added unconscious guilt, he'd withdraw, saying, "Other people think I have AIDS. They think I should keep to myself because they feel I'm infectious." If the woman with the gas mask had been in the misperceived position, she would have been wearing the mask because she felt that others could smell a terrible, poisonous odor emitting from her. The bulimic girl would have felt, even though she weighed only eighty pounds, that others could see fat on her body and that they thought her ugly, unacceptable, and guilty, because of this fat.

Anything in reality can be twisted around to rationalize the added unconscious guilt. In the misperceived position, the man who lived near the house that burned would have said, "My wife thinks that I'm guilty because she thinks I lit that fire." People with enough added unconscious guilt can always find a way to rationalize it because they have all of reality from which to choose a rationalization: aspects of themselves; aspects of the people, experiences, or current or past situations; events that they hear or read about. The man mentioned above heard about the fire, and because his increased added unconscious guilt was in the misperceived position, he rationalized it by saying, "My wife thinks I lit the fire."

When added unconscious guilt is high, the rationalizations may strain reality, sometimes to the delusional level, in order for the individual to find reasons why someone else thinks he is so inferior, inadequate, unacceptable, wrong, or guilty. If the rationalization doesn't make sense to someone else, it's because "He [that someone else] doesn't understand." We could assure the man that his wife doesn't think he lit the fire, but he'd say, "No, you just don't understand. I can tell by the way she looks at me that she believes I'm guilty, and it's because she thinks I lit that fire." Or we can tell the woman that no one can smell her hair, and she'll say the same thing, "You don't understand."

If the added unconscious guilt stays at this level, the individual may make what he believes to be reality, from his misperceived position, actually *become* a reality. For example, the man in the misperceived position feels, "My boss thinks my work is inferior." This man starts to spend too much time making sure that everything is correct until finally his boss says, "There *is* something wrong with your work," and he is fired because he converts what he sees as true in his emotional unreality into his true reality. Another example would be the woman in an office who feels, "My co-workers don't like me because they think I'm inferior, inadequate, and guilty." She feels that "They don't want me around them" and becomes withdrawn at work. After a time, her co-workers *do* stop asking her to join them for lunch, or to go shopping on the weekends, because she is so withdrawn and they perceive that she doesn't want to associate with them. She has made reality fit what she already believes based on her emotional unreality. She'll use the changed reality, that her co-workers, in fact, are now avoiding her, to confirm what she originally felt. She'll say, "You see, I was right all along—they don't like me and never have," when she's actually caused this reality.

In the misperceived position, as we saw in the self-felt position, added unconscious guilt can be lowered through the use of alcohol or drugs. Since alcohol and drugs lower both the unmet oral dependency need and the added unconscious guilt, they decrease the feeling that someone else thinks one is inferior, inadequate, unacceptable, wrong, or guilty. As an example, consider the man whose wife cannot get him out on the dance floor. His added unconscious guilt is in the misperceived position, so he won't dance because he feels that other people think he's inferior and inadequate, that his dance steps are unacceptable. After a few drinks, however, he no longer senses that others view him this way, and he'll get up and dance. After a few more drinks, he's dancing in the middle of the floor, and it doesn't seem to bother him. Then there are some people who don't want to leave the house because they feel that other people somehow believe they're inferior, inadequate, unacceptable, or unclean. But after they take certain prescribed or illegal drugs, they can go out because they no longer feel that others find them inferior, inadequate, or unacceptable. Going back to the mentally ill of the Middle Ages, we can theorize that beating a patient in the misperceived position would increase, not decrease, the added unconscious guilt. The person delusional in the misperceived position already feels maligned by someone else or others. Beatings would confirm this feeling.

We can see that the more there is of added unconscious guilt in the misperceived position, the more reality is distorted in regard to how we perceive that others regard us. Again, if the added unconscious guilt in this position can be lowered, then we are more likely to see reality as it actually is; we tend to see more clearly how others actually feel about us. With high added unconscious guilt, the unconscious deceives the conscious mind into believing that a distorted perception of reality is a clear one.

The third and final position of added unconscious guilt is the *projected position*. When the added unconscious guilt is in this position, the primary feelings are made referable to someone else or others. The person in the projected position sees someone else or others as inferior, inadequate, unacceptable, wrong, guilty, a failure, and headed for trouble. The rationalizations would be, "He's a failure because _____," "She's inadequate because _____." Again, the primary feelings and their rationalizations can be expressed in other phrases or in the vernacular: "He's garbage and stinks," "She's ugly and repulsive," "They're no good." More specifically, "She's no good at sports," or "He's no good in bed." Although one feeling may seem predominant in the rationalization, such as, "He's inferior" or "She's guilty," all of the primary feelings are present, and all of them can usually be heard if one listens long enough. As in the other two positions, the unconscious uses the feeling that makes the most sense in the rationalization. All of the primary feelings are present before the unconscious creates a rationalization, which, in the projected position, focuses the primary feelings on someone else, or on anything associated or identified with someone else, or on others.

For example, a man in the projected position might say to his high school daughter, "Your hair is unacceptable. It's entirely inadequate. You shouldn't go out with other people with your hair like that." He feels that she's guilty for getting her hair cut in the style that she chose.

He wants her to fix it some other way and frequently tells her, "Go look in the mirror and see how wrong you look." The daughter may or may not change her hair, but it is projected guilt on the part of her father that causes him to tell her she's so unacceptable. His primary feelings are projected to someone else, specifically, his daughter, and his rationalization is oriented toward her hair.

The individual has all of reality from which to choose a rationalization. For example, "He's inferior because he's uneducated," "She's unacceptable because she's poor," "He's guilty and worthless because he doesn't have enough Christian love." The rationalization could be oriented toward a past experience that someone else has had. One could say "He's unacceptable because he fought in the Vietnam War. That war was unpopular at the time, and many people protested against it. He didn't, and he's guilty for fighting in it. If he'd served in World War II, then it would be different. Those men were heroes."

A similar example would be an individual who knows a woman who had an abortion five years ago. He might say, "She's guilty because she had an abortion." This sounds logical. It's presented as though the woman had the abortion, then the individual felt that she was guilty. It's a deception. Actually, the individual is projecting guilt, projecting *all* of the primary feelings to this woman, and the fact that she had an abortion serves as a convenient rationalization. The feeling of guilt is emphasized because it fits best with the rationalization. If the individual's added unconscious guilt increases, his projection may spread out, and his rationalization may become oriented toward all women who have had abortions instead of just one woman. With even more added unconscious guilt, he will feel more strongly that something must be done about whatever his rationalization is oriented toward, in this case, women who have abortions. He may join a "Right to Life" group, and with enough added unconscious guilt to project, he will be marching on the state legislature and picketing clinics or hospitals that perform abortions. With even more projected added unconscious guilt focused this way, he might bomb an abortion clinic. Projected guilt could also be rationalized with the opposite orientation, and the person could join a "Right to Choose" group; with enough projected added unconscious guilt, she would also be marching, just carrying a different sign. Behind these contrasting reality manifestations could be the same amount of projected added unconscious guilt.

When the added unconscious guilt is in the projected position, there is often a need to "correct" whatever the rationalization is oriented toward. As the guilt increases, so does the need to "correct" what's seen as wrong. The guilt may be projected through socially acceptable rationalizations with public support. Fighting against crime and injustice are socially acceptable causes. The people who fight against what they consider wrong, immoral, or unjust are people with a lot of added unconscious guilt in the projected position. Those who fight the most intensely and seem to feel the most strongly about their causes are those with the most guilt to project.

If there is enough added unconscious guilt in the projected position, it may be projected in ways that are violent. Carrie Nation, for example, was a woman with a lot of added unconscious guilt in the projected position. She used the rationalization that alcohol and those who sell it are guilty, unacceptable, and wrong. In the 1880s, Carrie would go into Kansas saloons and smash them up with a hatchet; she became a celebrity for this behavior and Kansas marked its state highways for years with hatchet-shaped signs. The world champion fighter, John L. Sullivan, had a bar in New York City, and someone once asked him what he'd do if Carrie Nation came to his bar. He said that he'd pick her up and throw her out. However, when some of Sullivan's friends paid Carrie's way to New York, and she walked into John L. Sullivan's bar with her hatchet, he hid in a closet upstairs while she smashed up his bar.

War and terrorism are violent projections of added unconscious guilt. Fighting for a country's independence is a projection of added unconscious guilt with the rationalization oriented toward the tyranny of the current ruler. Projection of added unconscious guilt motivates terrorists; they rationalize their reasons for blowing up buildings or having someone assassinated. In war and terrorism, there is so much of the feeling that something must be "corrected" that people are willing to kill and to risk their own lives to "correct" it.

Many wars and some terrorist acts are based on prejudice. Prejudice is a rationalization for projected added unconscious guilt. The rationalization may be oriented toward the color of someone's skin, someone's ethnic background, or someone's religion. The guilt may be projected in ways that are less violent, but the basis is the same as for wars, terrorism, race riots, and discrimination. It's projected guilt with a rationalization oriented toward skin color, ethnicity, sex, age, religion, or any number of factors. The direction of the prejudice can be learned, but no one can be taught to hate. For instance, if a boy grows up in a home with relatives who are prejudiced against people of a certain religious orientation, this boy may grow up to have the same prejudice, but only if he has enough projected added unconscious guilt will he hate. If he has enough self-felt added unconscious guilt, he will not hate the people of a particular religion but will hate himself. Theoretically, one could be raised in an atmosphere to love everyone where there is no programming for prejudice. But one can always find something to hate when his or her added unconscious guilt builds up in the projected position.

If the added unconscious guilt increases quickly, there may be no rationalization for it, but the primary feelings will still be expressed in the projected position. Someone may say, "I feel he's inferior, but I don't know why," or "I just don't know why I don't like him." Given time, the person will usually come up with some rationalization. One woman having marriage problems recently told me, "I'm mad as hell at him but I don't know for what reason! I just know I'm mad at him for something—maybe it's unconscious and it will come to me later." She'll find something about her husband or his past or anything associated or identified with him that logically seems like a good reason to be upset with him, or to think that he is in some way inferior, inadequate, unacceptable, wrong, guilty, unclean, or headed for trouble.

After an individual finds a reality focus for the projected guilt, it may spread out if the guilt continues to increase. Feeling that one woman is unacceptable, using the rationalization that she had an abortion, may carry over to feeling that all women who have abortions are unacceptable, as we have seen. Or perhaps a father doesn't like one of his teenaged son's friends. He views this friend as inferior. The father may start out saying things like, "He doesn't even dress neatly," and go on to, "He needs a haircut, too," as his own added unconscious guilt increases. Eventually, with more added unconscious guilt, the father may say, "He doesn't dress neatly, he needs a haircut, he doesn't even keep himself clean, and, son, look where he lives. His father is worse than he is. I don't want you associating with him. Don't bring him into our home again." The feeling may also become more intense and, as we have seen, feeling that a group is inferior, using the rationalization that they are of the "wrong" religion, etc., can intensify into a riot, terrorism, or a war against that group.

The added unconscious guilt can reach the delusional level, where reality becomes distorted and strained, to rationalize the projection of primary feelings. The father who finds his daughter's hair unacceptable may have enough added unconscious guilt to reach the delusional level and begins to smell her hair rotting. Someone with added unconscious guilt in the projected position that has reached the delusional level might see a man with a blood blister and say, "Oh my God! He has AIDS," meaning that he's unclean, repulsive, unacceptable, or guilty. "I don't want to be around him; he shouldn't be around anyone." The person may tell the man with the blister "Go get tested for AIDS and stay away from other people because you're infectious!" But even if the man does this and the doctors tell him that he doesn't have AIDS, it won't be

enough for the person projecting the guilt because his added unconscious guilt has reached the delusional level. If the woman wearing the
gas mask at the state hospital had been in the projected position, she
would have worn the mask because she believed other people had terrible, poisonous odors.

If someone has a lot of added unconscious guilt, and can't find a
rationalization for it in some aspect of the person to whom he's projecting
or some past experience of that person, he may twist reality to form a
rationalization that makes sense to him. If the man who lived near that
fatal fire had had added unconscious guilt in the projected position, he
would have come in saying, "I have a feeling that my wife is the one
who lit that fire." What happened is that the man's added unconscious
guilt has increased. He projects the guilt to his wife, feeling that she's
inferior, inadequate, unacceptable, wrong, and guilty. When his unconscious can't find anything about his wife that will rationalize his primary
feelings, it uses the news item of the fire to create a rationalization. His
rationalization makes sense only to him, however. His wife may say "But
you sleep with me every night. How could I have lit a fire that night?"
But his reply is "Well, sometimes you get up during the night to get a
glass of water or go to the bathroom, and I don't even wake up. You
could have sneaked out of the house, gone down there and lit that fire,
then come back to bed, and I never even would have known it." If the
man's added unconscious guilt increases even more, instead of saying,
"I have a feeling that my wife is the one who lit that fire," he'll be saying,
"My wife *is* the arsonist. She's guilty of starting that fire."

If other people don't agree with the rationalization for projected guilt,
the individual will say, "You don't understand." If we tell the father that
his daughter's hair is in the latest style and looks very fashionable, he'll
say, "No, you don't understand. That may be the latest style, but for *my*
daughter, that's unacceptable." Or if we try to convince the woman at
the state hospital to take off her gas mask, she'll definitely tell us that
we don't understand why she must wear the gas mask; if she's in the
projected position, she believes she *must* protect herself from the poisonous odor emitted by other people.

If these people could lower their added unconscious guilt, they would
see that, for instance, other people do not emit poisonous odors or that
one's wife of several years did not get up in the middle of the night and
burn down a nearby house. In the projected position, added unconscious
guilt is lowered through the accompanying anger expression. We have
said that repressed anger becomes added unconscious guilt and that the
quantities of the two are equal. When the added unconscious guilt is in
the projected position, the added unconscious guilt is lowered by the

amount of anger expressed. The anger is expressed predominantly in communication, either directly or indirectly, through the transference process. The guilt is projected and the anger is released. In talking negatively about someone, we convey the primary feelings, and as we directly or indirectly express anger, the quantity of added unconscious guilt is thereby lowered. These are the specific dynamics involved in, first of all, accumulating or storing up anger that we referred to earlier when we looked at oral dependency need frustration, and second, expressing anger. It is stored up as added unconscious guilt in either the self-felt or misperceived position. When the added unconscious guilt is projected, anger is released. Most guilt is projected in getting rid of anger in the unconscious communicative process. Added unconscious guilt, which is derived from repressed anger, is projected to unconsciously perceived aspects of the listener, and the anger is released. The level of added unconscious guilt then decreases.

Again, in this position, alcohol and certain drugs may allow someone to express anger who would otherwise not do so because of fear of jeopardizing a relationship. As we have said, alcohol and certain drugs give the effect of lowering an unmet oral dependency need. This decrease in the unmet oral need may result in a decrease in concern about future oral dependency need gratification, so that a man who ordinarily would have said nothing about his daughter's hair may begin to project his added unconscious guilt and get angry about it after a few drinks. We shall see later on that the increased perception of oral dependency need gratification tends to allow the projection of added unconscious guilt.

As you can see, in the projected position the greater the added unconscious guilt, the greater the distortion of reality concerning how we feel about other people. But when the added unconscious guilt is lower, after we have expressed anger, we can see reality in regard to someone else more clearly.

If one had a choice, the projected position is probably the best of the three positions in which to be. Some people seem to remain fairly comfortable, emotionally, in the projected position. Their situations in reality are such that their projection of added unconscious guilt serves them in good stead. One example of a person whose projection of added unconscious guilt led him to reality success is General George Patton. Patton's rapid push through France and Germany astounded both the enemy and the Allies, and put him in the limelight. Someone who was with him told me that he'd take his jeep and drive down the road screaming at his men to go faster. When a German plane would appear over the column, the men would run for the ditches, including the officers.

Patton would stop his jeep, grab the officers bodily and pull them back onto the road. In a dramatic show, he'd cuss them out and tell them to get their men back on the road, moving forward again. His projected added unconscious guilt got his men moving. And that was just what was needed to get the Third Army across France so quickly.

I was presenting a course a few years ago for the continuing education of nurses. One nurse supervisor told me that she had some difficulty understanding this third position of projected added unconscious guilt. She said, "My job is supervisor and as such, I have to kick ass! That's my job! Are you saying that it's really my added unconscious guilt's projected position?" I said, "Yes, it is," and she put up a big fight which confirmed to everyone that she was a person whose added unconscious guilt usually took the third position. As an operating room supervisor, she would get after the doctors and nurses to keep the surgery schedule. She had no difficulty finding fault, placing blame, and getting angry. To her, it was just a job that anybody could do, but it took her added unconscious guilt in the projected position to do it well. It would not be a job for a person whose added unconscious guilt is usually in the self-felt position.

It was said of General MacArthur that he needed enemies the way other people needed friends. Without someone to love and with added unconscious guilt from frustrated oral dependency needs in the projected position, a person can find somebody to hate and can then go through life fairly comfortably. And some people do seem to go through life this way, to the dismay of others around them. In too many neighborhoods, there's at least one neighbor who can't seem to exist without a disagreement or an ongoing fight with another neighbor. If one neighborhood dispute is settled, then he starts another. As long as this person is projecting guilt to someone in the neighborhood, the person can remain fairly comfortable. If he doesn't have a fight going with a neighbor, then he is having marital problems, or he's sick with a malady no doctor can diagnose or cure, or perhaps he's depressed or phobic or having anxiety attacks. The neighborhood fight keeps him more comfortable at home. His added unconscious guilt is kept at a comfortable level.

In fact, these dynamics are also responsible for problems like child abuse. If a mother is not getting her oral dependency needs met in her own situation, she has a lot of oral dependency need frustration. This frustration becomes anger, and if she is too dependent on too few and must repress the anger, it then becomes added unconscious guilt. She may project this added unconscious guilt to her dependent child, through verbal abuse or even physical abuse because he or she is unable to move away from the relationship with the mother, even though it is abusive. Projecting guilt and expressing violent anger to the child lowers the amount of added unconscious guilt for the parents; consequently, the parent will feel better. Hence, the basis of child abuse is projected added unconscious guilt in those who are too dependent on too few and who use the dependency of the child to relieve an uncomfortable level of added unconscious guilt. A related dynamic is spouse abuse, where, with projected guilt, there is verbal and physical abuse of one's spouse. It is also becoming more common to see cases where people in the projected position abuse their elderly parents. In situations where the elderly person has become confused or suffers from physical problems that require him to be dependent on his children, these children, who have projected added unconscious guilt and are too dependent on too few, may verbally abuse the parent and eventually physically abuse him, as well. Referring again to the treatment of the mentally ill during the Middle Ages, those administering the beatings were probably people with high amounts of projected added unconscious guilt. We can speculate that even though the patient might not have felt better, those people doing the beating would have.

As you can see, perception is heavily influenced by the added unconscious guilt. The amount of unconscious guilt we have determines the degree to which our perception of reality is distorted. We distort reality to support the way the added unconscious guilt makes us feel, and our distorted perception of reality becomes inseparably intertwined with our emotional unreality. A fellow psychiatrist once told me that he had a patient in a psychiatric hospital with an extremely distorted perception of reality. This man believed he was dead, a zombie, with no feelings or emotions. His added unconscious guilt had reached the delusional level where he distorted reality to support his emotional unreality. This psychiatrist, who was new in the field at the time, tried to use facts of reality to convince the patient he wasn't dead. The younger doctor couldn't do it, however, because the patient's added unconscious guilt distorted the reality facts that the psychiatrist presented. The psychiatrist got so frustrated that he asked the patient, "Do dead men bleed?" The man thought for a while and said, "No, dead men don't bleed." So the psychiatrist pulled out a scalpel and stuck the man on the hand. When a drop of blood appeared, the man appeared greatly astonished, exclaiming, "By God, dead men *do* bleed!" Our own added unconscious guilt distorts our perception in like manner; if our added unconscious guilt were to become too high, we would become delusional, like this schizophrenic.

The way we distort reality is determined by the position of the added unconscious guilt. A few years ago, the "Son of Sam" murderer eluded police in New York City for a while and became nationally famous. The

police department was inundated with letters that fit into three categories, reflecting the three positions of the added unconscious guilt. The
first category of letters were from people who'd write, saying, "I am Son
of Sam! Arrest me!" The police would go out and talk with the individual,
only to find someone with a lot of added unconscious guilt in the self-
felt position. The next category came from people who'd say, "My neighbors think that I'm Son of Sam. Do something about this. I'm not Son
of Sam, but they all think I am." In their attempts to follow every lead,
the police would go and talk with these people, too, and again they'd
find someone with a lot of added unconscious guilt, this time in the
misperceived position. The third category came from people who'd write
in saying, "My neighbor is Son of Sam. I see him leave at certain times,
etc., so come and arrest him!" Again, the police had to investigate, and
again they'd find an individual with added unconscious guilt, in this
instance in the projected position. All of the letters can be classified
according to the three positions of added unconscious guilt. Whenever
a heinous or reprehensible crime is committed, the police receive these
three kinds of letters. In the self-felt position, the letter writers try to
turn themselves in. In the misperceived position, they feel that someone
else is trying to turn them in. And in the projected position, they're
trying to turn someone else in. These are all people whose added unconscious guilt is so high that they must twist reality to find a rationalization for it. The quantity of these letters indicate the number of people
in the community whose added unconscious guilt has reached the delusional level. One should note that the delusions of added unconscious
guilt differ from delusions of the unmet oral dependency need. The
compensatory delusions of the unmet oral dependency need are usually
delusions of grandeur: "I am someone famous—someone loved and
admired." The delusions of added unconscious guilt involve people who
are monstrously bad or evil, as in, "I am someone infamous—someone
hated or despised." These of course will reflect the position of the added
unconscious guilt, such as, "I am Adolf Hitler," "They think I'm Adolf
Hitler," or, "He is Adolf Hitler."

How we feel depends more on our emotional unreality than on our
true reality. Someone may have great problems in reality but with low
added unconscious guilt, can still be emotionally comfortable. For example, I saw a woman recently on TV who had no arms. She was born
that way, but she could do everything. She could type with a stick in her
mouth, paint with a brush in her mouth, and accomplish all sorts of
other things. She was raising her children, cooking, cleaning, and doing
it all remarkably well. When asked if she felt abnormal, she said, "No,
not at all." According to her reality, she *is* abnormal. If she'd had a lot

of added unconscious guilt in the self-felt position, she would have the feeling, "I am abnormal because I'm so inferior, inadequate, and unacceptable." She didn't however. Yet I see many people with two arms and normal appearance, who *do* feel abnormal, some of them most painfully so. Some feel so abnormal they don't want to be seen by anyone. If they looked in the mirror, they'd act repulsed by what they'd see. It's not reality that directly determines how we feel but our emotional unreality.

Increased added unconscious guilt distorts our perception of reality, not only the reality of the present but that of the past and future, as well. Words like "always," "never," and "constantly" are often used when an emotionally uncomfortable person talks about reality. We may hear, as reflective of each of the three positions, "I've *never* been happy with myself," "He's been *constantly* putting me down through this whole marriage," or, "He's *always* been a failure." In the self-felt position, one can say about the past, "I've always done something wrong"; about the present, "I'm always doing something wrong"; and about the future, "I'll always be doing something wrong." In the misperceived position, one would say about the past, "He feels I've always done something wrong"; about the present, "He feels I'm always doing something wrong"; and about the future, "He feels I'll always be doing something wrong." And in the projected position, "He's always done something wrong," "He's always doing something wrong," and, "He'll always be doing something wrong." The same can be seen with the use of "never" and "constantly" in all three positions.

These perceptions can be set in complex and lengthy rationalizations. These frequently begin with the memories of past rejection, as in, "You called me a stupid old bitch at last year's Christmas party, right in front of my friends, and I've *never* gotten over it!" When this rationalization is elaborated upon, it can serve as a basis for more guilt projection and anger expression. Or, as another example, "I shall *never* forget the way my mother looked at my brother, Robert, when he was leaving for Florida. 'Kiss me good-bye, Robert. I'm going to miss you so much!' I have *never* seen a more sincere expression of love and it *constantly* comes back to me. *Never* in her entire life has she *ever* looked at me with love. It's *always* been a look of disdain, a look of utter disregard for my need for her love." Or, "Throughout the entire marriage, he's been *constantly* putting me down. He's *never* really loved me. And he's *always* misunderstood me!" When the added unconscious guilt decreases, these perceptions of the past change. One may even forget or not care to remember that these things were ever said.

Oral dependency need frustration and the repression of anger, producing an increase in added unconscious guilt in the present, can also cause someone's perception of the future to become distorted. The resulting increased added unconscious guilt can distort perceptions not only of the past and present but of the future as well. I have heard people, regarded as highly successful, who have a bright future, say things like, "I have no reason to live. Everything I see in my future makes me want to die. My whole life has been nothing but disappointments; I can't ever remember succeeding at anything." Because the person doesn't seem to have suffered any hardship, misfortune, or other oral dependency need frustration, he and his family are at a loss to explain the change in perception in regard to the future.

Our perception of reality, in the present, in the past, and in the future is affected by the position and the amount of added unconscious guilt. A simple shift in position can cause drastic changes in perception, as can sudden rises in the level of guilt in any one position. If our guilt is in the self-felt position, it affects our perception of ourselves. If it's in the misperceived position, it affects the way we perceive how others feel about us. And if it's in the projected position, it affects our perception of other people. The more added unconscious guilt we have, the more our perception is distorted. There is increasing difficulty in distinguishing true reality and what the person is forced, by added unconscious guilt, to perceive of reality. The observation, evaluation, decision, action, and feedback cycle is affected by the underlying emotionality. Added unconscious guilt affects opinions, emotions, attitudes, and behavior, but always does so under a guise of intellectuality based on perceived "facts of reality." The person, of course, feels that he or she is observing true reality and simply must "face up to facts" not seen before.

If you wonder what position your own added unconscious guilt might be in, I have a test for you. Go to a high cliff, or to the top of a tall building, with someone else, and stand on the very edge. If you feel that you might lose control and jump, you're in the self-felt position; if you feel as if the other person is going to push you, you're in the misperceived position. And if you have an urge to push the other person, you're in the projected position. Although you probably don't think any of these things will happen in reality, if you had enough added unconscious guilt, your perception of reality could be so distorted that you would believe one of these things as factual; which one you would believe would depend on the position of your added unconscious guilt.

The distortion from high added unconscious guilt in any position creates then a *cognitive impairment*. This defect in the mental process by which knowledge of reality is acquired, evaluated, and acted upon is *not* based at all on any biochemical or anatomic abnormality. It's a defect with an origin all its own. In the next chapter, we'll see more of this nonorganic impairment in mental functioning.

CHAPTER 9
Secondary Feelings of Added Unconscious Guilt

The added unconscious guilt is more difficult to see when the primary feelings produce *secondary feelings*. The secondary feelings are merely extensions of the primary feelings into specific areas of a person's perceived reality. They tend to be more complex than the primary feelings. As such, they're more difficult to recognize, yet if one listens, one can summarize them in simple statements, such as, "I need to improve my work." "I need to improve my work" is a secondary feeling because it's based on the primary feelings, "My work is inferior, inadequate, unacceptable, or wrong." "I need to improve my work" is an extension of added unconscious guilt in the self-felt position. A secondary feeling, like a primary feeling, can be summarized in one sentence, but it too is usually presented in lengthy, elaborately constructed rationalizations. But if you listen closely enough, you can hear the primary feelings behind the secondary feelings.

Some examples of secondary feelings would be:

"I need to correct myself."
"I should be more attractive than I am."
"I need to accomplish more."
"I need to forego any pleasure."
"I need to feel more responsible."
"I shouldn't express myself."
"I should be more appreciative and grateful."
"I'm embarrassing to myself."
"I need to worry more."
"I need to check on my health more."
"I cause nothing but trouble."
"I need to be punished."
"I should apologize for my actions."
"I should isolate myself."
"I need to be other than I am."

These are all examples of secondary feelings when the added unconscious guilt is in the self-felt position. If the added unconscious guilt were in the misperceived position, the secondary feelings would be: "He feels that I need to correct myself," "She feels I need to be more attractive than I am," "They feel I need to accomplish more," etc. In the projected position: "He needs to correct himself," "She should be more attractive than she is," "He needs to accomplish more," and so forth.

The reason behind any secondary feeling is always the primary feelings, for example, "I need to be other than I am" because "I'm so inferior, inadequate, unacceptable, wrong, etc." Or, "He feels I need to be other than I am" because "He feels I'm so inferior, inadequate, unacceptable, or wrong," or, "He needs to be other than he is" because "He's so inferior, inadequate, unacceptable, or wrong."

I had a patient once who came in with the secondary feeling, "I'm going to flunk my exam." His feeling was oriented toward the future, but based on the primary feelings of the self-felt position—"I'm going to flunk" because "I'm inadequate as a learner," "I'm unacceptable for a higher position." He had been working at the post office for some time and was very familiar with all the regulations. But when he had to take a test, he'd freeze up and be unable to answer a single question because he felt so strongly that he was going to fail. In a similar case, one of my patients had a sixteen-year-old daughter who wanted to get her driver's license. She had a learner's permit and had no problem driving while her father was in the car. She had no difficulty with the written test. But once she was in the car at the Motor Vehicle Administration with a police officer in the passenger seat, she could not pass the test. She couldn't even shift the gears because of her secondary feeling that she was going to flunk the test.

Even though there are many phrases and vernacular expressions describing primary feelings, there are only half a dozen primary feelings. But many more secondary feelings branch out from these primary feelings. Since the secondary feelings are focused on some aspect of a person's reality, there are a great many more ways available to express secondary feelings. For example, the secondary feeling, "I'm going to fail" can be oriented toward some specific test. It could be sexually oriented as in the case of a man who thinks, "I'm going to fail sexually." This man might not be able to have sex with his girlfriend because he is so convinced that he's going to fail sexually, which is a manifestation of the self-felt position. In the misperceived position, he would feel that "she believes I'm going to fail sexually," and as a result he might not be able to have sex. The actress on the stage might not be able to perform when her misperceived added unconscious guilt suddenly increases because she is certain that "They (the audience) think I'm going to fail, to forget my lines." The reason she feels that the audience expects she's going to fail is because she feels that they see her as inferior, inadequate, unacceptable, etc. In the projected position, a father may feel that his son is going to fail in high school. With a sexual orientation, the feeling of "He's going to fail" becomes "He's going to fail sexually." The girlfriend may tell the man that sexually he's a failure, and blame any sexual problems in the relationship on him. This feeling of "I'm going to fail," "Someone else feels I'm going to fail," or "Someone else is going to fail" can be oriented toward any aspect of a person's reality, as can all the other secondary feelings.

It's easy to observe the relationship between the different primary feelings. There may be a semantic difference between being inferior and being inadequate, or being unacceptable and being wrong, but it's still easy to see that the feelings are closely related. The secondary feelings however may be very different; we may not recognize the common relationship between them until we look back into the primary feelings. They can even seem contrasting. For instance, it may be difficult to understand any relationship between "I need to work harder" and "I need to be less happy with myself." Or between "I need to apologize for my actions," and "I need to check on my health more." These feelings are so specific that we may not make the connection between them until we go back to the primary feelings behind them and then we can see that they are closely related.

The aforementioned feelings are in the self-felt position, but the relationship between secondary feelings is equally hard to recognize in the other two positions. For instance, a man in the misperceived position may feel that his wife doesn't care for him and, therefore, may suspect that she's having an affair. Such a feeling may seem hard to relate to, "They're watching me at work." But both stem from the primary feelings in the misperceived position. "She's having an affair because she doesn't care for me. She doesn't care for me because she feels I'm inferior, inadequate, unacceptable, and wrong." and, "They're watching me at work because they feel my work is inferior, inadequate, unacceptable, and wrong." Secondary feelings that stem from added unconscious guilt in the projected position may also seem unrelated. A man in the projected position may think his son needs to improve his grades in school. He may also feel that his son should apologize for his actions. These are secondary feelings, both stemming from the primary feelings, "My son's school work is inferior, inadequate, unacceptable, and wrong." and, "My son's actions are inferior, inadequate, unacceptable, and wrong."

There are secondary feelings where the relationship is more obvious, such as, the feelings, "I should withdraw" stemming from the self-felt position: "I'm inferior, inadequate, unacceptable, etc." Some more of these obviously related secondary feelings would be, "I am intruding," "I'm boring," "I see my faults too clearly," and, "I don't fit in." In the misperceived position, the secondary feeling is, "They feel I should withdraw," because of the primary feelings "They feel I'm inferior, inadequate, and unacceptable." Some related secondary feelings are: "They feel I'm intruding," "They think I'm boring," "They see my faults too clearly," and "They feel I don't fit in." In the projected position, "He should withdraw" because "He's inferior, inadequate, and unacceptable." Related secondary feelings would be, "He's intruding," "He's boring," "I see his faults too clearly," and, "He doesn't fit in."

Sometimes the secondary feelings of a position of added unconscious guilt are actually in opposition to one another. In the self-felt position, for instance, a man may feel, "I should work harder," stemming from, "I'm inferior, inadequate, and unacceptable." His work situation may require him to be around many people. He may also have the feeling, however, that because, "I'm inferior, inadequate, and unacceptable, I should withdraw." In his case, "I need to work harder at the office," and, "I should withdraw and stay at home" are conflicting feelings, yet they come from the same base: the primary feelings in the self-felt position. In the misperceived position, the secondary feelings would be, "They feel I need to work harder at the office" and, "They think I should withdraw and stay at home." In the projected position these same feelings would be, "He needs to work harder at the office" and, "He ought to withdraw and stay at home.

As another example of contrasting secondary feelings, suppose a woman with added unconscious guilt in the self-felt position has the secondary feeling, "I don't like myself (because I'm so inferior, inadequate, and headed for trouble.)" Yet at times, she also has the secondary feeling, "I need to check on my health more (because my body is so inferior, inadequate, and headed for trouble.)" With more added unconscious guilt these feelings increase. "I don't like myself" becomes "I hate myself," and "I need to check on my health more" becomes "I *have* to see my doctor." With even more added unconscious guilt "I hate myself" becomes "I don't even want to live," and "I *have* to see my doctor" becomes "I have to go from doctor to doctor until I find one who can treat me." It seems as if this woman hates herself so much that she *wants* to die, yet she's also running from one doctor to another because she *doesn't* want to die. These secondary feelings are in direct opposition to one another, but they have a common origin in the primary feelings of self-felt added unconscious guilt. We could create a similar scenario using someone in the misperceived position as in, "He doesn't like me—he doesn't even want me to live," but, "He thinks I need to check on my health more—he doesn't want me to die"; or using someone in the projected position such as, "I don't like her—I don't even want her to live," but, "She needs to check on her health more—I don't want her to die." The secondary feelings may seem contrasting but they all originate in the primary feelings.

The reality focus of the secondary feelings sets the manifest content for the person's communication of his emotional uncomfortableness and creates the deception as to the origin of that uncomfortableness. For instance, if my secondary feeling that "I need to accomplish more" is focused on my job, I will unconsciously try to resolve my emotional uncomfortableness through talking about my work situation. My work situation is seen as the origin of my problem. When the added unconscious guilt increases, we know that the primary feelings increase. The secondary feelings also intensify. For example, suppose the secondary feeling is, "I need to improve myself," which a man has focused on the reality of his physique. Since this man's feeling concerns his physique, he begins body-building with weights. The secondary feeling could be concentrate on any aspect of reality, however. Another man could say "I need to improve myself financially, so I'm going to go the library and read more about the stock market so that I'll make better investments." Or a woman could say "I need to improve myself as a Christian, get more involved in church, and pray more." As their added unconscious guilt increases, these people feel more of a need to improve themselves in the specific directions in which their feelings are focused. As the first man's guilt increases, he goes to the gym three times a week instead of one, and as it increases more, he goes every day. The second goes to the library more often as his added unconscious guilt increases. Instead of spending only an hour a week in church, the woman spends every afternoon in church work and prays more often when her added unconscious guilt increases.

Secondary feelings could be oriented to sexual attractiveness. A woman, for example, could believe she should improve herself by becoming more attractive. She may try to lose weight by dieting. As her added unconscious guilt increases, she begins to skip a meal now and then. And as her added unconscious guilt increases more, she may stop eating for days at a time, or she may start causing herself to throw up what she eats. A man might focus his "need" to become more sexually attractive on his receding hairline. As his added unconscious guilt increases, he thinks more about his hair. As guilt increases more, he make an appointment with a doctor to see what, if anything, can be done about his problem. With even more added unconscious guilt, he gets a hairpiece, all to make himself more sexually attractive.

The secondary feeling, from the misperceived position, "He feels I need to improve myself" intensifies as added unconscious guilt increases. If a man feels that someone else thinks that he should improve his physique, he may decide to lift weights and as the feeling grows stronger, he may lift more often. The same is true of the woman who feels, "The people at church believe that I need to be a better Christian. They want me to spend more time at church and pray more." An increase in her added unconscious guilt may then cause her to do this. Or the woman may go on a diet because she feels that her boyfriend thinks she should be more sexually attractive. With enough added unconscious guilt, the feeling may intensify to "He believes I shouldn't eat," and she may begin to fast. The person who feels that "My boss thinks I should work harder and longer" may be very successful in her job because she does work harder when the added unconscious guilt increases.

In the projected position, the feeling that "You should improve your physique" intensifies with increasing added unconscious guilt, and the man whose wife's added unconscious guilt is in the projected position causes him to go to the gym more often as her added unconscious guilt increases. The young woman may go on a diet because her boyfriend feels that "She should be more sexually attractive." A boss in the projected position could feel that "He needs to work harder and longer," and as the boss's added unconscious guilt increases, he expects the employee to work later each night. The boss could be outstandingly successful because he pushes his employees to work harder when his own added unconscious guilt has increased.

The secondary feelings can, though, become delusional with enough added unconscious guilt. For example, someone whose self-felt added unconscious guilt has reached the delusional level may manifest this guilt in the secondary feeling, "I should tear off my clothes, smear myself with ashes, and run naked down the street because I'm such a terrible person." In the misperceived position, this becomes "They tell me to tear off my clothes and smear myself with ashes and run naked down the street." If you were to ask this delusional person who "they" are, she might say someone specific, or she could say, "It's voices I hear," or maybe, "God tells me to do this because God knows I'm so bad." In the projected position, it becomes "He should tear off his clothes, smear himself with ashes, and run naked down the street." One could compensate for added unconscious guilt at the delusional level by saying, for instance, "I'm the best postal worker there is. I'm so good I don't even have to go in to work; I'm working all the time. I get work done in my dreams, in my sleep." This person is delusional, and feels he's compensating for the primary feelings by working hard.

Another secondary feeling in the self-felt position is, "I need to sacrifice something," or, "I need to mutilate myself." As we have seen, sacrificing by giving money to charity, for instance, can lower the self-felt added unconscious guilt. But when added unconscious guilt increases to the delusional level, the person who is feeling, "I need to sacrifice something," or, "I need to mutilate myself," may cut off an ear, for example. Or, in the misperceived position, they may cut off the ear because "She feels I need to sacrifice something," or, "She feels I need to mutilate myself." The Dutch artist Van Gogh, who cut off his ear, could have been feeling either of these things, based on his primary feelings in either the self-felt or misperceived position. In the projected position, the secondary feeling is, "He needs to sacrifice something" or, "He needs to be mutilated." If added unconscious guilt reaches the delusional level, the person with this projected secondary feeling may mutilate someone else.

With more added unconscious guilt, the secondary feeling could be, "I need to kill myself" because "I'm so inferior, inadequate, unacceptable, and guilty." It could become, for instance, "I need to take some cyanide with my headache capsules," from the self-felt position. The misperceived position would be, "They feel I should kill myself. They feel I need to take some cyanide with my headache capsules." The projected position is, "They need to be killed. They need some cyanide in their headache capsules." Such a secondary feeling at the delusional level may be the basis for a deranged person putting cyanide in drugstore headache capsules. It's that "They need to die" or "They need to suffer."

I have had patients whose feelings of, "I need to be punished," or, "I need to mutilate myself" have intensified enough that they have burned themselves with lit cigarettes. One woman who came to see me had burned and scarred her breast with a lit cigarette, manifesting that feeling of, "I need to mutilate myself; I need to be punished." Burning or scarring, mutilating and punishing oneself is a way of lowering self-felt added unconscious guilt. We can speculate that this woman's added unconscious guilt was lowered because she suffered pain. The misperceived position is, "They feel I need to suffer." The projected position is, "He needs to suffer." I know of cases in which the mother with this secondary feeling in the projected positon has burned her baby with a cigarette.

Another woman who came to see me had the secondary feeling, in the self-felt position, "I feel as if I have syphilis." She was a morally strict woman who attended church regularly, and hardly ever dated. Yet she believed she had syphilis, based on her self-felt primary feelings of, "I'm inferior, inadequate, unacceptable, wrong, guilty, and unclean." Her secondary feeling, which arose from the increased primary feelings, was, "I'm contaminated with syphilis." She'd been to a doctor who'd asked her how she thought she had gotten such a disease. She said that maybe she'd gotten it from a public restroom. Her self-felt secondary feeling had reached the delusional level, and no one could talk her out of her feelings, even though her laboratory tests were negative. If her feeling that she had syphilis later disappeared, it might appear that someone had talked her out of it. But it would only disappear if the added unconscious guilt decreased.

If one can decrease his added unconscious guilt, the intensity of his secondary feeling will decrease proportionally. This is true in each of the three positions. For example, a college professor, outstandingly successful in his department, came to see me a few years ago when he felt so pressured he couldn't function. He had a list that he kept of things that he "must" do. He told me that during the few months before he came in, the list gradually got longer and longer; he couldn't sleep at night because the list was so long, so urgent, and so constantly on his mind. He felt his problem was that he couldn't accomplish all the things he thought he should. The real problem was the gradually increasing added unconscious guilt. As his added unconscious guilt decreased, his list got shorter. He crossed off things that with higher added unconscious guilt he'd felt, *had* to be done. They didn't seem so pressing now. In the misperceived position, his list would have been of things that, for instance, he felt the department chairperson wanted him to do. In the projected position, a similar example would be the mother who makes a list of things that her teenaged son "must" do. In both of these cases, as the added unconscious guilt of the mother and the professor decreases, the lists get shorter and less urgent. As added unconscious guilt decreases, there is less avoidance of pleasure, less withdrawing from others, less of a feeling of being a burden or a bother to people, and less of a "need" to worry (or less of the feeling that others should avoid pleasure, or that others are a burden or a bother). Also, as the added unconscious guilt decreases, there is a proportionate increase in oral dependency need gratification, giving more of the feeling that "everything will be all right," which comes from oral dependency need gratification.

Sometimes added unconscious guilt increases, and although the secondary feeling may have a focus in reality, it isn't completely rationalized. An example of this is the master sergeant whom I saw in an army base mental health clinic. He had a lot of high personality core guilt traits, and he kept his men in top condition. But when he came in, he told me that for some reason he was afraid of inspections now. Before, he had always looked forward to inspections; he always had the top award. Now he worried about them, but he said, "I don't know why. I have the same commanding officer, and everything is the same in my work, but I just feel certain that I'm not going to pass the inspection." His secondary feelings of worry and expecting failure in the self-felt position were focused specifically on inspections, but he hadn't fully rationalized the feelings. Another patient was a construction worker from a nearby town. His job was to put girders up, which involved walking across them at great heights. He came in when for some reason he couldn't go up a building; he didn't trust himself to walk across the girders. He had been doing it for years, but rather suddenly he couldn't do it any more. His self-felt secondary feeling of, "I can't trust myself" or, "I might fail" was focused on the buildings, but he had no complete rationalization. If he'd been in the misperceived position, he might have felt rather suddenly, "My co-workers don't want me going up on the girders. They don't trust me." If his boss were in the projected position, the boss might have rather suddenly felt, "I don't want him going up on the girders. I don't trust him." All these feelings stemming from a sudden increase in added unconscious guilt are specifically focused, but not completely rationalized.

A woman whose added unconscious guilt was in the self-felt position recently came to see me. She was a very nice woman with a wealthy, well-respected husband; they had a six week old baby. But she came in because she had been excessively worried that she might hurt the baby accidentally. Then, as her added unconscious guilt increased, she developed a fear that she might lose control of herself and throw it down. When I first saw her she couldn't even hold the baby. She couldn't ride in the car with the baby because she "knew how easy it would be to lose control of myself and reach over and throw the baby out of the car window." She had self-felt secondary feelings of, "I'm not capable of taking care of a baby." "I don't trust myself," "I'm afraid I'll do something terrible," and, "I might lose control of myself." But she didn't know why she felt this way. Many new mothers have these same feelings but to a much lesser degree and they originate in self-felt added unconscious guilt.

Unrationalized secondary feelings have no specific reality focus. I've heard people say, "I feel down, but I don't know why," or, "I've been crying a lot, but I don't know why." Unrationalized secondary feelings go back to poorly rationalized primary feelings, such as, "I feel guilty, but I don't know why." An example of this lack of a specific focus is someone who says, "I've been having such a good time lately; I just *know* something terrible is going to happen." The person may not know why she has developed a sense of foreboding. She may attempt to use past memories to rationalize it, as, "I well remember how I went out and had so much fun two years ago, and the very next day my mother died." But what she is really feeling are secondary feelings like, "I don't deserve such pleasure." Beneath these secondary feelings are the primary feelings that have increased in intensity from her increased added unconscious guilt. The "I feel *so* inferior, *so* inadequate, *so* unacceptable, etc." leads to the secondary feelings like, "I should expect trouble or a deep hurt." As an unconscious secondary feeling, she believes that she's going to be punished for enjoying herself or that she'll pay a price for her pleasure.

These feelings that "I don't deserve any pleasure," "They feel that I don't deserve any pleasure," or, "They don't deserve any pleasure" are related to some other secondary feelings concerning anger, complaining, and criticism. In the self-felt position, for instance, one might have the feeling, "I shouldn't complain," because "I'm so inferior, so inadequate, and so wrong," which relates to "I'm undeserving," or, "I don't deserve any better, so I shouldn't complain." The more added unconscious guilt I have in the self-felt position, the more I feel that I shouldn't complain. The more misperceived added unconscious guilt I have, the more I'd feel that someone else feels that I shouldn't complain. The more projected added unconscious guilt I have the more I feel, "He shouldn't complain." "I shouldn't be angry," "She feels I shouldn't be angry," and, "He shouldn't be angry" come also from the underlying primary feeling of each of the positions of added unconscious guilt. Another accompanying secondary feeling might be, "I should put up with inconveniences and hardships," "They feel I should put up with inconveniences and hardships," "They should put up with inconveniences and hardships." Again, these secondary feelings are based on the primary feelings of the added unconscious guilt in each of the three positions.

Added unconscious guilt, we know, is lowered through the expression of anger, but these secondary feelings can put a damper on anger expression in communication. These secondary feelings can play a major role in the further build up of added unconscious guilt. In the self-felt and misperceived positions, they tend to inhibit the person's own anger expression, and in the projected position, they tend to inhibit someone else's anger expression. Increased self-felt added unconscious guilt causes a person to be more willing to put up with hardships and inconveniences, and to believe more that she should be grateful for what she has because she doesn't deserve any better, so she is less able to express any anger. Increased misperceived added unconscious guilt causes the person to believe that someone else thinks she should be willing to put up with hardships and inconveniences and that this someone else thinks she should be grateful for what she has because she doesn't deserve any better. She assumes this someone else feels she shouldn't express any anger. Increased projected added unconscious guilt makes a person feel that another person should put up with his hardships and inconveniences, and that he should be more grateful for what he has. This person believes that the other doesn't deserve any better and therefore shouldn't express any anger. These secondary feelings may put a damper on spontaneous talking. In the self-felt position, people have the secondary feeling, "I shouldn't say anything bad or anything derogatory about anyone or anything." With feelings like these, anger cannot be expressed directly, or even indirectly through transference. This thwarts the communication process which provides the easiest way to lower added unconscious guilt. Unless a person with these secondary feelings can lower the added unconscious guilt in the other ways that we've mentioned, it will build up and may do so rapidly. If someone's added unconscious guilt is in the projected position, these feelings may force someone else to find other ways to lower his or her added unconscious guilt, rather than in communication.

The inability to complain and the willingness to put up with hardship and deprivation, coming from the secondary feelings that "I don't deserve any better" and, "I should be grateful for what I have," can also lead to inequality in relationships. You sometimes see a couple in which one of the partners is extremely unattractive. The other partner may unconsciously be feeling, "I don't deserve any better." I have seen women who are outstanding executives, capable and successful, who are married to men who do nothing. The men are not successful; some are alcoholics; all of them stand in great contrast to their wives' success. You would think that a successful woman would marry an equally successful man. But in her unconscious, she has married an equal. In the business world, she has compensated for her added unconscious guilt, but in her personal life, she may be married to an absolute bum. She can offer all kinds of rationalizations, reality reasons why she married him and why she puts up with him. One also may see this with successful husbands who have wives that seem to do nothing. Many cases in other areas demonstrate this apparent inequality. For instance, the well-educated woman who marries the man who never graduated from high school, or vice versa. The unconscious secondary feelings like, "I don't deserve any better" may be involved.

People are abused by their spouses in a variety of ways because of these types of secondary feelings. In many cases a wife puts up with a husband when everyone, including her, knows he is having an affair or being sexually promiscuous outside the marriage. No one understands why she puts up with it. All her friends tell her to "kick him out," but she doesn't. Sometimes a man puts up with a wife who is the same way. He may be hardworking, while his wife is out having a good time with other men. He knows it, and so does everyone else, but he doesn't put her out. I've seen cases where all of the money and possessions in a marriage are in the husband's name. The wife has absolutely nothing, but says nothing. She may be feeling, "I don't deserve any better," where someone else might say, "Look, this marriage is a partnership, so the house is half mine, and we should have a joint bank account." The former just accepts it. It's gross inequality, but no one can make her change it. She'll say, "Oh, he's just that way." He may be "just that way," but anyone else, who felt she deserved better, would insist on greater equality. There are also relationships where two people live together and one of them does all the work. One of them shops, cooks, cleans, sets the table, does the dishes, etc. The other one sits in a chair and reads the newspaper or watches television. Either the male or the female can be the one doing all the work, while the spouse or roommate never helps. I see this type of inequality in both heterosexual and homosexual relationships. The secondary feelings are that "I should do all the work. I should be nice. I should put in this extra time." If you look at this relationship from the outside, objectively, you'd say, "That's an awfully unequal relationship."

One spouse may also verbally abuse the other. I had a patient tell me about her aunt, who'd been married six times and who had a terribly foul mouth. This aunt cusses out her present husband all the time, but he tolerates it. His secondary feelings must involve those like, "I should take the abuse; " "I deserve to be cussed out" because "I am so inferior, inadequate, and unacceptable." He may feel, "I'm fortunate to have a wife like this, and I really don't deserve any better." One spouse may physically abuse the other. We've already seen that someone in the projected position may abuse someone else. If the someone else is a wife with self-felt added unconscious guilt, she may take the abuse because she feels, "I'm lucky to have him," "I deserve to be punished," "I do things that cause him to act that way," or, "He has to put up with a lot living with me." She accepts the abuse and no one can talk her into doing anything to change that situation.

Many wives do not report being physically abused by their husbands. Others are very defensive about their husbands when spouse abuse is suspected, lying to cover the truth. One woman who came into the emergency room with a broken wrist told the doctor that she'd fallen off the doorstep of her trailer. When I asked her what really happened, she confided that her husband had angrily hit her across the wrist with a

tire iron. When I asked, "Why do you put up with that?", she replied,
"I couldn't go anywhere else. Who else would have someone like me?"
Yet she is especially nice, sweet, never says anything bad, and continually
waits on her husband hand and foot. Anyone else would be delighted
to have a wife like her. But she thinks, "I'm such a bad person; no one
would want me. I'm *lucky* to have the husband I do." In these situations
you often can't get the two people apart. What logically seems unequal,
with respect to the physical abuse, is felt as somehow equal, in an illogical
unconscious way, by the abused person. The abused person feels that
abuse is justified: "It's a price I have to pay for *his* putting up with me"
or, "I caused him to loose control of himself—it was really my fault."
Someone with less of the self-felt secondary feelings, "I don't deserve
any better," "I have no right to complain" would not put up so readily
with the abuse or inequality, and would be better able to express anger
through communication.

Another important aspect of communication which is affected by secondary feelings is oral dependency need gratification. The secondary
feelings that we have discussed, expressed in the self-felt position, such
as, "I am a bother," "I'm wasting other people's time," "I only cause
problems" inhibit the person's drawing oral dependency need gratification in communication. They cause a person to prefer not to be around
others who might have helped meet his oral dependency need. The
person is inhibited in talking to others if he feels, "They feel that I'm a
bother. They feel I'm wasting their time." If the person feels that someone else is a bother, or that someone else is wasting his time, then he
inhibits that other person's oral dependency need gratification through
communication. The more that someone isolates himself, or is isolated
because of someone else, the less likely his oral dependency need will
be met, and the more added unconscious guilt stands to accrue. If I am
a parent with a high amount of projected guilt, I might say to my child,
"You're a bother. Stop going over to the neighbor's house all the time,"
which would tend to keep the child from getting oral dependency need
gratification from the neighbors. In the self-felt position, the person
essentially feels, unconsciously, "I don't deserve to have my oral dependency need met." In the misperceived position, the person feels, "They
feel I don't deserve to have my oral dependency need met," and in the
projected position, the person feels, "He doesn't deserve to have his oral
dependency need met." The process of becoming and remaining emotionally comfortable through meeting the oral dependency needs in communication, which looked so easy to do, can thus be thwarted and made
much more difficult by high added unconscious guilt manifested in these
secondary feelings.

The secondary feelings of, "I need to work harder and longer" and "I need to avoid pleasure" could reflect themselves in reality success. "I need to worry more" about some focus in my business, or my military career, or my academic pursuits, etc., can also lead to reality success. These secondary feelings, added to the traits of high personality core guilt, can lead to outstanding success in any of the three positions, when they are focused on certain aspects of reality. They do this especially when high added unconscious guilt intensifies the high personality core guilt's traits. But high added unconscious guilt can also thwart the communication process, thereby inhibiting the lowering of the guilt and the gratification of the oral dependency need. A person could be successful in any field; yet with high personality core guilt and some of these secondary feelings, could avoid the spontaneous communication—that chit-chatting and gossiping—needed to become, and to remain, emotionally comfortable.

It may be difficult to differentiate in some rationalizations between primary and secondary feelings. Since we have defined secondary feelings as reality-specific extensions of the more generalized primary feelings, some rationalizations or explanations of emotional uncomfortableness previously given in earlier chapters as primary feelings might also fit as secondary feelings. "I feel like an outsider" may be viewed for instance as involving a single expression for the primary feelings. When it is elaborated upon by the speaker and made specific to a certain aspect of his reality then "I feel like an outsider" fits more as a secondary feeling. In other rationalizations, it may be quite evident we are hearing secondary feelings. This is particularly so when we can see that these secondary feelings are presenting as a result of, or as compensation for, the more nebulous, deeper-lying and less reality-oriented primary feelings. "I have to be superior" or "more desirable" or "more successful" or "in the best of health," or "I should be more tidy and better organized;" or "I should do anything or go anywhere for him" are clear-cut secondary feelings. These are all secondary feelings of the self-felt position that have corresponding counter-parts in the misperceived and projected positions. All imply a specific aspect of one's reality as the genesis of the feeling rather than that real origin in the emotional unreality.

What happens when secondary feelings having a similar specific orientation in a person's reality are clustered will be shown in the next chapter.

THE THREE POSITIONS OF ADDED UNCONSCIOUS GUILT

Self-felt Position:

I'm not a nice person.

Misperceived Position:

They feel I'm not a nice person.
They're insinuating I'm not a nice person.
They're telling everyone I'm not a nice person.
Etc.

Projected Position.

They're not nice people.

Note:

"Not a nice person" or "not nice people" is a
secondary feeling that can be complexly and
extensively rationalized.

CHAPTER 10
Conditions of the Self-Felt Position

Certain closely related secondary feelings seem to make up recognizable states. We will call these states "conditions." We all have these states, or conditions, at times, and how intensely we experience them depends upon the amount of unconscious guilt we have that is focused with a particular reality orientation into secondary feelings. These feelings make up the conditions, and the reality focus of the secondary feelings sets the orientation of the condition. A condition is not necessarily a pathological entity in medicine. Anyone can experience one or more of them when added unconscious guilt increases.

An example of a condition we've already seen would be the state of being withdrawn. The constellation of related secondary feelings would be such things as "I'm a burden and a bother," "I'm not wanted," "I don't fit in," and "I see my faults too clearly." The condition of being withdrawn, made up of such secondary feelings, which stem from the self-felt primary feelings "I'm inferior, inadequate, unacceptable, or wrong," is a condition of the self-felt position.

Another self-felt condition is anhedonia. Anhedonia, by definition, is an aversion to pleasure. The secondary feelings that make up the condition, or state, of being anhedonic are often oriented toward work. The person who is anhedonic foregoes immediate pleasures and would rather work. Such secondary feelings as, "I need to work harder and longer," "I shouldn't have a good time or enjoy myself," or, "I don't deserve any pleasure," resulting from the primary feelings that "My work is inferior, and inadequate," are characteristic of anhedonia. The more added unconscious guilt that is being focused into these primary and secondary feelings, the more anhedonic the person will be. This is the person whom we call a "workaholic."

When a person is in one of these conditions, she may give a rationalization for being so self-abusive or anhedonic, or why she has to seclude herself, or must work so hard. The rationalization is a deception, because the real reason is the build-up of self-felt added unconscious guilt.

Another condition is the state of being worried. It is characteristic of us all to worry at times. The feelings are concentrated in a certain aspect of a person's life, such as work or social activities. It can focus in one particular area and not in another. But with enough added unconscious guilt, the condition may spread throughout the person's life. As the added unconscious guilt increases, we develop, for instance, a "need" to worry. Life is such that we can always find something about which to worry. No matter how well we are, we can worry about getting sick, or just getting old. If we can't find anything in our personal lives to worry about, we can always resort to worrying about the rising crime rate, the economy, or the weather. That "need" to worry about something comes from the increased added unconscious guilt, focused on the reality of whatever it is that we worry about. The rationalizations that we present are that our perceptions of these aspects of reality are the cause of our worry. For instance, suppose someone is worried about a nuclear holocaust. She presents to herself and others, that it's because she's recently been reading about the stockpiling of nuclear warheads by the Soviet Union and the United States, and about how the two powers have enough nuclear weapons to incinerate the entire planet, and that's the cause of her worry. But that's not the real reason. Her unconscious is deceiving her. She's worried about a nuclear holocaust because her increased added unconscious guilt has pinpointed this aspect of reality. As the added unconscious guilt decreases, she'll be less worried about it, even though she has the same knowledge concerning the weapons. If she had read the articles when her added unconscious guilt was lower, she might have absorbed the information and it may have influenced her opinions or her political views, but she would not have been so worried. She may have said, "There's not really anything I can do about it, so why worry? Just live one day at a time, that's all I can do." A person can *only* "live one day at a time" when her added unconscious guilt has decreased enough so that she doesn't have such a great "need" to worry. It's a deception to believe that one *learns* to do this.

The condition of being worried can also be unrationalized. For example, suppose a woman is married to a salesman who travels around the country. Suddenly, when her added unconscious guilt increases, she might say, "I've gotten so worried about John. I'm so afraid that something's going to happen to him, that his plane is going to crash, and I don't know why. I've never worried about him before; he's been a salesman for the past fifteen years. Now for some reason I'm just so worried." She may be having nightmares about plane crashes; she may call this a premonition. The analysts would say that her worry is unconscious wishful thinking. But she's *not* unconsciously wishing that something would happen to her husband; this couldn't be further from the truth. Her worry is about the source of her oral dependency need gratification. Her worry would only look like unconscious wishful thinking if she later became involved in psychoanalysis, and, in time, began projecting guilt, using her husband as the reality orientation of her projected guilt to the analyst. It's possible that she could later project guilt to her therapist, using the manifest content of her mother or friend or her college professor, after coming into therapy because she was excessively worried about her husband. If she can decrease her added unconscious guilt, either by projecting it, or by any of the other ways that we've talked about for the self-felt position, she won't be as worried.

Another example of what the analysts would call unconscious wishful thinking is the man whose mother is in the hospital for an operation. He's very worried about whether she's going to survive the operation. He's so worried that he can't sleep; he's afraid that she's going to die. The analysts would say that he's unconsciously wishing that his mother would die during the operation. Again, this is not so. His unconscious primary feeling of impending tragedy has been given the reality orientation of his mother who is about to have an operation. He's too dependent on too few and he has a large amount of added unconscious guilt in the self-felt position showing itself as excessive worrying. His mother is identified with him; he's really worried that something terrible will happen to him and to something close to him.

A condition that often accompanies worry is insecurity and lack of confidence. The construction worker who can't go up on the girders is in this state. He used to walk across a girder, even sit with one leg on either side of it to eat his lunch, sixteen stories above the ground; now he is suddenly insecure, lacking confidence, and worried about going out on the girders. The doctor who suddenly can't perform surgery is in the same condition, and his feelings are focused on surgery. "I'm not functioning up to par (as a surgeon)," "I'm not as capable (as a surgeon) as I was," "I don't trust myself (to perform surgery)." All of these secondary feelings make up his condition of insecurity and lack of confidence. Both of these people might give reality-oriented rationalizations for their insecurity, lack of confidence, and worry. The surgeon could say, "I know I'm not functioning up to par because last week in surgery I forgot to ask for the right instrument." He gives this fact of reality as though it is the reason for his insecurity, his worry, and his lack of confidence. But his condition is not coming from his perception of reality; it's coming from within, from his increased added unconscious guilt. We use reality to deceive ourselves that our feelings originate there.

Sometimes, if we can't find any reason in our present for why we should feel so insecure, we can use a person, experience, or situation from the past to rationalize our insecurity and lack of confidence. For instance, I had a salesman come in to see me who was experiencing this condition. He'd become so insecure and lacking in confidence that he couldn't meet people or even talk to them on the phone. He told me, "Actually it goes back to when I was in the first grade. The teacher asked me to stand in front of the class and give a report on what I did over the summer, and I wet my pants. All the kids laughed at me, and I've always remembered it." It doesn't make too much sense. He'd been successfully selling things and meeting people before, but when he tried to think of the cause of his present insecurity, it was the only reality-oriented rationalization he could come up with.

Depression may also be a condition, or a set of feelings, that we all have to a degree at times. It is a state in which we are dissatisfied with ourselves, or an aspect of ourselves, or something associated or identified with ourselves. Other secondary feelings making up depression include "I dislike myself" or "I dislike (some aspect of) myself," and with more added unconscious guilt, "I hate myself." The primary feelings are behind these secondary feelings: "I'm dissatisfied with myself" because "I'm inferior, inadequate, unacceptable, wrong, guilty, a failure, and headed for trouble." If the depression is rationalized, the feelings are made specific to a certain reality orientation. Throughout history, the feelings of depression have been a part of the human experience. In the Old Testament Book of Samuel, for instance, King Saul suffered from depression and eventually died by falling on his sword. Many outstandingly successful people with the traits of high personality core guilt have had the primary and secondary feelings of increased self-felt added unconscious guilt that make up the condition of depression: "I'm dissatisfied with myself," "I need to improve myself," because "I'm inferior, inadequate, unacceptable, wrong, guilty, incomplete, and headed for trouble." Such people included Michelangelo, Benjamin Franklin, Samuel Johnson, Isaac Newton, Charles Darwin, Sigmund Freud, Winston Churchill, and many other well-known people.

Freud wrote a paper called "Mourning and Melancholia," melancholia being the word used in his time to describe feelings of deep depression. He wrote that mourning is not melancholia, that grief and depression are not the same. He proposed that grief occurs when a person has lost another person and must spend a certain length of time in mourning until he or she eventually fills the void that the other has left. When a person is melancholic, he wrote, he or she tends to stay depressed. But we can propose that the feelings making up mourning and melancholia or grief and depression are essentially the same. The difference between the two is that mourning or grief occurs in the person who is not too dependent on too few; he may become uncomfortable and grieve for a period immediately following a loss, but he makes adjustments in his emotional life that allow him to venture out emotionally and meet his oral dependency needs from others. If he loses someone emotionally close, the void is not as big, nor is it as difficult to fill. We can theorize that clinical depression may occur in people who are too dependent on too few; they don't go out as readily and fill the void that is left when they lose parts of people, experiences, and situations that gratified their oral dependency needs, or parts of people, experiences, and situations that were targets for anger expression.

A person can grieve if he loses someone to whom he is emotionally close, but if he doesn't have a high personality core guilt, his total unconscious guilt can be lowered enough so that he becomes comfortable again. He may always have special memories or a special place in his heart for the person that he's lost, but he'll function and be fairly comfortable. The person with the high personality core guilt, who is too dependent on too few, may become melancholic or deeply depressed, and the depression may last longer because she has more unconscious guilt. Added unconscious guilt, added to high personality core guilt, makes the unconscious guilt so high that this person has difficulty lowering it. The loss is a more massive oral dependency need frustration, producing anger, which must then be repressed if the person is too dependent on too few. The repressed anger, in turn, produces added unconscious guilt. The person with high personality core guilt finds it difficult to fill the void and her grief turns into melancholia because it is deeper and lasts for so long.

With depression, one can say, "I'm dissatisfied with myself," and one can specify it in certain ways. The specification is, however, a rationalization. A woman came in to see me because she was depressed and dissatisfied with herself. Her rationalization for her depression was that she had just turned thirty. She gave me many reality-oriented reasons why "It's all downhill after thirty." She said that she was past her peak; she was concerned about getting old: she could see a wrinkle that wasn't there before, and she thought she'd found a gray hair. She actually had to be hospitalized because she was so depressed. She recovered and I ran across her years later in a shopping mall. I remembered her and I knew that she'd had her fortieth birthday. I asked her how things were going, and she said, "Fine; everything's going great. I'm enjoying life." I reminded her that she was forty and her happy reply was "Life begins at forty!" If the rationalization she gave before had been the real reason for her depression, she should have been even more depressed at forty.

But she wasn't. Turning thirty was only a rationalization for depression that had its origin in an increase in self-felt added unconscious guilt. Her rationalization doesn't explain why some people turn thirty or forty, sixty or eighty, without becoming depressed. I know of one man who's ninety-four years old, driving his own car, dating women, and enjoying life. It also doesn't explain why some people who've turned nineteen or twenty are so dissatisfied with themselves that they commit suicide.

A successful stock broker I saw recently had focused his rationalization on his work situation. He came in depressed because he felt, "I should have done more at work." He had just finished three of the best months he'd ever had in selling stock, but he still felt that he could have done better. The feeling was coming from his added unconscious guilt in the self-felt position; he was too dissatisfied with what he had accomplished and was blaming himself for not selling more.

The secondary feeling, "I don't deserve anything good. I deserve to be punished" can be a part of depression and can produce some interesting rationalizations. I know of one man who told me that he gets depressed when he receives a bonus or a nice Christmas gift because, "I know I don't deserve it." Another man who is married to a woman he loves very much and who loves him, leaves for several weeks at a time to join a religious order because he feels that he doesn't deserve such a good wife. These two men believe they don't deserve anything nice because they feel that they are so inferior, inadequate, unacceptable, and guilty. When their added unconscious guilt increases, these feelings become more intense and they may become depressed. Their rationalizations focus on the nice things that they don't feel they deserve.

Because depression is a condition of the self-felt position these people also feel that they shouldn't complain, they shouldn't put the blame for their depression on anyone else, and they should look to themselves for the cause of their depression. They think, "I should blame only myself for my shortcomings." Because they don't want to put the blame on someone else or on some experience or situation, they often do not have a specific reason or rationalization for their depression. They often say, "I have no reason to be depressed," which goes hand in hand with, "I shouldn't complain." If we ask the person about his marriage, he readily tells us, "I have a fine wife. I couldn't ask for a better wife. I'm so thankful that I've got her. I don't see how she puts up with me." Or if we ask, "How is your job going?" "The job is wonderful. I have no complaint there at all," he characteristically will say. "Well, what about your friends?" "My friends are great. I don't see how they've stood by me, being the type of person I am. They're nicer to me than they should be." These responses are typical because these are people who are in the self-felt position. They won't point the finger of blame, criticize, or complain about anyone or anything. So they often end up saying, "I just don't know why I'm depressed. I don't know why I'm so dissatisfied and feeling down. I'm not enjoying life and I have no reason to be this way. I have every reason in the world to be happy. Everything is fine and it's always been that way. Things are no different than before I got depressed. So why am I depressed?"

In comes the psychiatrist, at this point, to tell them that it *must* be biochemical. The psychiatrists call this unrationalized depression an "endogenous depression," which, they say, is biochemically oriented and is due to a defect in the transmission of the nerve impulse, from a chemical imbalance in the neurotransmitters of the brain. This theory of chemical imbalance as the root of depression is now popularly accepted. If a person who is depressed can point the finger at someone else, to say "I'm depressed because of you," or "because of this experience or situation," then she won't be depressed for long because she's getting rid of anger, which lowers her added unconscious guilt. This person is already getting out of the self-felt position and is, instead, projecting guilt. But the person in the self-felt position will point the finger of blame at only himself: "There's something wrong with me"; "I'm just not myself"; "It's no one else's fault."

The biochemical explanation for depression gives the person with the self-felt secondary feeling of, "I don't know why I'm so down on myself" an acceptable rationalization for the depressed feeling. Now he can say, "I don't like myself because of a chemical imbalance in my body." But this self-felt feeling is analogous to the unrationalized projected feeling, "I don't know why I'm so down on him." It's the same entity, the added unconscious guilt, behind both feelings, but in different positions. We wouldn't give a biochemical reason or rationalization for the projected feeling. Some might then question whether we really have "endogenous" depression any more than we have "endogenous" hatred. The person in the self-felt position readily accepts the biochemical explanation because it fits with the self-felt primary and secondary feelings. He still doesn't blame anyone else and can say, "It's something wrong with *me* that's causing my depression; my neurotransmitters aren't functioning right."

Psychiatry differentiates between an "endogenous" and a "reactive" depression. "Reactive" depression is, as the name suggests, depression in response or reaction to some recognizable event in the person's life. We know that it's really rationalized depression caused by increased self-felt added unconscious guilt, not directly by an event in the person's life. Perhaps, too, "endogenous" or "biochemically-caused" depression is similarly a result of increased self-felt added unconscious guilt but without a reality-oriented rationalization. Psychiatrists tend to support the idea of "endogenous" depression because psychiatry has, of late, swung back into medicine. And biochemical abnormalities are a medical problem, out of the realm of concern for nonmedical professionals. Listening and counseling lend themselves to the treatment for "reactive," or rationalized, depression and are often left to the priests, ministers, rabbis, psychologists and social workers. This treatment is more easily facilitated when the person is given an opportunity to project guilt. The treatment is more difficult when the person, too dependent on too few, blames only himself.

Another common condition for those in the self-felt position is that of being phobic. The secondary feelings associated with phobia can be summed up as, "Something terrible is going to happen," focused in some area of reality. It could be, for example, the housewife who has an increase in her added unconscious guilt, which shows itself in a phobia connected with something that she has to do. The higher her added unconscious guilt, the more it will affect her life. This housewife might have to do the grocery shopping for the family, and when her added unconscious guilt increases, she may develop a phobia about the grocery store. She now has great difficulty shopping because she thinks something terrible is going to happen to her if she goes into a store. She begins to avoid the grocery store. If her added unconscious guilt is high enough, with the secondary feeling, "If I go to the grocery store, something terrible is going to happen," then even the mention of going to the grocery store bothers her. Her phobic condition worsens as her added unconscious guilt increases. First, she doesn't want to go into the store. Then she doesn't want to go into town, and as her added unconscious guilt further increases, she may only be able to go a mile or two from her home. She may, as her added unconscious guilt increases still further, get to the point where she doesn't even like to go into her yard and she may be confined by her phobia to her house. You can see that the secondary feeling of, "Something dreadful will happen if I go into the grocery store" has intensified to, "Something dreadful will happen if I leave my house."

Another phobia might be focused on elevators. Often the person who develops such a phobia has an office on the thirtieth floor and has to use the elevator every day. Suddenly, he might not be able to use the elevator if his added unconscious guilt quickly increases. If it had been a slower increase, he might have been able to get on the elevator and sweat nervously, praying until he reached his floor. But as his added unconscious guilt increases, he becomes unable to get on the elevator and he may not even be able to go near the building. As the added unconscious guilt increases, his phobia becomes more intense and it may begin to affect his cognition, his thinking. His "what if"'s begin to increase. He may think: "What if I get on the elevator and it gets stuck between floors?"; "What if I get stuck in the elevator and there's a fire in the building?"; "What if the supporting cable breaks?"

Like all the other conditions, phobias may be specifically rationalized. I was speaking on this topic at a workshop when a woman raised her hand and said that she had developed a phobia concerning airplanes. She said that the reason she had a phobia of airplanes was that several years earlier she had been on a flight to Florida when the plane hit an air pocket. It suddenly dropped six hundred feet; trays flew to the ceiling and people who were not belted in came up out of their seats. She said that it was most terrifying and because of this experience, she developed her phobia. We might speculate that what actually happened was that her added unconscious guilt had increased and then conveniently focused itself on airplane travel. It made sense to develop an airplane phobia and to point to this reality experience as its origin. But, again, it's a deception. The plane held two hundred other people and we could speculate that they did not all develop airplane phobias. Many of them probably still travel by plane. Her logical explanation is also refuted, by the case of Group Captain Sir Douglas Bader, one of the leading British air aces of the Second World War, who lost both legs in a flying accident. He did not develop an airplane phobia. He had artifical legs made for himself and he continued to fly for the duration of the war. The reality-oriented rationalization that this woman presented to explain her phobia is just that, a rationalization.

I recently saw a man with an airplane phobia who said that he developed his phobia after reading a newspaper article about a terrible plane crash. Since he read the article, he'd been unable to go anywhere by plane. Again, we could speculate that everyone who read that particular article did not develop an airplane phobia as a result. The article was a convenient reality focus for his increased added unconscious guilt. I've also seen people who have dog phobias. They may explain their phobia by saying, "When I was small, I was bitten by a dog. Now I can't get near a dog." But thousands of children are bitten by dogs and never develop dog phobias. Some who have never been bitten by dogs *do* develop dog phobias. So being bitten by a dog doesn't cause a dog phobia. It may give the logical direction that the phobia will take when the added unconscious guilt increases to such a level that it can cause the formation of a phobia.

The people whose added unconscious guilt is focused on some phobia seem to want reassurance that all of the "what ifs" that they can come up with won't come to pass. The more added unconscious guilt there is—showing itself in, for example, an airplane phobia—the worse things the person expects to happen if he were to travel by plane, and the more he demands reassurance that they won't happen. I read a letter to the editor of a widely circulated journal, written by an air transport pilot, which pointed out that everyone involved in the airline industry was human. Because all humans make mistakes, the only way, he said, to guarantee that there would be no air fatalities, would be to close down all the airports and stop flying altogether. A pilot of a major airline once confided to me, "There are only two types of pilots: those who have landed on the wrong runway and those who will." It's just part of reality to have to contend with bad luck, misfortune, and the frailties of being human. Reassurance, then, is not the cure for any phobia. It isn't always possible to guarantee that the elevator won't get stuck, that a bridge won't collapse, or that a dog won't bite. The only way to decrease the intensity of a phobia is to lower the self-felt added unconscious guilt that is its basis.

Sometimes people have unrationalized phobias. They can't get near a dog or ride in a plane and they know no reason for it. They say something like, "I just developed this phobia. I can't explain why I suddenly can't go in stores. I've never had a bad experience in a store in my life." If they can't come up with a logical rationalization, once again, the psychiatrist may help them find one. The more recent psychiatric literature has articles about the "endogenous phobia," theorizing that it's due to a malformation in the midbrain. At one large phobia clinic I know, the patients are told that these unrationalized phobias are caused by biochemical abnormalities that are genetic in origin. A stewardess suddenly developed an airplane phobia and couldn't fly. She could think of no reason why she'd developed such a phobia. She had read nothing about plane crashes in the newspaper, nor had she had any bad experiences while flying. She had been told by a psychiatrist that it was genetically caused. She did know of a relative with a phobia. But then, who doesn't? We know that flying was the focus of her self-felt feelings of increased added unconscious guilt. The "endogenous phobia" can be likened to the "endogenous depression." These people in the self-felt position don't have to blame anyone, or even a past experience or situation. They can accept the explanation of the biochemically-oriented psychiatrist and blame the problem on a malfunction of their own brains.

Another condition experienced by people in the self-felt position is the anxiety or panic attack. An anxiety attack is different from being worried or anxious. An anxiety attack is a sudden state in which the sufferer's heart pounds, he sweats, his stomach is knotted up, his pupils dilate and he feels that something absolutely dreadful is about to happen. Something conscious or, more likely, something unconscious triggers the attack. But the "need" to have an anxiety attack, like that "need" to worry or that "need" to have a phobia, is there already because of the increased added unconscious guilt. Some people know that "When I get on an elevator, I'm going to have an anxiety attack." Or, "If I get caught in a long checkout line at the grocery store, I'll have an anxiety attack." Anxiety or panic attacks are closely related to phobias, to excessive worrying, and to all the other conditions of the self-felt position. There are cases in which someone will go to the grocery store, have an anxiety or panic attack, and have to run out of the store. A store manager once told me that at the end of the day, he'll always find a half dozen or so half-filled carts left in the aisles. He knows it's because the people had had panic attacks and had left the store in a rush. I talked to a woman who told me that as long as she didn't feel trapped in the store, she could buy her groceries. But she had to use the "express" lane because the other lines were too long. So she could only get eight items at a time. She said that sometimes she'd have to go to the store five or six times in one day to buy all the things she needed.

Sometimes anxiety attacks may be rationalized if the person is consciously aware of a trigger for the attack. For example, "When I'm out around people, I'll have an attack—my heart pounds; I get sweaty; and I feel as though I'm going to die." Someone who has an anxiety attack is similar to someone in the projected position who suddenly vents all of his anger when he is triggered by one thing. The anxiety attack is a sudden manifestation of added unconscious guilt in the self-felt position. The trigger for sudden anger expression in the projected position and for the anxiety attack in the self-felt position may be unconsciously determined. It can be anything, any part of a person, experience, or situation. We may be unconsciously programmed by past people, experiences, and situations, to be triggered by certain things, but like a gun, a trigger must be accompanied by a charge. It's the increased added unconscious guilt that charges the gun.

Many times the panic attack is unrationalized. Again, research psychiatrists are now describing "endogenous panic attacks" that are postulated to arise from biochemical aberrations within the brain. When the patient himself can see nothing in his life that has changed in any way, such biochemical explanations are readily accepted. In fact, all the conditions of the self-felt position lend themselves well to theories founded upon aberrations within the brain of the patient.

Another self-felt condition is that of feeling stressed. We have recently seen seminars on how to handle stress springing up everywhere. Doctors tell us that stress can affect the heart and the rest of the body, and if we're under a great deal of stress, it can even throw our hormones off. The feeling of stress may be derived from related secondary feelings of the self-felt position, focused in a certain area of the person's life, such as his job. These feelings might include, "I'm not doing enough," and, "I should be an expert and know everything," and, "I'm in a precarious position, and if I don't work harder, something terrible will happen." As the feelings of, "I should," and "I have to" increase, one naturally feels more stress.

One might erroneously think that the stress is caused by reality. This may be only a rationalization for stress that is due to increased added unconscious guilt in the self-felt position. In the following case, we can see that it's a rationalization. I had a patient who was a highly decorated soldier of the Second World War. During the war in Europe, his job was to go on night patrol, and discover where the enemy armor, such as trucks and tanks, was being kept. He had a map on which to mark the coordinates of this armor, so that when he came back and notified his superiors, the artillery could shell the area. He told me that if he ran across an enemy soldier while on patrol, he would kill him. He did this every night and said that he must have killed twenty or thirty men by slitting their throats. He had traits of high personality core guilt and, as such, he tried to perfect his job. His knife was always sharp, his face well-camouflaged, and he carried nothing that made noise. He said he learned how to kill a man without allowing him to utter a single sound. If a job could be stressful, this one certainly should have been. If he were caught, he would have been killed immediately, But he said that "it was just a job." Not only did he feel very little stress, but he actually enjoyed it, rationalizing this by saying he was allowed to sleep late in the mornings. He felt so little stress because he was having more of his oral dependency needs met. While in the army, he was forced to maintain close emotional involvements with many people. He didn't have a choice. He was being kept emotionally comfortable by his fellow soldiers, who met his oral dependency need on a part basis and who accepted his projected guilt. When he left the army, he married a dance hall queen and the combination of his high personality core guilt and her possess-iveness caused him to cut off his relationships with others. She had a tendency to demand exclusivity from him, and because of his tendency to be too dependent on too few with his high personality core guilt, he wanted this exclusivity. Before he came to see me, he had quit his job making pantyhose because of perceived stress. His stress was coming more from the build-up of accumulated self-felt added unconscious guilt than any reality stress.

Like Bob, the Vietnam veteran we saw earlier, this man stayed comfortable when he was forced, by being in the army, to have friends and enemies, even though if we could measure stress, he was in a highly stressful position. But when he left the service and became too dependent on too few, his added unconscious guilt quickly increased and tended to be sustained. He felt stress in a comparatively unstressful position, so much so that he had to quit his job at the hosiery factory.

We've all known people who seem to be able to handle a demanding job and demanding community service while they're raising their children, and somehow managing to find the time and energy to do it all, yet they don't seem to be under stress. In fact, they seem to enjoy all of their activities. These are people who have many emotionally gratifying relationships, which help to meet their oral dependency needs and accept their projected guilt, which keeps their added unconscious guilt low. People with high personality core guilt, who accumulate high sustained self-felt added unconscious guilt when they get into situations where they're too dependent on too few, might have had depression, excessive worrying, anxiety or panic attacks, phobias or any combinations of these instead of experiencing stress. But if their high self-felt guilt and secondary feelings were oriented toward their work, they'd feel great stress. The feeling of stress may come much more from an increase in that self-felt added unconscious guilt and much less from those reality reasons that people give. If one gets involved in anything that tends to lower self-felt added unconscious guilt, or if one can shift self-felt guilt to projected guilt and thereby lower the level of added unconscious guilt, one will perceive less stress. Theoretically, then, one could perceive less stress even in a situation where there is more true reality stress.

Another condition of the self-felt position is neurasthenia. The busy counselor or the therapist will see a lot of patients who complain of weakness, tiredness, listlessness, and feeling drained of energy. These people say that they're not themselves, but if you ask them if they're depressed, they readily say "No, I'm definitely not depressed but I just have no energy." One patient recently told me "As soon as I get up in the morning, I feel as though I want to lie down. I always stayed up late evenings, but now, right after supper, I want to sleep. I used to love to play tennis, but now I'm too tired. But I'm certainly not depressed." The person appears overwhelmed by life, acts as though he's given up, and feels because of his self-felt primary and secondary feelings "I'm not myself," and "There's something physically wrong with me." It's an easily seen self-felt condition because, "It's no one else's fault, the problem is me."

Neurasthenia is, as a rule, incompletely rationalized; the person cannot specify the origin in reality terms, and he'll usually admit that he doesn't know why he feels the way he does. He may go to a doctor with symptoms of weakness, tiredness, and lack of energy, and the doctor will naturally think of many different physical conditions that could produce such symptoms. The physician may attribute the feelings to a vitamin deficiency, a hormonal imbalance, or perhaps to an "undetected sleep disorder." The person could be tested to see if he has an allergic condition, or if he's eating the wrong foods and has a nutritional problem. These medical reasons make sense, and the testing is readily accepted, but the condition is arising from unconscious secondary feelings of the self-felt position, feelings like, "I'm not myself" or, "I don't deserve to do fun things." Since enjoying life, for instance, is a "fun" thing, the person doesn't have the energy to do it anymore.

The feelings that make up the condition of neurasthenia seem to result when the added unconscious guilt becomes too excessive for the personality's compensatory traits, and a breakdown of those defenses results, as with the piano player we saw earlier. She had no energy to play the piano and felt that she was just not herself. She may have added she was not depressed. The secondary feeling here would be, "I need to improve myself but it's too much of a monumental job, and I don't have the energy to do it," so she gives up.

Hypochondriasis is a condition very closely related to neurasthenia. It is both the most unrecognized and most poorly understood condition in all of medicine. It may be the most financially costly condition or illness. It is a condition in which the secondary feelings are focused on one's physical health: "There's something physically wrong with me." All the secondary feelings have this orientation, including the feeling that something terrible but unforeseen and not recognized by the doctors is going to happen regarding the person's physical health. One can use anything about the body or physical health to rationalize this condition. It would be impossible to cover here all the remarkably different ways in which hypochondriasis can manifest itself. There may well be something physically wrong with the person. Everyone is in the process of aging. Arteriosclerosis, for instance, can even be detected in people who are in their twenties. Evidence of the aging process is present in all of our bodies. A pathologist once told me that he could perform an autopsy on anyone and find something that was not quite right, perhaps atypical or even abnormal. The anatomical and physiological norm is statistical and almost no one meets this theoretical norm. People differ in their body functioning; it's as individualistic as a person's fingerprints. All of this lends itself to the reality focus of hypochondriasis. These differences, rather than the increase in the self-felt added unconscious guilt, can become the reality oriented rationalizations that are seen as the origin of the uncomfortableness or pain.

A prominent component of hypochondriasis may be the secondary feeling, "I'm worried that I'm going to die." This feeling is derived from that primary feeling, "Something terrible is going to happen." The more added unconscious guilt there is, the more one feels this and the more one is convinced that this is factual and not just a feeling. One can't talk a person out of what he perceives to be his true reality. Similar to what we saw with airplane phobias, nothing can reassure a person that he's completely free of disease. We have no test to pick up that one cancer cell in the body that's going to multiply, spread, and produce the fatal cancer. Hypochondriacs may fear that they have an undetected fatal process or disease. They often "doctor-hop," from one doctor to another in search of confirmation for what they're so strongly feeling. They don't ever become emotionally comfortable until they have lowered their added unconcious guilt, and this is so whether they have an undetected cancer or whether they don't. There are people who do have undetected cancers or fatal illnesses who do not go to the doctor because they don't have a lot of self-felt added unconscious guilt focused in a hypochon-driacal way. They *should* go to the doctor, but they don't have that feeling that "something is wrong with me." They may have heart disease or diabetes, but they don't seem worried about their physical conditions until their diseases are in the last stages. For years, I had a patient who suffered from chest pains. He frequently went to the emergency room every time his added unconscious guilt increased a little and his hypo-chondriacal chest pains became more severe. He was overly dependent on his wife and she on him so that she would go into a panic every time he complained of chest pain and she would insist that he go to the emergency room. This went on for at least twenty years. Eventually though, he did have a heart attack. No one can tell you that you are not in pain or that you don't have a disease. One well-known political figure whom I knew had a physical exam and was told by his highly reputable doctor that he was in excellent health, but he died of a coronary the next day. I know a specialist in internal medicine who confided to me that he told a patient she was in excellent health after very carefully examining her, and the woman dropped dead on the stairs leaving the doctor's office.

If you were to go to your doctor with a smaller amount of added unconscious guilt, with an equivalent amount of hypochondriasis, the doctor might say, for example, "I think your thyroid may be a little off." So with a lot of testing he does find you are a little hypothyroid, which may be just an incidental finding. He talks to you about being hypothyroid and you to him, and he may give you some pills. You may come back telling him, "Those pills were no damn good! They've got horrible side effects!" Staying in the manifest content, he might reply, "Well, if those didn't work, let's try these," and may give you some different pills. He doesn't know, and doesn't care to know, about unconscious communication psychodynamics. He wouldn't believe that when you tell him, "The pills are no damn good," you're telling *him* he's no damn good, in part. You get your oral dependency needs met in part and indirectly get rid of some anger, which he obviously accepts. You feel better and he feels good about it because he feels he's successfully treated you for hypothyroidism. He doesn't consider you a hypochondriac at all when, in fact, you *were* hypochondrical. Your added unconscious guilt was easily lowered in the patient-doctor relationship. The people that he considers hypochondriacs come in with much more hypochondriasis from much more added unconscious guilt, and this treatment doesn't make them feel better.

A man in Michigan who had quit school in the sixth grade started practicing medicine several years ago. When he was eventually arrested for not having a medical degree, which was a felony, he was to be prosecuted. But the prosecution could not get enough witnesses because so many people came in with testimonials that they had gone to highly-educated specialists in Detroit, but that this "doctor" without even a high school degree was the one who'd cured them. He apparently met more of their oral dependency needs and could easily accept their anger. He was described as sincerely caring for his patients and, on top of that, he made house calls. Some say that a good quack can put a medical doctor out of business any day. But people don't really need to see quacks, for they can usually find doctors who will support their hypochondriasis. If, for instance, you go to your doctor with back pain and he or she can't find anything physically wrong, you can be referred to an orthopedic doctor who may readily operate. Or you can go to a chiropractor, who might tell you that "Your vertebral column is out of line and you need a series of adjustments." You interact with the surgeon or the chiropractor; you get personal attention and you even may have someone "laying on his hands." The medical profession provides a medically scientific manifest content for the emotional interaction which actually produces the cure. The emotional process is hidden from both the doctor and the patient. A quack or a faith healer, however, has the potential of producing the very same result using a different manifest content.

Lowering the added unconscious guilt makes the person feel better, regardless of his or her physical health. An ironic situation occurred when a patient was referred to a psychiatrist I know because his doctors could not find a cause for his intense abdominal pain. After exhaustive medical work-ups, his doctors concluded that the pain was psychological in origin. With psychotherapy several times a week that afforded more of a meeting of his oral dependency need and allowed him to project some guilt, he became much more emotionally comfortable, and he experienced much less pain. However, he suddenly died three months later, from a cancer of the head of the pancreas that was only discovered on autopsy. A person can be very physically ill or even dying, but if his added unconscious guilt is low, he may not be as worried as someone else with high added unconscious guilt focused in hypochondriasis. Remember, too, that the correspondingly high unmet oral dependency need will be reflected by an intolerance, or an exaggeration, of pain.

If the added unconscious guilt increases further, hypochondriasis can reach the delusional level. The hypochondriac who has such a large amount of added unconscious guilt may be convinced that he's dying of cancer of the pancreas even after a succession of doctors have told him he's not. Others may feel, "My body is filled with worms," or, "My brain is dead." As added unconscious guilt decreases, so do the hypochondriacal delusions. The person whose back pain was "unbearable" when his added unconscious guilt was higher, may begin to feel, when his added unconscious guilt decreases, "I still have my back pain, but I guess I'll just have to put up with it. Those damn doctors didn't help me at all. I've decided it's just something I'll have to live with." Before, when his guilt was much higher, he was telling others that he *couldn't* live with it.

Similar to those people whose added unconscious guilt is focused on their physical condition are those who think, "There's something mentally (or emotionally) wrong with me," when their added unconscious guilt increases. These people may voluntarily seek the services of a psychiatrist. I have seen a lot of people who have come in saying, "I think I'm crazy." In listening to them, it's easy to determine that they're in the self-felt position with greatly increased added unconscious guilt. One patient I saw recently was as nice a person as you'd ever want to meet. Nobody would want to have changed anything about him but he really thought he was "losing his mind," thinking that he was not functioning right mentally. This feeling is similar to those of neurasthenia where the person feels that he's weak and tired and just "not functioning right."

Hypochondriasis also ties in with perfectionism. For instance, I had a patient who tended to be hypochondriacal, always finding physical problems with himself. He finally stopped complaining about his health, but then complained about his new very expensive car. To him it wasn't running "perfectly," and he could hear a noise. First it was in the engine, then in the body, and finally in the wheels. He took his car from one dealer to another, like a doctor-hopping hypochondriac. He could tell, "Something's just not right with my car," but no one else could hear the noise. One can see the common relationship in the feeling, "Something is wrong with my car" and the feeling, "Something is wrong with me physically." He wanted his car in perfect condition as he wanted his health in perfect condition. His hypochondriasis subsided though when his added unconscious guilt focused itself on his car, which he identified with himself. This man exhibited the same traits, in regard to his business, where he demanded perfection and would frequently complain of finding things wrong that no one else could see. Sometimes this technique worked well, because he would often uncover problems, and this did make money for him. But there were other times when nothing was actually wrong. It still kept his employees looking.

The last condition of high self-felt added unconscious guilt that we will examine is obsessive-compulsiveness. Obsessive-compulsiveness is also linked to the compensatory trait of perfectionism, which is often found in those with high personality core guilt. With an increase in added unconscious guilt, the trait can intensify into a recognizable condition of obsessive-compulsiveness. In certain reality situations, obsessive-compulsiveness—which is an unconscious need to be obsessed with something, to organize, clean up, straighten, or somehow "make right" the added unconscious guilt—can be a definite asset. When added unconscious guilt increases, there is a greater tendency to be obsessive-compulsive, and in certain situations, this can lead to considerable reality success. This condition can also become a liability. Obsessive-compulsiveness is closely tied to the feeling that "something terrible is going to happen." One man who came to see me had to make the sign of the cross every time he came out of the bathroom. He couldn't pass the linen closet without doing it. When I asked him why he did that he said, "I have the feeling that if I don't do it, something terrible will happen." His deeper feeling is, "I should be punished unless I perform this ritual because I'm so inferior, inadequate, unacceptable, wrong, and guilty." Obsessive-compulsiveness is just another constellation of reality focused self-felt secondary and primary feelings.

A housewife told me that when she got emotionally uncomfortable, she had to have all the clothespins on the line facing a certain way when she hung out the clothes to dry. She was always a perfectionistic housewife, but with an increase in added unconscious guilt, her asset became a liability. She had to have the clothes hung just right, and folded in a certain way. She couldn't stand to have anything in the wastebaskets, and had to empty them immediately if she knew there was anything in them. Another one of my patients had been in the army and had captured a German soldier during the Second World War. The German's job was to booby-trap rooms as the German army retreated across Europe. He told my patient how he had discovered a way to get the high-ranking officers or NCOs to set off his trap. He'd put an explosive behind a picture on the wall and tilt the picture slightly. The people without the traits of perfectionism that accompany high personality core guilt would not be bothered by a tilted picture. But those with high personality core guilt who tended to be perfectionistic and, with more added unconscious guilt, tended to be obsessive-compulsive and would feel compelled to straighten the picture, thereby setting off the fatal charge. These were often the men who had become outstandingly successful because of their perfectionistic obsessive-compulsiveness, but here it became a liability in this particular reality situation.

I have many patients who are noticeably obsessive-compulsive when their self-felt added unconscious guilt is high. They come for other reasons, but I notice the obsessive-compulsiveness as well. Many of them, while talking to me, are lining up the pencils on my desk, and straightening the books, because everything has to be lined up just right. I have some patients who come in and brush any dust they see off the edge of the desk or the other furniture, because everything must be perfectly cleaned. Cleaning is a common focus of obsessive-compulsiveness; the added unconscious guilt must be cleaned up, because it's felt as a contaminant. Frequently, when self-felt added unconscious guilt increases, the person who becomes obsessive-compulsive frequently has to clean the bathroom, which is suggestive of the nature of the added unconscious guilt.

In the following example, you can see that many of the conditions we've discussed are present at one time; depression, excessive worrying, obsessive-compulsiveness, insecurity, lack of confidence, and stress are all a part of what this woman is feeling. A teacher who lives by herself came to see me. She said:

I've been so depressed that Friday night I got the shotgun out and was going to end it all, but I thought that it would make such a mess and mother would have to clean it up, so I decided against doing myself in as I know I should. Friday morning I got a telephone call from Uncle Bernie and Aunt Helen in California. They were flying in Saturday to spend the day with me. I was under stress all day Friday while teaching school just thinking about all that had to be done in preparation for the visit. As soon as I got out of school, I hurried home and started washing and waxing the kitchen floor. Well, after I waxed the floor, the wax was apparently so old that it turned yellow and I had to take the wax back up. Then I rushed to the store to buy new wax to rewax the floor. Then, when I was frantically grabbing the towels from the bathroom, I accidentally yanked the towel rack off. I was panic-stricken! I rushed to the hardware store to get the right replacement rack. It had adhesive backing, and after I put it up, I saw it was crooked. When I pulled it off to restick it, a piece of the plaster came off the wall. Then I had to get plaster and paint, and ended up painting the whole bathroom because the new paint didn't quite match the old paint. I noted the curtains in the bedroom looked dirty so I threw them in the wash and when I took them out I cried. The curtains had an insulated backing and apparently the hot wash water made the backing came off and the curtains shriveled up. I had to go to three different places before I found the right type of curtain. It was after ten when I got home and I was an absolute nervous wreck. I had to vacuum because the living room was a mess. I plugged in the vacuum cleaner where I already had my toaster and the warming oven and blew all the fuses. It was dark and I was running around in circles. I didn't have any extra fuses. I was at the end of my rope. Finally, I went next door to get a replacement fuse. I was at my wit's end but I just had to shop because Aunt Helen is a finicky eater, and I did want her to have the right food. Then I realized I had spent all my money on curtains and everything else. I just sat in the middle of the floor and cried, wishing I could die!

It's easy to see that this woman's conditions are all tied together. There is a commonality to all of these self-felt conditions of emotional uncomfortableness. One well-known psychiatrist[1] has written a book stating that these conditions all mask depression; that they are "depression equivalents," and that depression underlies them all. He did see the commonality in all of them. But rather than the many faces of depression, these self-felt conditions—none of which is more important than another—along with the conditions we'll see in the next chapter, are the many faces of added unconscious guilt. They are simply the realty mask of that underlying guilt.

1. Lesse, Stanley MASKED DEPRESSION Aronson 1983

CHAPTER 11
Misperceived and Projected Conditions

It's easier to fool someone if what we present looks plausible. Unconsciously we use reality to deceive ourselves and others. Hiding behind our reality-oriented Aristotelian thinking is the emotional unreality that is always influencing how we feel, how we act, and what we say. The secondary feelings of the emotional unreality determine what we say when we're emotionally uncomfortable. Closely related secondary feelings may make up a state or a condition that governs our behavior, including our verbal behavior. These closely related secondary feelings produce a wide variety of seemingly different states or conditions with many reality orientations, which we use to talk about our emotional uncomfortableness. These reality orientations, or manifest contents, are specific to each individual's situation and experience. The manifest contents can seem very different, but we're dealing with the same basic entity underneath. Because the condition determines the manifest content of the rationalization, it often influences the direction that the individual will take to seek relief from emotional uncomfortableness, the direction he will go, in reality, for help or treatment. Depending on where he goes for help or treatment, he will get varying and sometimes contrasting reality-oriented explanations of the cause of his uncomfortableness, which appear logical according to Aristotelian thinking. This becomes particularly apparent if one looks at the states and conditions of the misperceived position. We've seen how the states and conditions of the self-felt position can seem so different from one another when expressed in reality. They seem even more different from the conditions of the misperceived position.

We've already seen the condition of stress from the self-felt position with the secondary feelings of, "I should work harder," and "Unless I do more something bad is going to happen," etc. The condition in the misperceived position is made up of secondary feelings like, "They want me to work harder," "They don't want me to make a single mistake," "They expect me to fail," "They want to replace me," "They're not really satisfied with my work," and "They think my work isn't measuring up,"

163

etc. The reason for these secondary feelings is the added unconscious guilt in the misperceived position. "They feel I'm inferior, inadequate, unacceptable, and wrong," can focus itself on work, which is closely identified with the self and can lead to a condition of stress. In the misperceived position, the stress is seen as coming from someone else and the way that someone else feels about the person and his or her job.

For example, an executive secretary told me that her boss expected a certain amount of work to be on his desk "yesterday." She took home piles of work that she tried to finish during the day. She noticed though that after she got all the work finished on time, it stayed on his desk for several days before he even looked at it. She still felt, "My ass is constantly on the line," meaning that her job was always in jeopardy. "If he had the opportunity, he'd kick me out of that office." But, in reality, she did very good work, and her boss didn't think about firing her. He even told her, "Don't take extra work home." But she confided to me, "He didn't really mean that. He expects the work to be done on time." She determined what "on time" was (and feeling that it was "yesterday" implies that she could never accomplish her work on time), but she attributed the pressure and the stress of the job to her boss. Even if the boss expected all of the work to be done on time, the other people in the office, who are not in the misperceived position, wouldn't necessarily feel stressed by that. They might not take work home and might not feel they were about to be fired. This secretary feels stressed regardless of what the boss expects, in reality.

Another condition we have seen is that of withdrawal. In the self-felt position, the person feels, "I don't fit in," "I'm boring," "I should isolate myself" and withdraws. Conversely, in the projected position, feelings of, "He doesn't fit in," "He should isolate himself" could cause "him" to withdraw. But someone in the misperceived position withdraws because she feels, "They feel I should isolate myself," "They think I don't fit in," "They feel I'm boring and a waste of their time," and this person attributes her withdrawal to someone else or others.

Some of the other conditions that we saw in the self-felt position could also result from the misperceived position. Anhedonia, for example, in the self-felt position has secondary feelings such as, "I don't deserve any pleasure," and "I shouldn't enjoy myself." Anhedonia could also result from the misperceived secondary feelings, such as, "He doesn't think I deserve any pleasure," "He wants me to work all the time," and, "He gets upset if I spend any money on myself." Together, these feelings produce the condition of anhedonia, in which the person isn't able to enjoy life, seems to be working all the time, and attributes this to an emotionally significant other or others.

One condition associated especially with the misperceived position is hypersensitivity, being overly sensitive. Some of the secondary feelings that make up this condition are, "They think I'm strange," "They don't really accept me," "They're ready to laugh at me about _____[the way I look, the way I talk, my education, etc.]" The primary feelings of the misperceived position are at the root of hypersensitivity: "They feel I'm inferior, inadequate, unacceptable, wrong, etc." The feelings may be focused on a specific aspect of the person's appearance, behavior, experience, or situation. I had a patient who was a highly successful business executive, well-known and respected in the community. He was overly sensitive because he could not hold a glass or a cup and saucer without his hand shaking. He had many business and social functions to attend. When he attended a business meeting, he'd have to hold his cup and saucer with both hands or it would shake and rattle. If it were a glass at a cocktail party, his hand would shake so the ice would rattle and the drink would spill. He got so that he couldn't even hold the glass with both hands. He had all types of ruses that he used to avoid having to hold a glass or a cup and saucer. He'd excuse himself during coffee breaks at the meetings; he told hosts at cocktail parties that he was trying to cut back on his drinking, and, when offered a soda, that the carbonation bothered his stomach. When his hypersensitivity increased, he could not bear to be seen with a cup or glass in his hand.

A teacher I know was hypersensitive about his body. His wife came in to see me and said that even though she'd been married to him for seven years, when he went from the bathroom after a shower to the dressing room, he kept himself wrapped in a towel. She'd ask, "Why do you need the towel? I'm your wife." But he always used it, being very sensitive about how he looked, feeling that she found his body in some way inferior, inadequate, unacceptable, or wrong. This case ties in with those of the many people who cannot undress in front of their partners. They undress alone in the dressing room or the bathroom. I knew one very attractive young woman who had been a runner-up in a national beauty pageant. Yet she could not undress in front of her husband. She had to get into the closet to take off her clothes. Other people can't have sexual relations in the light; all the lights must be turned off, because they're so sensitive about their bodies. The body is only one focus for the condition of hypersensitivity, however. It can be focused in any aspect of the person's reality.

A condition made up of misperceived secondary feelings that is quite common is jealousy. Focused on a marriage or love relationship, this condition includes secondary feelings like, "She's getting tired of me," "She finds me unexciting," "She isn't satisfied with me," "She'd rather be with someone else," and the primary feelings are behind them. "She's getting tired of me" because "she feels I'm inferior, inadequate, unacceptable, etc.," for example. If these feelings are focused on a marriage relationship, one person can get jealous if the other is simply in the company of someone of the opposite sex. The spouse in the misperceived position sees this as a threat to the relationship. The wife who doesn't want her husband working alone at the office with the secretary and the husband who has to know where his wife is at all times are good examples of jealous spouses. I have known several women whose husbands require a minute-by-minute account of where they've been each time they leave the house. I talked to one woman who actually had to let her husband examine her underpants for any traces of a sexual encounter every time she went anywhere without him. His jealousy was so intense that he checked even if she went to the grocery store for twenty minutes. The jealousy in the marriage relationship could extend to people of the same sex, for the same reasons, but without any sexual orientation. The husband might say to his wife, "I don't like you spending so much time with your girlfriends. You feel that they're more important than I am." The same secondary feelings that were previously focused on members of the opposite sex are here pinpointed on friends of the same sex. Jealousy doesn't have to concern the marriage relationship; it can be a part of any relationship. For instance, "They don't care about my work; they're interested in someone else's," is one of jealousy's secondary feelings, focused on a job or work situation.

Jealousy can create problems in the relationship sphere because it implies a lack of trust. If it's sexually or romantically oriented, it can cause problems when the other person denies any sexual or romantic interest in someone else or becomes angrily defensive about such interest. The jealous person may believe that the other is lying, that the other really *is* interested in somebody else. The jealous person may do all sorts of things to check on the other person, which can also cause problems in the relationship. I knew an excellent teacher who had many of the secondary feelings making up jealousy. She sometimes taught night school, so she had to leave her husband at home alone. She thought that he might sneak off and meet someone else while she was gone, so in order to check on him, she would place a popsicle stick under the rear wheel of his car. If he backed the car out of the driveway, the tires would mark the stick. She could tell from the tire tracks that the car had been moved. He would say, "I went up the street to buy a paper," or "I wanted a bag of potato chips to eat while I watched the game, so I went to the store," but she never believed him. It seemed to her that he always had an excuse for why he'd used the car. Because of her jealousy, he began to feel that he had to explain his every move, that she didn't trust him. The jealousy caused problems in the relationship. Jealousy can lead to accusations. Checking on the other person with popsicle sticks, checking clothing, or giving the third degree does little to help a relationship at all, and does not guarantee of faithfulness. Instead, it tends to erode the relationship because there is no mutual trust.

The feeling of trust comes from the meeting of the oral dependency need; it makes a relationship better. The more misperceived added unconscious guilt, the more jealous a person is and the greater the tendency to weaken the relationship. We've already mentioned a case in which a man was not having an affair until his wife's jealousy led to accusations. His wife's accusations and her lack of trust frustrated his own oral dependency need. With a high unmet need, he was more vulnerable to having an affair which met his oral dependency need. If his relationship with his wife had been a more comfortable one that more easily met his oral dependency need, he would have been less vulnerable and less inclined to go elsewhere to have his emotional needs met.

Another condition that can result from added unconscious guilt in the misperceived position is paranoia. Some of the secondary feelings of the paranoid condition are, "They're trying to ridicule me," "They're watching me," "They're following me," "They're saying bad things about me," "They're trying to punish me," or "They'll try to blame me if anything goes wrong." The reality focus of paranoia can be very specific. For example, I saw one woman who believed "They're trying to poison me," focused on the canned goods that she bought at the grocery store. She'd go to the grocery store, buy a couple bags of groceries, unpack them, and put the canned goods on the shelves. Then thinking they'd been poisoned, she'd throw them all out. She shopped at one grocery store, then another, trying to find one where "they" weren't trying to poison her. She rationalized her paranoia by saying, "That can just didn't look right," or "Those labels had a funny color." She interpreted her perceptions in the light of her misperceived added unconscious guilt that was focused on, "They're trying to poison me."

The woman in the following excerpt, who previously had won a national commendation for her work, focused her paranoia, her feelings that "They have it in for me," on her work situation:

There are some people in the office who are harassing me, who are antagonistic to me, and who are always trying to work against me. For instance, they'll ask me personal questions, like what did I do last night, which is absolutely no business of theirs and is only done to interrupt me in my work. I would never ask them such personal questions. They get me all upset so that I can't work as the boss expects I should. I told him I definitely know that some of the work I turn in, is credited to someone else. They're a close-knit bunch and have always excluded me, even though I've tried so hard to be friendly. The other girls in the office will purposefully hide material that I need for my work. It's as though they don't want me to do an adequate job, so they can get rid of me. They mess up work that I do and then I get blamed for it. Of all my co-workers, Marge is the one who has it in for me the most. She wants to get rid of me, even though I've tried to get along with her. I think it's because she has a sister who wants my job. She actually followed me into the ladies room the other day and I saw her fumbling in her purse to get a small can of hair spray. Then when she used it, a distinct change came over me. I felt weak and dizzy, and more irritable and that's not like me at all. It was so strange. I asked her if she had been following me, and whether she wanted to harm me. When she moved her hand a little as if she was going to hit me, I quickly left. I couldn't work the rest of the day after that! It was so upsetting! I can understand that she wants my job for her sister, but don't you think that trying to physically harm me is going a bit too far?[1]

A condition of misperceived added unconscious guilt, which is closely related to jealousy and paranoia is feeling victimized. The secondary feelings of victimization include, "They're trying to take advantage of me," "They don't treat me right. They treat everyone else nicely, but they treat me like they don't really care about me, and I can tell they'd like to get rid of me." The feeling of being victimized is often focused on the work situation and it may be supported by other people. Someone who feels, "They don't treat me right at work. They treat everyone else nicely, but they don't treat me right," may go to a union, for instance which may support him.

Victimization has an interesting relationship to jealousy. Someone who feels victimized may believe that he or she is not being treated fairly, usually in a work or social situation, and can often get support from his or her spouse. The husband or wife will often agree with the paranoid feelings. Yet the jealous person feels that the husband or wife is not treating him or her right, and may get support from friends or co-workers. I know one teacher who says that he's not treated right; that "they" never did accept him when he started to work at this particular school. I know other teachers at this same school who tell me otherwise. Yet this teacher is ready to go to his union with the complaint that "They're not treating me right. They give me the worst classes every year." He also gets support from his wife, who agrees, "Yes, I know they don't treat you right. They never have treated you the way they do everyone else who works there." She supports his feelings of being victimized with mutually shared projected guilt. When they both feel this way, their marriage seems much better. The marriage would not go well if their misperceived feelings were oriented toward each other.

Someone who feels victimized feels discriminated against and this feeling may be supported by other people. Sometimes a person of a particular race, ethnic background, or sex gets into the misperceived position and then feels victimized. He or she believes that he or she is being victimized or discriminated against because of skin color, or country of origin, or sex. He or she can then go to certain federal or state governmental organizations with his or her complaint of racial or sexual discrimination. Or, in the armed services, he or she can complain to the inspector general or to the commanding officer. When I worked in the mental health clinic of a military base, I saw quite a few people who felt discriminated against. I could tell from their stories that many of them simply had increased added unconscious guilt in the misperceived position and were interpreting the facts according to their feelings of being victimized. But they were being well supported by the attention they received and the subsequent investigations. If they'd been working in a factory, they would have been supported by the union and, rather than the inspector general, the shop steward would have come in to check things out.

I know of a woman whose paranoia served her in good stead. She had the feeling, "They're trying to poison me," which eventually oriented itself specifically to her drinking water. When her added unconscious guilt increased, she was more convinced "they" were trying to poison her drinking water. She finally took a sample of the water to the local health department where tests showed that her water was indeed poisoned. Chemicals that her husband had used on the lawn to kill the weeds were seeping into the well. Her paranoia had good results, but she had the water tested not because she thought that chemicals could be contaminating the water, but because she felt that someone was trying to poison her. Her case is similar to that of the hypochondriacal person with headaches who finally doctor-hops to a neurologist who then finds a brain tumor.

Another example of beneficial paranoia, which fits with what we've said about all the conditions follows. I know a successful businesswoman whose paranoia is a great asset. It is focused primarily in her business relationships, where she feels, "People are out to get me." She can cite many examples where other people in the business world have been, as she puts it, out to "screw you over if they can." But because she is a little paranoid, she can think of all the different ways that people might try to take advantage of her, and because she anticipates them, she thereby prevents them from ever getting the upper hand. In the realm of business, the suspicion of the paranoid condition can be in one's favor. Theoretically, if you worked for the Internal Revenue Service, a little paranoia would help you to find more lawbreakers because you would suspect every return you examined. A person who's a little paranoid in regard to walking down dark alleys is less likely to become the victim of crime. In certain reality situations, being a little paranoid, or any of these other conditions could be of help.

As we saw with the self-felt position, when added unconscious guilt in the misperceived position increases, the feelings that make up the various conditions intensify. The person feels *more* stressed, *more* hypersensitive, *more* jealous, *more* victimized, and *more* paranoid. When the executive secretary's added unconscious guilt increases, she feels as if she must have a certain amount of work on the boss's desk in less time. So she takes home more work, after working overtime at the office. The wife of the man who was hypersensitive about his body noticed that on some days, when he was "even less comfortable than usual," he had the towel wrapped more tightly around himself from his knees to his chest, and hurried more quickly from the bathroom to the dressing room. When his added unconscious guilt increased, he was more hypersensitive about his body; his feelings that "She finds my body inferior, inadequate, and unacceptable," intensified. With an increase in added unconscious guilt, the jealous woman who suspected her husband of having an affair with his secretary will more actively accuse him of it.

When the added unconscious guilt decreases, all the feelings become less intense. When the secretary's added unconscious guilt decreases, she takes only a little work home and she leaves the office at five, with everyone else. This is because there is less of that feeling, "He expects me to work harder." Sometimes, when the hypersensitive man's guilt decreased, he'd be less careful about holding the towel up around his body. His wife told me that at times, when she knew he was more emotionally comfortable, he would be quite lax with his towel. She told me that the way he held his towel was a good barometer as to how things were going in his life and how comfortable he was feeling. The jealous woman, when her added unconscious guilt decreases, is more likely to believe her husband when he says that he'll be late because he has some work to finish at the office. After the teacher's added unconscious guilt decreased, he said that people were beginning to be nicer to him at work, which he rationalized was due to the union's intervention. The behavior of the other people hadn't changed, and even though the union might have intervened, his perceptions at work had changed. Since his feelings of being victimized had decreased, he interpreted the behavior of others less in the light of his feeling that "They're not treating me right; they don't care about me."

An increase in added unconscious guilt would make someone in the paranoid condition more paranoid, as we see in the following example. A man who had the feeling, "They're talking about people who work the second shift [his shift at the factory]," with more added unconscious guilt, might say, "They're talking about me." The feelings might intensify to the delusional level if there were more misperceived added unconscious guilt where he might say, "I hear voices talking about me" when no one else is around. These delusional voices might say that the person is no good, or make other insulting statements about the person's work, which demonstrates the connection with the misperceived primary feelings that "They feel I'm inferior, inadequate, unacceptable, etc." Instead of a work orientation, the voices may be oriented sexually. For instance, if he believes that homosexuality is wrong, they could tell him he's a homosexual. With even more added unconscious guilt, the voices might be oriented to both his work *and* his sex life. They could instead be oriented to anything in his reality.

Another feeling of the paranoid condition which could increase to the delusional level is the feeling that, "*They're* trying to control my thoughts." In the self-felt position, this feeling would be, "*I'm* trying to control my thoughts," and you'll sometimes hear people say, "I'm trying to keep my mind on God all the time," which is a way to counter the feelings of guilt, inadequacy, and unacceptableness. In the projected position, the feeling is "I'm trying to control *his* thoughts," and you can see this feeling when a parent, for example, tries to control the thoughts of a teenager who, perhaps, is beginning to use obscene language. But in the misperceived position, "They're trying to control my thoughts" can be a feeling of the paranoid condition, and it can increase to the delusional level when someone thinks, "They *are* controlling my thoughts."

As a final example of a condition of the misperceived position reaching the delusional level, consider the woman that I knew who was so hypersensitive about her body she had to cover herself with a towel or robe when she walked in front of the television. She believed that the people on television were looking at her and finding her unacceptable. As her added unconscious guilt decreased she could recognize that this action was irrational but she would still cover herself because she felt better when she did. When her added unconscious guilt decreased further, she could streak nude by the television without it bothering her too much. In this example, one can also see the close relationship between hypersensitivity and paranoia which both, as do victimization, jealousy, and stress, come from misperceived secondary feelings.

An individual will tend to give a reality-oriented reason for his feelings. He may explain his perception that someone is laughing at him, like the music teacher who said that the children knew she hadn't studied the piano for as long as the other teachers. She could also have cited evidence, as in, "Many times I see them whispering about me during my class," or, "Sometimes when I walk into the classroom, they suddenly stop laughing." Someone else might cite as evidence that her husband is having an extramarital affair from perceptions like, "There was a cigarette butt in his ashtray, and he doesn't smoke." In reality, her husband may have given one of his co-workers a ride home, but the wife's jealousy, coming from her increased added unconscious guilt in the misperceived position, colors her interpretation of reality. She uses this "evidence" as a rationalization for her jealousy. What is being presented is that these observations of reality are *leading* to her feelings of jealousy, when it's actually the increased misperceived added unconscious guilt in her emotional unreality that creates the jealousy feeling. Then the observations of reality are used to build the rationalization as though the feeling is secondary to these observations.

Sometimes, however, the conditions of the misperceived position can be unrationalized or incompletely rationalized. Someone could say, for instance, "Why don't they accept me at work?" or, "I don't know why they're so against me at church." A woman in psychotherapy told me, when her misperceived added unconscious guilt had increased, "They're following me again," feeling that other motorists were following her down the road. When I asked her why, she replied, "How the hell do I know? I wish somebody would tell me!" Although some people who feel victimized may say, "It's because of my sex," "It's because of my religion," or, "It's because of my race," others who'll say, "I don't know why people in my office don't treat me as an equal." One woman told me that she had a sudden urge to check her husband's ashtrays and wastebaskets for traces of lipstick or makeup on cigarette butts and tissues, but she also told me that she had no reason to do so. "He's always been faithful to me, and he's given me no reason whatsoever to be jealous," she said. "If I ask him where he is, or where he's been during the day, he'll tell me; he doesn't try to hide anything from me. Yet I've developed this urge to check on him." The reason behind her behavior is her increased added unconscious guilt, in the misperceived position producing the secondary feelings that make up jealousy, such as, "He now wants to replace me," and "He's not satisfied with me anymore." These secondary feelings are extensions of the misperceived primary feelings: "He's now feeling I'm inferior, inadequate, unacceptable, etc."

The poorly rationalized jealousy of the woman in the preceding example could cause problems in her marriage. The feelings making up her jealousy are unrationalized, such as, "I don't know why he wants to replace me," and "I don't understand it, but he's just not satisfied with me anymore." Other unrationalized feelings of the misperceived position that can lead to problems are those like, "I don't know why he's avoiding me all of a sudden," and "I can't see any reason why he's not interested in me anymore," or "I don't know why he just doesn't seem comfortable (or happy) around me anymore." These feelings could combine with feelings like, "He wants to replace me with someone else," to form a condition of jealousy, that could destroy the relationship. The feeling could begin as, "I *feel* he wants to replace me with someone else," and become, as misperceived added unconscious guilt increases "He *wants* to replace me with someone else." With even more added unconscious guilt it becomes, "He's *got* someone else." I talked to a woman recently who was very upset because, "My husband ignores me. Suddenly, it seems he'd rather watch television or read a book than talk to me." Because her added unconscious guilt, in the misperceived position, has increased, she no longer perceives that her husband cares about her. Yet she has no logical explanation for this observed change in his behavior. This demonstrates how one's observation of reality is directly influenced by the emotional unreality and, specifically in this case, by increased added unconscious guilt in the misperceived position.

We have seen that groups or constellations of some particular secondary feelings in the self-felt and misperceived positions make up conditions. Projected added unconscious guilt can also produce secondary feelings which form certain conditions. In any of the three positions, one could have the same amount of added unconscious guilt producing primary and secondary feelings. But with the different reference of the feelings, in each position, the implications are remarkably different. For instance, in the self-felt position, the condition of stress is made up of feelings like, "I should work harder." In the misperceived position, it's made up of, "He feels I should work harder." But in the projected position, the feelings, "He should work harder," could put stress on someone else. The secondary feelings in the projected position which make up certain states or conditions have a psychodynamic commonality with those in the self-felt and misperceived positions but the implications are remarkably contrasting.

One condition of the projected position is being hypercritical, or finding fault with someone else. Many secondary feelings could make up this condition with varying reality focuses, but they could be summarized as, "They must get it right," "They must be perfect," and these come from the primary feelings: "He must not be inferior, inadequate, unacceptable, wrong, guilty, failing, unclean, or destined for trouble." In certain reality situations, being hypercritical could put stress on someone else. The feelings could be in regard to a work situation where the person in the projected position could say, "You're not working hard enough," "Your work isn't good enough," and "I demand perfection from you." If the person in the projected position is the boss, her condition might put an employee under a great deal of actual stress. It might also cause anhedonia in him or his fellow workers.

One can also see this condition in marriages where one partner demands perfection of the other. This partner in the projected position seems to be constantly finding fault with his spouse or anything associated with the spouse. He could say that the other is not measuring up in regard to the way she dresses or cooks or talks, etc. One spouse might tell the other, "You don't handle the children right." Fault-finding could have a sexual orientation; one partner could be hypercritical of the sexual relationship. One spouse could say, "Your friends don't measure up," or "I don't like your relatives and particularly your Aunt Mary coming over here all the time without even calling first." In these last two cases, the friends and relatives are associated with the other person and the spouse in the projected position is saying, through them, "You don't measure up."

I had one patient who was married to a successful surgeon from a nearby city. She told me that at times he would come home and find fault with things that hadn't been done to his satisfaction. One of the things he particularly criticized was that she did not always keep the plants watered. He'd come in, see the wilted plants, and yell at her, "I built you this half-million dollar house, and you sit here doing nothing while I'm out working myself to death! I've given you everything, and you can't even water the damn plants!" When I later talked to him, he *was* hypercritical, just as his wife had said. He told me, "I'm a perfectionist and I built her this nice house just the way I felt she wanted it. But I come home and I find the plants wilted. I have to shut lights off. She's always leaving the attic lights on and the lights on in the closet. Or she'll leave an upstairs window open and turn the central air conditioning on. That just drives me up the wall." This man was a perfectionist, and he expected his wife to be perfect in every detail. This expectation of perfection intensified or lessened reflecting the amount of added unconscious guilt he accrued. His idea of perfection, his wife later told me, included not only having her dressed "perfectly" but having all the shades in the front windows at the exact same level. He would find fault with the wife because sometimes she'd leave the master bedroom shades down all day. His perfectionism worked well with his surgery. He always made sure he'd done everything exactly right, which led him to outstanding success in the operating room and an excellent reputation in his subspeciality. But when his added unconscious guilt increased and his increased perfectionism spilled over into his marriage, his constant fault-finding caused problems in his relationship with his wife. Added unconscious guilt in the projected position, when taken home and projected to spouse and children, can lead to severe emotional problems. The person with the high personality core guilt whose added unconscious guilt is in the projected position fails to see what he is doing at home and may utilize his reality success as proof that the way he sees things is the correct way and that his criticism is appropriate.

In the following example, a woman speaks of her father who was the most critical of her when she was growing up:

I remember my father as the perfect fault-finder. He could always find something wrong about anybody or anything. In fact, he seemed to enjoy finding fault. Discovering a flaw in any person or thing actually made him feel good. It seemed to give him pleasure if he could put somebody down. I know because he did it to me all the time. Nothing I ever did went without his criticism. As a teenager, if I parked my car in front of the house, he'd tell me what was wrong with doing that; yet if I parked in back, he'd find something to criticize in my doing that. He had a need to constantly find fault, criticize, harass or pressure. I actually think he enjoyed making people miserable. And if my mother pointed it out to him, he would defend his criticizing by saying that he was doing people a favor by telling them about their faults so they could correct them.

A multimillionaire with high personality core guilt, projected his added unconscious guilt to people who worked in his beach house, one of whom was seeing me for psychotherapy. The millionaire only stayed in the house occasionally, but he expected his table set for supper and his bed turned down every evening in case he decided to fly in and spend the night. He was a fanatic about cleanliness and orderliness. Everything had to be dusted and spotless and it all had to be done in a certain way. If it wasn't done his way, he unloaded his added unconscious guilt by finding fault with everyone who worked in the house. His fault-finding worked well in his business, where he demanded perfection from his employees. However he was often looking for new people to work in his beach house after the previous ones had quit because of his excessive criticism.

With increased added unconscious guilt, the person in the projected position tends to be *more* demanding, *more* hypercritical and the fault-finding intensifies. I heard one man say about his wife, "She can't cook right; she doesn't use the eating utensils right; she can't make love right; she doesn't talk right; she can't even walk right; and she doesn't choose the right kind of friends." This man had a lot of added unconscious guilt to project, so he demanded perfection. He though determined what was perfect and imperfect. Before his added unconscious guilt increased, he might have only found fault with her cooking, or perhaps only with her friends, not with everything that she did. This example shows a deception that can occur in regard to the origin of a marriage problem. It would seem that the problem is arising with the wife's inability to "cook right," "choose the right friends," etc., when the problem actually originates in the husband's increased added unconscious guilt in the projected position. His ability to project guilt implies that he is getting support from outside the marriage, whether from his work situation, a friend, or even a lover.

The more added unconscious guilt there is, the more the projection is presented as if it has a basis in reality. The multimillionaire claimed he found fault with his employees because they didn't have his bed turned down in just the right way. He would use reality as though this were the origin of his need to express anger. It is the same with the surgeon who would say that he found fault with his wife because she didn't water the plants, or the father who criticized his daughter for parking the car in the wrong place. These are rationalizations for the projection of added unconscious guilt. If the wife had the plants watered and the shades drawn right, her husband would have found something else to criticize. The daughter pointed out that her father not only objected to her parking in front of the house but in back as well.

In that case example, the father said he pointed out faults so that they could be corrected. As added unconscious guilt increases, the fault finder has more of a "need" to correct the imperfection, the target of projected guilt. It could be the way his daughter parks the car; it could be her husband's relatives; it could be any "injustice," "sin," or "corruption." Those leading the fight against any of these things are often those with a lot of added unconscious guilt in the projected position. They are often people with high personality core guilt and who are too dependent on too few such that a high level of added unconscious guilt can be continually sustained. Projected guilt is always being replenished in this too dependent on too few situation. People with high personality core guilt and high intelligence who focus their guilt on some issue can present sound logical arguments and many times they do correct whatever they believe is wrong. Perhaps this is the basis for social progress.

However, with too much added unconscious guilt in the projected position, the person may strain reality in order to rationalize the projection of added unconscious guilt. Terrorists sometimes strain reality in this manner. The more a person strains reality, the less likely he or she will be able to attract supporters. The closer to the delusional level the person gets, the more likely it will be an individual action, like one man's attempt to assassinate the president of the United States.

Sometimes the unconscious can't seem to find a logical rationalization and the projection of added unconscious guilt remains unrationalized or poorly rationalized. A wife who has a sudden increase of added unconscious guilt in the projected position might say about her husband, "I don't know why, but I just don't want him near me anymore. I cringe now if he touches me, but I don't understand it. There's no reason that I can think of." As one can imagine, this sort of poorly rationalized guilt projection can cause marital problems. But the origin of the feeling, in the projected position, "I don't want him near me," is the same as that of "He doesn't want me near him" and "I don't want to be near myself" in the misperceived and self-felt positions.

In the projected position, anger comes along with the projected guilt. Projected guilt is an expression of that anger which was previously repressed to form the added unconscious guilt. The more added unconscious guilt a person has, the greater the "need" to express anger. The projected position allows the expression of this anger, and this "need" to express anger goes hand in hand with the "need" to find fault or criticize. As the added unconscious guilt decreases, there is less of this "need." For instance, a man could live with a woman who leaves the cap off the toothpaste. Some mornings he comes out of the bathroom yelling, "Why the hell can't you put the top on the toothpaste?!" At other times, she can leave the top off and he doesn't say anything about it because, we can theorize, his added unconscious guilt is lower. Like any other condition of added unconscious guilt, when the added unconscious guilt decreases the criticism becomes less intense.

The condition of abusing alcohol could arise from the secondary feelings of added unconscious guilt in any of the three positions. In the self-felt position, the secondary feelings may be, "I drink to feel less stressed," "I drink to feel less of a need to work harder," "I drink to feel less unwanted," "I drink because I'm dissatisfied with myself," "I drink to escape myself." These thoughts come from the primary feelings so the person is actually saying, "I drink to make myself less inferior, less inadequate, less unacceptable, less wrong, less guilty, less a failure and less destined for trouble." The more added unconscious guilt that someone has in the self-felt position, the more intensified these feelings are and the greater his "need" to drink. As the added unconscious guilt decreases, the "need" to drink is reduced. The secondary feelings of alcohol abuse, in the misperceived position, would be, "I drink to lessen the feeling that you [they] expect me to work harder," "I drink to lessen the feeling that you're [they are] dissatisfied with me," "I drink to escape the way you [they] feel about me." Behind these secondary feelings are the misperceived primary feelings "They believe I'm inferior, inadequate, and unacceptable." The greater the added unconscious guilt, the more intense the primary and secondary feelings and the greater the "need" to drink. In the projected position, "I drink to lessen my dissatisfaction with them," "I drink to escape my feelings about them," are secondary feelings that lead to alcohol abuse. Alcohol lowers the feeling that, "They're inferior, inadequate, and unacceptable," that one has with projected added unconscious guilt.

Remember, alcohol will also lower the feelings associated with an increased unmet oral dependency need. The lack of emotionally gratifying relationships, perceptions of rejection from significant others, and loneliness, can also produce a "need" to drink in order to lower the level of the unmet oral dependency need. Anyone who abuses alcohol, then, does so for two different sets of reasons: *one*, in order to lower the unmet oral dependency need, and *two*, to lower the added unconscious guilt in one of the three positions.

The conditions of stress, depression, neurasthenia, anxiety attack, phobia, hypochondriasis, anhedonia, paranoia, jealousy, hypersensitivity, fault-finding, alcoholism, and many others are all rooted in added unconscious guilt in one of the three positions. The sudden appearance of one or more of these conditions in a person may be rationalized by the person. For instance, someone may say, "I never worried about my heart until I read an article on heart disease." The problem seems to have arisen after having some reality experience. One girl told me, "I didn't start worrying about cancer until my friend's mother died of it, and now I can't get it out of my mind." It seems as though the friend's mother's death caused her worry, but this is a deception. The experience only provides a focus for the already increased added unconscious guilt. It's analogous to the electrons that build up in a thundercloud and then coalesce into a lightning bolt that strikes a tree. It's the lightning and the struck tree that we see, not the electrons that had built up. Saying that the friend's mother's death caused the fear is like saying that a tree caused the lightning that struck it. The sudden fear of heart disease or cancer is analogous to sudden jealousy or the sudden expression of anger. The man whose fender was dented and who shot the driver that dented it, is a good example of the sudden appearance of coalesced added unconscious guilt. We said before that the man's anger had built up and he let it all out to the driver who dented the car. Now we can see that the added unconscious guilt had increased and then shifted to projected guilt, coalesced in a reality focus, allowing him to express his anger. The other driver provided a focus for the guilt, and it struck with an intensity that equaled the amount of added unconscious guilt. We can see that the driver who dented the fender did not cause the anger that was expressed. Likewise, the woman dying of cancer did not cause the girl's worry.

Another example of the sudden appearance of the added unconscious guilt is a patient I had who was unable to use a public men's room if there were other men in it, a type of hypersensitivity. He said that he never had the problem until he read a letter to a leading advice columnist from a man who had the same problem. Again, the focusing of the already increased added unconscious guilt was the cause of his sudden hypersensitivity, not reading the other man's letter.

The origin of the increased added unconscious guilt may be most difficult to see for there often is no discernible whole person, experience, or situation frustration of the oral dependency need. The oral frustrations might have all occurred on a part-oriented basis. Or rather than oral frustrations, there may have been undetectable accumulations of added unconscious guilt from losses of previous targets, both on a whole or part basis, for guilt projection. This, we know, can occur particularly when a person is too dependent on too few. The presented rationalization seems more logical as the cause of the condition. It's more understandable than the unconscious process of accumulating added unconscious guilt.

Many research psychiatrists believe that unrationalized conditions of depression, anxiety attack, phobia, or alcoholism are caused biochemically. Genetic and biochemical theories for the etiology of these conditions sound logical and scientific, and are easily understandable. They seem readily accepted by professionals, patients, relatives, and the public at large. Perhaps, though, looking for a biochemical explanation involving imbalanced brain microchemistry for any of the conditions is like trying to conclude why the Catholic Church has been working so well for almost 2000 years by examining only the molecular make-up of the mortar between the bricks of a cathedral. In examining the different mortars, one could find some interesting molecular structures. One might find that some mortars don't hold the bricks together as well as others, or that the lack of certain ingredients in mortar causes the bricks to come apart. All of this may be true, but it somehow fails to explain what makes one church function well for years and another fail to function. The reason may not be in the mortar between the bricks, even if differences are found. It would be a big deception if a theory of why a church functions well or not well is presented by those mortor specialists as due to what occurs minutely between the bricks.

Psychiatry, of late, has too emphatically embraced the notion that "the roots of mental illness lie at the cellular level." Saying that any unrationalized condition of added unconscious guilt is biochemical in origin may be a big deception. Psychiatry may be propagating this deception. To theorize that these conditions are the result of biochemical abnormalities is very logical and it does make sense. Consequently, it's a lot easier to get funding for such research. Researchers don't receive million-dollar grants from the government or private foundations for just listening. Perhaps the psychiatric research that needs to be done and is long overdue is not in the ivory tower of the laboratory, but out in the community, and not with microscopes and test tubes, but with an ear.

1. Adapted from: PSYCHODYNAMICS OF THE EMOTIONALLY UNCOMFORTABLE, Warren H. Green Publishing Company, St. Louis, MO 1979

CHAPTER 12
Comparing the Three Positions of Added Unconscious Guilt

Everyone knows that snow, ice, rain, fog, clouds, and steam are really different forms of the same basic thing. Yet they appear to be quite contrasting. You can see variations within each form as well. There are many different types of rain, and there are different forms of clouds. One Eskimo tribe has thirteen words for snow because they have distinguished thirteen types. This is analogous to added unconscious guilt. It appears in many different forms. We can make another analogy. Students of human behavior who examine added unconscious guilt must avoid the mistakes of the three blind men who examine the elephant. Each man feels a part of the elephant, and each comes away thinking that he knows what the whole elephant is. One man feels the tail and concludes, "The elephant is like a rope." Another man touches the animal's side and concludes, "No, the elephant is like a wall." The third feels the leg and says, "Oh, no, you're both wrong, the elephant is like a tree." But students of human behavior must touch the entire elephant to really get a good understanding of the whole animal.

We have looked at each position of added unconscious guilt and seen its different forms. As we can see ice, water, and steam have very different consequences, we can see that each position of added unconscious guilt has very different consequences, too. But we must keep in mind that ice, water, and steam are different forms of the same entity. Likewise, each of the positions—the self-felt, the misperceived, and the projected—are different forms of the same entity: added unconscious guilt. Like water with its various forms, we can appreciate the great variations that added guilt can take without losing sight of the fact that beneath or behind what is so contrastingly different is a common entity. So let's in this chapter compare the three forms of added unconscious guilt in an overview.

In the self-felt position, someone negatively labels him or herself. In the misperceived position, he or she feels negatively labeled by someone else or by others. In the projected position, he or she negatively labels someone else. The higher the added unconscious guilt in each position, the more intense the negative labeling becomes while the lower the added unconscious guilt, the less intense. The negative labeling will have a specific reality focus in each of the three positions. The consequences of each position are quite different, but calling yourself a failure, feeling that someone else calls you a failure, or calling someone else a failure (to use failure as an example of negative labeling), all come from the same basic added unconscious guilt. So do the feelings, "My work is inferior," "My wife thinks I'm unattractive," and "His son's reading preferences are no good." Even though these feelings sound so different, they all arise from the same entity. One can have depression leading to suicide, marriage problems leading to divorce, or a neighborhood crusade to eliminate pornography. But like snow, rain and steam, they are all forms of the same thing.

In the self-felt position, the person makes derogatory remarks about him or herself or about anything associated or identified with him or herself. In the misperceived position, he or she feels that others are making derogatory remarks about him or her or about anything associated or identified with him or her. And in the projected position, he or she makes derogatory remarks about someone else or about others or anything associated or identified with them. With enough added unconscious guilt in the self-felt position, someone can actually loathe him or herself. In the misperceived position, he or she can feel loathed. And in the projected position, he or she can loathe someone else or others.

People in the self-felt position seem to have a "need" to belittle or degrade themselves. They're down on themselves. They don't seem to respect, approve of, or even want to be around themselves. If we listen to people in the misperceived position, they seem to "need" to feel that others belittle or degrade them. They feel put down. They feel that others don't respect them or approve of them, and that others don't want to be around them. And people in the projected position seem to have a "need" to belittle or degrade other people. They're down on somebody else. They don't seem to respect or approve of others; they don't seem to want to be around other people. When we listen to people talk from the self-felt position, we may reach the conclusion that they need to think better of themselves. If they were in the misperceived position, we'd conclude that they need to feel that others think better of them. And if they were in the projected position, we'd say that they need to think better of others. The person in the self-felt position asks himself, "How can I be a better person?" The person feels he doesn't "measure up" and wants to improve himself. In the misperceived position, he asks, "How can others perceive that I'm a better person?" This person feels that someone else feels, or others feel, he doesn't "measure up" and that someone else or others want the person to improve himself. In the projected position, it's, "How can someone else or others be a better person or people?" The person feels someone else doesn't "measure up" and wants this someone else to improve himself.

The person in the self-felt position, who, because of her primary and secondary feelings is always down on herself often appears to have an *inferiority complex*. The more added unconscious guilt there is in the self-felt position, the more an inferiority complex may be evident to other people. It's not evident to the person, for she feels that she is simply perceiving facts of reality. Someone with an inferiority complex seems verbally abusive to herself. She may say, "I'm strange, weird," "I'm so ugly and fat," "I don't do anything well." An example of someone with an inferiority complex is the young teacher who came to see me. She was good in her field and several times had been given the "Outstanding Teacher of the Year" award. Anyone who knew her would say she was an exceptionally nice woman. She brought a paper on which she was going to list her assets and her liabilities, as a popular magazine had suggested for people who were down on themselves. She had made a long list of her liabilities, but she said she couldn't think of a single asset. She tearfully told me, "If I am to be perfectly honest, there isn't a single thing I can put in the asset column!" She was feeling, "I'm not O.K.," which encompasses many other feelings that make up an inferiority complex. An inferiority complex stresses only certain of the primary and secondary feelings of the self-felt position. Someone in the self-felt position though may not appear to have so much of an inferiority complex; she may instead emphasize the feeling of impending trouble or disaster. Or she may experience stress, depression, phobias, excessive worrying, or anxiety attacks. But usually when someone is in the self-felt position, you can see some evidence of a not so underlying inferiority complex, even if she is more blatantly exhibiting some other manifestation of the self-felt added unconscious guilt or emphasizing one of its primary feelings more than others. These people always show a problem in accepting themselves.

The person in the misperceived position, whose primary and secondary feelings cause him to feel put down by others, has what we could term a *rejection complex*. The rejection complex is completely analogous to the inferiority complex of the self-felt position; it involves the emphasis on the same feelings but with a different reference. Again, a rejection complex is not evident to the person, though it may be to others, because that person feels he is simply perceiving facts of reality. If the teacher who came to see me had been in the misperceived position, she would have said, perhaps referring to another teacher, "He doesn't think I'm

O.K." With a rejection complex, someone feels that others are verbally abusive to him. He may feel, "She thinks I'm ugly, because she suggested that I change my hair," or, "He said that we should change our eating habits because he thinks I'm too fat." "He tells me that everything I do is wrong" is another perception of someone with a rejection complex might have. These people show a problem in feeling accepted by others.

We should recognize that true reality can range from a situation in which the person *is* being rejected, but doesn't feel rejected, to one in which the person is *not* being rejected in any way, but feels rejected. In the former case the person's perception is being influenced by a high level of oral dependency need gratification, while in the latter the person's high level of misperceived added unconscious guilt is causing him to perceive rejection where absolutely none exists. Between these two situations is a mixture of the emotional unreality and true reality which the unconscious must handle.

In the projected position, when these feelings are made referable to someone else, we could say that the person has a *fault-finding complex*. The fault-finding complex is analogous to the self-felt inferiority complex, where the person finds fault with him or herself, and to the misperceived rejection complex, where someone perceives that others are finding fault with him or her. Someone with a fault-finding complex finds fault with others and is always putting someone else down. This person seems to show a problem accepting someone else. It may be totally or it may be some aspect of the other person's past or anything specifically associated or identified with that person in the present. This unacceptance may even be made referable to this person's future. Again, having a fault-finding complex is not evident to the person, though it may be to others, because that person feels that she is simply perceiving facts of reality. If the teacher with the list had been in the projected position, she would have said about someone else, "He doesn't have a single asset," feeling, "He's not O.K.." These are the people who verbally abuse others. They may say, "He's strange, he's weird," "Maybe she wouldn't be so ugly if she changed her hair," "You should go on a diet; you're too fat," or "You can't do anything right." Although these complexes seem different and appear to be different in origin, they all stem from the same basic added unconscious guilt.

In the self-felt position, the feelings that are emphasized may make up a *guilt complex*. Feelings that are common in a self-felt guilt complex are, "It's my fault," "I'm to blame." A detailed rationalization oriented to reality usually accompanies the expression of the feelings associated with a guilt complex and are presented as though that reality is the origin of the feeling of guilt. Someone could say, for instance, "I caused my grandfather's fatal heart attack because I was too heavy a child for him to carry." As another example, a short time ago I talked to a woman who said, "I feel so guilty, and whenever I look at my son I break down and cry because I remember that I actually considered getting an abortion when I was pregnant with him ten years ago. How could I have thought such a terrible thing?" This woman's guilt complex is easy to see. Her self-felt feelings, with the emphasis on guilt, are coming from a rise in her added unconscious guilt in the present, but she is blaming something that happened ten years ago as a rationalization for her guilt complex. Her thoughts of having considered an abortion are a rationalization. They are not the origin of her feelings of guilt at all. Yet she believes they are, and although she probably won't tell anyone else about this except her therapist or counselor, the therapist or counselor will probably also believe they are. A rationalization is never the origin for the feeling. This becomes even more evident when we contrast what this woman said with another rationalization for guilt that I recently heard. Another woman told me that she felt dreadfully guilty because she *didn't* consider an abortion some years before. She said that her husband had dropped out of college to support her during the pregnancy and now, because he never got his degree, he has to do manual labor. "I feel so guilty that I break down and cry every day when I see him leave for work because I know he's not doing what he wanted to do," self-felt added unconscious guilt *in the present*, and her decision not to have an abortion is but a rationalization that creates her guilt complex. Her rationalization contrasts interestingly with the first woman's rationalization and demonstrates that, as with the inferiority complex, someone can always find something in reality on which to base her feelings, in this case, a guilt complex.

People in the misperceived position feel that someone else is giving them a *guilt trip*, or that someone else feels they are to blame. They'll say, "She's trying to make me feel guilty," or, "He tries to give me a guilt trip whenever I talk to him." Or, "She's a master of the guilt trip," which implies that the person is perceiving, "She feels I'm guilty." Someone in the misperceived position might say, "Mother thinks I caused my grandfather's fatal heart attack because she thinks I was too heavy a child for him to carry." The misperceived feelings of guilt are there but they are felt as being placed there by someone else. If the person were not in the misperceived position, nobody would be able to give him or her a guilt trip. In the self-felt position, one gives oneself a guilt trip; in the misperceived position, one believes that someone else is trying to make him feel guilty, even if, in reality, this is not the case. If the other person doesn't say anything to "try to make me feel guilty," then it's often felt as implied, as evidenced by, "I can tell by the way she looks at me," or, "I can tell by the way he acts when I come into the room." Or one may present other reality-oriented rationalizations as to why the other person tries to make him feel guilty. But whether in the self-felt or misperceived position, the guilt-oriented rationalization comes from the increased added unconscious guilt.

The person who actually does try to make someone else feel guilty is in the projected position. This person feels that someone else *is* to blame, or that someone else *should* feel guilty. He usually gives an explanation of why the other person should feel guilty, but, again, it's a rationalization. He might say, "You ought to feel guilty for not going to visit my sister in the hospital after all that she's done for you," or "You should feel guilty about behaving like a fool at the company picnic," or, "You caused your grandfather's fatal heart attack because you were too heavy a child for him to carry." The mother might say to her teen-aged son, "You should be ashamed of yourself for going out with your room looking like a tornado hit it." The other person may or may not feel guilty, depending on how much added unconscious guilt he has in one of the other two positions and how that guilt is focused. For example, if the teenager's mother says, "You should be ashamed of yourself," and the young man has plenty of friends to gratify his oral dependency need, his room may very well stay messy. However, if he's too dependent on too few and has a lot of added unconscious guilt in the self-felt position, he may feel guilty and clean his room instead of going out. If he works hard at cleaning his room, foregoing any pleasure, he can, we know, decrease his self-felt added unconscious guilt and feel less guilty. Pleasing his mother by cleaning his room may improve his oral dependency need situation with her and might decrease the amount of added unconscious guilt she projects to him. Once again, the relationship between the three positions may be difficult to see, but if we look deeper, below the rationalization, we can readily see that the feeling of guilt is coming from recently increased added unconscious guilt in one of the three positions and that the rationalization provides a deceptive origin for that guilt.

Another interesting aspect of the self-felt position is what we could call a *failure complex*. The failure complex can be an orientation of the added unconscious guilt to the future. The person in the self-felt position may feel that he or she is going to fail. Remember the postal worker who couldn't take a test because he was sure he'd fail, and the girl who could not drive a car when faced with the driving test because she felt that she was going to fail. Neither of them may feel that he or she is a failure in the present or that either has been a failure in the past, but each is very sure that he or she *will* fail. In the misperceived position, the person feels that someone else expects him or her to fail, and in the projected position, the person feels that someone else is going to fail. The failure complex, coming from either position, could spread out to include the person's past and present.

The inferiority complex emphasized the self-felt primary feelings of inferiority, inadequacy, and unacceptableness and self-felt secondary feelings like, "I'm ugly," or, "I can't do anything well." The guilt complex emphasized the primary feelings of guilt and wrongness and secondary feelings like, "It's my fault," or, "I'm to blame." Emphasis on the secondary feeling, "I'm going to fail," produces the failure complex. With the emphasis on different primary and secondary feelings, in the self-felt position, someone could be self-punishing. *Masochism* emphasizes secondary feelings like, "I deserve to be punished," "I should hurt myself," "I should suffer pain or humiliation," or, "I deserve to be punished, hurt, abused, humiliated or tortured." These secondary feelings are analogous to those that we saw in the inferiority complex, the guilt complex and the failure complex, but now they seem to make up the complex we know as masochism. Masochism does not require a sexual theory for its development as the psychoanalysts propose. The basis of masochism is not at all sexual. The need to hurt oneself can, however, take on a sexual orientation, just as the inferiority complex, the guilt complex, or the failure complex may take on a sexual orientation, but it, like those complexes, may focus solely on other aspects of reality. The psychodynamic base of masochism is not sexual; it's the self-felt added unconscious guilt arising from all those ways that we have seen that can increase added unconscious guilt. It doesn't have to take a sexual orientation at all. A masochist may cut or burn himself in other than a sexual area. He may decide to scar his face. With enough added unconscious guilt, he may decide to kill himself in one final act of punishment.

Masochism can, however, have a sexual orientation, as can feelings of inferiority, guilt, and failure. Masochism with a sexual focus can produce some interesting sexual preferences. A masochistic woman may have rape fantasies, which are sexually-oriented manifestations of this need to be hurt or punished. This type of fantasy also incorporates anhedonia, that feeling of "I don't deserve pleasure," with a sexual orientation. However, one may or may not see the anhedonia in other aspects of her life as well. She may unconsciously think, "I don't deserve any pleasure. However, if I am attacked and raped, I can have sexual pleasure because it's not really *me* that's initiating it; it's somebody else who's doing it *to* me against my will." Rape fantasies are not uncommon and many women have told me they have them.

I recently saw a capable, successful business woman who confided that she could only have sex when she would tell her husband that she was going into the bedroom to "take a nap." He knows when she says that that he can wait a few minutes, then tip-toe into the bedroom and have sex with her. It's as though they're playing a game, with her pretending that she is asleep and that she really doesn't know what he's about to do or what she's about to enjoy. This "game" fits with her self-felt added unconscious guilt; she doesn't feel that she deserves pleasure. But that same anhedonia and masochism in regard to her work have made her most successful in reality.

One can see other aspects of masochism with a sexual orientation. For instance, some people, both males and females, want to be tied to the bed to have sex. Again, this preference is not uncommon. With their arms and legs tied to the bed, they unconsciously think that they're not really participating in the sexual pleasure; it's being forced on them. Others cannot become sexually aroused unless they are being verbally abused with the most foul or obscene words. Still other people want to be beaten or have physical pain inflicted upon them before they can experience sexual pleasure. Some people even like the beating to be accompanied by the threat of being killed. These masochistic sexual preferences, bondage and dominance, stemming from self-felt added unconscious guilt, are not uncommon among members of either sex. Adult bookstores make fortunes selling materials depicting such practices. Some men become sexually aroused by women in black leather boots and Nazi outfits, cracking whips at them, because they have added unconscious guilt in the self-felt position which is sexually-oriented. Pictures and films of the same are sold in surprisingly large numbers. Some people, as we've said, actually want to have pain inflicted upon them. The pain assuages their added unconscious guilt so that the feelings, "I don't deserve pleasure" and "I deserve to be deprived" decrease, and they can allow themselves to experience sexual pleasure. These are the people who have to be beaten or hurt before they can enjoy sex. Prostitutes can tell bizarre stories about the strange things involving sexual masochism that some of their customers request. There are also people in the self-felt position who cannot have sex unless they've been drinking. Alcohol is similar to being beaten, in this case, because it lowers the added unconscious guilt enough to allow the person to experience sexual pleasure.

In the misperceived position, *paranoia* is analogous to masochism. The paranoid person feels that somebody is out to take advantage of her, to "use" her, to hurt her, to punish her, or even to torture her. Someone else is verbally abusive, threatens physical abuse, or threatens to kill her, according to the perceptions of the paranoid person. Paranoia can also have any focus in reality at all. Like masochism, its origin is not in sexual psychodynamics as the psychoanalysts believe, but in the increased misperceived added unconscious guilt. The paranoid person could believe that someone is trying to poison her, as in the case of the woman who thought her groceries were poisoned. Or the paranoid person could believe she is being followed, as did the woman who felt that the other cars on the highway were following her.

Paranoia can have a sexual orientation as in the case of a woman who feels that someone is following her in order to rape her or otherwise sexually abuse her. A psychiatrist friend of mine saw a successful enlisted woman who happened to be the daughter of a nationally-known general. She claimed that she had been raped on a military base where she had been recently assigned. This caused a scandal because a military base is supposed to have higher standards of discipline and personal safety, with more enforced regulations than the outside world. But she made the accusation that she'd been raped, and it quickly produced an extensive investigation. Although she described her assailant, no positive identification could be made so there were no arrests. Furthermore, it was discovered that the door and the windows of the room where she reported that the rape had occurred were locked from the inside and showed no evidence of any break-in. The base gynecologist, upon examining her right after the alleged attack, could find no evidence of rape. But still she claimed that she'd been raped. Her father in Washington got involved and ordered the base commander to find the assailant and arrest him or the commander's own military career would be at stake. Even a congressman looked into the case, but no arrest was ever made. This woman later visited my friend at the mental health clinic on another base because she was depressed, and her "nerves" were bad, she said, due to the rape. My friend's evaluation of her case was that she hadn't been raped at all and that she was paranoid. Her added unconscious guilt in the misperceived position had built up, and her paranoia had reached a level that caused her to believe that she had been raped. She was a person who didn't have many close friends and always had difficulty making any friends. She was new to the particular base where the alleged rape occurred, and, in throwing herself anhedonically into her work because she felt that her new supervisor expected it, hadn't become close to anyone. She had left her only close friend at her previous military base. Her traits suggest that she had a high personality core guilt and that, with the difficulties of a new location, it would have been easy for her to accrue a lot of misperceived added unconscious guilt.

Analogous to masochism and paranoia is *sadism*. Sadism emphasizes the same feelings as masochism and paranoia but in the projected position. Secondary feelings like, "He deserves to be punished," "I should degrade him," "I should abuse her," and, "I should torture her" are emphasized in sadism. Like masochism and paranoia, sadism is a manifestation of added unconscious guilt; it does not have a sexual psychodynamic base as the psychoanalysts have proposed. It can be oriented to any aspect of reality. We have spoken of a woman who burned her child with a cigarette. Many cases of child abuse and spouse abuse involve sadism, and this sadism may or may not show itself in the person's sex life. It is the projected added unconscious guilt that makes the person want to abuse, mutilate, torture or even kill someone else.

However, as with masochism and paranoia, sadism can have a sexual orientation. Someone may "need" to be verbally abusive in order to become sexually aroused. Or the person must physically abuse someone to experience sexual pleasure. He or she may want to tie the other person to the bed, to beat the person, or even to threaten the person with death. He or she can then have sex with someone because this other has been abused or punished. The adult bookstores also make money from this sort of clientele selling them magazines, books, and movies. People whose feelings and fantasies of sadism are sexually-oriented find these materials to be a "turn-on." Again this sexually-oriented sadism is not uncommon; prostitutes can tell bizarre stories of hurtful and often disfiguring experiences to which they have been subjected by sexual sadists.

Sometimes in relationships that involve sex, one person wants to tie the other to the bed, but the other person objects. Or one person may want to be tied to the bed and the other does not want to tie him. Sadism and masochism can cause incompatibility in sexual relationships. But if the sadist marries or becomes sexually involved with the masochist, they may be very compatible sexually. One abuses and the other seems to love it. One feels, "I deserve to be punished and hurt," the other feels, "He or she deserves to be punished and hurt,"; sexually, they can live in bliss. This is completely analogous to a frequently occurring form of spouse abuse. One is sadistically abusive; the other masochistically accepts this abuse. They want no interference from outsiders who attempt to intervene to stop the abuse. They're compatible in an abusive relationship, like two consenting adults may be compatible in any sexual relationship. It is only when one person who is masochistic becomes less this way with a decrease in self-felt added unconscious guilt that the person is more prone to get help to stop the abuse.

There are people who like to be verbally abused or who like to verbally abuse, but only when they have an increase in added unconscious guilt. The amount of added unconscious guilt in the self-felt position may determine whether or not a person would like to be tied to the bed. If the person in the self-felt position's masochism is sexually-oriented, she may derive sexual pleasure from being verbally abused. As the added unconscious guilt increases, she may want to be whipped. The added unconscious guilt could increase to the delusional level; the feelings of "I don't deserve pleasure," "I deserve to be punished, abused, and mutilated" increase so much that the man may attempt to cut off his penis. The woman may burn or attempt to cut off her breasts. With sexually-oriented paranoia, someone may feel that she is being followed by someone else who is going to rape her. As her added unconscious guilt increases, she may become more and more convinced that she will be raped. If it reaches the delusional level, she might believe that she has been raped, as the general's daughter did. If projected added unconscious guilt increases, the person whose sadism is sexually oriented could want to beat someone instead of just verbally abusing him. If it reaches the delusional level, he could burn the breast of or castrate someone else believing perhaps that the someone else is a witch or the devil. The intensity of the secondary feelings that make up all these different complexes increases or decreases reflecting the level of the underlying added unconscious guilt.

There seems to be a great difference in wanting to be hurt and wanting to hurt, in having a rape fantasy and thinking that someone is following you in another car, in abusing a child and becoming sexually aroused by being tied to a bed. But all of these different behaviors come from added unconscious guilt. All of them in their common origin are similar to, "You should be ashamed of yourself," "I feel guilty because I thought of having an abortion," "They think I'm ugly," and, "She's never really loved me but only married me for my money." Although it can be very different in its behavioral manifestations in reality, the added unconscious guilt is at the root of all of these expressions and behaviors. They're all deceptively different parts of the same elephant.

Someone in the self-felt position with a lot of added unconscious guilt often has a detectable inferiority complex, a guilt complex, and a failure complex, to some degree, as well as a certain degree of masochism. We can see the psychodymanic commonality between putting oneself down, feeling guilty, feeling that one is going to fail, and feeling that one deserves abuse and not pleasure. Many of these feelings and behaviors could all be summed up in the second feeling, "I'm dissatisfied with myself," for whatever reality-oriented reason given. With more added unconscious guilt, this becomes, "I dislike myself," and with still more, "I hate myself." With still more added unconscious guilt, one might feel, "I deserve to die," and may make arrangements to kill himself. If his added unconscious guilt increases enough, he does kill himself. The increased added unconscious guilt in the self-felt position is the cause of suicide. A rationalization is only incidental. Recently, I saw on the national news that a farmer had lost his farm because of economic problems and had committed suicide. It looks as if he lost the farm and, therefore, committed suicide. But losing the farm didn't *directly* cause him to commit suicide. Thousands of other farmers who are losing their farms don't commit suicide. Thousands of others each year who don't seem to have lost anything of value do commit suicide. Other people, who have had millions of dollars and seemingly, therefore, every reason to live, have committed suicide. It's the added unconscious guilt that is the direct cause of the suicide, not a rationalization that looks as if it makes sense. If losing the farm had anything to do with this farmer's suicide, it would have been that he met his oral dependency needs and got rid of added unconscious guilt by working hard on his farm and talking to his farm hands. Perhaps when he lost his farm, he lost much of his oral dependency need gratification, and he may have had no close confiding friends with whom to talk over his problems. But even if this were the case, it's still his added unconscious guilt that directly caused the suicide. If one has enough accrued added unconscious guilt in the self-felt position, he'll find a reason to kill himself, whether he loses a farm or not. One might easily speculate about this farmer who lost his farm and accrued a high level of added unconscious guilt, that if his added unconscious guilt had taken the projected position, he might have shot and killed the banker who held his mortgage. If one has enough projected added unconscious guilt, even though he hasn't lost a farm, he can always find some other rationalization under which to kill.

In the misperceived position, the commonality is between, "They put me down," "They try to give me a guilt trip," "They think I'm going to fail," and "They feel that I deserve abuse." These feelings can be summed up as, "They are dissatisfied with me" for whatever the reality-oriented reason. With still more added unconscious guilt, "They dislike me," for whatever reason, and with even more, "They hate me," then, "They feel I deserve to die." With still more added unconscious guilt, "They are going to kill me," as the person becomes even more paranoid.

In the projected position, "I should put them down," "They are guilty," "They are going to fail," and "They deserve abuse," can be summed up as, "I am dissatisfied with them," for whatever the reason may be. With still more added unconscious guilt, it becomes, "I dislike them," and with even more, "I hate them." With still more added unconscious guilt, the person feels, "They deserve to die" and makes plans to kill "them." If the added unconscious guilt increases enough, the person will actually kill; any reason given is just a rationalization.

Added unconscious guilt in the projected position is the basis for murder. In the misperceived position, it's the basis for paranoia, and in the self-felt position, for suicide. Suicide, paranoia, and murder, then, are completely analogous. The analysts have always theorized that suicide is murder, turned 180°. What we are presenting is that added unconscious guilt is at the root of suicide and of murder and that both suicide and murder are completely analogous to paranoia. All three behaviors have a common relationship; they are all manifestations of added unconscious guilt in the extreme. Each of these behaviors is like the tail, the side, and the trunk of the elephant; they are all parts of the same entity. Like ice, rain, and steam, all three appear to be different entities in reality with different consequences. The characteristics may appear to be most contrasting; consider, for instance, the characteristics of a person feeling unlovable, with those of a person feeling that someone else (perhaps even the person he loves) finds him unlovable, and finally a person who feels that someone else is unlovable (perhaps even her child). Each person in each case not only contrasts with the others, but also the consequences in reality are contrasting. The same is true of murdering someone, believing that someone is going to kill you, and killing yourself. All may appear contrasting in reality yet are essentially added unconscious guilt.

We can see the added unconscious guilt in regard to the way it influences how man thinks and feels from the three different positions throughout recorded history. One of the oldest books known to man is the Bible, in which we can interestingly see reflections of the positions of added unconscious guilt. In studying the Bible, one may conclude that the Old Testament seems to have a different philosophy from that of the New Testament. In the Old Testament, we want to feel that God is with us, and we are admonished to keep His commandments, one of which we have already seen—the first commandment: to worship only God and to have no other gods before Him. In doing so, God will protect us from our enemies. The Old Testament God, we learn, can get very angry. We do not want to bring the wrath of God down upon ourselves by not keeping His commandments. It's important that He doesn't get angry at us, but rather that He gets angry at our enemies. In the Old Testament we are told that although He may be slow to anger, He is a punishing God. If we keep His commandments, He will punish our enemies and not us. The philosophy of the New Testament, in contrast to the Old, is that God is love and that God is a forgiving God. We are admonished to turn the other cheek, to walk the extra mile, and to put others first. In contrast to the Old Testament, we are told to love our enemies. This is in contrast to the Old Testament where God is often killing people such as the Egyptians, the Canaanites, the Philistines, to name just a few. Added unconscious guilt is clearly taking the projected position. The New Testament philosophy has a message for people in the self-felt position who feel that they deserve to turn the other cheek, that they should walk the extra mile and that they should willingly bear their crosses. These people are more guilt-laden; they already feel sinful and feel the need to atone for their guilt and sin. To "love your enemies" almost implies masochism because our enemies are out to hurt us.

A person in the self-felt position may feel sinful if his rationalizations are taking a religious orientation. He may be worried about going to heaven and may feel that he is living in sin. He wants to concentrate on God, to keep thoughts pure and clean. It's this person, when his added unconscious guilt has increased, who feels that he might lost control, jump up in the middle of a sermon and yell something obscene, thus feeling even more of a need to keep his thoughts clean. I had one patient, a grey-haired pillar of the neighborhood church, who came to see me dreadfully fearing that she might stand up in church during a sermon and yell, "Fuck you!" thereby showing everyone how sinful she was. The feeling, "I need to be other than I am," takes on a religious orientation. The person may feel, "I'm not a good Christian so I need to be saved." He is not satisfied with the way he is religiously; he is not pious enough. I've had patients, in the self-felt position, tell me that they've almost worn out their jeans at the knees from praying so much. These people feel that they've been living in sin, they are living in sin, and they will be living in sin unless they change themselves and their behavior.

The person in the misperceived position feels that someone else believes she is sinful, that she should be other than she is. This person may feel, "They don't think I'm a good Christian and they know I need to be saved." This person believes that others are not satisfied with the way she is religiously and that others feel that she is not pious enough. If this person wears out her jeans at the knees, it's because, "The other people at church (or "my priest" or "minister," or "my mother,") feel I should pray more." She might say that others feel she has been, is, and will be living in sin unless she changes her behavior.

Someone in the projected position feels that others are sinful and should be worried about going to heaven. He feels that someone else "needs to be other than she is." Proponents of religious faiths that proselytize might easily use added unconscious guilt in the projected position. As such, they might feel that a group of nonbelievers are living in sin and they they should change their ways. These nonbelievers have to be shown, the proponents feel, that they're religiously wrong (and religiously inferior, inadequate, unacceptable, and headed for trouble) and that, as such, they should be worried about going to heaven.

Certain well-known passages from the Bible can be seen from the three positions. Verses like, "The meek shall inherit the earth," preach a promise to people in the self-felt position. In the New Testament, where a woman is about to be stoned for the commission of adultery, Jesus said to the crowd, "He who is without sin cast the first stone." The people in the crowd must have all been in the self-felt position because the woman was not stoned. If he had said the same thing to a crowd of people in the projected position, the woman would probably have been stoned to death in a matter of minutes. There do seem to be many people in this world with lots of added unconscious guilt in the projected position. Some have enough to kill for religious reasons. Wherever the Pope goes, he must ride in a car with bullet-proof glass because there have already been several attempts on his life. We could speculate that if Jesus were to come back to earth, He'd have to do so in a bullet-proof car, otherwise someone with a high enough level of added unconscious guilt in the projected position would surely shoot Him. But note that this very same amount of added unconscious guilt taking a religious orientation in the self-felt position makes, by contrast, a saint.

Taken from the three positions, certain Biblical teachings have very different connotations. For instance, someone in the self-felt position may ask, "What greater gift is there than for me to lay down my life for someone else?" But someone in the misperceived position feels, "They feel that there is no greater gift than for me to lay down my life for someone else." Someone in the projected position might ask, "What greater gift is there than for you to lay down your life for someone else?" Only a person with increased added unconscious guilt in the self-felt position could think of no greater gift. A person with an equal amount of guilt in the projected position might come up with a lot of painful ones.

We can also see certain things from more recent history from the three positions. For instance take Nathan Hale, a hero of the American Revolution. He was a schoolteacher who was captured by the British as a spy and sentenced to hanging. Before his execution he said, "I regret that I have but one life to give for my country." Such great acts of patriotism are always inspired by the self-felt position of high levels of added unconscious guilt. In the misperceived position, he would have said, "They regret that I have but one life to give for my country." In the projected position, the sentencing judge might have said, "I regret that you have but one life to give for your country." During the Second World War, the Korean War, or the Vietnam War, a young man might have said, "They feel I should serve my country," from the misperceived position with "they" representing his family, or other Americans, or maybe the Draft Board. The self-felt position is, "I should serve my country," and the projected, "He should serve his country."

It has been said that the written history of man is but a record of wars. Wars have been fought for countless reality reasons: to gain territory, to gain the power to govern that territory, to overthrow governments, to stamp out certain religions and to propagate others, to break away from a country, for ideological reasons and many others. But these reality-oriented reasons for wars are not the actual cause of the wars. War itself is a patriotic rationalization for murder that is supported by society, and murder, we've already learned, is projected added unconscious guilt in the extreme. One might theorize that acts of terrorism and wars will continue as long as there are large amounts of added unconscious guilt in the projected position. But without added unconscious guilt in the projected position, how would one correct that which "should" be corrected? It takes high levels of projected added unconscious guilt that can be sustained to stamp out injustice, crime, corruption, sin, and those "false" religions. The projected position, in making others wrong, makes the person feel he or she is right in perceptions of just what these categories are.

Rationalized high levels of added unconscious guilt in each of the three positions can produce vastly contrasting behavior. Great acts of "good" and terrible acts of "evil" have a common basis in added unconscious guilt—they're just different parts of the same animal.

CHAPTER 13
Understanding the Most Important Psychodynamic Relationship

Now that we understand some of the consequences of added unconscious guilt in the three positions and see the commonality between them, let's take a step back to observe the relationship between added unconscious guilt and oral dependency need gratification. Their relationship is like that of two children playing on a seesaw. As one child goes up in the air, the other goes down. So, too, with added unconscious guilt and oral dependency need gratification; as one increases, the other decreases. The consequences of this inversely proportional relationship, in regard to the feelings the two entities produce, are rather interesting. In this chapter, we will look more closely at the relationship and its consequences.

The more oral dependency need gratification we have, the better we feel about ourselves. Oral dependency need gratification is the origin of a good self-image and of self-esteem. Oral dependency need gratification is the source of a sense of self-worth. These feelings about the self, of course, can always be rationalized and given some deceptive source in reality. However, when our oral dependency need gratification decreases, so does our sense of self-worth, our self-esteem, and our good self-image. Some people say, "You need to learn how to think better of yourself." We see books and magazine articles that claim to teach us how to improve our self-image. But we cannot *learn* to value ourselves; we can only improve our feelings of self-worth, our self-image and our self-esteem through an emotional, not an intellectual process. With added unconscious guilt, we have a low sense of self-worth, low self-esteem, and a poor self-image. We can see reflections of these feelings in each of the three positions. All of these things can be rationalized by using something in reality that makes sense, but they too have an emotional origin, tied to added unconscious guilt.

As we saw in Chapter Two, with increasing perceived oral dependency need gratification, one is better able to withstand discomfort, frustration, stress, and pain. In medicine now, a popular issue is PMS, or premenstrual syndrome. One of the most respected medical centers on the East

197

Coast now has a PMS clinic. A woman suffering from PMS character-istically has depression, irritability, a lack of energy, a low tolerance for stress and frustration, and pain. These symptoms are given a biological explanation; many doctors believe the changes in a woman's body just before and during menstruation cause them. There is no way to measure the physical pain that these biochemical changes may cause. And one can never say that a person is not feeling pain. The feeling of pain is never imagined; so when a woman with PMS complains of pain, we know she's experiencing pain. One may also say, "Who wouldn't get depressed, tired, and irritable if one's having severe pain?" It's a good argument, for the severity of perceived pain is not measurable; "severe pain" is always in the eye of the beholder. But when a woman with PMS is un-consciously perceiving more oral dependency need gratification, she won't perceive the pain as severe. When the woman is unconsciously perceiving much less oral dependency need gratification, pain will be experienced as more severe. Similarly, someone may complain of head-ache. There are clinics for people who have degrees of constant pain that nothing seems to help. Again, we are not saying that these people are not having pain. However, if we see that the person does not have an emotional involvement in a wide sphere of oral dependency need gratifying relationships and, particularly, is too dependent on too few, we can surmise that he has less ability to withstand pain.

If the person is perceiving more oral dependency need gratification, the better able he is to put up with any pain. For instance, a man may have a severe headache but when some of his good friends come over and say, "Let's go to a movie," he may go out. If we were to observe him during that evening, perhaps we wouldn't see too much evidence of his headache. If he'd stayed at home, he might have gotten the hot water bottle out, taken some aspirin, lain on the couch, and complained about his pain. Get this man with the headache out among other people, where he's getting his oral dependency needs met, and his head doesn't seem to bother him as much. With more perceived oral dependency need gratification, he might not experience his headache so severely because he'd have more of an ability to withstand pain, discomfort, stress, and frustration.

In contrast, consider added unconscious guilt. Accompanying the added unconscious guilt is an inability to withstand pain. As added un-conscious guilt increases, oral dependency need gratification decreases. That same man with a headache has a low level of perceived oral de-pendency need gratification and a high level of unmet oral need and added unconscious guilt. With that high level of added unconscious guilt he has less ability to withstand pain. But when he is out with his good friends, he projects some added unconscious guilt so that his guilt level is lowered. Now he has less added unconscious guilt, because of his emotional involvement with his friends, and he is better able to withstand pain. The importance of being able to perceive oral dependency need gratification *and* being able to project guilt in the relationship sphere should be apparent. Inversely proportional as the two processes are, they dovetail each other in producing the same outcome. In this example, it's less experienced pain for the man with the headache who gets off the couch and gets emotionally involved with his friends.

Many doctors believe that more than ninety percent of headaches are attributable to stress. When our added unconscious guilt is up, we have a greater inability to withstand the pressure that comes with the secondary feelings we've discussed. But when our oral dependency need gratification is up, we perceive less tension. We cannot learn to put up with stress any more than we can learn to put up with pain. Some people, for instance, do have to endure pain because of severe physical problems. If someone has injured his back, for example, and has a lot of pain, it doesn't help to tell him, "You'll have to learn to tolerate the pain." Meeting more of his oral dependency need and decreasing his added unconscious guilt make him better able to contend with the pain. He is also better able to contend with any stress.

As oral dependency need gratification increases, we have more of a feeling of contentment, but as added unconscious guilt increases, we feel more discontented with ourselves, or we feel that someone else or others are discontented with us, or we feel discontented about someone else or others, when the discontent is viewed from all three positions. A man came in to see me several years ago, and told me that he knew that he was nice looking, at the physical peak of his life, with a good job, making a lot of money, and had every reason, in reality, to be content. But, he told me, he was depressed and wanted to commit suicide. He contrasted himself to a boy he had seen a few days before he came in. He said that a car had driven up to his house and a boy got out and came to the door, collecting for an organization to benefit the mentally retarded. The boy was obviously mentally retarded and deformed, with every reality reason to be depressed, but he had a big smile on his face that radiated happiness. It's oral dependency need gratification that gives that feeling of happiness, not anything in reality. It's the increased added unconscious guilt which makes us feel unhappy.

With oral dependency need gratification, we believe that everything's going to be all right. We feel secure. But with added unconscious guilt, we feel insecure—that everything is not going to be all right. This feeling ties in with worrying, anxiety attacks, phobias, paranoia, and many of the conditions which we've seen before. This feeling that everything is not going to be all right increases and decreases along with increases and decreases of the added unconscious guilt. If we have more oral dependency need gratification, we feel more that things will be all right and that we will have good luck. But as our oral dependency need gratification decreases, we have less of the feeling that we are lucky. As added unconscious guilt increases, we feel more unlucky and more like things aren't going to turn out well. I had one patient tell me that with his luck, if opportunity ever came knocking on his door, he'd probably be out back emptying the garbage.

Closely related to the feeling of luckiness, oral dependency need gratification brings a feeling of hope. Some people who have received the death sentence, if they're getting oral dependency need gratification, have the feeling of hope for a last-minute reprieve. Similarly, if people who are dying of cancer are having their oral dependency needs met, they can be optimistic about their recovery, and be hopeful about a cure. They feel that they're chosen for good things to come, and there's little or nothing to worry about. They feel that when they pray, God listens. Opposing these feelings, which are fostered by oral dependency need gratification, are those which accompany added unconscious guilt. Added unconscious guilt gives the feeling of hopelessness, the feeling that there's much to worry about, and the feeling that God is deaf to one's prayers. One patient stated this feeling as, "When I pray, I feel God's out to lunch." Or, as another said, "God has more important things to do than to listen to me." A person can be in perfect health and be convinced that something is physically wrong and he's going to die. He can go from one doctor to another who tells him that he's in good health. But he may still believe he's going to die because of added unconscious guilt, and he lives like a person who's condemned to death with no hope of a reprieve. As you can see, hypochondriasis is closely tied to this feeling which accompanies added unconscious guilt. A hypochondriac with his low level of perceived oral dependency need gratification and his high level of added unconscious guilt, stands in sharp contrast to the cancer patient with the feelings of hope and good luck that come with high levels of perceived oral dependency need gratification and low levels of added unconscious guilt.

The feelings of bad luck, of being chosen for bad things, of hopelessness, of pessimism, are all tied to added unconscious guilt. And the feelings of good luck, of being chosen for good things, of hope, of optimism go along with oral dependency need gratification. All of these feelings then, come from the emotional unreality. We use our perception of reality to support the way we already feel. We can see that all of these feelings that accompany oral dependency need gratification fit together in such a way that they overlap somewhat. They all increase as oral dependency need gratification increases. So as our oral dependency need gratification increases, so do our good self-image, our self-esteem, our sense of self-worth, our ability to withstand stress and pain, our satisfaction with ourselves, our sense of well-being, our feelings of contentment, hope, luckiness, our feeling that everything is going to be all right, and our optimism. We feel better able to handle trouble and the unforeseen, more invulnerable, indispensable, strong, and complete. Likewise as our added unconscious guilt increases and decreases, so do our poor self-image, our lack of self-esteem, and of self-worth, our inability to withstand stress and pain, our dissatisfaction with ourselves, as do our feelings that things are not all right, our feelings of discontentment, hopelessness, unluckiness, our feeling that everything is not going to be all right, and our pessimism. We feel more unable to handle trouble and the unforeseen, more vulnerable, dispensable, weak and incomplete. As you can see, these feelings all fit together, dovetailing each other; a reality-oriented rationalization cannot explain the origin of them.

Other feelings are closely related to the ones we've already mentioned. With oral dependency need gratification, we feel knowledgeable. There is a similarity between feeling knowledgeable and being satisfied with oneself; we're satisfied with what we know. We feel our knowledge is complete. This feeling also increases and decreases, depending upon the amount of perceived oral dependency need gratification. Added unconscious guilt, on the other hand, provides a sense of ignorance or doubt, and of dissatisfaction with what we know. We believe our knowledge is incomplete. This feeling could also be connected with the feeling that everything is not okay and the hypochondriasis which could come from this feeling. We may feel, for instance, that the doctor isn't telling us everything. We might say, "Sometimes doctors don't tell people when they're going to die. I'd rather have him come right out and tell me. How do I know when he says that I don't have cancer that I really don't? Maybe he's trying to keep it from me." A frequently heard variation of this is "The tests were negative but you know as well as I do that labs do make mistakes—and with my usual bad luck, the lab made an error and sent my positive results to someone else, and I got someone's negative results. So I end up still not *really* knowing if I have a fatal condition or not!" This sense of ignorance, of not knowing something one should know, also increases and decreases, depending upon the amount of added unconscious guilt. This feeling of ignorance can be felt from any of the three positions of guilt.

Along with this feeling of ignorance goes the one of incompetence.

With oral dependency need gratification, we feel competent. Closely associated with these feelings is that of completeness or accomplishment. With oral dependency need gratification, we are satisfied with what we've accomplished. With added unconscious guilt, we feel a lack of accomplishment, in each of the three positions. We believe that we, or something associated with us is acceptable, with oral dependency need gratification. But with added unconscious guilt, we feel unacceptable, possibly in regard to the amount of knowledge we have or in regard to a job being completed, and this feeling can be taken from the three positions, as can all of those associated with added unconscious guilt.

Oral dependency need gratification fosters a feeling of belonging, togetherness, and closeness. Individuals who have a lot of their oral dependency needs gratified do not feel alone, even if in reality they are alone, for example, exploring a polar icecap. I remember a famous painting that shows Charles Lindbergh's plane, a tiny speck in the masses of clouds above the ocean. The title of the painting is "We," which suggests that even though Lindbergh was alone, miles from the nearest human, he did not feel alone. People with a high level of oral dependency need gratification do not feel alone, even if they are by themselves. But with high added unconscious guilt, one has a feeling of isolation, alienation, and distance. With high added unconscious guilt, one can feel alone when he's in a crowd, surrounded by people. He can feel that nothing connects him to other people and that he's alienated from others, even if he's in the same church, the same class, the same age bracket. He may have a lot of reality characteristics that would seem to connect him to others, but he still feels alienated and alone.

A sense of being related is enhanced as oral dependency need gratification increases. One has the feeling of "fitting in" or being affiliated with others. In contrast, increasing added unconscious guilt enhances a feeling of "not fitting in" and of being unrelated. I remember a young unmarried professional man who came to me depressed and describing his recent trip to the courthouse to find the "proof" for his feeling that he wasn't related to his parents, that he was not their biological offspring. He had developed an intense feeling of not fitting in with his family and a feeling of being unrelated. He told me of his great surprise to find he hadn't been adopted. He had felt so strongly what he termed "that adopted feeling." Yet, I know of many others who were adopted and who don't have that "adopted feeling." They have a feeling of belonging, of togetherness, of "fitting in" and of being related. That's because they perceive enough oral dependency need gratification to feel this way.

One man I knew, a lay preacher, who had a feeling of not belonging, said, "Everywhere I go, I feel I don't belong; I stand out like a guy in a black tuxedo and brown shoes." He was a perfectionist, and he had anxiety attacks, which, as we've seen, are both related to high unconscious guilt. But he eventually got involved with other people and began perceiving more oral dependency need gratification and he later said, "I used to feel embarrassed if I made a mistake and even if I didn't, I'd still have anxiety attacks for fear of doing so. Now I can stand up and give a sermon, and if I make a mistake, it doesn't bother me, because I know that we're all one family in God. I don't have to be perfect; I'm just human." With more oral dependency need gratification, he now has a sense of belonging to "one family in God." He added that the congregation didn't mind a mistake or two: "As long as they get the message, that's the important thing." He now thinks that his sermons are perfect, even though he may leave out some words or misquote a Bible verse. He's satisfied with what he presents, and he believes that it's accepted because of his increased level of oral dependency need gratification. With his previous low level of oral dependency need gratification, he wasn't satisifed with his sermons and couldn't accept them, even though every word of every verse was quoted correctly.

As oral dependency need gratification increases, there is more of a tendency to think positively, and as oral dependency need gratification decreases, there is less of this tendency. We tend to think positively about anything in our reality, as in the preceding example. As the lay preacher's oral dependency need gratification increased, the man began to think positively about his sermons. With added unconscious guilt, we have a tendency to think negatively. As added unconscious guilt decreases, we have less of a tendency to think negatively. If we say, for instance, "You're the greatest" to someone who is thinking positively, with oral dependency need gratification, that person will think, "He means I'm the greatest person and that I have a lot going for me" or "She thinks I'm the greatest tennis player on the courts (or the greatest cook, or the greatest lover, etc.)" But if we say, "You're the greatest" to someone with high added unconscious guilt, who is thinking negatively, the person will think, "He means I'm the greatest failure" or anything negative or unpleasant.

With oral dependency need gratification, we tend to dwell on the pleasant, we look forward to pleasant things, and we look back on pleasant things. We tend to remember our past successes and the fun we've had in life. With added unconscious guilt, we are apt to dwell on the unpleasant and to anticipate unpleasant things. Our memories are of misery and failures in regard to the three positions. We tend to remember bad times and embarrassing situations if our added unconscious guilt is in the self-felt position. Or else those bad times are remembered in regard to the misperceived or projected positions. With oral dependency need gratification, we are likely to have pleasant dreams, and with added unconscious guilt, our dreams tend to be unpleasant with a manifest content that reflects the position of the added unconscious guilt. For example, if one's added unconscious guilt is self-felt and focused in an elevator phobia, she may dream that she's on an elevator that suddenly plunges down 30 floors. Or if her added unconscious guilt is misperceived and focused in paranoia, she could dream that something is chasing her, and with even more added unconscious guilt, that it catches her. Unpleasant dreams are similar to unpleasant memories and come from added unconscious guilt made very specific to the individual.

I had one patient tell me that her nightmare was that the bathroom toilet was overflowing during a big dinner party. Occasionally, someone will tell me that he dreamed of garbage being thrown around or dumped. Such things clearly reflect the added unconscious guilt. Whatever is feared most in a person's condition or complex usually becomes the focus of nightmares. If one is frightened, for example, of spiders, her bad dreams will more than likely contain lots of spiders. In regard to decreasing added unconscious guilt, I recently had a patient in the hospital who suffered anxiety attacks and terrifying nightmares, containing spiders, which she feared. She would awaken and run screaming down the hospital hallways. After being in the hospital for a couple of weeks, eventually perceiving more gratification of her oral dependency needs and decreasing her added unconscious guilt, she told me one morning as I made rounds that she was awakened that night by a nightmare. "I dreamed there was a spider loose in my bed but (smiling pleasantly) then I dreamed I caught him and threw him out!"

There is a tendency as oral dependency need gratification increases, to identify with the capable, the adequate, the complete, the acceptable, the clean, the beautiful. We identify with people or things that are successful, innocent, right, healthy, perfect, able to handle trouble, with the omnipotent, the omnicient, the desirable, the justified, the proper, the respected, the favored or blessed, and with those having good luck and many assets. We identify with life and living. In short, we tend to unconsciously identify with the positive aspects of people or things, experiences and situations. Such identifications increase or decrease depending upon the amount of perceived oral dependency need gratification. As added unconscious guilt increases, we are more likely to identify unconsciously with the incapable, the inadequate, the incomplete, the unacceptable, the dirty, and the ugly. We identify with people or things that are unsuccessful, guilty, wrong, sick, imperfect, unable to handle trouble, with the helpless, the ignorant, the undesirable, the unjustified, the improper, the disrespected, the disfavored or even cursed, and with those having bad luck and many liabilities. We identify with death and dying. These feelings of unconscious identification with the negative aspects of people or things, experiences, and situations increase and decrease along with increases and decreases in our added unconscious guilt.

With oral dependency need gratification, one tends to identify with the winner, the victor, or the advantaged. But with added unconscious guilt, one tends to identify with the loser, the disadvantaged, or the underdog. There are people who feel that the underdog is the unborn fetus whose "rights" are being curtailed and they identify, in part, with that. On the other side of the abortion issue, some believe that the underdog is the pregnant woman who should have the right to make decisions concerning her body, and they identify, in part, with her. The "underdog" with which to identify is in the eye of the beholder, just as the "villain" for one's projected added unconscious guilt is also in the eye of the beholder. Some people see the Israelis, who have had no homeland for two thousand years, as the underdogs, yet others see the Palestinians, who have been moved out of their homeland, as the underdogs. Depending upon one's identifications, the "villain" changes. In Tennessee, some people saw the snail darter, a small fish on the verge of extinction, as the underdog, and fought the construction of a dam that would have further endangered the species. Others saw the farmers, who needed the water the dam would have provided, as the underdogs. Those who become most vociferous have the most added unconscious guilt with which to make an identification with a cause and the most to project within that cause.

This identification—both with the positive, with oral dependency need gratification, and with the negative, with added unconscious guilt—is important in communication. We have previously seen that spontaneous communication provides a way to gratify the oral dependency need. When someone listens to us, he or she is making us the center of his or her universe. By talking to him or her, we meet our oral dependency need. We have also seen that communication provides a way to lower added unconscious guilt. We can also, by means of this identification, meet some of our oral dependency need through listening to someone else. It works this way. If we have enough oral dependency need gratification to be comfortable, and someone speaks to us about the positive aspects of people, things, experiences, or situations, we tend to identify with these things, and this identification causes an increase in our oral dependency need gratification. It's as if the unconscious thinks, "He or she is somehow talking about *me*, in part," which meets the oral dependency need. If someone says, "It's a beautiful day," for instance, the unconscious of the comfortable person thinks: "He or she thinks *I'm* beautiful." If we then say, "Yes, it is a beautiful day," then we and the person with whom we're communicating are mutually supporting each other's oral dependency need gratification. An interchange like this one is an example of mutually supported likes that mutually meet oral dependency needs.

Mutual likes, we saw earlier, cause mutual support for oral dependency need gratification, which plays a part in the unconscious selection of and the maintaining of friendships. Common targets for projected guilt, or mutual dislikes, also as we have seen, play a part in this unconscious selection and maintenance process. Because of this identification with the positive, brought about by oral dependency need gratification, friends often share many of the same interests: the same activities, the same books, the same sports, the same movies, the same politics, the same religion, etc. For example, someone might say to you, "I like going to the beach. I love to lie on the sand and swim in the ocean." If you say, "Well, I do too. I love the smell of the salt in the air and I like to feel the sand between my toes," then you have mutual confirmation and support of unconscious oral dependency need gratification. The interchange is oral dependency need gratifying for both people involved, just the same as it would be if both were projecting guilt onto a common target. It's easy to see that these two people might decide to go to the beach together, exchange more mutual confirmation of oral dependency need gratification, and become friends. Someone who likes to go to the beach tends to have a friend or friends who also like to go to the beach. Two friends who like to go to the beach identify with the positive aspects of the beach, and when these aspects are mentioned in spontaneous communication, it mutually meets their oral dependency needs.

Because this identification results from, and also increases, oral dependency need gratification, those who have the most oral dependency need gratification are the best able to accumulate more. Those with the least oral dependency need gratification, thus the most added unconscious guilt, have the hardest time accumulating it in spontaneous communication. When these people engage in spontaneous communication, they identify with the negative aspects of people, things, experiences, or situations. If a person has a high level of added unconscious guilt and someone speaks to him about these negative aspects, as in, "What a horrible day!", his unconscious tends to think, "He somehow thinks *I'm* horrible." The less oral dependency need gratification and the more added unconscious guilt he has, the less he tends to identify with things that are spoken favorably and the more he tends to identify with things that are spoken of unfavorably. This identification with the unfavorable, with high levels of added unconscious guilt, can affect communication in an adverse way. In opposition, the identification with the favorable, with high levels of oral dependency need gratification, can affect communication in a positive way. These unconscious psychodynamics involved in mutually supported projected added unconscious guilt and enhanced oral dependency need gratification play a most important role in why the more emotionally comfortable person is seen enjoying the company of others. The converse is also true where the more emotionally uncomfortable person, with his low level of oral dependency need gratification and high added unconscious guilt, identifies too readily with projected guilt and identifies too little with the favorably spoken of. This person doesn't enjoy the spontaneous communication of others and is often uncomfortable around them.

In order to give an example on a reality level of how this identification works in spontaneous communication, consider a patient of mine. This man is a carpenter, an overly conscientious perfectionist in his work. He has the traits characteristic of high personality core guilt, which means that he often has to contend with high added unconscious guilt. His high personality core guilt assures that he won't get rid of his added unconscious guilt easily because he avoids gossip or chitchat and tends to stay by himself. His perfectionism, however, led him to be an excellent carpenter. He sometimes worked with another carpenter, named Oscar, who was not a perfectionist. Oscar was more "laid back" and easy-going. The first carpenter came in to see me and told me that his boss had come by the previous day to tell both men who were working together, "You're both doing a great job, but you're not setting the world on fire for speed." My patient got all upset over this remark and couldn't work. He made up an excuse that he felt ill and went home early because, he told me, he remembered the second part of his boss' remark. He didn't really hear, or couldn't remember, the first part. He later mentioned this to Oscar. Oscar wasn't bothered by the remark at all; he said that he only heard the first part and either didn't hear or couldn't remember the second part. Oscar, who had less added unconscious guilt, heard or remembered only the favorable aspect of the boss's remark, and was quite pleased with it; while my patient, with more added unconscious guilt, remembered only the unfavorable aspect and was not only displeased, but upset.

Even though the boss did mention something unfavorable, because Oscar did not have a substantial amount of added unconscious guilt, he did not perceive the negative part of the remark as being aimed at him. If someone says to us, "What a horrible day!", and our oral dependency need gratification level is up while our added unconscious guilt is down, we will not identify unconsciously, in part, with the comment. Even though the other person unconsciously, using transference language, *is*, in fact, talking about us in part, we do not perceive it. We may listen to the remark, and we may even mutually *support* it. For example, if our oral dependency need gratification is high, and someone says, "What a horrible day!", we don't get the unconscious message that "He thinks I'm horrible;" instead we might respond with a little projected guilt ourselves by saying, "Yeah, I hate the cold." But as added unconscious guilt builds up, in the misperceived position, we tend to think, "He feels I'm horrible."

As added unconscious guilt increases, there is more of a tendency to perceive that when someone else talks about anything unfavorably, she may be talking about us. This perception, that the other person is some-how equating us with the subject being described does not meet our oral dependency need. So the accrual of added unconscious guilt is like the accumulation of oral dependency need gratification, in that, the more we have, the more we tend to accrue, and we tend to accrue it more easily. Ironically, the very person with the greatest unmet oral dependency need, and the greatest *need* to meet his or her dependency need in spontaneous communciation, is the very one who has the most problem doing so, while the person with much less unmet oral dependency need has little difficulty in meeting his or her oral dependency need in spontaneous communication.

If a person says to a friend of his who has a low level of unmet oral dependency need, "I hate going to the beach because sand gets in my shoes, my hair and my car," then she will probably support what he says. Even if she may like the beach, she will probably say something like, "Oh yeah, I know what you mean. I like the beach, but the sand can be a bother at times." However, if he says the same thing to someone with a high level of unmet oral dependency need, that person will tend to think unconsciously, "He feels that I'm comparable to sand in his shoes and I must really be a bother," or "I'm as annoying as sand in someone's shoes." This interchange would not be oral dependency need gratifying for someone who has the most need for such gratification. People with the most oral dependency need gratification, then, have few problems in making and keeping friends. The dynamics of unconsciously perceived mutual confirmation of oral dependency need gratification allow the accompanying guilt projection to go on in friendship. This unconscious process can take place under any manifest content.

It has already become evident that the emotional unreality affects our perception. The more added unconscious guilt, and the more unmet oral dependency need we have, the more distorted our perception of reality will be according to one of the three positions of added unconscious guilt. The more oral dependency need gratification we have, the more we tend to see reality as it truly is and as oral dependency need gratification decreases, the less we tend to perceive reality as it truly is. As added unconscious guilt decreases, our perception of reality is less distorted. A good example of this distortion is the person who thinks he's found in another person the perfect answer to his unmet oral dependency needs, when others who see the second person as she really is, can see so clearly the mirage.

Reality, for each individual, is whatever he perceives it to be. Even though he does not perceive reality as it truly is, for him, the perception of reality is his reality. For instance, if a father sees his son as being "no good," that is his perceived reality. No one is able to talk him out of it because, for him, "My son is no good" is a fact of reality. This perceived reality will not change until the father's added unconscious guilt decreases. If I believe that I'm bad, no one else is going to change my mind. No book or magazine article or any class is going to change my mind. Only I can change my mind, if my added unconscious guilt decreases. The same is true if I think that others feel I'm bad or that others don't accept me. These misperceived views make up my reality. My perception will only make up my reality. My perception will only change if my added unconscious guilt decreases. If you don't agree that my perception is reality as it truly is, then I'll say as one of my patients did, "You just don't see it as I do. You may as well tell me that it's dark outside at noon, and sunny at midnight as try to change my mind about what I perceive to be reality." Someone can be intelligent and well-educated, but his or her perception of reality will always reflect his or her high added unconscious guilt. Perception is influenced by added unconscious guilt, and perception can be grossly distorted if the added unconscious guilt is high. It is important to recognize that because perceptions of reality are so affected by one's underlying emotional unreality, what one concludes about his or her past, his or her present and his or her future reality always has a degree of distortion.

Some of the expressions we use show how oral dependency need gratification and added unconscious guilt affect perception. With oral dependency need gratification, we tend to see the weather as "partly sunny." But the same day is "partly cloudly" with increased added unconscious guilt. Or consider the following: an older woman who goes to church often, belongs to a garden club, is active with her children and grandchildren, and who has a high level of perceived oral dependency need gratification may look at her fuel tank in the middle of a howling snowstorm and see that it is "half-full." She may see no reason to worry. But this same woman, if she were to stay at home and were not active in the church or with her family, with high added unconscious guilt, would worry because the tank was "half-empty." This latter woman may be staying by herself because of high personality core guilt. Some people *do* stay alone much of the time because of their high levels of unconscious guilt, not because of physical problems. An unfortunate number of older people who would like to be involved with others *must* stay by themselves because they have neither family nor friends who can visit them or provide them with transportation. These people, too, when their unconscious guilt rises, would tend to see the fuel tank as "half-empty." Many people with physical handicaps somehow find ways to become involved with other people and are more comfortable if they do so. In contrast, many with no physical handicaps with high personality core guilt, manage not to get involved with others and are more emotionally uncomfortable as a result.

Man is the most intelligent animal that has ever lived, and prides himself on his intellectual abilities. He may tend to overlook, however, that he can be the most emotional animal as well, and that when so, those intellectual abilities take a secondary and supportive role. The more added unconscious guilt one has, and the more unmet oral dependency need one has, the more one will distort reality and simply use the intellect to support the distortion. For instance, if I feel I'm bad and unacceptable, my feeling is coming from my added unconscious guilt, but I'll use my intellect and my education to support what I already feel. I could say I'm no good because I went into psychiatry, not neurosurgery, and come up with all sorts of nice intellectualizations to support what I perceive to be a fact of reality.

The man who perceives his teen-aged son as bad will use his intellect to support this perception. He may say that his son is bad because he smoked pot, dressed poorly, ran around with the "wrong crowd," and was a discipline problem in school. He uses reality to support his feelings which are actually coming from his own emotional unreality. Our perceived reality then is unconsciously determined to a degree by our emotional unreality. We then use our intellect to support our often erroneous perceptions without realizing it. If someone else points out an error in our conclusions about reality, we use our intellect to refute what was said. The more intelligent one is or the more well-educated one is, the better he or she is able to do so. Someone who is intelligent and well-educated, with a lot of added unconscious guilt, is good at supporting and defending these distorted perceptions of reality. However, someone with less intelligence and education still manages to hold onto his or her distorted perception. The more intelligent one is, the better the case he presents in support of the distortion, but regardless of intelligence level, he cannot be talked out of what he perceives to be true reality. We deceive ourselves by thinking that our perception of reality is true reality when it's actually being distorted by our emotional unreality. We attempt to deceive others by intellectually supporting our perception, but if our added unconscious guilt is high enough, others can readily see the distortion. It's when the added unconscious guilt is lower that the deception is subtle.

When the added unconscious guilt decreases and a person no longer feels the same way, he often uses his intellect to explain his change in perception as due to a perceived change in reality, rather than a change in the emotional unreality. He might say that the change is due to some intellectual endeavor. For instance, the parent may say that he's "learned to accept" his son. Or someone may say, "I've learned to accept myself," or "I've learned to take one day at a time." The person who previously had a high amount of misperceived added unconscious guilt can with lower guilt now say, "I've learned to say 'no' to others," or "I've learned to put myself first a little." These misperceived secondary feelings have decreased, and someone who once said, "They expect me to say 'yes' " and "They expect me to put them first," now says, "I've learned to ignore their demands." The person who previously had a high amount of projected added unconscious guilt can, with lower guilt say, "I've learned to overlook the shortcomings in others." The intellect, the conscious functioning of the mind, always gets the credit for the change. But it's a big deception because the unconscious, the emotional unreality, is responsible for the change in perception. We don't teach a person to value him or herself; we can't teach someone how to go out and make friends, and we can't teach someone how to communicate and get his or her needs met, or how to have fun in life. We don't teach a person how to cope with life. People can do these things, not because of anything they've learned, but because the added unconscious guilt has been lowered. Learning, or the intellectual side of man, however, is always given the credit. And this deception is even fostered by psychiatry.

Even such prestigious organizations as the AMA give learning the credit. In a recent AMA newsletter, there was an article on transcendental meditation groups which claimed that if one learns how to meditate and imagine beautiful, peaceful places, he can gain a sense of serenity. It's presented as though the serenity is a result of this intellectual endeavor to learn. We know it's more from the changed emotional unreality that has occurred from the subtle, unconscious interrelating of perceived "parts" of the transcendental meditation group's interactions. The same is true of behavior modification, used to "cure" phobias. Phobia clinics use "cognitive" therapy to stop people from thinking of the dread-ful "what ifs." One is told that he can *learn* to put the phobia out of his mind through conscious endeavors. He is told he can control his thinking and he can *learn* to think positively. But the real reason for the resulting positive thinking and more intellectual control is the decrease in added unconscious guilt, and the increase in oral dependency need gratifica-tion. Anything one tries that increases oral dependency need gratification and lowers added unconscious guilt, under any manifest content, would result in the same change to positive thinking. The focus of the involve-ment in reality does not have to be on the phobia.

Similarly, a course in assertiveness training cannot "teach" people how to have more self-confidence. One doesn't learn self-confidence. One feels it. Someone with a lot of added unconscious guilt in the self-felt position isn't going to learn to put himself first, or to accept himself. He can read every book written on the subject of assertiveness training, but until he lowers the self-felt added unconscious guilt, he will be not able to do it. There are many people who've never read a book, or who have never taken a course in assertiveness training who *do* accept themselves and who *do* put themselves first with no problem at all. Others who have read all the books on assertiveness training they can find still can't do it. By joining a course on assertiveness training, a person can become more assertive. But it's not by a learning process. The irony is that he could have become more assertive, if he had joined any course, regardless of its orientation, particularly if he enjoyed it and was socially active with the other members. I have seen people who have failed these courses on assertiveness training. They failed because it's not something that can be learned; they had high added unconscious guilt and high unmet oral dependency need that didn't get lowered. Any self-help book, of course, is aimed at a particular problem in reality when the actual problem is so often in the emotional unreality. But people don't recognize the real problem because it's too nebulous and too illogical; it doesn't make sense. The real problem is the unmet oral dependency need and the increased added unconscious guilt made from bits and pieces of frustrations, repressions, etc.

The added unconscious guilt distorts perception of past, present, and future reality. Conscious thinking supports this distorted perception, so that it may look as though the intellect is responsible for a change in perception. But when the added unconscious guilt is high enough, it distorts perception enough so that others notice that the perception is not coming from reality. No one can talk the person out of his or her distorted perception, however, only lowering the added unconscious guilt can change it. Involvement in any experience or situation where the person can find support for guilt projection and meet his or her oral dependency needs can lower the added unconscious guilt, bringing about a change in perception. A well known popular writer once said, "Don't focus on your past failures; concentrate on your past successes." This sounds like very good reality-oriented advice, but it's worthless! Someone with high added unconscious guilt cannot do it because the added unconscious guilt distorts his or her perception of the past. And the person with low added unconscious guilt doesn't need the advice because he or she will do it anyway.

It becomes evident, now that we know the problem is added unconscious guilt, that the orientation of the different talking therapies really doesn't make much difference. The manifest content hides the process of lowering the added unconscious guilt. At a certain level of added unconscious guilt, however, therapies or books or classes involving cognition can work. For instance, if you read a book that tells you to go out and make friends, talk about anything, get your oral dependency needs met, and project guilt, if your added unconscious guilt is low enough, you'll be able to do it. But as added unconscious guilt increases, you become less able to do it. You tend to become more and more incapacitated as your added unconscious guilt increases. Self-help books seem to appeal to someone with high personality core guilt, who wants to do it *himself*, who doesn't want to rely on others, and who'd rather read them than talk to other people. Ironically, self-help books can work for those people who need them the least. A.A. can tell someone, as they do, to "take one day at a time," but the person who can take the advice is the one who's doing it anyway. But if she has a lot of the feeling that "so many things *must* be done, and I have such little time," she can't take a day at a time. When she can take one day at a time, it's only because the added unconscious guilt has been lowered enough to allow her to do so. All the different types of reality-oriented therapies allow a manifest content and spontaneous communication, which are actually decreasing the added unconscious guilt.

Man is the most emotional animal and his intellectual supremacy may, at times, be only a myth or a deception. If there is intellectual supremacy, then it is only when the added unconscious guilt is low enough and the oral dependency need is being comfortably met. But when the unmet need and added unconscious guilt increase, this intellectual supremacy proves to be false. Unfortunately, the person usually doesn't know that he has lost this intellectual supremacy and his ignorance compounds the problem of a distorted reality. Sometimes, however, a person does recognize that his emotions are determining his behavior. For instance, when the unmet oral dependency need increases, people will sometimes become involved with someone about whom they might say, "My mind is telling me I should not be seeing her, but my heart wants to." These people may fall in love easily, and later, when they're going through emotional grief, they'll often say "Why didn't I listen to my head instead of my heart?" One young woman, in looking back with more projected guilt at such a relationship, queried, "What I want to know is where the hell was my shit-detector when I met that guy?"

The greatest achievements for the good of humanity are made by man, yet ironically the most inhumane things imaginable are also done by man. No other animal can rival man at his best—or man at his worst. This contradiction comes from the emotional unreality. Man commits unbelievable acts of sadism and cruelty, but he also commits awesome acts of love and devotion. Because reality demands the use of logic, the intellect and knowledge may be erroneously given a determining credit for such events rather than the emotional unreality with all its illogic. A psychiatrist friend of mine is seeing the daughter of a leading child psychologist. Her father, with all his knowledge of child-rearing practices, seemingly should have raised a more emotionally comfortable daughter. Another case is that of a well-known psychiatrist who had written considerably on interpersonal relationships and who died in a psychiatric hospital. Doctors, as a group, have one of the highest suicide rates in this country, and the specialty in medicine with the highest suicide rate, ironically, is that of psychiatry. The intellectual knowledge of human behavior doesn't seem to help in living happily. It certainly doesn't seem to help in preventing suicide. If the intellect were so supreme, then to solve a problem of phobia, depression, anxiety attack, low self-esteem, stress, etc., all we'd need to do would be to read a book and become knowledgeable. Many people with emotional problems are advised by newspaper columnists to seek "counseling," which implies an intellectual solution based on advice. But what is really needed is for the emotionally troubled person to go out and talk to a professional who will *listen*. In this way, the person can get some of his or her oral dependency needs met and project a little added unconscious guilt.

There is a smorgasbord of therapies, offered to people who are emotionally uncomfortable, ranging from analysis to Zen. The most recent count reveals that there are well over four hundred brand-name therapy techniques being offered at the present time. All of these therapies have different reality orientations, some of which contradict each other. But all of them seem to work, for some people, some of the time. The proponents of each therapy believe that theirs is the one true therapy, whether it's analysis, behavior modification, or transcendental meditation. In an overview of these therapies, it becomes evident that one particular therapy may seem to work better for some individuals, while for other people, a different therapy seems to work better. The one that works the best for a given person is often the one that fits with the orientation of his rationalizations, or the way in which his added unconscious guilt is showing itself in reality. It doesn't make much sense to ask a man with an airplane phobia and who doesn't drink to go to A.A. instead of to a phobia clinic. Theoretically, he could go to A.A., and solve his problem of an airplane phobia. The person with a drinking problem, who is ordered by a judge to attend A.A. can possibly meet his oral dependency needs and lower his added unconscious guilt through his involvement in A.A. and stop drinking. However, if he were ordered to play bridge two or three nights a week, he could very possibly see the same results. With his high added unconscious guilt on top of the high personality core guilt, it might take a court order with supervised probation to get him regularly involved in any activity involving spontaneous communication. What is becoming evident, then, is that there is no one true therapy. All the therapies and a good share of most quackery are oriented toward reality, and they all provide different intellect-oriented manifest contents for the emotional process of lowering the added unconscious guilt.

Quackery is a multibillion dollar business in the United States and the AMA has been its longtime foe. But if it is a multibillion dollar business, and people seem willing to pay for it, and even to give testimonials for its efficacy, then it must be doing something. What it is often doing is lowering the added unconscious guilt and the unmet oral dependency need, in a subtle emotional way. It is possible to become emotionally comfortable in what the AMA calls quackery. Just because we can't measure it, or see how it works, we don't have to call it worthless. Just as there are, and have been for thousands of years, many religions, some working best for certain people, others for other people, there are many therapies with little or no scientific basis that do work for certain individuals. Like those religions, the therapy works the best if its proponents truly believe in it. The most effective priests, ministers, or rabbis have always been those who sincerely believe that theirs is the one true religion, those who tend to be less ecumenical. And the best therapists are often those who believe that theirs is the one true therapy; those who tend to be less eclectic. One can understand the dynamics of human behavior very well and still not be as good, with respect to meeting the oral dependency need of others, as someone who has little or no understanding of the "scientific facts" of human behavior. For example, remember the social worker at the state hospital who knew social work and also was so good at meeting the oral dependency need of others. She felt that the dynamics of human behavior was not in her domain, but as far as meeting the oral dependency need and accepting projected guilt, she was one of the best.

We have seen that people with a lot of added unconscious guilt find it most difficult to participate in activities that include spontaneous communication. Added unconscious guilt gives a tendency to identify with the negative aspects of people, things, experiences, and situations, making it difficult to meet the oral dependency need through communication. Another feeling that comes from added unconscious guilt which is related to low self-esteem, insecurity, pessimism, etc. is that of a lack of trust. I read in a newspaper not long ago, a letter written to a leading advice columnist. The letter came from a woman who had just married a man who had been married before. During the man's previous marriage, he and this woman had had an affair. Now, the woman says, she finds it hard to trust him. The advice columnist wrote that this mistrust is the price that the woman must pay for helping the man to cheat on his former wife. But, the reality of this has nothing to do with the feeling of mistrust. It comes from increased added unconscious guilt. Someone who has never cheated on a spouse is not guaranteed the trust of that spouse. The feeling of mistrust comes from a build-up of added unconscious guilt, in the misperceived position. Oral dependency need gratification does enhance a feeling of trust which is there whether the spouse is cheating or not. Likewise, increasing misperceived added unconscious guilt enhances a feeling of mistrust whether or not the spouse is cheating. The reality of past cheating or not cheating is of far less importance than the present emotional unreality. This woman's rationalization for her mistrust is logical and it makes sense, but it's not the real reason. Trust and mistrust come directly from one's emotional unreality.

As oral dependency gratification increases, so does freedom of behavior. The trust, security, ability to cope with stress, identification with the positive in communication, pleasant memories and dreams, optimism, and general satisfaction with the self that all accompany oral dependency need gratification allow freedom of behavior. But the mistrust, insecurity, inability to cope with stress, identification with the negative in communication, unpleasant memories and dreams, pessimism, and dissatisfaction with the self, coming from the added unconscious guilt, limit freedom of behavior. The emotional unreality exercises control over how we feel and how we behave and more strictly, does so when the added unconscious guilt is high. As oral dependency need gratification increases and decreases, so does freedom of behavior. As added unconscious guilt increases, there is more inhibition: in the self-felt position, in regard to feeling unacceptable or guilty, for doing or not doing something; in the misperceived position, in regard to feeling that others will not accept us or feel we're guilty for doing or not doing something; and in the projected position, in regard to feeling that someone else is unacceptable or guilty, for doing or not doing something. As added unconscious guilt decreases, there is less inhibition with respect to all three positions.

Having seen the teeter-totter relationship between the results of increasing and decreasing oral dependency need gratification and added unconscious guilt, it's now time to look more closely at the most dynamic and intriguing position—the misperceived position.

CHAPTER 14
The Misperceived Position

We admire reflections of intense love with certain reality focuses. We all admire for instance a great love for God, for country, for fellow man, or for a worthy cause. Underlying any intense love, however, is a high unmet oral dependency need. This love that we admire so much in others and often seek to a certain degree ourselves has a negative side, particularly when the intense love is focused on another individual. Some counselors and therapists feel that love is one of the biggest causes of man's emotional grief. Many people have come to me saying, "If only I hadn't fallen in love . . . " Often, relationships involving intense love, that begin "heavenly," turn too soon into "hellish" ones. In fact, it is more likely that a relationship will turn "hellish" the more it is initially perceived as "heavenly." What determines the need to search for "heaven" is that high unmet oral dependency need.

The misperceived position can guarantee a high unmet oral dependency need, an intense thirst for love. It can propagate the tendency to go through life being frustrated by one intense relationship after another. The person with increased added unconscious guilt in the misperceived position seems to search, throughout life, for happiness but never seems to find it. These people look for happiness in a human relationship, but true happiness, as we already know, is found in the emotional unreality, in unconsciously perceived parts of people, experiences, and situations. True lasting happiness is found through diffusion, not in one human relationship. I had a patient tell me with tears streaming down her face, "All I've ever wanted in life is to love and be loved in return. Is that asking too much? What's wrong with that?" On the surface, it would seem that there is nothing wrong with her desire for love, that it's not asking too much. But after looking at the misperceived position in detail, we'll be able to see that there *is* something wrong in her statement.

In the self-felt position, the person feels that he does not deserve love, which is really, on its most basic level, oral dependency need gratification. This person, when his self-felt added unconscious guilt is high, will often block attempts by others to give him love. With high added unconscious guilt in the projected position, this person will attempt to prevent the someone else from receiving love, or oral dependency need gratification,

feeling that the other person doesn't deserve love. But in the misperceived position, the person *wants* love, but feels that someone else or
others who are emotionally significant are preventing him from receiving
love.

An individual in the misperceived position feels that "She doesn't feel
I deserve love," or oral dependency need gratification. Characteristically,
the person in the misperceived position is seeking love, seeking positive
recognition, seeking approval and acceptance, but feels that somebody
else is, or others are, withholding it. She will often ask, "How do I get
others to like me?" She really wants some emotionally significant other
to love her, but she can't perceive that the other loves or even accepts
her. She can't perceive it because of those primary and secondary feelings
of the misperceived position, "The person I love thinks I'm too inferior,
inadequate, unacceptable, etc. He'd rather not be with me." Because she
wants to love so intensely, if her unmet oral dependency need and misperceived added unconscious guilt are high enough, she tends to concentrate this desire on one individual or on too few people. She is like
the infant who has to concentrate love, or oral dependency need gratification, on one or a few people. Because she concentrates her love,
seeking it intensely from one person in reality rather than through a
diffusion process, she ends up being too dependent on too few, which
is characteristic of the misperceived position. In listening to someone in
the misperceived position, it becomes obvious that the person is too
dependent on too few, or as we've seen earlier, too emotionally immature. The misperceived position tends to foster emotional immaturity.
It effectively thwarts the diffusion process. In fact, the more misperceived
guilt one has, the more it tends to cause a person to regress from being
more emotionally involved with others to being *less* emotionally involved
with others and too dependent on too few.

As we have seen, the misperceived position can be presented or expressed in a variety of ways. The feelings are the same as those in the
self-felt or projected positions but they are being attributed to someone
else. We may hear things like "He's implying I'm _____," "He's probably thinking I'm _____." Another commonly occurring one is "He
acts as though I'm _____." Any of the primary or secondary feelings
could be substituted for the blank, and, as always, "she," "my boss," "my
wife," "they," "others," "people," "everyone." could be substituted for
"he." These introductory statements are expressions of the misperceived
position. A secondary feeling in the misperceived position would be
something like, "They don't like me because I'm not working." Remember, the self-felt position of this is, "I don't like *myself* because I'm not
working," and the projected position is, "I don't like *him* because he's
not working." The person with increased added unconscious guilt in the

misperceived position is unable to perceive, in the work situation, a meeting of his oral dependency need which is what he would like to have. Another would be, "She looks at me as irresponsible and lazy if I take a day off or slow down a little." Another example of being unable to perceive oral dependency need gratification involving the work situation would be, "My boss feels I should be working all the time." In emotionally significant relationships outside the work situation one might hear as misperceived guilt increases, "You act as though you don't have a minute for me" or "He tries to make me look as if I'm the weak one in the marriage," "She wants to get rid of me," "He talks down to me." Feelings like these don't lend themselves to oral dependency need gratification.

The person in the misperceived position who is too dependent on too few seems to be making other people too important. It is apparent that the person is placing too much emphasis on how somebody else regards him. We don't see this in the other two positions. In the misperceived position, people are continually looking for evidence that others feel favorably about them, that others like them, that others appreciate them. But they can't see any evidence because they're feeling, "He doesn't care about me," "She doesn't accept me," "They don't like me." The more misperceived added unconscious guilt there is, the more intensely the person feels this way. This is precisely when there is a correspondingly equal amount of unmet oral dependency need and, thus, a greater urgency to meet that need. Involvement with others may be lessened as the person increasingly feels, with rising misperceived guilt, "He won't allow me to leave the house," or, "He doesn't want me seeing my friends," or, "He thinks I'm up to no good if I'm not at home." Another feeling one hears is, "He expects me to work at home and he doesn't want me to have friends in to sit and chat."

Another characteristic of the misperceived position is that of trying to please or others. This results from the situation of an increased emotional need for others, and an increased blindness to any gratification. So the person tries to do whatever she can to change this frustrating situation. She is trying to change the situation that she perceives by trying to get others to show that they care about her, that they accept her, that they like being around her, and that they like her. She can't see when someone else actually *does* care about her, accepts her, likes her, or appreciates her. She becomes even more frustrated when she tries so hard to please someone else, and still can't recognize that she has pleased the other person. It's increased misperceived guilt that makes a person believe that her efforts to please are never reciprocated. The person may remark, "I've been her friend but she hasn't been mine." This person has tried to please others but feels that the attempt to please has failed. One woman that I saw tried very hard to please her husband. One evening, after working all day in her job, she hurried to the grocery store, bought some expensive shrimp with her hard-earned money, rushed home and cooked a fabulous gourmet dinner before her husband came home. But after her husband came home, she did not perceive that he appreciated it. She felt that he didn't care about the amount of work she'd put into the dinner. They had a big fight, which ended with her throwing the whole dinner onto the floor. She screamed, "Look at all the trouble I went to fix this for you!" and he yelled back, "Who the hell asked you to fix the shrimp dinner? What did you want me to do, jump up and down and do cartwheels when I came through the door?" Even if he had gotten visibly excited about dinner, she could not have perceived that she'd pleased him because of her high added unconscious guilt in the misperceived position.

The situation may seem like a "reverse psychology," to someone with a large amount of added unconscious guilt in the misperceived position. The harder the person tries to please, the less he is able to perceive that others are pleased. Yet with lower added unconscious guilt in the misperceived position, the less he feels this "need" to please, the more he perceives that others are pleased. For instance, I've heard people say, "The more I try to please him, the less he appreciates it, but then it seems when I don't even try to please him, the more appreciative he appears," or "The nicer I am to her, the worse she is to me; but it seems the worse I am to her, the nicer she is to me." Someone with now de-creased misperceived added unconscious guilt told me, "I really didn't think this marriage would float, but when I finally got to the point where I just didn't care any more, he seemed to get better."

An example of these dynamics would be the woman that I saw, who used to fix a separate breakfast for her husband to let him sleep until the kids left for school. She had an increased "need" to please from increased misperceived guilt. After the kids had eaten and she'd done all their breakfast dishes and sent them to school, she would cook another entire breakfast and then call her husband. But she didn't perceive that he appreciated it. One day, when her added unconscious guilt in the misperceived position had greatly decreased, as well as her unmet oral dependency need, and she no longer felt such a "need" to please, she told him that he could "get his ass out of bed and come down to breakfast with the rest of the family." He told her, she said, that he was *glad* she'd finally said that, because he thought it was nicer to eat breakfast with the family. She got positive support for curbing her extra efforts to please him, it seemed. Now that she's not trying to please him, she can see that he's pleased. This seems like some form of "reverse psychology." The same thing could happen in a work situation or for example, "The more

I try to please my boss, the less she seems to appreciate it." One can see a similar situation in a parent-child relationship, as in, "The more I do for those kids, the less they appreciate it; but now that I don't do so much for them, they seem more appreciative of what I do." It could also happen in a church situation, where someone in the misperceived position is doing charitable work. He or she might say, "The more I give of my time, the less the others seem to appreciate it."

It doesn't seem to make sense, but we can understand this "reverse psychology" by seeing that it fits so well with increased added unconscious guilt in the misperceived position. Perceived appreciation is inversely proportional to the level of misperceived added unconscious guilt. Since added unconscious guilt is always equal to the level of unmet oral dependency need, the more one has of a "need" to see appreciation, the less they will be able to see it if they're in the misperceived position. Conversely, the less "need" one has to see appreciation from others, the more there is of a tendency to see appreciation.

As an example of what deceptively appears as an unresolved parent-child problem from the distant past, rather than a problem of the present, consider a middle-aged unmarried college professor I know. She is the head of her department and known for her excellence in teaching. She's also in the misperceived position; she feels at times an increased "need" to please and to be admired, yet she is unable to see when others are pleased with her or admire her. In talking to me about her personal life, she said "I've spent my whole life trying to please my mother and have never succeeded no matter how hard I've tried. If I got all A's, that was never enough for her—she would want me to get the top grade in the class and nothing less. Yet it was always all right for my brothers and sisters to get C's and D's. She and I have never gotten along. She gives so little yet she expects so much of me. She's never satisfied with me and I'm not accepted by her as my brothers and sisters are. Just last weekend she had a family picnic. She invited my brothers and sisters, my aunts and uncles and my grandmother. But did she invite me? No! Sure, she said, 'Why don't you come over for a picnic on Saturday,' but that was the morning of the picnic. Everyone else seemed to know about it days in advance. If she'd *really* wanted me there, she would have invited me ahead of time." One can see that this woman has an increased level of added unconscious guilt in the misperceived position. She can't see that her mother is proud of her accomplishments and wanted her to come to the family picnic. In fact, this woman's brother later told me, that the picnic was an informal picnic and that "no one had received engraved invitations," or had been asked more than a day or two ahead of time, the way his sister expected. It was the professor's increased misperceived added unconscious guilt that made her unable to recognize her mother's love for her.

Another characteristic that should be apparent by now is a *blocking effect* that comes from the secondary feelings of the misperceived position. We see this blocking effect with the college professor. The person in the misperceived position seeks approval, recognition, acceptance, and respect. The person wants to be liked, and wants to feel that others admire him, but the secondary feelings are saying, "She doesn't approve of me," "He isn't pleased by me," "They don't accept me." These secondary feelings produce a barricade, or a block, to the perception of oral dependency need gratification. This block on oral dependency need gratification, characteristic of the misperceived position, causes a snowballing effect. The more the person requires meeting the oral dependency need, the more the person is frustrated. In being too dependent on too few, or too emotionally immature, the resulting anger tends to be repressed, creating more added unconscious guilt. With increased added unconscious guilt the greater the block of the perception of oral dependency need gratification. A person caught up in this snowballing process will tend to perceive greater and greater rejections.

The block causes someone in the misperceived position to interpret the behavior of others in regard to feeling rejected. Whatever someone who is emotionally significant to that person does or doesn't do will be perceived—or really *misperceived*—as a frustration of the person's attempt to meet the oral dependency need. For example, one woman I knew said of a neighbor, "She couldn't invite me to dinner in person; she had to do it over the phone." This invitation to dinner becomes a rejection or a frustration of the oral dependency need. I heard someone else say, "Bob called me when I was home sick from work; he was probably only checking on me to see if I was really at home." What one would think would be oral dependency need gratifying, is misinterpreted as frustrating. The block causes a twisting around of perceptions, all done unconsciously, but viewed as factual and supportive of the block. To show this twisting, look at this example. Suppose someone visits a neighbor and notices a new painting on the wall. She says to the neighbor, who she knows paints, "Did you paint that picture?" If the man is more emotionally comfortable, he'll say something like, "Why yes, do you like it?" If she says, "It's beautiful; I love it!" then he'll be pleased and the interchange will have been oral dependency need gratifying. However, if he has a high added unconscious guilt in the misperceived position when she says, "Did you paint that picture?", he might say something like, "You didn't think I was capable of painting that, did you?" If she says, "I love it, it's beautiful!" he might add, "I'm really offended that you didn't think I painted it!" He twists the perception and blocks out any meeting of his oral dependency need. He cannot perceive acceptance, favorable recognition, or admiration, even when it is so obviously offered. Another woman I saw recently said about her husband, "He only stays with me because he's afraid of what people would say if he left." Her feelings are, "He doesn't love me," "He'd rather be with anyone than have to stay with me." But when presented with the fact, "He's staying with you. Doesn't that mean something?", she says, "He only stays with me because he's afraid of what people would say if he left." She twists the perceptions around and blocks out the fact that he's staying because he loves her; she effectively blocks out any oral dependency need gratification.

Another example of the block is, "I only hear from the children when they need money." This statement came from a retired man with several adult children; when they visit him, he believes that the only reason they do so is to get money. He does give them some money every time they visit, but he feels that they expect it. The higher his misperceived added unconscious guilt, the more he feels, "They *expect* me to give them money" and the more he also feels, "They don't *really* love me." He can't understand that they visit him because they love him and want to spend some time with him. He has a block on their love for him. I heard a retired woman say of her children, "They only come to see me if they want a free place to stay in Florida." But her children spend their vacations visiting their mother because they do love her. She blocks out this love, however, when her added unconscious guilt in the misperceived position has increased. She wants so desperately then to see evidence that her children love her, but when they provide it she can't see it. It's misperceived as a rejection.

The block produces a *no-win situation* for someone else. The person with a great amount of added unconscious guilt in the misperceived position will twist any statement or behavior around to manifest the block. For instance, in the previous two examples, if the children visit, the parents don't recognize that the children love them, but if the children did not visit, the parents would be equally convinced that the children did not love them. The woman does not perceive that her husband loves her if he stays with her, but she surely would not believe his love if he left. It is the misperceived position that is the basis for the "rejection complex," so the person is going to perceive rejection, regardless of reality.

The person in the misperceived position will twist innocuous statements, pieces of casual conversation, around, into a rejection. For instance, I knew a successful professional woman who told me about a recent visit to her mother-in-law. She reported "His mother said, 'Come again when you can stay longer.' God, that made me mad! I stayed there for two hours. What did she think—that I've got nothing to do all day except sit on my ass and chat? She must think I'm a leech on her son. Why can't she say, 'Thanks for coming' the way my mother would have?" The mother-in-law made a seemingly innocuous statement, but this woman, who already has the misperceived secondary feeling and, as such, a perception of reality as, "My mother-in-law doesn't like me," twists it around to make it a blatant rejection. To someone with increased misperceived added unconscious guilt, there is no such thing as an innocuous statement. The person is always suspiciously thinking, "She is telling me she doesn't like something about me." Not only the communication but the observed behavior is searched for confirmation of the rejection that is being felt because of the increased misperceived guilt. Even what is not said or what is not done has the potential for being misconstrued to make the reality proof of the rejection that is actually coming from the person's emotional unreality. The person in the misperceived position will examine innocuous statements and observed behavior wondering, "What did she *really* mean by that?" We don't need a biochemical explanation for this unrationalized perception of rejection. It is equated with the unrationalized depression, phobia, and anxiety, of the self-felt position, or the unrationalized dislike or hate of the projected position. Because of those increased primary and secondary feelings of the misperceived position, the person has the capacity to twist any statement, that would be innocuous to anyone else, into a rejection. This perceived rejection can be well rationalized, poorly rationalized, or unrationalized.

The misperceived position can also produce the feeling of being *used*, which is simply a variation of being rejected. We've already seen this feeling in the examples of the parent who felt that his children used him to get money, and the parent who felt that her children were using her to have a free place to stay in Florida. Someone could also feel used in the work situation, as did the woman who told me, "He speaks so nicely to me at the office, 'Good morning, Carole,' but it's all a damn front. I know he hates my guts. He's just using me until he can find a replacement, then I know he'll nail my ass and can me." Or, someone could feel used in regard to a sexual relationship. I've heard many people who I know are in the misperceived position say, "She's only after my body," or "He's only dating me for sex." One woman even said to me, "He just masturbates in my vagina—that's our sex life." These feelings of being used come from the inability to perceive any oral dependency need gratification. Because of the increased misperceived guilt, the person is feeling, "He doesn't care about me because he finds me so inferior, inadequate, and unacceptable."

The feeling of being used can particularly show the no-win situation. The person in the misperceived position wants to feel needed but can't perceive that he or she is needed; instead, he or she feels used. For example, one woman who belongs to a church group told me that she felt rejected when she wasn't asked to work on a committee. Whenever she was asked, however, she felt used. Or as another example, a house-wife told me, "It really upsets me when Bill (her husband) cleans up around the house. It's as if he likes to point out what a slob I am." But at another time, she'd said, "I wish Bill would help around the house. It upsets me to think that he just uses me to keep his house clean." In a sexual situation, if a spouse is *not* having sex with the person, it's because the spouse doesn't care about the person. But if the spouse *is* having sex, the person is being used. Even in dating situations one will see evidence of this same thing. A young woman that I knew, who had a high misperceived added unconscious guilt, was upset after several dates with a young man because he didn't make some sexual advances. "It would indicate to me if he made a sexual advance that he thinks something besides that I'm an old slob that he's stuck with for the evening." But if the reality of this dating situation was that the young man did make a sexual advance, then it would have been interpreted as, "What type of person does he think I am? He just wants to use me." The block and this feeling of being used create no-win situations for those people with increased added unconscious guilt in the misperceived position and for those who are involved with them.

Sometimes it is difficult for people in the misperceived position to substantiate with any facts how they believe someone else feels about them. They then resort to saying things like, "I just picked up bad vibes from him," or "It was his attitude," or "It wasn't *what* she said, it was *how* she said it," or "I could tell from her body language." If we argue with the person who says, "I picked up rather obvious signals that I wasn't welcome," and try to tell her that she is perfectly welcome, she then may say, "I'm not stupid, I can tell when I'm not wanted!" But it's the increased misperceived secondary feelings that are telling her that she is not wanted. The person feels it's from perceived attitudes, nuances, subtleties, signals, "vibes" and "body language."

In regard to a compliment, which these people cannot accept, we'll often hear, "She was only being sarcastic, because I know how she really feels," or "He didn't really mean that; he just said it to be polite." Compliments are characteristically taken in regard to the feelings of rejection that are already there. One frequently hears, "People can be such fakes and phonies. They're not honest with me about how they feel." It seems as though people in the misperceived position would like us to be "honest" and tell them that we don't like them. However this they'd certainly take as a rejection too. What they want most is to *feel* that we do like them, but if we *say* we like them, we're not being honest.

We can't even do nice things for these people without their perceiving the acts as rejections. A guest with increased misperceived added unconscious guilt may twist his hostess's act of turning on a hall light into a rejection, saying, "You don't have to turn that light on for me! I may look that old and enfeebled to you, but I'm not! Sure, I'm not as young as I used to be, but I can still find my way around." How a simple complimentary act can be taken as a gross rejection, and bitterly resented, is again exemplified by the student taking French, who gets a letter, written in French, from a friend: "He wrote to me in French because he thought I was so stupid that I wouldn't be able to read it. He was just trying to show me up as the ignoramus. Well, I fooled the bastard! I didn't have any trouble reading his letter. He'd never believe it, though. But I really fixed him when I threw his letter in the waste basket and I'll be damned if I'll answer it!"

Because of the block, others may conclude that it's like a *bottomless pit* to try to please the person with high misperceived guilt. The others can shovel in attention, consideration, time, effort, praise, and love, but the person doesn't recognize any of it and demands still more. It's like putting sand down a rat hole; it just doesn't fill up. It's because the attention, the consideration, and the love of others are all being blocked by the person's increased added unconscious guilt in the misperceived position. No matter what they do for this person, it's never enough; what they do just doesn't seem to count. What this person really needs most is not shovelled-in love but a way to decrease the misperceived added unconscious guilt and its block.

The person who can't perceive the oral dependency need gratification is always trying to figure out a way to see real evidence that the other loves her, or even just likes her. She may make a *hostile demand*, such as, "If you *really* liked me, you'd do _____," or "If you *really* love me, you won't do _____." For instance, suppose a man has to go on a trip for a week which is very important to his success at work. But his wife, with increased guilt in the misperceived position, demands, "If you *really* loved me, you'd cancel that trip and go with me to my bridge tournament." So the man cancels the trip, but she still can't perceive that he loves her and the tournament turns out to be an emotional disaster for her. She still perceives rejection; it's an example of the "bottomless pit," the nowin situation, and also the hostile demand. Sometimes the other person does not do what the person demands and this then will be the "proof" of how the person feels—that the other person doesn't really care about her. Fulfilling the hostile demand appears to be most crucial to attaining emotional comfortableness or serenity in the relationship. It is supposed to show her that the other person really does care about her, that the other does like or love her. But we later realize that it doesn't matter whether or not these demands are fulfilled, because we can't show these people that we like them or care about them or even that we love them.

This block reminds me of the story of the monkey and the flagpole. The monkey is climbing the flagpole so that people will look up and see his great accomplishment, but when they look up, they see a part of his anatomy that he'd rather keep hidden. The further up he goes to seek favorable attention, the more unfavorable attention he gets. The part of his anatomy that he reveals completely negates his accomplishment. The person in the misperceived position seeks the limelight on what he feels to be an asset but it seems as though that limelight becomes instead a spotlight focused upon a liability. He perceives any recognition or attention that he does receive as unfavorable, just like that monkey up the flagpole.

We can see examples in people we'd think would be basking in the limelight of public recognition or national acclaim. Judging by the amount of attention, recognition, and admiration they receive, we would think that they have an abundance of perceived oral dependency need gratification. They are constantly in the public eye, receiving tons of fan mail, and pages of press coverage. Yet we know, from the unhappy lives of these people that they seem to have high unmet oral dependency needs and are *not* emotionally comfortable. It's the misperceived position that causes people like these to perceive the limelight as an unfavorable spotlight. We can see many of these people, not only in the field of entertainment, but also in any other reality endeavor, where they've been highly successful.

Because the person is too dependent on too few and has a concentration of his or her unmet oral dependncey need, focused on too few individuals, this person tends to become involved in love-hate relationships. The greater the block, the more there is a build-up of still more misperceived guilt, and the more the person becomes emotionally immature—regressing toward dependence on one person. That regression to one source for drawing oral dependency gratification and getting rid of anger is directly proportional to the amount of misperceived guilt. What, in the emotionally comfortable person, is usually done diffusely, subtly and successfully, becomes concentrated, blatant, and unsuccessful. In the exclusive relationship, where the person is almost totally emotionally dependent on someone else, one sees the most intense love-hate relationships. If someone is still dependent on a *few*, rather than exclusively dependent, then one can see a love-hate relationship to a lesser degree. In any love-hate relationship, there often seems to be a continual swinging from a love side to a hate side with very little, if any, "like," or comfortable relating in between.

This brings us to one of the most interesting characteristics of the misperceived position. The position seems to have two sides: a *self-felt side* and a *projected side*. The self-felt side is similar to the self-felt position, except that the self-felt position is more permanent. The self-felt side of the misperceived position is not permanent. The person may be on the self-felt side temporarily but then may swing to the projected side, which is similar to the projected position, but, again, less permanent. What we have seen so far of the misperceived position is the *mid-line stance*. The primary feelings, "He feels I'm inferior, inadequate, unacceptable, guilty, wrong, and incomplete" and all of the secondary feelings arising from those of the misperceived position are from this mid-line stance. The self-felt and projected sides are similar to the self-felt and projected positions in regard to the primary and secondary feelings and in regard to lowering the added unconscious guilt. When someone is on the self-felt side, he can lower his added unconscious guilt in any of the ways that we mentioned for the self-felt position. And on the projected side, he can lower his added unconscious guilt in the same way as can people in the projected position.

When someone is on the self-felt side, he feels, "It's *my* fault; *I'm* to blame." On the projected side, "It's *his* fault," or "*He's* to blame." The mid-line stance is, "He feels I'm to blame." The misperceived mid-line stance, as another example, might be, "He doesn't love me; he doesn't really care about me." On the self-felt side, one would see, "But I don't love myself; I don't really care about myself." And on the projected side, one would see, "I don't love him; I don't really care about him." "She thinks I'm impossible to live with," "He feels I created the marriage problems," and "She feels I contribute nothing to our relationship" are expressions of the mid-line stance. On the self-felt side, these become, "I am impossible to live with," "I do create the marriage problems" and "I'm the one that contributes nothing to our relationship." On the projected side, these are, "He's impossible to live with," "He created the marriage problems," and "He's the one that contributes nothing to our relationship." In the work situation, "They feel I'm lax and irresponsible," is a mid-line expression with, "I am lax and irresponsible" being the self-felt side and, "They're the ones that are lax and irresponsible" being the projected side. The more added unconscious guilt there is in the misperceived position and the more the person is too dependent on too few, the more the person will tend to swing from the self-felt side to the projected side and back. While in the mid-line stance, the person simply feels rejected.

One can stay on either side for an extended period of time, particularly if the misperceived added unconscious guilt is at a lower level. It is increasingly more difficult to stay on one side or the other as the misperceived guilt increases and as the diffusion process reverses toward concentration. In selecting someone with whom to live, if one chooses an individual on the self-felt *side* rather than in the self-felt position, he'll be in for some grief when that person swings to the projected side. If he chooses someone who is in the self-felt *position*, he's chosen a saint, and she will stay that way. If he chooses someone in the projected position, she will be critical and always finding fault, and she will tend to stay that way. If he is sure that the person is in the self-felt or projected position, not just on the self-felt or projected side of the misperceived position, then he knows what's in store. But if the person is on the self-felt side, he probably has some unpleasant surprises ahead. If the person is on the self-felt side, she may appear very nice and self-sacrificing, accepting blame and responsibility for mistakes, and professing love, putting others first, doing for others, and not getting angry. But when the person swings to the projected side, her behavior is exactly the opposite.

If we listen to someone in the misperceived position, we can often hear him swinging back and forth, particularly when he is emotionally upset. For instance, when a wife who is in the misperceived position is upset, on the projected side, she may say, "He's not a good husband and he doesn't treat me right. He's had an affair. He's always going out drinking and coming home drunk. I don't see how I put up with *him*!" But then when she swings to the self-felt side, she says, "I know I haven't been the wife I should have been and it seems as though all I do is bitch and complain. If I didn't do that, I wouldn't have driven him to another woman, and he wouldn't drink so much. It's my fault; I don't see how he puts up with *me*!" Someone like this woman will often present the projected side and just when one is beginning to understand that the person described is some son-of-a-bitch, she will swing to the self-felt side and present contrasting evidence that it isn't that way at all and that she herself is the son-of-a-bitch. After presenting either the self-felt side, or the projected side, she will pause, sigh deeply, and preface the contrasting side's argument with, "Maybe I'm seeing this all wrong." After presenting the projected side, for instance, she may pause, sigh, and say, "It may be my fault. It usually is," or "I probably caused it." Or, "I'm just feeling sorry for myself," by which they really mean, "I deserve this kind of treatment," and "I shouldn't complain." Or after saying that the problem is the other person's fault, the person briefly pauses and may say, "I'm not saying that it's *all* his fault," and then present the entire problem again, this time from the self-felt side. Sometimes the person presents the projected side, then pauses and says something like, "You probably don't believe me; nobody usually does," and then goes on to present the self-felt side's, "Nobody *should* believe me." "Nobody believes me" is, of course, the mid-line stance of misperceived position with, "I don't believe myself" being the self-felt side and "I don't believe him" being the projected side. After giving evidence that "He has a sick and twisted mind" or "She should see a psychiatrist," then evidence is presented that "I'm the one with a sick and twisted mind" and "I should see a psychiatrist." "He doesn't know how to love a person" is countered with, "I don't know how to love a person." The "He feels I don't know how to love" is the mid-line stance conveying rejection.

This swinging which characterizes the misperceived position is really the psychodynamic basis for *ambivalence*, which is a mixture of feelings. Like a pendulum swinging back and forth, the very emotionally uncomfortable person goes back and forth from the self-felt side to the projected side. On the projected side, one hears, "He has *no* right to expect this added work from me," and on the self-felt side, "He's got *every* right to expect this added work from me." On the self-felt side it's, "I could do better", and on the projected side, "She could do better." On the self-felt side, "I created the problem," and on the projected side, "He created the problem." These are all examples of ambivalence, of this swinging back and forth. These people are often left wondering, "Is it *me* or is it *him*?" They're never sure, because they're always swinging back and forth. And no answer from anyone else could be correct because of the tendency to swing; no side is permanently held. With enough added unconscious guilt, the person can reach the delusional level on either side. It is interesting to note that one of the earliest writers on schizophrenia found that ambivalence was a prominent characteristic of the condition.

When the person has a large amount of added unconscious guilt in the misperceived position, he may appear to be "schizophrenic" or split in his thinking. The person appears "nutty" when it is difficult to get at the "meat" of what is so ambivalently said. Various other expressions describing this "craziness" suggest the ambivalence of the misperceived position. "Loony," for example, means literally resembling a loon, a bird which spends part of its time under the water and part out of the water. "Squirrelly" refers to the small animals who seem unable to go from point A to point B in a straight line. This is shown particulary when they attempt to run across a busy street. They'll go halfway, then back a quarter of the way, then go three-quarters of the way, then back to the halfway point, then finally, they may reach point B. They can't seem to decide whether they want to go to point B or not. "Batty" is a similar example, because the flight of a bat is never in a straight line. The direction these animals take seems indecisive and not goal-directed, as does the thinking of people with greatly increased guilt in the misperceived position. These people don't follow a straight line, with respect to what they're presenting, because they're swinging back and forth. Another related expression is, "She's going off in all directions." These people can't seem to "get it together." Other examples of this are: "He's not all there," "He's got a screw loose," "He's not playing with a full deck"—all implying that "he" doesn't complete what "he" says on one side, because "he" is swinging back and forth. Sometimes we'll hear college kids put this in the vernacular with, "He can't get his shit together." These colorful metaphors that we all have probably heard suggest the swinging back and forth from side to side of the misperceived position.

The ambivalence of the misperceived position sometimes makes it difficult to commit suicide. Someone who is on the self-felt side may want to, or may even attempt to commit suicide. But he or she does so ambivalently, as seen in the following cases. I knew of a woman, on the self-felt side, who tried to commit suicide by shooting herself. But she showed her ambivalence about it by shooting herself in the hand, on the local hospital lawn, in plain view of emergency room personnel. A psychiatrist once told me that he'd had a patient who was ambivalently suicidal, and went to the Chesapeake Bay Bridge, which is the highest bridge on the East Coast. But the man prepared to jump from the lowest span of the bridge, at noon, when traffic was especially heavy. Traffic stopped, and many people got out of their cars to prevent his suicide. These people have the same difficulty trying to commit murder. They often can't hold anger or hatred long enough to do it. For example, I knew of a husband and wife, who were making passionate love in the bedroom during a cocktail party. The next day he was in the emergency room with a minor stab wound; his wife half-heartedly tried to kill him, and, of course, he refused to press charges. Another example is the wife of a pharmaceutical representative, who was upset because her husband, who was always a little paranoid, was sleeping with a gun under his pillow. She told me she was afraid she'd wake up some night, and while still half asleep, grab the gun and either shoot herself (self-felt side) or shoot him (projected side).

Because of this swinging back and forth, anger on the projected side of the misperceived position is never held as it is in the projected position, as you can see from the above example. It's always ambivalently expressed anger. If anger is expressed, it is not as successfully done as it is in the projected position, because it is usually focused on someone who will not support the projection of guilt and will probably project guilt back. The projected guilt and expressed anger are only temporary, and then when the person is back on the self-felt side, he or she feels apologetic and to blame for the incident and feels guilty about having expressed the anger. This is opposed to the projected position, in which the person expresses the anger, feels it's justified, and is never apologetic. It's never ambivalently expressed. Only in the misperceived position, will the person express anger on the projected side and then, on the self-felt side, say, "I'm so sorry. I shouldn't have yelled at you. It's really my fault," or "I'm sorry I shouldn't have beat you." The anger in the misperceived position is always ambivalent. The love is also ambivalent. When someone in the misperceived position has an intense love, this love may swing back and forth as the person swings from side to side. She will profess a love for someone at one time and then not love him at another. A confusion of loving and not loving, hating and not hating, befuddles both partners. When both the anger and the love are directly expressed and interchanged with the other emotionally significant person's misperceived position, the situation quickly becomes even more chaotic!

The ambivalence of the love-hate relationship is evident in many cases of spouse abuse, as it is in the following:

I provoke him when I know I shouldn't. It can't be his fault completely. I shouldn't blame him as I know he loves me. He always feels so guilty after he's done those things that I feel sorry for him. It's as though he loses control of himself. It's my fault, and I shouldn't blame him. I've got to face up to that. God only knows I'm not perfect. I'm far from it. At times, I wonder why he ever married me. We've got to find out who's to blame if we're going to get this marriage where it use to be, and where it ought to be now. I don't know whether I'm sick, or whether he is. I do know that if he's sick, and if I really do love him, then I should give him understanding and another chance. I'd want him to do that for me if I were sick. That's what love is supposed to be like. I don't want to turn him in to the authorities. He'd never forgive me for that if I did, and I would never forgive myself. I'd rather hurt myself than have him suffer like that. He hasn't had it easy in life, and he's had to put up with a lot in living with me. I don't want to make it worse for him. There's been enough suffering already. Why should more be involved? I only want to give him love. Punishment not only isn't the answer, it would be wrong. And two wrongs don't make a right. I want things to be right in my marriage. I do get pleasure out of doing nice things for him. I'd rather pamper him than be pampered myself. That's the way I am. But I wish he'd do some nice things for me once in a while. He hasn't done anything nice for I don't know how long. But then he says I don't deserve it the way I've been acting. And maybe I don't. I can't really say I've been the wife I should have been to him lately. There are too many things in the past, too, that I'm guilty of. But, believe me, he's been no angel either! He can get so ugly at times. He's threatened to kill me many of the times he's beat me. He'd kill me right now if he knew I was talking to you about him. What's wrong with him anyway that he gets so abusive? He beat his other wife the same way he does me. He'll use any excuse at all to beat me. I often wonder if he doesn't have something physically wrong—you know—like a brain tumor, or maybe a hormonal imbalance. He could be very ill. He won't go to a doctor. And he's against my coming here. He thinks we should work out our own problems, and maybe we should. We don't need outside interference. We only need each other. He does need help, but *I* want to help him. I want him to need me. I knew he was a wife-beater when I married him, but I also knew what his ex-wife was like, and she was asking for it with the things she did. I thought I could change him by giving him all my love. I still think I can. But at times I think he's incapable of giving me love and that I'm married to a sadist. I sometimes wonder if he ought to be arrested before he does kill me. I never told anyone how he broke my arm last year. I told everyone I fell and did it myself. If he's a sadistic wife-beater, he ought to be locked up. [Pause] He says he's not. And maybe he isn't. He deserves another chance. It's only fair. I mean, I'd want him to give me another chance, if the situation were turned around. He means well and I've got to believe him. He is my husband, after all. We've got to work it out together—just the two of us. I'm going to stop coming here and see if both he and I can try to love each other more and hurt each other less—that's all we both want.

The ambivalence, the love-hate relationship, and the situation of being too dependent on too few are painfully evident in this passage. And we can see that this spouse abuse will continue.

The misperceived position is the position of being too dependent on too few. It is the position of ambivalence and of the love-hate relationship. If you listen to a person with increased guilt in the misperceived position talking about the person that he seems to hate so much, you might well ask, "Well, why don't you just leave her?" But then the person seems to imply, "Oh, I can't, because I love her." And if you were foolish enough to advise, "Then why don't you stay with her," the response would be, "But I can't because I hate her so." What becomes apparent is that there is no solution in reality. They can't live *with* each other, and they can't live *without* each other. This seemingly unsolvable dilemma comes from being too dependent on too few, concentrating the oral dependency need and anger expression on one person. The solution of this dilemma can only come in an emotional unreality with an emotional process involving emotional diffusion. It doesn't come with intellectual advice.

Accusations can arise from the secondary feelings of the misperceived position. Feelings like, "He doesn't love me," "She doesn't care about me," "He's not comfortable around me" become, "You don't love me!" "You don't care about me!" "You're not comfortable around me!" "You don't listen to me!" "You want to hurt me!" "You're deliberately trying to make me miserable!" "You don't understand me!" "You want to get rid of me!" These accusations may be put into question form, like, "Why do you hate me?" "Why do you hurt me?" "Why are you angry with me?" or, "What do you want from me?" They are frequently found in emotional arguments but presented as factual. In these arguments, one hears the misperceptions, the twisted conclusions, the "bottomless pit," and the no-win situations. They all can be rationalized at length using the past, present, and future. The arguing becomes more intense if each partner is contending with a high level of misperceived added unconscious guilt.

A recent article in a popular magazine stated that over half the marriages in America break up over arguments about money. It went on to say that the real underlying problem is that "most couples start yelling before they ever try talking." We know that's because there's a "need" to yell. A nationally-known marriage counselor has said that underlying all marriage problems was a communication problem. But he wasn't looking quite deep enough. Although money may be a popular manifest content, underlying the communication problem is always increased guilt in the misperceived position. So another characteristic of the misperceived position is a communication problem.

Naturally, the ambivalence of love and hate will create communication difficulties for not only that person but also his or her listener. Some of the problems in communication arise from intensified secondary feelings like, "He doesn't listen to me," "She isn't interested in what I have to say," or "He doesn't want to talk to me." These feelings block oral dependency need gratification, which appeared, for the emotionally comfortable person, to be so easy to get in spontaneous communication. The unconscious communicative process, which meets the oral dependency need and allows the projection of guilt, appears to be so simple, but intensified feelings of the misperceived position can greatly complicate it. The process is only simple for those who have much less added unconscious guilt in the misperceived position. But once it increases, the block begins to build up. What then results is that even when this person is with other people, the person can't meet his or her oral dependency need. It may seem at first hard to understand that the person prone to alcohol abuse, who appears to be getting involved, talking to other people, still falls "off the wagon" and gets drunk. We can speculate that he had high misperceived added unconscious guilt and that those intensified primary and secondary feelings blocked the meeting of the oral dependency need. Another secondary feeling that blocks the meeting of the oral dependency need and creates communication problems is, "She doesn't understand me." A feeling like, "She doesn't understand me" implies that it's a waste of time to try to communicate, which, of course, blocks oral dependency need gratification. In the following example, the woman's misperceived added unconscious guilt causes problems when her husband tries to lower his own guilt. Her husband, a farmer, needs to express the anger he has accrued because of oral dependency need frustrations that have nothing to do with his relationship with his wife. But since she already feels, "He thinks it's *my* fault; he blames *me*," he can't express his anger without her "taking it personally." She came in to see me, and said, concerning her relationship with her husband, "All he does is gripe, bitch, and complain when things don't go right on the farm. It's as though it's all *my* fault, and I'm the cause of the water standing in the fields that rots the crops, or the drought that dries them up. Nothing ever is his fault; it's all my fault. I can't stand it any longer and if I don't get away I'm going to go crazy."

Such communication problems prevent the diffusion of the oral dependency need and the diffusion of projected guilt, leaving the person too dependent on too few. Through talking to someone else outside the love-hate relationship, the added unconscious guilt in the misperceived positon can be lowered. All those characteristics of the misperceived position become less intense. This is the solution for the problems of the misperceived position.

CHARACTERISTIC COMPLAINTS OF THE MISPERCEIVED POSITION

Mid-line Stance

I DON'T FEEL UNDERSTOOD

From: "He doesn't understand me."

I CAN'T BE MYSELF

From: "He feels I shouldn't be myself."

WE CAN'T TALK

From: "He feels I shouldn't express myself."

I DON'T FEEL LOVED

From: "He feels I'm not lovable."

I DON'T FEEL INCLUDED

From: "He feels I shouldn't be included."

I DON'T FEEL EQUAL

From: "He feels I'm not equal."

Self-felt Side

I'M TO BLAME FOR MY NOT . . .

feeling understood."
being able to be myself."
being able to express myself."
feeling loved."
feeling included."
feeling equal."

"There's something wrong with **me**."

"Maybe it's all **my** fault!"

Projected Side

HE'S TO BLAME FOR MY NOT . . .

feeling understood."
being able to be myself."
being able to express myself."
feeling loved."
feeling included."
feeling equal."

"There's something wrong with **him**."

"Maybe it's all **his** fault!"

CHAPTER 15
Results of the Misperceived Position

Some people don't seem to know how to pick out a good mate. At times they may think they do, but later they know they didn't and wish they did. In fact, they'd give anything to find that perfect mate. The answer to why they must search so diligently for that perfect mate lies in the misperceived position. When the secondary feelings of misperceived added unconscious guilt intensify, the high unmet oral dependency need tends to be focused on another person, or on a few other people. The people with increased added unconscious guilt in the misperceived position are looking for love. I've had many patients come in, like the woman in the previous chapter, who say that all they want in life is to love and be loved in return. The problem is that the increased misperceived added unconscious guilt makes these people unable to see any evidence of what they want. They become blind to the very thing that they want the most.

Because they want this love so intensely, they often demand not just a relationship with too few, but an *exclusive* relationship with one person. They want to be the center of this other person's life. All of their attempts to meet their oral dependency needs become focused on this one relationship. When we look at their lives, we can see a history of repetitive increases in misperceived added unconscious guilt and one exclusive relationship after another that has ended in grief. Even if we ask them about their high school days, they'll often tell us that they found one person with whom they "went steady" for several years. They'll tell us too, that this relationship was emotionally intense and exclusive. When that relationship broke up, they became involved in another similar exclusive relationship. They'll tell us that they never did date many different people. Characteristically, these people have one "best friend" and that's it. They don't have a wide sphere of friends. And since this is the position that is characterized by paranoia, these people seem to feel, "It's me and my only friend against the hostile world." After high school they may struggle along with the same unhappy relationship or they may continue to have one exclusive relationship after another, and often, one marriage after another. They have not matured emotionally, diffusing the oral dependency need so that it is gratified on a part-person, part-experience, part-situation basis. These people are looking for intense love in an exclusive relationship. The intensity of the love is directly proportional to the level that the misperceived added unconscious guilt has risen because of the block on any perception of oral dependency need gratification. When other people look at these relationships, they conclude, "She's *too* dependent on him," or "He's *too* dependent on her." These people will often rationalize their "need" for an exclusive relationship by saying things like, "Well, isn't that what marriage is? Shouldn't one partner depend on the other? Shouldn't he be the only important person in my life? Why should we have to need others when we have each other?" These rationalizations seem to make sense in reality and it's difficult to refute them. But these people become *overly* dependent in one relationship. Though they may be involved with other people, it's not an emotional involvement from which they can diffusely draw oral dependency need gratification. They all too likely perceive rejection, discrimination, or victimization in their involvements with others.

Throughout their lives, these people continue to involve themselves in exclusive relationships. Their secondary feelings create the block, intensify the unmet oral dependency need, and the relationship becomes doomed to failure. For example, I knew of a sixteen-year-old girl who was verbally and physically abused at home. She wanted to get out of this hellish situation and find "heaven," so she got married. She married someone who also had an intense need for love, derived from his high level of misperceived guilt. Then her spouse verbally and physically abused her in the same type of exclusive, intensely emotional relationship she'd had with her parents. She still doesn't see that her basic problem is that she's continuing to be too dependent on too few. The cure as she sees it is finding "Mr. Perfect."

The high unmet oral dependency need of someone in the misperceived position tends to attract other people in the misperceived postion. One person can "see" the high unmet oral dependency need in another and it's attractive because it's the person with the high unmet need who can reciprocate an intense relationship. The emotionally comfortable person doesn't have this high unmet oral dependency need so they are not so attractive; they are not the type of people who are, for example, going to put a note saying, "I love only you," "I miss you so much," or, "I can't live without you" in the other person's lunchbag or coat pocket. The person with increased guilt in the misperceived position will do this sort of thing. I've known people in the misperceived position to write, "I love you" on the top of the butter, if they know that the other will be using it. Or to leave small love notes on the windshield of the other person's car so that she will read them when she goes to the parking lot after work, or to send flowers often, for no particular reason. A person in the misperceived position needs this kind of continual attention and desires an exclusive involvement and another person in the misperceived position is the very one who will try to give such love. Therefore, these exclusive relationships are usually between two people with increased guilt in the misperceived position. Initially these exclusive relationships are characterized by being so "heavenly" and so "loving," which is a direct reflection of the high unmet oral need and that unconscious wishful thinking we previously saw in regard to the transference.

Another thing that attracts two people in the misperceived position is their similar past histories—histories of not just poor, but often tragic, relationships. They'll say things like, "Both of us have been through living hells, but now we have each other. I know she understands me because she went through the same horrendous things I did." One woman recently said to me, "While I was in the hospital, I met someone unbelievably nice. His nerves were shot and he was being treated for an ulcer. We were attracted to each other right off. We're both so sensitive and we've both been through so much hell for so long. His wife treated him like dirt, just like John [her husband] treated me. His wife never cared for him and John didn't care for me. His wife feigned love and John was the greatest actor I ever saw. His wife just used him the way John used me. When he said that his wife took away his masculinity and castrated him, I told him that John had taken away my womanhood. I didn't even feel like a woman until I met Ralph in the hospital. He was so easy to talk to. He was so understanding and so starved for love . . . " Being "starved for love" reflects Ralph's high unmet oral dependency need. But the reason that this woman found it easy to talk to Ralph was because they shared a past history of failed relationships. The failed relationship does not have to be a marriage. Two people could share a poor relationship with their parents, their siblings, their children, etc. This common past reality allows a common manifest content in talking about how others have treated them badly, never loved them, used them, and put them down. We don't see this situation with the other two positions of added unconscious guilt.

When two people with high unmet oral dependency needs find each other, they have the tendency to form quickly an intense transference. One person will then be likely to make the other greater than he is in reality, using unconscious wishful thinking. When the person finds someone, it's usually after a previous relationship hasn't worked out. After a relationship fails, this is the person we saw earlier, who says, "I've had it with men. I'm *never* going to fall in love again." Then she finds someone, and feels that this is the person she has been looking for all of her life: "Mr. Perfect." She is so happy, and in her unconscious wishful thinking, because of the intense transference coming from the high unmet oral dependency need, she has made this person greater than the other actually is. The other person becomes her reason for happiness. Where before, she might have felt like dying and may even have attempted suicide, she again has a reason for living. For example, the woman who met Ralph in the hospital continued to say, "I don't think I really knew what love was like until I met Ralph. He's perfect in every way. I can't believe how wonderful he is. We're perfect for each other and so happy together. Where before I wanted to end it all, now I want to live. If I could spend all the rest of my life with him and only him, I'd be the happiest woman. He feels the same way. That's the kind of love I've always wanted. I still sometimes wonder about his love, in that it just doesn't seem possible that anyone as nice as Ralph can possibly love someone like me . . . " You can see that this woman has made Ralph greater than he really is when she says things like, "He's perfect," "How wonderful he is," and "Anyone as nice as Ralph . . . " The person in the misperceived position has a tendency to say all these kinds of things: "He's the most wonderful man I've ever met," "I can't believe such a sweet, beautiful woman could love me." The other person has become the sole source of happiness.

But then the trouble starts. The two become exclusively involved with each other and lose any targets that they may have had for the expression of anger. The person in the misperceived position cannot tolerate even indirect expressions of anger, so problems soon begin to develop in the "heavenly relationship." One person may have said, "My mother is always putting me down. She's constantly on my back." Then the other says, "I'll take you away from all that," partly because he wants to do so much for the other person, and because, "I don't want you angry or upset." But many times, he takes the other person away from those people, experiences, or situations used for targets of projected guilt. If one person complains about his or her job, the other may say, "Change your job. Quit!"

The relationship becomes too concentrated in regard to emotions. It becomes an emotional powder keg for projected guilt. One person in such a relationship told me, "I gave up all my friends for Joe; Joe *demanded* it! He didn't even want me involved with my own children and insisted on my moving away from them. Joe was always finding fault with them and I did agree that all they did was use me. He didn't want me to go to lunch with the office gang, and I will admit that all they do is talk about one another, so I had to quit doing that. He wanted me only involved with him. It was what appeared to make him happy. And I was willing to do it, because I loved him. Joe even had me give up my dog, because he said I got too worried about her. I think that it was really because Joe wanted me for himself, and couldn't bear the thought of sharing me with anyone or anything else. Things went well for a month or two. We were so happy together—happier than I've ever been in my entire life. Then Joe began to accuse me of putting him down, making him feel useless and worthless. He became supersensitive and accused me of being supercritical. And I accused him of the same. We both had changed. Our love turned to hate and now all we do is fight." Joe had taken away this woman's targets for guilt projection and now she's beginning to project guilt in the relationship itself. The guilt isn't projected indirectly or metaphorically but is too often projected directly.

In another example, I knew a woman from a lower middle class family who married a very wealthy man. They soon developed an exclusive relationship. This man, in wanting to take her away from her past situation, told her that he didn't want her to work. "I make more than enough money for us both and I don't want you working. I want you to be there when I get home and to greet me with a kiss and a smile," he said. But she told me, "He says my smile is usually a snarl. How can I smile and look happy when I feel so unhappy? I can't hide it. He buys me expensive clothes, jewelry, a nice new car, and anything else I want. But I feel like a bird that's lost its ability to sing, trapped in a gilded cage." All of this woman's other relationships have been cut off. She had moved away from her family and her few friends to be with her husband and she has no work situation that would give her targets for the guilt projection that could keep her added unconscious guilt at a more comfortable level.

Often, when the exclusive relationship begins, the person who has a high unmet need has added unconscious guilt on the self-felt side, which looks so attractive because of all the self-felt characteristics. These people will do anything for others; they put others first; they work hard; they take the blame; they don't get angry, etc. These characteristics, along with the capacity for intense love coming from the high unmet need, are most attractive to other people in the misperceived position. But then the person swings to the projected side, targeting anger at "my no good children," "my goddamned stepmother," "my ex-husband, that S.O.B.," or "that stupid bunch of hypocrites I work with." The other person, meaning well, takes her away from the children, the stepmother, the ex-husband, or the work situation. What the other person is actually doing is removing the targets for projected guilt.

People with increased guilt in the misperceived position are characterized by demanding exclusivity and by having one intense relationship after another. As we've noted, these relationships can be marital, sexual, or parental, but they can also be with friends. These people don't have many friends; they're the ones who say, "I have lots of acquaintances, but only one good friend." So when these people lose a close friend, they don't have many others to turn to for the part-person, part-experience, part-situation equating for guilt projection. Since they don't, their added unconscious guilt quickly goes up. But they can't project guilt in the exclusive relationship without causing problems, and when they do project guilt, the relationship quickly begins to deteriorate. After the failure of an intense emotional relationship, the person often says, "I'll never fall in love again," but then finds someone else, usually another person with increased guilt in the misperceived position and with a high unmet oral need. Each person may temporarily lower added unconscious guilt by projecting guilt and expressing anger, indirectly, at the person with whom he or she was previously involved. For a very short time, the relationship may appear "heavenly." But then the two will start cutting off relatives, friends, employers, co-workers, church members, even pets, and the relationship soon becomes as "hellish" as the previous one. The auxiliary sources of oral dependency need gratification and the targets for projected guilt are removed.

The exclusive relationship, where two people are almost totally involved with each other, could go well if the person's misperceived added unconscious guilt stays on the self-felt side. Here the person will develop one or some of the conditions associated with the self-felt position. For instance, an individual exclusively involved could have a good marriage relationship, but be hypochondriacal, phobic, or have anxiety attacks. Or the person could be abusing alcohol or drugs. In the following example, the man's hypochondriasis protects this exclusive relationship with his wife. His guilt has not swung to the projected side because it is focused on the self-felt side, on his headaches. "I can't put off these headaches any longer. When these headaches strike me, I almost go blind from the pain, and the only way I can endure them is to lie down in a dark room. No medication seems to help, and believe me, I've tried everything. I've gone to one doctor after another but so far no one has been able to find the cause of my headaches or anything that relieves them. I've even tried chiropractic and praying, but that didn't help. And my wife is so worried. I don't know what I'd do without her. Dr. Brown wants to put me in the hospital for another set of exhaustive tests. I don't want to go, but she insists, so I'll probably be in the hospital for three or four weeks, much as I dread it." If this man's added unconscious guilt shifted to the projected side, his hypochondriacal headaches might cease but he'd probably develop problems of the very same magnitude in his relationship with his wife.

Another manifestation of the exclusive relationship is the desire to "become one" with the other person. These people want to be "islands in the stream," just the two of them. In some religions, one of the goals is to "become one" with the supernatural, and perhaps that sort of "becoming one" works. But to "become one" with someone who is less than divine usually doesn't work, and it can often create severe problems. For instance, when on the self-felt side, with lots of added unconscious guilt, a person will often inconvenience himself for others, and will be self-sacrificing, which may have made him most attractive. But when he "becomes one" with that exclusive other, he will tend to make the other person do the same thing, which may be resented by the other. As an example, consider a retired high-ranking army officer I knew whose misperceived added unconscious guilt was often on the self-felt side. His brother is the wealthy chairman of the board of a nationally-known company. I saw the officer's wife, who is exclusively dependent on him, and a hypochondriac with back trouble. This woman had back pain that no medicine alleviates. She finally found a surgeon who would operate on her back. That didn't solve her back problem, but only compounded it by giving more of a reality basis for her intractable pain. She then went to a medical center, several hours drive away, for still another operation. Her husband went to pick her up in his Volkswagon. Her brother-in-law had told him, "Take my limousine; she can stretch out on the back seat." But her husband said, "No we'll go up in the VW!" That made her extremely angry at her husband. Because her husband is on the self-felt side he was holding her to his self-sacrificing ways. When she leans toward the projected side, she brings this incident up, telling how her "damn thoughtless husband made me suffer all cramped up on the back seat of a VW!" When she's on the projected side, her back pains aren't as severe. Her marriage problems are, though.

Someone in the misperceived position, whose spouse is on the self-felt side, once complained to me, "He never takes a vacation. Before marriage, he took me everywhere and bought me all kinds of presents. And we were always eating out. Now it's just the opposite. We never spend any money on ourselves. He gives to the church, and to charities, but he won't do anything for us. Everyone else goes to Florida in the winter; we stay here. He can afford a vacation but he doesn't take me any place. He doesn't need to work anymore; he's already made a fortune. He could easily retire so we could travel and enjoy ourselves. Why has he changed?" In this example, the hard-working anhedonic traits of high personality core guilt can be seen in the husband, whose added unconscious guilt is on the self-felt side. He expects his wife now to forego pleasure, along with him because he feels that she's part of him. They both have "become one."

Since added unconscious guilt in the misperceived position blocks perception of any oral dependency need gratification, these exclusive relationships become burdensome as the added unconscious guilt in the misperceived position increases. When the relationship began, it might have been light, fun, and carefree. And it was this way because the two people were emotionally involved with enough other people. Their relationship with these other people took up the projected added unconscious guilt. Their oral dependency needs were more diffusely met so that there were fewer demands made upon each other. Jealousy and possessiveness were less of a problem when the oral dependency need was met more diffusely. But as they cut off these other relationships, their own became more and more exclusive, and as their added unconscious guilt increases, the relationship begins to deteriorate. Each person begins to impose responsibilities upon the other. When these are not perceived as being met, the person may feel that he or she is being treated unfairly. As they become more exclusively dependent on each other, added unconscious guilt can quickly build up in the misperceived position. They may begin to feel that the other hurts them on purpose. The intensifying secondary feelings of the misperceived position may lead to the perception of "mental cruelty." I've heard these people often say, "I'd rather take a physical beating than have to put up with this terrible mental cruelty."

As a relationship gets more burdensome, innocuous statements or questions posed by the other person begins to be perceived as rejections, as in the case of the young woman who said, "I'm taking a night class at the community college and if I come home early, my parents ask 'How come you're home early?' You know, as if they're thinking I've been kicked out of the class. If I come home late, they ask 'How come you're home late?' You know, as though they think I've been out running around with men. God! I've got to get out of that house and get an apartment of my own before they drive me crazy!" It's the hypersensitivity, the twisted thinking, and the block on oral dependency need gratification of the misperceived position which cause the relationship to become an unbearable burden.

An instance of a relationship that was initially enjoyable and has become a burden to both is shown in the following example. The woman uses body language to perceive a rejection from the man she's dating. She swings from the projected side to self-felt side, as she goes from accusing him to blaming herself for the feelings which she perceives that he has. She says to him:

I wasn't going to stop over tonight, because you really made me mad the other night, the way you acted. And don't tell me you don't know what I'm talking about! You couldn't wait to get me out of this apartment. Don't deny it! It was so obvious it was embarrassing. Did you have some chick waiting around the corner for me to leave? It's all right. You have no obligations to me. I only ask that you be honest with me. I've told you before that if I'm intruding you should let me know. I know you've got more important things to do than spend time with me. But last time, you acted as though you couldn't wait to get rid of me. I saw you glancing at your watch and looking longingly at the door. Did you think I was going to sexually assault you? You seemed afraid of me. Well, if it'll make you feel any better, I don't have sexual designs on you. I just came over to talk to you because it was *you* that wanted *me* to stop by. *You're* the one that asked me! That's what I don't understand. If you feel that I'm a burden, just say so. I can take it. Don't act as though you're stuck with me and you can't wait until I leave, like you did the other night. I know I'm not the best of company and I know I can be terribly boring. So I can understand why you want to get rid of me. Just please be honest about it!

What she actually wants is a show of love, or proof of this man's love, but any such show or proof is blocked; her added unconscious guilt has increased because she's removed targets for projection. If he denies he wanted to get rid of her, then she perceives that he's not being honest.

When people perceive rejection and bitterness in a relationship, they tend to return rejection and bitterness. One client of a marriage counselor was advised to remember that "you'll catch more flies with honey than vinegar," when there was an apparent need to show her husband love, not hate, in order for him to reciprocate. The client, who had a high level of misperceived added unconscious guilt on the projected side, illustrated the worthlessness of intellectually-based advice in resolving emotional problems, in her reply, "Why doesn't he show *me* love first? I'll be glad to show him I care for him if he can show me *first* that he cares for *me*! How can I act all sweet and loving to him when I'd like to brain the son-of-a-bitch with a brick!" After perceiving rejection, this woman's added unconscious guilt has swung to the projected side. Her need to brain her husband with a brick is better verbally expressed to someone other than her husband. In doing so, she will have less of that need to project added unconscious guilt to her husband. The solution, then, is not based on advice but involves a subtle emotional process involving transference language.

The swinging back and forth of the misperceived position causes some people to say of their spouses, "I thought I married a Dr. Jekyll, but he's turned out to be Mr. Hyde." They may also say, "But you'd have to *live* with him to know what he's *really* like. If I brought him in here, he'd charm you, the way he charms everyone else who isn't with him all the time." When the relationship began, this woman saw that man as "Mr. Perfect" or Dr. Jekyll; she made him greater than he was. But as the relationship became more exclusive, she developed a block on oral dependency need gratification, so she could no longer see that he loved her. Also, as the relationship became more exclusive, his targets for projected guilt were cut off and he now must project his added unconscious guilt to her. Thus, she perceives that he has changed from Dr. Jekyll to Mr. Hyde. She had been in the mid-line stance of the misperceived position, feeling, "He doesn't love me," "He's cruel to me." But if she tells someone else, "He's turning out to be Mr. Hyde," she's leaning toward the projected side. Telling someone else about a "Mr. Hyde" also implies that she's getting emotional support from this someone else, and with emotional support, someone who had been in the mid-line stance of the misperceived position tends to swing to the projected side. As one begins to lean to the projected side he or she will unmask Dr. Jekyll, revealing a Mr. Hyde. Mr. Hyde is only seen with projected guilt.

When someone begins to see her spouse, or a friend, as Mr. Hyde, she is contrasting the now-perceived emptiness in oral dependency need gratification with the intense happiness she initially felt in the exclusive relationship, when she had less misperceived added unconscious guilt. This is further contrasted if that misperceived guilt had been lying toward the self-felt side when the relationship began. The emotionally significant other was viewed as a greater than real, and "too good to be true," as far as a source of gratification. But now, with projected guilt, the person says things like, "He used to call me several times a day, just to tell me he loved me and how much he appreciated the things I had done for him. Now he only calls if he wants me to do something or to check to see if I'm home working as he expects. I don't get the feeling he loves me. In fact, I've begun to pick up hints that he not only doesn't care about me; he really wants to get rid of me." The woman in this example had added unconscious guilt on the self-felt side, which is now in the mid-line stance and leaning toward the projected side. With more emotional support, she'll lean still further toward the projected side and see clearly the Mr. Hyde. She'll feel that the Dr. Jekyll she saw before was a false front or a cruel joke and that Mr. Hyde was always present.

In the following example, you can see not only the swinging, or the ambivalence, of the misperceived position but also that the woman involved has duplicated her previous failed relationships and has rationalized the demand for exclusivity, which are also characteristic of this position.

He is in no way the person I married a year ago. That beautiful relationship we had is gone. I actually thought I was the happiest woman in the world when we married, but I must be the unhappiest now. But am I to blame? Have I really changed? Or do I somehow pick husbands who have a hidden capacity to be sadistic? I've read where some women always marry alcoholics even if the man never drank a drop before the marriage ceremony. Each time I've married, I thought for sure that I'd found the one perfect husband for me. They all seemed, at first, so exceptionally nice, so loving, and so willing to make me the center of their world. That's what I want in a husband. Maybe that's all wrong. Why do they all turn out to be so sadistic? Maybe I have some unconscious masochistic need that turns my husband into a sadistic brute. Why is it we can't find the beautiful love we had before? I don't want any sadistic-masochistic relationship. I want an equal love, an equal respect, an equal trust, and an equal need for each other in the marriage. Instead, I've been sadistically tortured. I don't understand it! Do I do something that makes a good man turn into someone bad? It makes me wonder, when I meet my ex-husbands and they seem to have changed back into how they were before I married them. Do I cause the men I marry to treat me in a way I wouldn't treat a dog? It's never long after I marry them that they begin to treat me like a doormat. I've known other women who've married men who seem worthless to me, but their marriages last. Mine don't! And this one is not going to either, unless he changes back to the person I married. But how do I get him to change back when he doesn't think he's changed at all? Or is it me that somehow must change first? Who's at fault, anyway?

When these people swing to the "hate," or projected side, they feel that the other person has changed and is the cause of the problems, but then they swing to the self-felt side and feel that they must have caused the change in the other person. "When you point the blame at someone else with one finger, you have three pointing back at yourself" is a saying people on the self-felt side of the misperceived position will remember when they couldn't decide in which direction the finger of blame should be pointed when in the mid-line stance.

The same love-hate relationship which we've seen in regard to marital relationships can occur with a parent and child. When I give workshops, someone usually asks, "If you meet a child's oral dependency need, and *spoil* him, is that going to help make him comfortable later in life?" To "spoil" a child is not to meet consistently his oral dependency need. When a child's oral dependency need is consistently met early in life, he begins to venture out, diffusing his guilt projection and anger. Parents and children can end up having love-hate relationships where there's no "liking" in between. One such couple that I know hired an expensive limousine to take their son and his date to a high school prom. But the next day, they were beating him. They go back and forth. They may say something like, "You ungrateful thing! We got you that limousine, we buy you everything you want, and look what you do." Spoiling a child is an example of the intense love, on the love side of a love-hate relationship that will be negated by the hate side later. These parents are often too dependent on too few. They're overly dependent on their own children. Their children could emotionally mature better if they were simply and consistently "liked" and not subjected to spoiling.

The love-hate relationship of the misperceived position can result in murder-suicide if there's enough added unconscious guilt. The added unconscious guilt on the projected side can be sufficient for murder, and on the self-felt side, sufficient for suicide. Every so often, one will read in the newspaper about someone who has murdered a spouse or lover, then committed suicide. This type of murder-suicide represents the culmination of the emotional turmoil that can be found in the exclusve relationship. The feelings behind the murder on the projected side involve, "You must die" and "If I can't live with you, then no one else is going to." After killing the lover or spouse, the person swings to the self-felt side and feels, "I must die" and "I can't live without you—I'm not going to live with anyone else." In the projected position, we know that murder comes from the secondary feeling, "*He* deserves to die," and in the self-felt position, we know that suicide results from the secondary feeling, "*I* deserve to die." But in the misperceived position one has the contrasting feelings of intense love and hate, which, with enough added unconscious guilt, can result in a murder-suicide. It doesn't have to. One could have, instead, any of the conditions characteristic of self-felt guilt, and have any of the conditions characteristic of projected guilt. The reality focus of the increased added unconscious guilt doesn't need to be on each of the partners. We already know that a high enough level of added unconscious guilt to produce a suicide in the self-felt position may instead manifest itself as severe hypochondriasis. And a high enough level of added unconscious guilt to produce a murder in the projected position may instead manifest itself as a crusade against immorality. Behind it all, regardless of its reality manifestations lies the basic problem of being too dependent on too few.

CHAPTER 16
More Results of the
Misperceived Position

To better understand the results of the misperceived position, consider a small child going downtown with his mother, who holds him tightly by the hand. She has to know where he is at all times. At home he has to get his mother's permission to play outside his own yard, even if only to play with the kids next door. He has certain limits, set by his mother, where he can play, and his mother may often tell him, "Don't get out of my sight." She wants to know where he is and what he's doing at all times. If he strays, she may get angry and yell at him. This is analogous to someone in the misperceived position who is too dependent on too few. He may feel, at times, like this little child or appear to others to be this way. He may have high personality core guilt and a very important position in reality, yet he is getting "jerked around" by some emotionally significant other or others. When someone is too dependent on too few, like this little child, he can be jerked back and yelled at if he wanders too far away or goes places where the exclusive other feels he shouldn't go.

Such people suffer a loss of freedom. They must be careful about what they say or do because they don't want others to think they're inferior, inadequate, unacceptable, or guilty, when they're leaning to the self-felt side. They're always afraid of displeasing the emotionally significant others on whom they are too dependent so they tend to hold back on angry feelings. A fifteen-year-old girl, for instance, came in to see me just the other day and began to complain about "Margie." Margie was her "best friend"—in fact, her only friend. The girl told me, "If I buy a sub, Margie expects me to offer her a bite; then when I do she'll eat three-fourths of the whole thing! But if she buys a sub and I ask her for one small bite, she'll say, 'Well, who the hell paid for this anyway?' It's things like this I have to put up with. I put up with it again and again, afraid to say anything for fear she won't like me, until finally I explode when I can't take it anymore. I try to hold back my anger, but it builds up over incidents just like this until I have to let it out. Then Margie calls me a mental patient and won't have anything to do with me for a week." This

250

girl feels that she *has* to accept unfair treatment from Margie, and obviously lacks the freedom Margie has to say and do what she wants.

Such people may have demands placed upon them by the emotionally significant others, on whom they're too dependent. These demands consist of "dos and don'ts" which restrict their freedom in communication and behavior. For instance, a patient of mine told me that he was dating a woman who wouldn't go to certain restaurants because she knew that he'd taken his ex-wife there, so these restaurants are taboo. Another person told me that she and her fiance can't go to a particular beach because her fiance knows that earlier she fell intensely in love with someone else at the beach. The previous relationship is gone, but the beach is "off-limits" because it reminds him that she's been involved with somebody else. I've seen people who couldn't wear certain colors, who couldn't use particular perfumes, or who even had to change friends because the person demanding the exclusive relationship wanted to block out memories of the other's intense past relationships.

Often the person will not realize that he is manipulating the other and the manipulation is rationalized, as in, "I only ask her to do that for her own good." Sometimes a person may feel manipulated, and complain that he feels "like a puppet on a string." He may say that someone else is "pulling my strings"—that he can't determine his own behavior but this someone else is continually in control. These people wish they could *learn* to pull their own strings. But this is only possible by becoming less dependent on too few. They have to become emotionally involved with more people. And they do when they begin to complain to someone else about what they feel they must endure at home. When the person complains of being manipulated, he is swinging to the projected side. As he is telling somebody else, he is meeting the oral dependency need by having that person listen. He is also projecting guilt to the listener, who in the subtle transference, is the manipulator, in part. That emotional process of becoming more involved with more people is beginning to take place. But it will tend to be prevented by the person manipulating, for this person prefers to keep the other in a situation where manipulation is easy.

Some other ways of manipulating include saying things like, "I'll feel guilty if you do that," "You're going to make me cry," or, "If you do that, you'll hurt my feelings." Statements like these bother the person, because he doesn't want to hurt this other. This sort of manipulation is more from the self-felt side as opposed to something like, "Don't do that, or I won't like you anymore," which is more from the projected side. Manipulation can occur on both sides of the misperceived position.

Alcoholics who are involved in an exclusive relationship can often manipulate their spouses into behavior that supports their drinking. Al-Anon calls the people who are manipulated in such a way "enablers." An enabler, who is overly emotionally dependent on the alcoholic, allows him to get by with behavior that anyone else would not tolerate. The enabler puts up with the physical abuse that often accompanies a drinking problem. The man may go on a drinking spree and be in danger of losing his job, but his wife will offer to call his boss and say that her husband is ill. If the "enabler" were less dependent, she would not put up with the problem. She would be more likely to simply tell the person, "*You* face the music—it's *your* responsibility. I won't make excuses for you." But instead, the "enabler," who feels, "I'll do what you ask because I want you to like me," is manipulated into allowing the person to keep his alcoholic condition. We can recognize the same dynamics in other situations, not involving alcohol, where someone is too dependent on too few. One person "enables" the other to get by with behavior that somebody else would not tolerate. We can see it, for instance, in regard to hypochondriasis, where one spouse enables the other to remain hypochondriacal. He might say, "You went to the doctor and he said there was nothing wrong with you. I'll take you to another doctor who'll find out what's wrong. Don't you listen to that doctor who said it was all your nerves. We'll find somebody else who'll repeat the tests." The spouse who says such things is also an enabler.

As we have said, when a person in the misperceived position gets emotional support, she tends to swing from the self-felt side to the projected side. This dynamic fact may doom a relationship in which the people are too dependent on too few and where misperceived guilt is increasing. At first, the wife may have been on the self-felt side, with a high unmet oral dependency need, appearing very attractive to her husband. She is on the self-felt side because she is not involved enough with others to get the emotional support to take the projected side. She may appear very nice, with an attractive inferiority complex, though she might also show a little tendency toward depression, excessive worrying, or perhaps a social phobia, or maybe just feeling stressed. But when another person gets involved and gives emotional support, she will begin to swing to the projected side. Her husband may then get the projected guilt, either directly or indirectly. On the self-felt side, she might have been anxious, worried, hypochondriacal, obsessive-compulsive, in chronic pain, etc., and this other person feels that he or she can help with these manifestations of the woman's emotional uncomfortableness. Then, when she gets involved with this other person, she gets enough emotional support to project guilt, and problems begin to develop in the relationship. The depression, the panic attacks, the hypochondriasis, or the tendency to worry lessens. If one wanted to maintain comfortably an exclusive relationship with someone, he might be able to do so by preventing her from talking to her friends or to anyone else. In this way, she will keep on having anxiety attacks or stay phobic, or remain hypochondrical, but the relationship will more than likely go very well. If she starts seeing friends, or talking to others, including professionals, she may begin to get support from them and may begin to swing to the projected side, and the relationship may begin to sour. An example of this is the husband who angrily tells his wife, who has been recently seeing a psychologist for her social phobia, "We never had a marriage problem until you started seeing that doctor!"

When one person swings to the projected side, a "need" to fight may begin to become apparent. The person who is now on the projected side has a "need" to project guilt, to criticize, to argue, and to fight. The more this person tends to criticize, to find things that are wrong, to pick fights, the less she tends to be depressed, hypochondriacal, worried, phobic, stressed, anxious, or troubled by pain. The emotional support that facilitates this swing to the projected side can come from friends, relatives, co-workers, classmates, or neighbors. It may come from a professional listener in a therapy situation. Since the person with whom she is exclusively involved cannot accept anger very well, the person must project in some other relationship which may be, but is not necessarily, a professional relationship. When she is on the projected side, with a listener, she can lower the added unconscious guilt. However, her manifest content may involve that other person of the exclusive relationship and it may appear that the new involvement is threatening the relationship or causing it to deteriorate. Someone who is too dependent on too few may talk about the exclusive other to her counselor, priest, minister, rabbi, psychologist, psychiatrist, social worker, confidante, or friend at work. If the exclusive other finds out about it, he may then try to end the friendship or professional relationship. He might say, "I don't want you talking to that counselor, because you're making it seem as if *I'm* to blame for all our problems." The person can often be manipulated into cutting off a professional relationship, or even a friendship, and the person may then swing back into more pronounced hypochondriasis, depression, worry, anxiety, phobias, stress, pain, or addiction. Most often, the only way the professional involvement can continue is when both partners are seen together or actively included, or when the orientation of the manifest content is biochemical in nature.

If the professional relationship is not cut off, the resulting marriage problem can be treated by seeing just one individual. It's more difficult to do, because the other partner objects. He is often jealous and afraid of being talked about. He is afraid that the exclusive relationship will deteriorate or be terminated as a result his partner's treatment. But it is possible to make the marriage better by seeing just one of the couple. A person not knowledgeable in these dynamics may well wonder how this could be done. It seems analogous to recommending treating an elevator phobia by asking the person to go to Alcoholics Anonymous. But by seeing one person who's involved in a severely problematic marriage, the marriage may improve and if so it's because the person can talk with someone else. The support from simply being listened to allows the person to swing to the projected side, which lowers added unconscious guilt. Usually when a person does come in with increased guilt in the misperceived position, she is ambivalently blaming her partner for the problem, saying, "Get him in here—he is the problem. He doesn't treat me right; he doesn't love me; he won't allow me to have any friends; he tells the children I'm no good," which are comments typical of the projected side of the misperceived position. But after the person has been involved for a time, she may begin to query, "He's acting so much nicer to me at home, and starting to appreciate all the things I do for him; did you talk to him?" Or, "He doesn't seem to mind if I have my friend over and he doesn't try to turn the children against me—have you spoken to him?" No one has talked to the other person; what has happened is that the added unconscious guilt has been lowered in the professional relationship. Thus the block is lowered and the person can see the appreciation, the love, and the gratification that was blocked before. The person no longer sees the constraints on freedom or the rejection that she saw before.

When two people are too dependent on too few and they have a fight, they may make up afterward and may profess again their love and their vows of exclusivity to one another. Later when one gets on the projected side, one might say that, "These fights chip away at my love. They've taken something away." These statements are from the projected side and they imply support from somebody else. The relationship can worsen and the love diminishes when one person begins to "smear" the other with projected guilt. The person can begin to do this and do it consistently if he is getting support elsewhere. The other relationship may or may not include a sexual aspect. The expressed anger in the once-exclusive relationship, however, may be less ambivalent, as emotional support tends to keep the misperceived added unconscious guilt toward the projected side. The things that the two fight about may be any of the perceptions of the mid-line stance of the misperceived position, but where the blame is attributed to the other. It may be something like, "He can't accept my past. He can't forget about that affair ten years ago and he's always throwing it up to me!" Of course, the self-felt side is, "*I* can't accept my past and *I* can't forget about that affair ten years ago and *I'm* always throwing it up to *myself*!" On the projected side, the other is blamed for not being able to leave things in the past. Even if the other person says that he can accept the past, the person with the increased misperceived guilt replies with, "He says he accepts it but he really can't" and continues to take the projected side with, "He'll throw it up to me with snide remarks or innuendos."

Nice things that the person did willingly, on the self-felt side, are now resented on the projected side. "She expects me to do _____" may, in fact, be bitterly resented. The person did do nice things, perhaps wait on the other, hand and foot, put the other first, let the other make all the decisions, but he did these things willingly. The person felt he *should*, from guilt on the self-felt side. But now, as he swings to the projected side, "I will put you first" becomes "You *expect* me to put you first and I *resent* it!" Or, "I resent you're thinking I should wait on you hand and foot!" One woman told me, about her husband, "It's really not fair! He has me cook dinner, clean the house, and do the laundry after I get home from work, and he doesn't lift a finger to help me." On the self-felt side, she used to do these things willingly because she wanted to do them, and may even have insisted on doing them. But now that she's on the projected side, she sees them as unfair and resents doing them.

On the self-felt side, one person might have seen the other as greater than he was in reality, as is interestingly shown in the remarks of a wife now on the projected side of the misperceived position:

I've gotten so I resent his being so Goddamned *perfect* all the time. I resent how it makes *me* look! You don't know what it's like to live with someone who's always so nice, so superior, so consistently right, and so self-righteous. It gives me the feeling that ["according to him"] I'm some low-down bum that ought to be ever grateful for living with a person who's so perfect. Every day I see him and I'm reminded of how others see me. [Note that the "according to others" has been dropped.] I'm the one who comes from the wrong side of the tracks; I'm the one that has had so much trouble earlier in life; I'm the one that has sinned so; and I'm the one who's not well-educated, while he's the one who came from a nice family; he's the one who never went through the trouble I did in earlier life; he's the one that's never sinned the way I have; and he's the one that's so well-educated. Living with him makes me seem so damn imperfect by contrast. I shouldn't have to put up with this. It's like living with Mr. Goody-Two-Shoes, complete with halo, and I'm getting sick and tired of it. Everyone thinks he's so great and they all marvel at his accomplishments. What can they say about me, except something bad? I actually think it was a big mistake to have married him. I should have married someone on my level so I wouldn't be so painfully contrasted all the time. I've felt this resentment growing within me for a long time and now I can see where it's coming from. I had to talk to you about it because I can't talk to him. He can't see what he's doing to me. He doesn't understand how I feel. He knows as well as I do the background I have. But it's not my fault that I didn't go to college. Is it my fault that my parents weren't as well off as his? Why am I made out to be so inferior? When I try to tell him how I feel, he makes me feel like I don't know what I'm talking about.

The very qualities that this woman saw in her husband when she made him "Mr. Perfect" are now resented because her added unconscious guilt has shifted from the self-felt to the projected side.

We've already noted that one can differentiate the self-felt side from the self-felt position because the self-felt side is only temporarily held. Another difference is that the feelings of the self-felt side are more concerned with other people or another person. On the self-felt side of the misperceived position, others are always important; one is trying to please others. In the self-felt position, however, one tends to be working toward some goal that is not so person-oriented—perhaps a goal in academics or business or scientific research. It doesn't involve an exclusve relationship in which one is too dependent on too few. For example, the biochemist who is constantly working in his laboratory trying to develop a new cure for some illness is in the self-felt position. His oral dependency need seems to be met more in his work. Contrast him to a person on the self-felt side, who has a past history of poor relationships, and who seems to be working on trying to please an exclusive other or too few others. A person in the self-felt position lowers his added unconscious guilt by working hard; he doesn't appear to have such a great unmet oral dependency need that is oriented to other people, and characteristically, he does not fight with others. However, a person on the self-felt side may have a large unmet oral dependency need oriented to others and may too easily swing to the projected side to get rid of added unconscious guilt.

On the self-felt side, the person has a history of poor relationships and of continually searching for a concentrated meeting of the oral dependency need. The person on the self-felt side has often had periods, between intense relationships, of little or no involvement with others, during which she feels as one of my patients did, "If there is reincarnation, I want to come back as a rattlesnake, so that people will just leave me alone." The person on the self-felt side may appear to be as nice as someone in the self-felt position, a saintly Dr. Jekyll, but is known to have the vile temper of a Mr. Hyde when he or she swings to the projected side.

This Mr. Hyde begins to emerge when the person gets emotional support elsewhere and the relationship begins to sour. One may begin to resent even the things that he previously wanted in the relationship. Where before on the self-felt side, he wanted exclusivity and to "become one" with the other person, on the projected side, he may begin to complain of being "smothered." Where before he may have said, "I want to be with her always, sharing everything in my life with her," he now complains, "She's smothering me. I don't want her hanging on me all the time." This person may be getting some oral dependency need gratification from a new job or a new friend and is not as totally dependent on the other as before. Therefore, the person now swings to the projected side and resents the "smothering" dependence—that same dependence he previously demanded.

The projected added unconscious guilt can cause one to want some emotional distance from the exclusive other. The other person, who doesn't get emotional support from any other source, wants to maintain the closeness and exclusivity, but the person who's on the projected side begins to pull away. Sometimes the added unconscious guilt on the projected side, manifested in this resentment of the "smothering" of the exclusive relationship, gets so high that the person may say something like, "I don't even want him to touch me and I cringe if he puts his hands on me." She may complain that as far as the household chores, money, effort, and love, she is giving ninety percent while the other gives only ten. She may say, "I'm tired of always giving and getting nothing back." This person is definitely getting oral dependency need gratification elsewhere. This desire for distance and the block on oral dependency need gratification that are being focused on the other person usually herald the demise of the relationship, which had seemed so "heavenly" at first.

The person may even say that she feels better when the other person is gone. A wife, for instance, may say, "I feel better when John is on one of his business trips. Then I don't have to keep the house as spotless as he wants. When he's home, he expects me to wait on him hand and foot, but while he's away, I can relax." The fact that she no longer wants to know what "John" is doing at every moment, is not so worried about "John's" faithfulness, and is more relaxed and more comfortable when he's gone implies that she's getting oral dependency need gratification elsewhere. She may have been having lunch with the woman next door a few times a week, or she may have been confiding in other friends with whom she bowls, or plays tennis, or shops. Saying, "While he's away, I can relax" does not necessarily mean that she's having a sexual affair, but then perhaps she is meeting her emotional needs in an extramarital sexual relationship. But it may be as simple as being able to have "Mary" over when "John" is gone, because "John gets upset if I spend a lot of time with Mary." When "John" is away she can relax, because she can neglect all the things that she feels "John" expects of her.

The person may resent not being able to relax or "to be myself" when the other is around. Another woman told me, "The only way I can be myself is to get away from Fred. He won't let me be me. Whenever I'm with him, he's trying to control me or make me other than I am. If we go to a cocktail party together, he'll imply that I'm wearing the wrong dress or that I'm eating too much and offending the host, or maybe I'm not eating enough and offending the host. If he's not running me down, then he's saying that I shouldn't have talked about a certain subject, or maybe that I should have told the person something I didn't think of. He always wants me to be other than I am. I get the feeling that I'm under a microscope and he's always looking for flaws. It's as though I'm on stage and have to act in a certain way, where I can't really be myself. When I'm without Fred, it's entirely different. I feel free to be myself and I can say or do anything that I want. When I'm with him, it's as though I have to act in a certain way, or else he'll disapprove. In order to feel good, a person has to feel like she can be herself. I don't get that feeling at all in my relationship with Fred." Because she feels that Fred expects her to behave in a certain way, she feels that she can't be herself, and she resents Fred for inhibiting her behavior so much so that she likes to be away from Fred.

The individual who resents the "perfection" and the "smothering" of the other person and the things that she feels the other expects may begin to feel trapped by the situation. She may wish she could escape the situation where she perceives pressure and stress coming from her partner. It can even involve the lovemaking, when one partner feels that the other expects to make love and the former feels obliged to do so, "even though I don't enjoy it anymore." This person doesn't want to make love because her oral dependency needs are now being met more though friendship, work, the church, social activities, or in another relationship, and the sexual partner is being imbued with projected added unconscious guilt. The person may not be sexually involved elsewhere; she may be only emotionally involved.

This feeling of being trapped is perhaps the origin of what psychiatry terms the *hostile depression*. This hostile depression of the misperceived position is unlike the self-felt condition of depression. With the hostile depression, the person is angry about being trapped and is projecting added unconscious guilt. These people come across as being depressed, but we can also see the projected side in their anger at being trapped in the situation. The situation could be a job, a marriage, an exclusive friendship, or any exclusive relationship in which the person feels trapped. Where the self-felt condition of depression involves the secondary feeling, "I'm dissatisfied with myself," the hostile depression of the misperceived position involves, "I'm dissatisfied with my marriage (or my job, my church, etc.)." If we ask the person in the self-felt position why he is depressed, he might say, "Well, I just took a good look at myself (or "what I've accomplished" or "what is associated with me")." But if we ask the person in the misperceived position why he is depressed, he would be more likely to say, "I'm trapped in this Goddamned marriage," or "I'm trapped with this damn roommate," or "I'm trapped in this damned job." This similarity between depression in the two positions is that both include a lack of hope. The depressed person in the self-felt position feels no hope of ever changing, of ever being less "inferior, inadequate, unacceptable, wrong, or guilty." The depressed person in the misperceived position feels no hope of getting out of the entrapping situation. He may feel, "I'm expected to stay in _____," filling in the blank with whatever he perceives to be an entrapping situation. This hostile depression is different from the self-felt depression because one can see the projected guilt so well.

The hostile depression implies *a need to escape.* The person would like to get out of the entrapping situation. The woman in the following example uses her relatives' opinions as a rationalization for staying in a church in which she feels trapped. Her desire to escape comes through clearly. She told me:

I've come to the conclusion that I'm so inhibited and so concerned about how others are going to judge me because of the church. When my mother didn't want me, she gave me to a Catholic orphanage that raised me and now I see that for the rest of my life, I'm going to be trapped into being what I was taught to be. I remember the sisters teaching me the 'discipline of the eyes,' where I was taught to feel sinful if I were only to look at anything that might tempt me away from the straight and narrow path. The church has kept me from enjoying life, as other people apparently do—has limited my pleasure, and has controlled my behavior through the years. The church has really done a job on me! It's no wonder that I have no sexual feelings and can't even reach climax with my husband. The church has made me feel guilty if I don't attend Mass each week and has always made me feel like a sinner. I'm trapped in a religion I don't want and that holds me in a state of unhappiness. I can't leave the church now because I don't want my relatives talking about me. They talk enough about me already. It's the church that has made me so concerned about doing the right thing that I can't enjoy life. I'm stuck with a husband I don't love and I'd divorce right now if it weren't for the church. I'd leave him immediately except everyone would take *his* side and blame *me* for breaking up the marriage and I know the church would disapprove. That's the way it's been all my life. I can't do anything pleasurable without feeling that the church would disapprove. It's because of the church that I have to suffer. I'm trapped with an inhibiting conscience that the church has given me.

This woman would like to make her escape from the church, but, characteristically for the misperceived position, she's ambivalent about it; she rationalizes not doing so.

The man in the following example recognizes his "need" to escape and he does escape temporarily. He described his "escape" as follows:

I took the trip to Florida to get away from the pressures of work that were building up. All the responsibilities of that place fall on my shoulders alone, although I never get credit for anything I do—that is, do *right*. I'll get credit for anything that goes wrong, whether it's my fault or not! I get tired of having to please others all the time and I resent having to make everyone happy at work. That's why I didn't bring Cindy with me. I guess it was a disappointment to her because I know she wanted to go. But I would have had the same pressure of trying to please her and trying to make her happy. I have enough obligations and responsibilities. Then, too, I didn't want the hassle of being scrutinized and judged by her. I wanted to relax and take it easy and not be accountable to anyone. If I had brought Cindy to Florida with me, I would have gone through my usual routine of 'What do you want to do?' and 'Where do you want to eat tonight?' And then she would have given her usual answers of 'Whatever *you* want to do,' 'Wherever *you* want to eat.' That's the way she is, but it puts pressure on me, wondering if the place that I choose is the one she really wanted. I know, too, that she works hard in her job and I would have felt that I'd have to show her an especially good time. She'd expect it, and that's more pressure right there. Rather than that, I decided to go to Florida alone. It's not what I really *wanted*. It *had* to be that way. I will admit that it did get pretty lonely down there and I did miss Cindy. All I did was worry about her, and what she was doing. She probably took the opportunity to go out with someone else.

This man feels trapped by the exclusive relationship, and by his work situation, and he feels a "need" to escape. His worry and his loneliness suggest his ambivalence about his "escape."

Many times, if a person does escape an exclusive relationship in which he had felt trapped, he will send for the other person. He misses the other so much because he is still too emotionally dependent. I've known people who've "escaped" to the other side of the country and have then sent a bus ticket or a plane ticket to their exclusive other. I've seen people who move back and forth from one coast to the other, escaping the relationship, and then going back to the spouse, lover, parent, etc. This is similar to the woman who changed all the locks on the outside doors of her home on her attorney's advice then gave the new key to her husband from whom she'd separated, or to the woman who in an effort to leave her husband, took all the money from their joint bank account, moved it into another account, and then put both names on the new account. These people all feel the "need" to escape but they're still too dependent on too few and too ambivalent about making the break from the exclusive other.

The person wants to be free from the fighting, the bickering, the hurts, the expectations, the stress, the pressure, and the past unappreciated love of the exclusive relationship. The desire to be free implies though that the person no longer needs the other as much, to meet the oral dependency need, because the person is getting support elsewhere. He wants to get away from the other individual, from that experience, or from that situation that is being imbued with his projected added unconscious guilt. The person who wants to be free may leave his family, marriage, job, school, or roommate, in order to be free of the emotional uncomfortableness that he perceives as coming from the particular relationship or situation. One patient put this as, "I wish I were a little bird so that I could just fly away from it all." The meaning of suicide notes that say something like, "free at last" is that the person, who has been unable to escape the turmoil and demands of exclusive relationships in life has sought to escape and to become free, through death. On the self-felt side, other than resorting to suicide, the person can escape into chemical addictions. Or his need for escape lessens or disappears as he develops phobias, anxiety attacks or perhaps hypochondriasis.

This "need" to escape, to be free, may involve simply a temporary desire to be alone. The person may want to get away from the turmoil of an intense relationship, which is really the turmoil of being too dependent on too few. I had a woman come in who complained that a nearby church, due to recent vandalism, had begun locking its doors at night. This woman liked to go in the middle of the night and sit quietly in the church thinking. She, and others like her, have had uncomfortably intense relationships, and they just like to be by themselves, trying to figure out what went wrong in their lives. This wanting to be alone reflects the misperceived position—this desire to sit alone and "just think." I have many patients in the misperceived position who just like to sit by the ocean, alone, and think, looking across the water, seeing peace and tranquility. Likewise, there are quite a few people who like to go off in the woods alone, seeking a Thoreau-like experience of thinking in the quiet solitude. We all may have a need to be alone like this, to a lesser degree. But people in the misperceived position with high added unconscious guilt, who feel trapped by intense relationships, have this "need" to an intense degree. They "need" to have a chance to think over their misery, their grief, and the frustrating complexities of their lives, is created by increased guilt in the misperceived position.

These people may also turn to pets. The dog has been described as "man's best friend." We could safely say that this description comes from the dog's appearing to have such a big unmet oral dependency need, more so than other animals. People can get their oral dependency needs met from a pet. And pets, too, may be subjected to abuse when they are utilized for guilt projection. Someone in the misperceived position may physically abuse his pet as a result of the same type of love-hate relationship that he could have with another person.

In trying to escape the complexities and pain of human relationships, people can turn to lower animals, or they can turn to higher beings, to gods and goddesses, or to some divine being. The entire history of man, as far back as recorded history reaches, includes some form of religion. Man's ever-present need for religion perhaps reflects, to a degree, the misperceived position, the disappointments in the interpersonal relationship sphere, and the turning away from human relationships. Perhaps it is the misperceived position that necessitates religion. A person can find contentment in a god and talk to this divine being, feeling that the god listens. And if this person is able to have a good relationship that is a source of oral dependency need gratification, the person is better off. But this person can only have such a relationship when he has drawn enough oral dependency need gratification from parts of people, experiences, and situations from which the divine relationship can be then concretized in reality.

The resentment of an exclusive relationship, which brings about the "need to escape," and the hostile depression, can also produce a desire to retaliate against the emotionally significant other. With more added unconscious guilt on the projected side, the person may retaliate against someone with whom he had been exclusively involved. Again, retaliation implies oral dependency need gratification coming from somewhere outside the exclusive relationship. People can retaliate or get even in a variety of ways, such as, "I'm not cooking his breakfast for him anymore," or, "She's not getting my paycheck anymore." The feelings, on the projected side, are something like, "If she doesn't love me, if she doesn't listen to me or understand me, if she won't care about me, then to hell with her," and the person retaliates.

One way of retaliating is to have an affair. "He doesn't love me, so I'm going to find someone else who does" or "He hurt me so I'll hurt him" may be the feelings behind such an affair. The person with the high unmet oral dependency need that can come from a blocked perception of gratification and is characteristic of the misperceived position is more vulnerable to having an affair. This person may not necessarily be looking for an affair as a form of retaliation. Because of the unmet oral dependency need, there is a "need" to make another person greater than he actually is. There is also a need to talk to someone who will listen because the other in the exclusive relationship is perceived as not listening or not understanding. So the person decides to find someone else who will listen and understand, and eventually becomes sexually involved. In time, the affair simply duplicates the exclusive relationship which the person wanted to escape.

The affair may last longer when it's more a part of the emotional unreality and not concerned so much with reality. For instance, some people have affairs but don't see the other people very frequently, perhaps only once every few months. I have seen people who've been involved in the same affair for twenty years, but they're separated so much by distance, that the affair is more in their emotional unreality than in their reality. They'll come in and say, for example, "I love Jim so. I can talk to him where I can't Tom. Jim seems to understand where Tom can't. But I only see him twice a year. We'll talk on the phone from time to time, and he seems to keep me going. I can put up with my husband better because of Jim."

An affair that does not last long is one in which the person with high misperceived guilt "escapes" the hated exclusive relationship, and becomes involved with the other person who was providing intense emotional support. For instance, if the woman in the above example left her husband Tom and moved in with Jim, she might become totally involved in reality, and the relationship with Jim probably wouldn't be any better than the one with Tom. She might then say to her counselor, when that relationship starts to deteriorate, "I'm beginning to see that Jim reminds me of Tom." Or, "Jim is just like Tom! I can't believe I didn't see it before." With infrequent meetings, reality prevents the people from getting too emotionally close. A wider sphere of emotionally signficiant relationships is better maintained. With the transference and unconscious wishful thinking, the people who are physically distant may *feel* close, but in reality, they're not. It's more a part of the emotional unreality. It's analogous to someone who's involved in a religion, which provides a lot of support.

The affair does not have to be sexual. People can find emotional support from platonic affairs. But it *is* an affair because the person must conceal it. The person is being emotionally unfaithful to the exclusive other by meeting his oral dependency needs elsewhere. He must have this platonic relationship behind the exclusive other's back. He has to sneak out to talk to the other person and to get his oral depdndnecy needs met. These platonic affairs can also last a long time, if meetings are infrequent. But if the people meet too often, these affairs too can turn into love-hate relationships.

In the exclusive relationship itself, the resentment discussed in this chapter, causes problems in communication. One person is unable to talk to the other because it seems as though the other has a "need" to fight, a "need" to argue, a "need" to project guilt and find fault or criticize. One person, or both, may project too much guilt, too intensely, into the relationship and consequently the two cannot talk. They each need someone else to listen and support their guilt on the projected side. The guilt is more easily accepted when it is projected indirectly, which these people, because they're too dependent on too few and too intensely involved with each other, find difficult to do. The person in the exclusive relationship needs a listener outside of the exclusive relationship, one who won't refute the projected guilt, one who will not take advantage of his vulnerability to start a sexual affair, and one who does not give reality advice. The person needs someone who will just listen and give emotional support, without saying "You're seeing it all wrong" or giving advice like "Leave your husband" or "Move out." This someone must be able to understand the ambivalence of the person and allow the expression of this ambivalence with support. If he can find this on a part-person, part-experience, part-situation basis, he would be better off finding it that way than on a whole-person—experience—situation basis. It is here that the professional "therapeutic listener," under whatever guise of reality, is most needed.

CHAPTER 17
The Necessity of the
"Therapeutic Listener"

We have already recognized that communicating with ease becomes progressively less possible as a person becomes more emotionally uncomfortable. Emotional uncomfortableness has an adverse effect on both the talking and the listening aspects of communication. The best listener in the communicative process is the emotionally comfortable person who has an interest, for whatever reason, in the reality focus of the speaker. A high level of added unconscious guilt makes the emotionally uncomfortable person a poor listener. The best listeners for those who are emotionally uncomfortable are people who are listening as a part of their profession, where they have a logical reality reason to listen and are not listening in order to project their own added unconscious guilt. We can call someone who essentially listens, within some reality orientation that seems logical and makes sense, a "therapeutic listener." There is a need for some sort of reality-disguised "therapeutic listener," to relate to those who are emotionally uncomfortable and prone to intensify a whole-person transference relationship in order to draw oral dependency need gratification and to project added unconscious guilt.

People in the self-felt position may appear to be good listeners, particularly when they empathically identify with the maligned, the disadvantaged, the unfortunate, the worried, and the sick. Since they may volunteer little, if anything to the communicative process, their reluctance to speak allows someone else more time to talk. They may say, "I listen to everyone else's problems, but I keep mine to myself," or "I feel like a psychiatrist, as everyone comes to me with his troubles, yet I can't solve my own!" These people are particularly attractive to those who have high levels of added unconscious guilt in the misperceived and projected positions. They have more of a need for someone else to listen, so that they can use the transference to draw oral dependency need gratification and to project guilt, directly and indirectly. Because people with self-felt added unconscious guilt tend not to talk spontaneously, they do not attract the more emotionally comfortable person, who is more prone to be in a give-and-take communicative relationship, with more mutual oral dependency need gratification and more mutual guilt projection. The emotionally comfortable person may not want to continue a communicative relationship with someone who provides no input of pleasantly reflected oral dependency need gratification and stimulating guilt projection. Instead, these emotionally uncomfortable people attract other emotionally uncomfortable people, whose added unconscious guilt is in the misperceived position.

We have seen that a high level of misperceived added unconscious guilt blocks oral dependency need gratification, and unambivalent guilt projection; it also causes the person to be a poor listener. We have observed that a large amount of misperceived added unconscious guilt can produce a "rejection complex" and hypersensitivity. A listener who is hypersensitive or has a "rejection complex" will be apt to perceive rejection, degradation, and criticism in the spontaneous communication of others. Such a person is often unable to participate in a give-and-take relationship, one with mutual oral dependency need gratification and mutual guilt projection. But the person becomes particularly unable to listen when he is with a person who is projecting a large amount of added unconscious guilt.

Because of the primary and secondary feelings, a person in the projected position feels that someone else doesn't deserve, and should not have, oral dependency need gratification. He feels that this someone else should not spontaneously communicate, chitchat, or waste time in "idle talk." The person may rationalize that the other has too much to do, and that he doesn't have enough time "to sit around running his mouth." The person may make remarks that imply, "I don't like him," or "I don't care what he has to say—it's only drivel." An increase in projected added unconscious guilt intensifies the deprivation, the sadism, the anhedonia, and the insignificances of communicating that this person applies to someone else. This person prevents someone else's oral dependency need gratification, under reality-oriented "reasons" why that someone else can not, should not, and must not "feed" emotionally in spontaneous communication. With more projected added unconscious guilt, the person becomes more dogmatic, critical, and overbearing. He can stifle the attempts of someone who is too dependent on too few to draw oral dependency need gratification in spontaneous communication, by subjecting the other person to this concentrated guilt projection. The person with high projected added unconscious guilt may make it difficult for anyone else to talk by criticizing, interrupting, wanting the other to remain silent, and showing little or no interest in the other's communication. This person prevents the oral dependency need gratification that the other, who is at a stage of development of being too dependent on too few, could have had if this would-be listener had not had high projected added unconscious guilt.

The person with high added unconscious guilt in the projected position also tends to prevent others, from projecting guilt or expressing anger. He may feel that someone else's anger expression is unjustified and unwarranted; that the other is too inferior to express anger. The person may consistently convey the message, "You have no right to be angry," to someone else. This damper on the guilt projection of others may be well-rationalized. Someone who is more emotionally comfortable does not put such a damper on either the oral dependency need gratification or the guilt projection of another.

These individuals with a high level of added unconscious guilt in the projected position do not make good listeners, in that they have such a need to project their own guilt and to express their own anger in the communicative process. They may do so with a concentrated concern for a particular subject. The subject may be too narrow to be used metaphorically by others. People with high projected guilt may seem to have such a need to talk and so little interest about someone else's topics of conversation or opinions that they can't listen. They are often too interrupting, and too talkative to be good listeners in the communicative process that, for the most emotionally comfortable person, allows a *mutual* meeting of the oral dependency needs, a *mutual* projection of guilt and an expression of anger within a *shared* topic of conversation.

One can see that a high level of added unconscious guilt in any of the three positions can cause communication problems. Too much added unconscious guilt in any position can prevent a person from drawing oral dependency need gratification in spontaneous communication. It can also prevent a person from projecting the guilt in any position, including even the projected position, since concentrated projection may cause others to withdraw from communication with the person.

Particularly interesting are the dynamics involved in a parent whose added unconscious guilt is in the misperceived position but who oscillates between the self-felt side and the projected side. Here the child is first subjected to a side that is similar to the self-felt position and then subjected to a side that is similar to the projected position. There is no consistent meeting of the child's oral dependency need because the ambivalence of the parent ensures, with guilt projection, a frustration of that need. Emotional maturity is thwarted and rather than diffusing oral dependency need gratification, the child remains immature, overly dependent, and "spoiled." Listening to communication between parent and child where "spoiling" takes place we can readily recognize the ambivalence that is so characteristic of the love-hate relationship. Such a relationship can occur between any two people caught up in being too dependent on too few, but it can become emotionally disastrous for the child seeking maturity. Emotionally comfortable parents who ensure communication that is consistent in oral dependency need gratification, consistent in projected added unconscious guilt acceptance, and not under the influence of intense transference factors, allow the child to mature successfully. The best parents for making emotionally comfortable children are emotionally comfortable themselves.

If we look again at the spontaneous communication of emotionally comfortable people, we can see how the transference process works in expressing mutual oral dependency need gratification and in projecting guilt, subtly and indirectly. For instance, suppose Martha tells Jean that a mutual acquaintance, Susan, is nice, or fun to be with, or accomplished. Psychodynamically, Martha is referring to an unconsciously perceived aspect of Jean that is favorable. Susan, then, is a symbol in the manifest content, unconsciously equated, in part, with unconsciously perceived attributes in Martha's immediate transference relationship to Jean. If Jean is emotionally comfortable, she will unconsciously identify with the positively described Susan and will draw oral dependency need gratification from this identification. In Jean's unconscious, she is Susan, or the part of Susan being favorably described. The emotionally comfortable listener unconsciously perceives pleasantly described people, experiences, or situations with a self-reference. Psychodynamically, this also is correct; the speaker is referring to an unconsciously perceived aspect of the listener.

But the emotionally uncomfortable person with a high level of misperceived added unconscious guilt tends not to make such an identification. If Jean had a large amount of added unconscious guilt in the misperceived position, she would, instead of identifying with Susan, feel envious, jealous, perhaps angry, and feel that she is being unfavorably compared to Susan. Jean might think, "Martha's making Susan out to be so great, and in contrast, she feels that I'm so insignificant, inferior, etc." In this case, Jean does not draw oral dependency need gratification, instead she perceives rejection, which is oral dependency need frustrating.

Suppose that Martha does not like Susan, and in talking to Jean, describes Susan as inconsiderate, boring, and stupid. Susan is a symbol in Martha's manifest content for some unconsciously perceived aspect of Jean. Martha is projecting guilt, and expressing anger, not only to Susan, but more significantly, to Jean. In reality, the guilt is projected to Susan. But in the emotional unreality of the transference, Jean is unconsciously equated, in part, with Susan. But if Jean is emotionally comfortable, she accepts the projection of guilt without perceiving any personal reference. She has a level of oral dependency need gratification that gives her a feeling of self-acceptance and makes no identification, conscious or unconscious, with Susan. She may even share in the guilt projection using Martha's manifest content, agreeing with Martha that Susan is inconsiderate, boring, and stupid, and thereby supporting Martha's guilt projection. When Jean does so, "Susan" becomes metaphorical for an unconsciously perceived aspect of Martha that is involved with Jean's projected guilt. Here the metaphor is mutually used to project added unconscious guilt thus showing dynamically the benefits of gossiping. We saw in an earlier chapter that in the communication of emotionally comfortable people, a mutual, unconscious, and part-oriented projection of guilt takes place in the transference, unrealized by either speaker or listener. If Jean had high misperceived added unconscious guilt, this would be an example of the no-win situation, where no matter what Martha says about Susan, Jean perceives rejection. And at the other extreme, if Jean's added unconscious guilt is low, and her oral dependency needs are being met diffusely, no matter what Martha says about Susan, Jean will *not* perceive rejection, even though Martha is, in part, rejecting Jean.

The unconscious part-equating and transference in spontaneous communication work to allow the emotionally comfortable person to project guilt and to meet the oral dependency need. Indirect guilt projection to a listener is more effective in lowering the added unconscious guilt than if that guilt were directly projected to the person, in that indirect projection provides an unthreatened continuation of oral dependency need gratification. Also, when guilt projection is mutually shared and supported, the listening is a means of meeting the oral dependency need of the listener. When both speaker and listener are emotionally comfortable, neither perceives the latent reference in the guilt projection to the other. Instead, they perceive the mutual support for each other's guilt projection as oral dependency need gratifying.

It would seem that it's so easy to meet the oral dependency need and to project added unconscious guilt in spontaneous communication. It *is* easy for those who are already emotionally comfortable; they remain so by using spontaneous communication for oral dependency need gratification and indirect projection. Most of the emotional uncomfortableness in the world is resolved in this way, through spontaneous communication of daily relationships. I've been trying to get this message across for years; if only people would listen! It's talking and listening that cures, not the subject matter of the talking. The subject talked about doesn't make one bit of difference. We know that one subject may be just as good as another. Of course, the subject one chooses is important to him at the moment. But theoretically, any subject will do. Many people become emotionally comfortable by talking out their emotional problems without realizing that they're doing it.

Those who have the highest unmet oral dependency need and the most added unconscious guilt—the emotionally uncomfortable—are the very ones who have the most difficulty in communicating. Most emotionally uncomfortable people, as we've also seen, don't realize that their problems in communication originate in the emotional unreality, coming from perceptions that have been distorted by added unconscious guilt. Often, they feel that they can solve their problems intellectually, by reading books on how to make friends, how to be well-liked and popular. They don't realize that these things cannot be learned; their problems must be solved *emotionally*. Resolving emotional uncomfortableness is not an intellectual process; it only appears to be. Any emotional uncomfortableness is always resolved through an emotional process.

Because they want an intellectual solution, these people also think that they must know what their problems are in order to solve them. But we already understand that we can resolve emotional problems without knowing what they are, using any manifest content. We could solve our emotional problems by talking to a co-worker about our bosses, or by talking to someone on the bus about yesterday's baseball game, or by talking to our spouses about the children's grades in school. We know that any manifest content has the capacity to work. A person's manifest content is a vehicle for the latent content, and it doesn't matter what that manifest content is; it always has something to do with the immediate transference relationship between the speaker and listener. That transference relationship has the capability of resolving the emotional problems. This problem resolving capability occurs naturally and deceptively, under an intellectually oriented or reality-oriented cover. The emotionally laden latent content lowers the added unconscious guilt by projection. But the emotionally uncomfortable person does not realize that she can solve her problems by talking about anything.

The individual with the most communicative difficulties characteristically has a high personality core guilt, which makes the communicative process even more complex. Those with high personality core guilt, as we have seen, have little time to indulge in spontaneous communication; they want to be "independent," to need no one, to waste no time. These people often end up being too dependent on too few, with too much retained added unconscious guilt. A tendency to have the added unconscious guilt in the misperceived position further complicates the process, because, as we've seen, the misperceived position is where the most intense communcation problems lie. To complicate the problem even more, as we've also seen, people with a high level of misperceived added unconscious guilt tend to become involved in exclusive relationships with others who similarly have a high level of misperceived guilt. So those with the greatest need for good listeners are often involved exclusively with poor ones.

The "therapeutic listener" can help uncomfortable people under any reality orientation of the emotional problem. They can use phobias, panic attacks, alcoholism, hypochondriasis, marital problems, stress, analysis, or dream recall for the manifest content. They can see a psychiatrist or psychologist with a particular orientation, a counselor or therapist of some type, or a dream analyst because any manifest content has the capacity to solve the communication problem. The real solution to emotional uncomfortableness lies in the unconscious emotional unreality, not in the reality of the particular brand of therapy they choose nor in the reality of the manifest content. The easiest solution to emotional uncomfortableness of any form involves meeting the oral dependency need and lowering the added unconscious guilt and this occurs in the emotional unreality on the level of the transference language. One of the more popular therapies today is cognitive behavior therapy, which assumes that depression and phobias have an intellectual origin and that someone can learn to overcome the negative thinking and learn to think positively. But we already know that someone cannot *learn* to think positively. He or she only begins to think positively when he or she begins to become emotionally comfortable. The reason that cognitive behavior therapy works for some people is that it provides an acceptable manifest content for lowering the added unconscious guilt and meeting the oral dependency need, which in turn causes less negative, and therefore more positive, thinking. Reality oriented therapies create a big deception, in that the real reason for their success is their provision of a manifest content and a good listener for emotionally uncomfortable people who are usually in the misperceived position. One of the leading hypnotherapists in the country once confided to me that hypnosis did nothing but provide a reality reason for involvement and to provide a workable manifest content acceptable for those people so inclined to hypnosis as a "cure" for whatever they felt their problem was.

As these people become more emotionally comfortable, communication improves and they have less "need" for a "therapeutic listener" in whatever guise. This is illustrated by a story a psychiatrist once told me. He was conducting group therapy with a dozen or more men and women suffering with phobias and anxiety attacks. They would meet at his office once a week in the evening for a two hour session. In time, they all got more comfortable with each other. After their group therapy session they began to meet at a local restaurant for coffee, where they would sit around and chat for an hour or more longer. The psychiatrist told me that eventually no one was showing up for group therapy but all the members would simply turn up at the restaurant. They were getting just as much out of meeting together once a week at the restaurant as they were in group therapy and it was saving them one hundred dollars each. One of the group told me that they all missed the psychiatrist at their weekly gathering but they decided not to invite him to the restaurant for fear he might send them a bill afterwards.

We have already learned that the transference is more intense in the relationships of the emotionally uncomfortable. Transference language has great therapeutic potential in a relationship with a good listener. In the therapy or counseling situation there is a tendency, depending on the type of therapy, for the therapist to do more listening than would the other person in an ordinary transference relationship. Therapy attracts those people with a higher unmet oral dependency need, and the combination of these two factors produces a more evident transference relationship and, therefore, more evident transference language. We will see examples of transference language that is very evident, but we should remember that the same process is taking place in all of our relationships. In other relationships, among emotionally comfortable people, the transference is more diffused and more difficult to see than in a relationship of one person who is primarily the speaker to another who is predominantly the listener.

The person who seeks a therapist or counselor is usually on the self-felt side and wants help with her problem, seeing herself as its cause. She feels that she needs to see a therapist. However, as the therapist emotionally supports her, predominantly by listening, her added unconscious guilt will begin to lie more to the projected side. Take for an example, a married daughter who came to me when she became depressed. She was obviously too dependent on too few and her increased misperceived added unconscious guilt was lying to the self-felt side. With emotional support, this guilt would swing to the projected side. On this side, she would find fault because of her rather twisted perceptions, unload a little guilt when she expressed anger over these perceptions, and then swing back to the self-felt side. But each time she was on the projected side, the misperceived guilt was decreased a little more. When she returned to the self-felt side, her depression was thereby decreased. One time she came in, angrily telling me about a recent visit to her mother, saying, "All my mother did was to go on and on about how great my brother is! She had to tell me all the details of how well he was doing in college, all the nice girls he was dating, and how educated he was becoming. It was as if she was contrasting *me* with *him*! It made me sick! She probably feels that *I'm* doing poorly because I don't have a nice high paying job while trying to raise three kids, and that *I'm* no good because I didn't go to college, went around with the wrong type of boys, and married the wrong person. I resent how she regards my brother, and that she didn't say one thing good about *me* the whole time I was there! She's *always* put me down. I would like to hear her, just once, say something nice about *me*! No one ever says how well I'm doing and what I've accomplished! I always hear how well my brother is doing."

To tell this woman that her problem is that she can't identify with the positive in communication and draw oral dependency need gratification is not the solution for that problem. To try to get her to see that when her mother talks in a positive way about her brother, the mother is atually talking in a positive way about an unconsciously perceived aspect of her would be futile. The answer is to lower the level of her misperceived added unconscious guilt. That's all that is necessary. Her guilt is on the projected side in this example, and though it may swing back to the self-felt side, there'll be less of it. In fact, where the person initially may have felt she needed to see a therapist, she soon may feel the therapist is seeing the wrong person.

Many analysts feel that no anger expression means no progress in therapy. This belief fits with our theory for the therapeutic benefit of counseling or even just talking in that anger expression decreases the amount of added unconscious guilt and lowers the unmet oral dependency need. Once the person is able to swing to the projected side in a transference relationship where he does not have to receive a load of projected guilt in return, perhaps disguised as "good advice," the person is able to lower the added unconscious guilt. He then can begin to see things more as they really are. He becomes less phobic, less hypochondriacal, less depressed, less prone to abuse alcohol or drugs, and less distorted in his perceptions. The projected side allows expression of the anger that's had to be repressed, because the person was too dependent on too few, thereby lowering the added unconscious guilt.

In the exclusive relationship, one person characteristically supports the other in his reluctance to meet the oral dependency need elsewhere. It's important, in trying to help the person, to get him to talk to someone outside of the exclusive relationship to meet the oral dependency need. If you just listen to the person, under any manifest content, showing him that you're interested in his manifest content, he will begin to swing to the projected side, which is the key to lowering his added unconscious guilt. That manifest content he expresses may be incorrect, unrealistic, unscientific, unreasonable or even outrageous. But when it involves projected guilt in a therapy or counseling or even a chitchatting situation, it's therapeutic.

There is always a problem in that while on the self-felt side, the person feels guilty about meeting her oral dependency need and feels undeserving of and afraid to accept oral dependency need gratification. Someone on the self-felt side will often make remarks like, "I shouldn't be sitting here when I've got too much to do at home," "I'm afraid to get involved with someone because it seems I always end up hurting the person," or perhaps, "You shouldn't waste your time on me—I'm a hopeless cause." Such a person resists the emotional feeding through talking that necessarily precedes the expression of anger that will allow the added unconscious guilt to decrease. Once the oral dependency need begins to be gratified in a relationship though, guilt projection isn't too far behind.

The woman in the following example is reluctant to meet her oral dependency need. But she has received enough gratification to be able to project some added unconscious guilt. In her transference language, she speaks of this reluctance to "feed" emotionally, using as a manifest content her reluctance to physically "feed" while projecting guilt to her husband who she feels is making it more difficult for her to resist this "feeding." She implies that she feels the therapist is forcing her to "feed" when she says, to her therapist:

I don't like Frank [her husband in reality; the therapist, in part, metaphorically] going shopping with me. Whenever he's along, I always end up with groceries I never wanted at all. I'm trying to stay on a budget. I only get the essentials for the family, but he'll buy all those exotic and expensive foods that I try to avoid. When I go to the store, I try to shop as quickly as possible. Not Frank—he wants to examine everything and wants me to try this and that. He'll say, 'Say, look at this . . . I bet this is good!' Frankly, what he has usually turns my stomach with just the thought of eating it. I never was much on trying new or different foods. I mean, I always ate because one was supposed to eat in order to live. Maybe that goes back to my childhood when we didn't have much food. (Note the latent, emotional implications here). Times were hard, and I often went to bed without anything to eat. Frank feels eating should be a pleasure. But I'm afraid to let myself go. Because I didn't have enough food as a child, I'm afraid that if I let myself go now I'd become a regular glutton. I've seen too many people get fat and repulsive from eating too much. I watch very carefully what I eat, but with him bringing home extra food, it's getting more and more difficult.[1]

In the preceding example, the woman was resisting oral dependency need gratification on the self-felt side. It may seem that the person is metaphorically projecting guilt, but in listening to the person for a long period of time, perhaps even with other reality orientations, we can determine that comments that seem to be guilt projection are metaphorical self-references, in part. In the following excerpt, we can see that this next woman is more accepting of oral dependency need gratification. In her manifest content, her garden is metaphorically, in part, her therapy situation:

The garden is coming along very nicely. Two months ago, I was ready to let the whole thing go to weeds. I thought it was a waste of time. I didn't care if the flowers lived or died. Nothing was going right. [And it did seem this way in her therapy.] There was too much rain, and for a while what did come up just got washed away. Too much rain at the wrong time isn't good. Then when I needed rain, there wasn't enough. I had just about given up on the garden, but you should see it now. [Smiles warmly.] The marigolds are all in bloom, bushy and hardy. I never dreamed it would turn out so well. I think I owe a lot of the success with this garden to my husband [an unconsciously perceived aspect of the therapist]. At first he didn't seem to care whether I wanted a garden or not. It was 'Sure, you can have a garden, but you do all the work yourself.' And I have done most of the weeding. But he's done a lot of the other things for it. He's fertilized it, watered it regularly, sprayed for bugs, edged it with a fence to keep the rabbits out, and clipped the dead blossoms to keep the flowers blooming. He says it's his way of relaxing. And I think he's telling the truth, since he never did like to work. [Laughs.] My neighbor [another aspect of the therapist] admired it and wants me to join the garden club. I have to laugh, because I always thought the garden club was a waste of time, and because I couldn't grow anything, I wouldn't fit in with them. It's been a surprise to me, how well the garden has come along. In fact, my garden looks better than many of theirs. I think it's been a real boost to my ego and morale to know I can do this. I feel a lot better about myself. I've really enjoyed working in it with my husband. It was something I didn't want to do and I resisted at first. I just got interested little by little. Now I look forward to my time in the garden. I intend to keep on with it. I've already picked out a few plants for next year that I didn't dare try this year, as I've heard that they're so difficult to grow in this climate. But I think I'll give them a try and my husband said he'd help.[1]

By telling her therapist about her garden, and her surprise and pleasure that it's going so well, this woman is latently expressing her surprise and pleasure that her therapy is going so well. She also recognizes her initial resistance to getting involved and getting some of her oral dependency need met. She felt that meeting her need was a waste of time, because she was on the self-felt side. Now she has found that she enjoys oral dependency need gratification.

The early expression of anger, in therapy, is often very ambivalent.

It may be followed by remarks like "I'm coming across like a nagging old bitch," or, "You're probably thinking I'm an ungrateful person that no one could ever please," which expresses the swing back to the self-felt side in the first example and in the latter, to the mid-line stance. The person may present a convincing reality-oriented rationalization for his or her guilt projection, but then may follow this with, "How can you listen to this garbage?" Another way to express the swing is to present the projected side and then say, "You probably think I'm making all of this up, and maybe I am—maybe I'm not seeing things right—it certainly wouldn't be the first time." The anger expression is ambivalent and after the person has expressed some anger, he may feel guilty about it, and think he shouldn't have done it.

This anger expression can cause problems for the inexperienced therapist who does not recognize its ambivalent nature. Because of the swing, the therapist must not give support that is too vigorous, or too concrete in regard to the reality orientation of the rationalization. Support is best expressed nonverbally, with an understanding nod or look, without a reality orientation. For instance, if an emotionally uncomfortable woman says, "I can't stand my husband," the therapist should not jump in and say, "Well get away from your husband—leave him!" The woman will swing back to the self-felt side and present something like, "Well, he has to put up with so much from me." The therapist must recognize that he cannot enthusiastically support either the self-felt or the projected side, because the person cannot stick to any one side. Support that might be appropriate on one side, becomes inappropriate with the return to the other side. Furthermore, by telling the woman to get away from her husband, the therapist conveys a latent message for her to get away from *him* since he is her husband in part.

It is important, however, for the emotionally uncomfortable person to get onto the projected side and to express anger. It's also important to the continuation of a relationship that this anger be expressed in metaphor, so that it is disguised for the listener. The best therapeutic listeners, the ones who are able to keep the process ongoing, are those who understand transference language, and can continue tc monitor the person's latent content while staying within the reality orientation of the manifest content. Even in this type of relationship, it's still better that the anger expression be disguised for the speaker. Someone who calls her therapist a son-of-a-bitch directly, for example, is unlikely to continue that relationship. It's much better, in regard to helping this person, to let her call her boss or spouse a son-of-a-bitch, meaning the therapist, in part, but using the metaphor. Then the person will feel that she can continue the therapeutic relationship, and she can lower her added unconscious guilt still further. When a relationship is ongoing and oral dependency need gratifying, the diffusion process is enhanced in just this way. It isn't enhanced when directly projected guilt and expressed anger terminate a relationship. The person may be temporarily more emotionally comfortable but the comfortableness won't last if the person is still too dependent on too few. The therapist must unavoidably deal with directly projected guilt and expressed anger because the more emotionally uncomfortable person tends to be more exclusively dependent. As such, this person will transfer this situation into therapy, where one may see all the characteristics of a love-hate relationship. It is here that the experienced therapist can show his or her skill in handling both sides of this directly expressed relationship. As the person becomes more comfortable and simultaneously, less dependent on too few, his feelings tend to be expressed metaphorically and not directly.

In the next man's latent content, one can see that he's talking about his therapist in part. As his added unconscious guilt decreases, one can also see how his perception shifts. He was a graduate student who had been depressed and had had feelings of inferiority and inadequacy on the self-felt side. But he has now swung to the projected side and can express anger. As he does so, his perception of the therapist changes:

The sociology department [a reference to the therapy situation] is so damn passive. It really irks me to think of how little they do for the graduate student. They simply provide the setting, and the student *himself* has to do all the work, mapping out his own program, and setting his own goals. The department won't even help with a curriculum problem. It's a kind of, '*You* work it out . . . it's *your* problem' attitude that makes me so damn mad! I'm beginning to see things differently now about that department. And to think I thought it was the very best department in the whole university. Now I can see those little flaws I couldn't see before. And one of them is the department's passivity. [Long thoughtful pause.] I got a warning ticket last week for reckless driving [a reference to the previous expression of anger]. I really deserved it too. I didn't have the car under control the way I should, and furthermore, I was bucking traffic going the other way. I've got to watch myself more. Lately, I've gotten so I yell and scream when anything makes me mad. If I'm at a light and the driver in front [the therapist, in part] hasn't started moving, I'll give him a blast on the horn, and yell, 'Come on you bastard! Get going!' [Laughs.] I was *never* like that before. I guess I'm frustrated at the school. It's not giving me all I think it should, so I take out my frustrations on the highway rather than get expelled. But that's not right now, is it? [Therapist shrugs.] I get mad at people whom I know I shouldn't be mad at. Instead of a warning ticket, I should have gotten a fine! It surprised me that a state trooper [another perceived aspect of the therapist] can be so tolerant![1]

This man unconsciously perceives an aspect of his therapist that he feels is too passive and too slow. Toward this aspect, he projects guilt.

But as the therapist accepts his projected guilt, he begins to perceive that his listener is tolerant.

Once the person is on the projected side, he will make comments like, "I don't know if he has been this way all the time and I just didn't see it," or, "Have I gotten more perceptive lately and am seeing things I didn't see before?" or, "She should be here in this chair, not me!" This is similar to the man saying, "I'm beginning to see things differently now about that department. And to think I thought it was the very best department in the whole university. But now I can see those little flaws I couldn't see before." The person sees faults that he overlooked before because now he is perceiving the person, experience, or situation from the projected side.

As the man who was beginning to perceive his therapist as "tolerant" was doing, the person with emotional support and the oral dependency need gratification that comes from projecting guilt to an accepting listener can start to realize that anger expression in the therapy situation is not destructive. His anger expression begins to be viewed as not hurting the other. This is because there is less added unconscious guilt on the self-felt side, which would produce feelings that anger expression is harmful, wrong, and unacceptable.

Transference can also resolve ambivalence. Perhaps the person is not involved to the degree of a love-hate relationship, but she can like some aspects of another person and dislike other aspects of that same person. She may draw oral dependency need gratification from one or more unconsciously perceived aspects of the person and project guilt to other aspects. This is the process by which the love-hate relationship is resolved. Even if the ambivalence is of a lesser degree than that of the love-hate relationship, it still may not fit well with reality. Using metaphorical transference language, one can express this ambivalence in a way that makes sense. One does this best with a "therapeutic listener" who is less prone than the nonprofessional to refute distorted perceptions. The metaphors and the analogies reflect the ambivalent feelings and appropriately reflect the swinging from the self-felt to the projected side and back. Each time the added unconscious guilt takes the projected side it is lessened. Its acceptance by the listener aids in the diffusion process.

For example, in the following we can easily see that the woman likes certain aspects of her therapist and dislikes others. She can project guilt at the aspects she dislikes, yet still accept oral dependency need gratification from the aspects that she likes because of the distance afforded by the metaphors of her transference language. She had taken her daughter, Mary, to a surgeon to have a small growth removed, which could also be symbolic, latently, for the "removal" of her added unconscious guilt. Each of the doctors that she mentions is an unconsciously perceived aspect of the therapist:

That Doctor Green [one perceived aspect of the therapist] is so mean. He just can't be civil. He can't say anything without insulting a person. He's so over-bearing and thinks he's so great. I'd just love to buy him for what he's worth and sell him for what he thinks he's worth. I'd make a fortune! [Laughs] Mary [a metaphor for an aspect of herself] just can't stand him. I wouldn't blame her for kicking him the way he spoke to her. He talked to her like a dog, as if she was nothing but a bother, and as though he couldn't have cared less about her. But Dr. Smith [another unconsciously perceived aspect of the therapist] is just the opposite. [Smiles warmly] He explains things if you don't understand them. He's always so patient and understanding, and makes you feel at ease. Nothing is more important than you, when you're with Dr. Smith. Dr. Green is always gruff. He told Mary to shut up and quit complaining, and that she was being a cry baby. Now, how in the hell does he know whether it's hurting her? The stupid ass! He asked her, 'What are you, a little infant or something? I thought you were a lot bigger than this.' That made her feel terrible. I thought she was doing very well for a little girl of only ten. Now she just abhors going to see him. Every time she goes to the surgery clinic [a latent reference to the therapy situation] she hopes and prays that she'll get Dr. Smith. Actually, I hope and pray she does too but I tell her that sometimes you can't avoid the Dr. Greens of life. I tell her that she's got to expect a little rain now and then with the sunshine. I hate to say it but I think I would have been proud of Mary if she had just up and kicked Dr. Green instead of being like me, trying to grin and bear it. I don't think a person should have to take anything like that from someone, even if he is a doctor, do you?[1]

Sometimes the transference language is so obvious that it's surprising that the person doesn't realize that he or she is projecting guilt to the listener. In the following example, the man's gestures make his trans-ference very evident. Sitting in my office, this man was complaining about his wife's housekeeping. "Everything's so damn dusty. I don't think she knows how to clean and yet it's suppose to be her job [a reference to therapy and his added unconscious guilt]. She can't see it when it's right out in front of her. You can pick up dust just by running your hand across any piece of furniture." As he was saying this he ran his fingertips across my desk picking up a load of dust. He then held his fingertips out in front of me to make his point. He then went right on to say, "She's a dirty housekeeper. I've even noticed cobwebs in the corners by the ceilings," and he looked up to one corner of my office and I did to, and there *was* a big cobweb. He went on talking about what a poor house-keeper his wife was, acting out what he was saying about her, never realizing that he was talking about an unconsciously perceived aspect of me.

Often, a person will present something using one metaphor or analogy and then, if you listen for a long enough time, he or she will present the same emotional problem using a different metaphor or analogy. Yet the manifest content deceptively seems to be spontaneously chosen, like simple chitchat or gossip, with no purpose or direction.

The lawyer in the following example is also unaware of his transference language, which is rather evident to an outside observer. He talks about his wife and Henry, both of whom are different aspects of the therapist. Henry is a young man, just out of law school, that this lawyer has hired to help with a heavy work load. You can see that the man is expressing some ambivalence toward the therapy situation, at this point:

Well, things are good and bad. First of all, I think my wife understands me better than she ever has before. I didn't think she was capable of this. She knows I'm moody, but now she seems to accept me. She's been much more patient with me, and that's what I've needed most. We've done a lot of talking to each other lately than we have ever done in all the past years of marriage. She's been a big help to me and I appreciate her. [Therapist smiles.] But I'm worried about Henry. His attitude is bad, and all he does is sit there and watch me. I'd like to see a little activity on his part for a change. I hate to keep going over things with him that I think he ought to know already. He's paid enough to know it all. I dislike going over every case in detail with him before he can take any load off of me. I get so irritated with him at times for not seeing things on his own, or going to the law books [psychiatry books?] and looking them up ahead of time, instead of asking me. He waits until *I* bring them up, and that's not really helping me at all. I could actually do the work myself in less time, and at less expense, if I didn't have Henry trying to help me! I have to spend time with him to show him what a certain law problem is. So I end up paying him for my time. [Therapist: "That doesn't seem right".] It isn't! What annoys me the most is having to stop and explain things to him. I keep hoping that it's going to be easier on me in the long run, because once he gets it, he's going to lighten my load. In the meantime, it's making me damn mad at times, while at other times it's damn depressing! I had planned to get more work done than what I'm getting done now. I'm even further behind because of him. And that doesn't make much business sense because it was getting behind in my work that made me depressed. I can see problems that I just can't put into words. It takes time to explain it all to Henry, and then I don't think he understands half the things I explain anyway. I have a tendency, too, to want to do things myself rather than take the time and effort to explain them to others. I think the whole problem, at this time, is whether I can accept the fact that I've got to show him the problems, and how I want them to be worked through, so he can help me later.[1]

In his next session, this lawyer again talked about Henry in his manifest content. Once again, the transference language is easy to see, but this time, the man is able to project guilt unambivalently at unconsciously perceived aspects of the therapist. He began this session by saying:

I think I'm going to have to light a fire under Henry. He's just too damn slow for me. He just sat there all day yesterday and watched me work. It gripes the hell out of me because I can see so much work that has to be done but he won't go out of his way to look for it. No sir! He just sits there and waits for me to point it out. He's not taking any responsibility or any worry off of me, and that's what I really wanted a partner for. [Therapist: "Sure".] At this point he's just collecting money from me. That's all! And lately he's been telling me about all the money he could be making by working with somebody else as a full partner. He doesn't know it, but now I'm considering letting him go. [But "Henry" does know!] If he thinks he can make more headway with someone else, then he can go get someone else. [Therapist: "That's right!"] I get tired of leading him around by the nose. He's got no initiative, no push at all, and if he doesn't get on the stick, he not only won't be a full partner with me, but he [points finger emphatically at therapist] won't even be associated with me! And I get tired of his going home right at four p.m. every single working day. Now that *really* gripes the hell right out of me because there's so much work to be done. He knows it! Yet it doesn't seem to bother him a bit! Come quitting time, he just gets up and leaves. I'm used to working on a problem until it's done, and done right! I've always been that way—at least when I wasn't depressed. I guess Henry can't be hurried up. But I'm mad about it and I'll tell him so![1]

No matter how obvious the transference language seems to the listener, he or she should not try to interpret it for the speaker. Interpretation does not help the person. If you stop to interpret, to analyze the person's transference language, you introduce the illogical emotional unreality, and put the brakes on the spontaneous flow of the manifest content. That which is unconscious does not fit with reality. The person will often only deny that the interpretation is correct. Also, because his mouth is open, the speaker is meeting *his* oral dependency need, no matter how correct or incorrect he may be in reality. In any therapy situation, under any manifest content, it does the emotionally uncomfortable person little good to subject him to continual interpretations of what he is saying latently. Intellectualism doesn't help, but letting the person talk does, so the experienced therapist keeps within the metaphors and the analogies of the manifest content. This holds true even in psychoanalysis.

Interpretation can backfire. I saw a woman several years ago, who came in one morning depressed because her son had called from college and had not asked about her; instead, he'd asked about the family cat. I jumped right in, wanting to boost her poor self-image and sagging morale, and said, "But when he asked about the *cat*, he was asking about *you*, in part!" The woman quickly responded with, "Oh, I should have known, because his exact words were, 'Is that cat acting as *crazy* as he usually does?' " Because of her high level of misperceived added unconscious guilt, she even used the interpretation of her transference language to support her feeling that "my son [the therapist, in part] feels I'm inferior, inadequate, unacceptable, wrong, or just plain crazy." Interpreting someone's transference language often places you in such a no-win situation.

The real progress in therapy or counseling comes on the projected side. It's similar to how people stay comfortable in other relationships. When they swing to the projected side, they're keeping their added unconscious guilt down. Often, the guilt projection is not as easy to see in other relationships, because it's less intense and more diffused, but it is still there. If the therapeutic listener interrupts to interpret even the most blatant transference language, he will not allow his client to express that often ambivalent anger. It's best just to let the person talk spontaneously, without interpreting.

When the person is allowed to keep talking, and the therapeutic communicative relationship becomes ongoing, the transference will begin to become more complex. The person begins to draw oral dependency need gratification from and project guilt to differently perceived aspects of the listener. In the following example, a teen-aged girl is contrasting her driving instructor and her father, each of whom embody different aspects of the therapist. The driving instructor is equated with the aspects of the therapist that the girl perceives to be kind, considerate, and understanding, while her father is equated with the aspects that the girl perceives as fault-finding and impatient. The girl began the counseling session with:

I'm really enjoying my driving class. At first, I was leery of it, and felt sure that I wouldn't be able to continue with it, because I usually get so nervous and uptight. On the last test, I got an "A." My instructor was proud of me. [Smiles warmly at the therapist.] She didn't come right out and say that, but I can tell she thinks a lot of me, and, of course, I think the world of her. She did tell me that if I continued much longer in the class she was going to adopt me. [Laughs.] I wouldn't mind being her daughter either! She's so understanding, and so patient. She's consistent. She never gets angry, even when I make mistakes. She makes learning to drive fun. She's just the opposite from my father. [Here she introduces the opposing facet of her ambivalence.] He can be one way at one time and just the opposite another. I was out practicing driving with him the other day [a latent reference to a previous therapy session] and he was on me all the way. I like to take my time, and I don't like to be hurried. I know he means well, but he got me all upset, right in the middle of traffic, when I was trying to make a left hand turn: 'Go ahead! What are you waiting for? Do you want to get smashed in the rear? Get going!,' [The girl is expressing, meta-phorically, her misperceived secondary feeling that the therapist wants her to go faster in therapy, but here the experienced therapist will let her get her feelings out, without jumping in to correct her misperception or to defend him-self.] That got me all shook up and I stalled the car in the middle of the oncoming lane. Then he really got on me. He was yelling and screaming. I just sat there crying. [Her therapy sessions were often characterized by "stalls" where she would sit quietly and cry.] He said I was the worst driver he ever saw, and that I shouldn't be behind a wheel or ever have a license. He said that I was nothing but a typical woman driver. He always has to put me down. Even when he just looks at me, I can tell he's criticizing me. I wasn't even sitting right in the car, according to him, and we hadn't even begun to drive! Then I wasn't holding the wheel right. I've never been able to do anything to please him. Yet, I've got to have him with me, since the law requires an adult in the car as long as I only have a learner's permit. And no one else in the family has a driver's license. [Therapist: "You should have put him in the trunk then."] Why didn't I think of that! [Laughs warmly] That's where he belongs! [Laughs again and then becomes serious] Getting him into the trunk would be like belling the proverbial cat![1]

When the communicative process is ongoing, the person imbues some aspects of the listener with projected added unconscious guilt, and draws oral dependency need gratification from other aspects. Earlier, when the relationship served only as a target for guilt projection, or as a source of oral dependency need gratification, the transference language might have been easy to see. But as therapy or counseling progresses and the person starts to use different metaphors and analogies for unconsciously perceived aspects of the listener, she is already becoming involved with more people. Her diffusion of the oral dependency need makes her transference language become more complex. It becomes even more complex when certain metaphors are used to encompass aspects of the listener and aspects of the self. Also making the process more complex is a "part" interrelating, different parts of the person relating to different unconsciously perceived parts of the listener. The unconscious tends to be ambivalent; the more uncomfortable the person, we already know, the greater the ambivalence. But as the person diffuses her oral depen-dency need, more parts become involved and the transference is not as "simple" as it has been in the previous examples.

As an example of this more complex transference, consider the girl who came for counseling because of a school phobia. She developed the phobia when she was emotionally involved with too few people and had repressed too much anger; she spent most of her time at home with her mother. But with emotional support, she began to get involved with some of her friends. The different unconsciously perceived aspects of her counselor are conveyed in Barry, Bruce, her mother, Jane, and the policeman, while the unruly children and Helen convey aspects of herself. The geometry class and the little grocery store on the corner refer to the counselor's office. The counselor helps keep her manifest content going, which keeps the communication spontaneous. In talking to her counselor, the girl said:

I haven't missed a day of school yet. [Smiles warmly.] I even went to my geometry class this week, which I usually hate with a purple passion. I've been feeling a lot better and haven't had any of those panicky feelings I used to have. I think it's because Barry is treating me nicely right now. Before he was ignoring me, and that made me feel terrible because I felt left out. Before that he used to pick on me and was always finding fault with me. All the other kids knew what he was doing to me, and I think that's why I didn't want to go to school. He'd get me all mixed up in my feelings. When he *wasn't* with me, I was mad that he wasn't; and when he *was* with me, I was mad that he wouldn't leave me alone. He's not picking on me now. He's really changed. [Pause.] Maybe it's because he found out I've been interested in Bruce a little. Bruce treats me in a way I don't really deserve. [Counselor: "You don't deserve?"] I mean he's *too* nice to me. He always lets me do exactly what I want to do. He'd give me anything that I want. [Counselor: "He thinks a lot of you."] Yes he does. He's too perfect for me and too agreeable. [Pause—then becomes serious.] Sometimes what I want isn't best for me. I'm immature and Mother has always told me I want too much and that I'm too demanding. I don't think it's good for me to get too involved with a person like Bruce. [Thoughtful pause.] I mean, I kind of have the feeling with him, that if I insisted on lying down in the middle of a busy highway because it felt good to me, he'd say it was alright with him. Do you see what I mean? [Counselor: "I see."] I need someone who can say 'No' to me, and Bruce isn't that kind of person. [Another thoughtful pause.] I had a strange dream last night. I dreamed I got mad at my best friend, Jane. I don't know why I dreamed something like that as I've never been mad at her. She's always been such a good friend ever since the beginning of the school year. In the dream I was mad because she wouldn't help me take care of my unruly children who were clamoring for attention. I know what that's like from baby-sitting with some little monsters. Children can be such a bother. But the dream is ridiculous as I'm not even married. I don't have any children. I'm a long way from being married and settled down with one guy. [Counselor shrugs.] I wonder why I dreamed of getting mad at Jane, except she does turn me off when I talk about myself.

[Pause] Remember Helen? [Counselor: "The girl that got pregnant and had to get married?"] Yes, that's the one. She's getting along much better with her husband. It makes me feel good to know that she's happier. [Smiles warmly.] She use to be depressed and hardly said anything. All she did was cry and she didn't know why. Now she's more talkative and I've been spending a lot of time with her. Now I know how her husband didn't treat her right in the past. I've been helping out in the little grocery store on the corner doing what I can. That's where she works. It's not easy work but she needs the money [i.e. oral dependency need gratification]. I've heard the store is under surveillance because they suspect people are taking dope. The police think they might be getting it at the little store. We try to run the store right and we have kept some people out. I will admit that some of the characters that come into the store aren't the best type. And I know some are on dope. We had a man come in last week and tell Helen that the store shouldn't cater to teenagers. He said it was bad for the business. He said: 'You get teenagers in here and it'll be just a matter of time before the business goes bankrupt.' I don't see how he has any right to talk, as he doesn't even work himself. He just sits around all day stirring up trouble and telling others what to do. Helen can't stand him. She'll tell him so too. Why he comes back when he knows how Helen feels about him is beyond me. She's done every-thing to make her feelings known to him, including insulting him right to his very face. She doesn't put up with things as much now as she used to do. She'll give it right back. [Counselor: "I'm glad she does."] Just the other night, a fellow came to the house and Helen let him in. He didn't identify himself but began asking her a whole bunch of personal questions that were none of his business! He was snooping! When she told me later what he looked like I recognized that he was a plainclothes policeman. It didn't even occur to Helen at the time she was answering all those questions that he was a damn cop! She thought it was one of her husband's friends. She started telling him things, without even think-ing, because she's that way—you know, real trusting of others. Once she gets talking, she can't shut up. [Laughs.] I'm a little that way at times. He must have thought she was having a dope party. He never said what he wanted. Never said what he was going to do. Just wanted to get her talking freely, letting her think he could be trusted and that he was a friend of her husband's. Finally she said that she had to go, so he told her he'd be back next week. I would have slammed the door in his face. She wants to get away from things like that. [Counselor: "I don't blame her."] Jane and I have decided that as soon as I turn eighteen this summer, we're going out to California. We've got our plans made and Mother isn't going to stop me. Oh, maybe I'll come back and see her sometime later. But I think it would do me good to get away from her for a while.[2]

In the preceding example, one can see the complexity of the trans-ference language. As the person's misperceived added unconscious guilt decreases, the metaphors become more complex. She perceives different aspects of the therapist; some are guilt-imbued and others are oral dependency need gratifying. The metaphors of transference language can reflect not only the extremes of love and hate, but also many more subtle states in between. At the same time the complexity indicates the person's increased involvement with other people in her reality. Involvement in therapy coincides with improved relationships with more people, and this increased involvement with others makes more metaphors available. These other people can be used, in the transference language, to reflect differently perceived aspects of the therapist or different aspects of the person himself. No longer does the person have unconscious aspects of simple love or hate. Unconscious aspects of the self expressed in metaphor and analogies reflect a variety of likes and dislikes. As the metaphors become more complex they reach a point where it would take volumes to explain them. This is a sign, however, that the emotional process of diffusion is taking place, and at the same time, the transference and its language is becoming less evident.

The transference process works best when the person is unaware of it. Sometimes, however, when the person is too dependent on too few and forms such an intense transference, he or she will become aware of his or her own transference language. It's similar to a Freudian slip, which is a fleeting unveiling of the latent content. For example, a woman who had been involved in therapy had a lot of unmet oral dependency need so her potential for forming an intense transference was high. When the therapist began to meet her oral dependency need, her transference language was easily "read." It's easy to see in the following excerpt from a therapy session that what she talks about is her therapy in part. She has an uncanny way, every once in a while, of picking up on the fact that what she is talking about has something to do with the therapy situation. In this example, she's talking about her husband in reality and says:

He sits there at the table as if he knows everything and that really irks the hell out of me. I'd like to kill the bastard at times. [Suddenly pauses and looks embarrassed.] Now I'm not talking about you! I wouldn't be sitting her if I felt that way about you. I'm talking about my husband. [Therapist: "Oh, I know you are."] He lets the children ["Children" is a frequently occurring metaphor for oral dependency needs as in "I can't leave my husband because of the children"] go and they get into everything. He doesn't care. They take things apart, pull things out and then leave them out [a reference to how she perceives therapy—getting into things, taking things apart, pulling things out]. I've got things stored away that I don't want gotten into but he lets them. He lets them run loose all over the place. Sure, they love to be with him, but I swear it's a zoo at 708! [That was the therapist's street address.] Oh, I'm sorry! [Blushes.] What did I say that for? [Covers her face with her hand.] Oh, I'm very sorry! I meant 803 Pearl Street.

Her Freudian slip revealed her latent content to her, but it also thwarts the spontaneity of the process because this woman is reluctant to project guilt in the therapy situation.

Another woman once told me, "I'd like to tell my boss that he's an uncaring idiot. [She blushes.] Now I'm not talking about you! I don't feel you're uncaring at all. [Pause.] Well, sometimes I feel you are maybe just a little bit. [A long thoughtful pause.] Well, sometimes, come to think of it, you are downright uncaring. But you're certainly not an idiot. [Long thoughtful pause, then laughs.] You know, come to think of it I *could* be talking about you! Oh, well, I always say if the shoe fits, wear it!" This second person is much more comfortable in expressing anger than the first who has to watch that anger isn't more blatantly expressed. The difference between the two people is how much their oral dependency need is diffused. It's the diffusion of the oral dependency need that eliminates the threat of expressing anger.

In order for the person to be comfortable in expressing anger, he must get past that initial reluctance to do so which comes from the self-felt side and swing to the projected side. Initially, the person makes comments, on the self-felt side, like, "I should discontinue because I could sit in here talking all day," or, "I shouldn't come back as this could go on for years." But it rarely does, because once he gets some oral dependency need gratification, he will swing to the projected side and will begin to lower his added unconscious guilt. He will no longer feel like such an intrusion or a bother to other people, so he will expand his relationship sphere. He may even be able to express anger directly to the therapeutic listener, because now he is not too dependent on the therapeutic relationship for oral dependency gratification.

What we've tried to do in this chapter is to elucidate the "therapy" that is included in the everyday communication of the emotionally comfortable person. We have tried to show, in the therapy situation, what goes on much more subtly in the spontaneous communication of someone who's more involved with other people, experiences, and situations, someone who meets the oral dependency need and projects guilt diffusely. The same dynamics that we can see in the therapy situation exist, in a more complex form, in the more comfortable person's communication. And, having explored these dynamics, we can now move on to examine the deception involved in all therapies with a reality orientation, for in any therapy, there is a relationship that contains these same psychodynamics of communication that have such a capacity to lower the troublesome added unconscious guilt.

1. Adapted from: THE THERAPEUTIC LISTENER, Robert E. Krieger Publishing Company, Melbourne, FL 1974
2. Adapted from: COMMUNICATION BREAKDOWN, Warren H. Green Publishing Company, St. Louis, Mo 1975

HOW PSYCHOTHERAPY REALLY WORKS

THE MISPERCEIVED POSITION

MID-LINE STANCE
They feel I'm not a nice person.

SELF-FELT SIDE:
I'm not a nice person.

★

PROJECTED SIDE:
They're not nice people.

★★

Swings

As Added Unconscious Guilt Increases

★ Each time on this side the rationale for involvement in psychotherapy or counseling is provided —
   Augmented by the Unmet Oral Dependency Need

★★ Each time on this side the listener is "they" in part —
   Equated by the transference
   Amount of Anger expressed depends on Guilt projected
   Added Unconscious Guilt is quantitatively lowered
   Perceived Oral Dependency Need gratification increases proportionately
   Unmet Oral Dependency Need decreases by the same amount

★ Now less Added Unconscious Guilt for the manifestations of the Self-felt Side

CHAPTER 18
The Kaleidoscopic Deception in Treatment

There are a few more big deceptions which Aristotelian logic has hidden from the conscious mind, and in order to uncover these, let me tell you about Gretchen. Gretchen is a highly intelligent, well-educated, very articulate, and attractive woman, the wife of a plant manager for an internationally known company. Her mother was a college graduate and her father a high-ranking military officer. The family frequently moved from one area of the country to another because her father was required to change posts every three years. Both her mother and father wanted the best for her as a child but also expected the best from her. She always tried to do her best and attained top grades and honors in both high school and college. She characteristically was an "independent," hard-working, often "driven" person who always put work before pleasure. She was perfectionistic and had obsessive-compulsive traits. She excelled in whatever she put her mind to. Anyone knowing Gretchen would rate her as an exceptional wife and mother. Her home was always a showpiece in every way. Her two children are now grown and have attained positions of outstanding success in their professions.

Gretchen's husband, George, has a personality very similar to Gretchen's, which comes from a high level of personality core guilt. Perhaps their similar personalities attracted them to each other. He didn't come from the type of home that reflected success, as Getchen did. His father was an alcoholic, often unemployed, who finally deserted his family when George was eight years old. The family was poor and there were times when there wasn't enough money for food. George was often physically beaten and verbally abused by his stepfathers. He was a juvenile delinquent in his teen years, but after graduating from high school, joined the army where for the first time he felt he had a home. After his three year enlistment, he went to college on the G. I. Bill, excelled in business management, and graduated with top honors. Those same personality characteristics that Gretchen showed in the home served him in good stead in business. He was hardworking, perfectionistic, and obsessive-compulsive. These traits were always assets in his work. He tended to worry, but about the things in business that *needed* to be worried about. He rapidly rose in his company and soon became the youngest plant manager the company ever had. He would often be sent to different parts of the world, for several weeks at a time, where plants were not producing at expected levels and would quickly turn these around to make them profitable. Gretchen would proudly tell how he could work thirty-six hours or more, without food or sleep, to get a plant moving again. He was good at finding fault, placing blame, and demanding corrections. He would find things wrong or imperfect and would insist that they be immediately corrected. He drove himself and those who worked for him toward outstanding business success. His rise within this company was meteroric but like Gretchen, he despised idle chitchat, gossip, or small talk. And like Gretchen, he was always work oriented.

Because of his work, George and Gretchen often had to move from one geographical area to another. Once Gretchen's husband got a plant functioning well, he'd be transferred to still another. These moves were difficult for Gretchen and her children, but she always made the best of it. Her two boys, always the center of her life, are now gone from home. They're busily involved in their professions and have little to do with their parents, so a relocation now creates problems for Gretchen. She has never worked outside her home; the family always lived well on her husband's six figure annual salary.

Being a person who doesn't really enjoy other people, Gretchen, because of a recent move, leaves behind her only close friend who had helped meet her unmet oral dependency need. She also leaves behind the targets for her projected guilt that were necessary to keep her guilt at a comfortable level. She becomes too work oriented and too isolated in her new home. She begins to avoid relationships in which someone with less personality core guilt and less guilt-intensified personality traits would involve herself. While the children were young, she associated more with other people. In performing the duties of a dedicated mother to her boys, she was forced to get out and meet new people and was able on a part-person, part-experience, and part-situation basis to meet her oral dependency need and to project her added unconscious guilt. Her personality core guilt traits were kept at levels where they were assets rather than liabilities to her. But with the children gone, there are fewer reality reasons to get involved with others. After this last move, she spends her time getting the new house just the way she wants it. She becomes not just too dependent on too few, but almost exclusively dependent on her husband, and, for the first time, begins to develop emotional problems.

George on the other hand, is always forced into an emotional involvement with others because of his work. He can meet his unmet oral dependency need on a part-person basis at the new plant. And he has plenty of opportunity to project guilt by finding fault, criticizing, blaming, and demanding corrections at the new plant. His traits may be more intensified at times but the added unconscious guilt is never at a high enough level to turn them from assets to liabilities. So Gretchen's husband, because of his work, is able to go from one area to another with no evidence of any manifestations of emotional uncomfortableness. The work situation always provides an emotional involvement with others— a forced involvement that Gretchen, who doesn't go to work, doesn't have. He remains more emotionally mature while Gretchen slips back toward emotional immaturity with increasing added unconscious guilt in the misperceived position. That involvement with others is the key to understanding how he can remain comfortable.

Gretchen, with almost no chance to meet her oral dependency need inside her home, with a husband away for most of his waking hours, begins to change. She begins to show signs of emotional uncomfortableness from either the self-felt or the projected side, or else from the mid-line stance. With a build-up of added unconscious guilt perhaps leaning to the projected side, Gretchen might begin to find fault with the new area. She may criticize the people, perhaps making remarks like "Never in all my different moves have I ever found people more backward than here." As her guilt takes the mid-line stance, she might complain that she has never found people more "clannish," and that people in this new area don't make her feel welcome. She may feel they don't accept her and are unfriendly. Projecting guilt as she does, seeing "imperfections," "inadequacies," and shortcomings in the people of this area tends to close off any possibility of forming friendships that could make her and keep her emotionally comfortable. So she spends her time at home with a much more restricted sphere of relationships than she had at the previous place. She's alone much of the time. When George does come home, he may not want to listen to Gretchen tell how bad this new area is. He may tell her it's part of his job to live here and they both must adjust to it. He may say he has enough to contend with at work and doesn't want to listen to her complaints. If her guilt were on the self-felt side, she might begin to feel a little depressed, a little hypochondriacal, a little too worried, or perhaps too obsessive-compulsive about where things have to go or what she has to do in the new house. Perhaps on the self-felt side, she would be more obsessed with cleaning or perhaps more concerned about how she looks. But having the added unconscious guilt on the projected side spares her from all this.

Gretchen, who is less to blame than the situation in which she now finds herself, begins to show a problem in adjusting to the area. On the self-felt side, her constant cleaning or her exaggerated need to have things organized may begin to bother her husband. Her complaints about her physical health may begin to try him. Consequently, he may begin to withdraw from her and may begin to find other activities—perhaps golf on Saturdays or Sundays with plant executives, which he may rationalize as expected of him as part of his job. Gretchen may then be even more isolated. From increased added unconscious guilt in the misperceived position, she begins to feel he'd rather not listen to her and would rather spend his time with others. Gretchen may begin to realize, without necessarily blaming either herself or her husband, that she can't talk to her husband. And when she can't even talk to her husband, her misperceived added unconscious guilt increases still more. On the projected side, she becomes even more critical of the area and its people; or she begins to show even more of all the manifestations we have already seen that reflect added unconscious guilt on the self-felt side.

We know that Gretchen now has difficulty in lowering her added unconscious guilt in the day-to-day manifest contents of a relationship sphere. Those intensified core feelings of inferiority, inadequacy, unacceptableness, and guilt; those compensatory pressures toward perfection; and her sensitivity or intolerance to imperfections as she may see them make it most difficult for Gretchen to chitchat or gossip with even her husband. That accompanying pressure to work, to organize, to clean, or to get rid of that which symbolizes the increased added unconscious guilt will make any chitchatting or "idle talk" very low on her list of priorities. There's no time to sit and talk when there's "too much to be done" and when her husband doesn't show any inclination to talk with her. Staying at home she begins to develop communication problems with her husband that are so characteristic of the misperceived position. She begins to feel, "I can't talk to him," and in a confusion of ambivalent feelings, blames herself on the self-felt side and him on the projected side, perhaps rationalizing this with midline perceptions that he doesn't seem interested, doesn't seem to understand, or doesn't seem to have the time. Her intensified secondary feelings cause her to withdraw from involvement with others, to avoid contact with others, and to isolate herself. She feels too different from others, that others find her too different, or that others are too different from her to involve herself. She develops avoidant behavior. She begins to create rationalizations to explain to herself and others as to why she must do this. She may soon reach a point where it is beyond her ability to involve herself with others voluntarily. She would have to be forced by someone else or others to be involved.

It is at this point that Gretchen's added unconscious guilt has increased to such a level that it begins to create a major *disabling* problem for her no matter how it might show itself in her reality. Her increased added unconscious guilt has made her too sensitive to be involved with others if it leans to the self-felt side. Or it has made her too critical of others if it leans to the projected side. Or it makes her feel too much that others don't really accept her if it takes the mid-line stance. On any of these sides, it becomes more and more difficult for Gretchen to resolve her own problem, no matter how her increased added unconscious guilt and unmet oral dependency need show themselves, in any other than a professional relationship. With much less misperceived added unconscious guilt, she could have resolved her problem in spontaneous communication with a friend. She is now beyond the point where a friend could help. Her being too sensitive, being too critical, or feeling too unaccepted and the ambivalent swinging back and forth through all these different feelings tend to force her toward some type of professional involvement.

We already know that Gretchen's level of added unconscious guilt in the misperceived position can present itself kaleidoscopically. A simple turn of the kaleidoscope and a different picture results. It's the same amount of guilt though. What seems like one problem in reality can be replaced by another reality problem that may appear to be totally different and completely unrelated, with very different recommended specific treatments or solutions. Even within the self-felt side a whole array of shifting conditions can be evident depending upon which secondary feelings are coming to the fore. Different secondary feelings and their accompanying rationalizations may come into focus producing a different predominating condition. Depressions may appear to lift but phobias, or anxiety attacks, or more pronounced obsessive-compulsiveness, or hypochondriasis, or incapacitating poor self-images, guilt, or feelings of inferiority or failure may then develop—all with very different pathways in reality for possible solutions. But the same level of added unconscious guilt can continue.

For instance, suppose Gretchen began to drink heavily when her misperceived added unconscious guilt increased. She may feel that she is becoming an alcoholic when she recognizes that her drinking is interfering with her life. Or from the mid-line stance, she may feel that her husband is thinking she is becoming an alcoholic. She doesn't want to participate in A.A. but wants to prove to herself that she can do it herself.

She wants to show herself and her husband that she can control her drinking and even stop drinking. That's the same resistance that we saw earlier to involving herself with others that comes from the intensified traits of high personality core guilt, as well as that "need" to avoid others that comes from increased misperceived guilt. Maybe she could lower a little of the misperceived guilt by self-sacrifice, deprivation, and by working harder at home. However, unless she is able to keep this up to lower the guilt, more will accrue. The opportunity for continuing to perceive rejection is still there when she's almost exclusively dependent on her husband and too prone to be in the mid-line stance of her misperceived added unconscious guilt.

Suppose Gretchen does prove to herself and others that she can stop drinking without going to A.A. Suppose she won't touch a drink. Now, however, Gretchen may begin to complain of headaches—terrible, incapacitating headaches. She may go to several different doctors for treatment but nothing helps until she finds one doctor who tells her that her headaches are a form of migraine. He assures her that anybody that hasn't had migraine headaches doesn't really know how bad they can be. He prescribes Percodan tablets, an addicting drug, and she finds that they do help. They seem to "knock that headache." But she finds it necessary to take these regularly during the day.

The same amount of added unconscious guilt is there; it's just taking a different shape or form. No longer is drinking a problem, instead she's addicted to her medication. Those people in A.A. would, more narrowly, see this as just another manifestation of Gretchen's problem with chemical addiction. They would tell you that she's simply substituting one addiction for another. We don't see it that way—we know her problem is that of an increased unmet oral dependency need and an increased added unconscious guilt in the misperceived position. We admit that had she joined A.A., she probably wouldn't have had the problem with migraine *or* the problem of addiction to Percodan. However, it's a big deception to conclude that her basic problem is a chemical dependency. Suppose when Gretchen stopped drinking, she began to have anxiety attacks instead of headaches. She's neither drinking nor taking addicting pain pills, but her added unconscious guilt is at the same level. She now goes to a psychiatrist who puts her on a benzodiazepine, a type of tranquilizer with an addiction potential which she later abuses in an attempt to control the anxiety attacks. She abuses her tranquilizer because her added unconscious guilt is still at such a high level. Again, the deception continues when A.A. or Narcotics Anonymous will point out that she is still manifesting the basic problem of chemical dependency and has simply substituted the tranquilizer for her addicting pain pill. Again, had she involved herself in Narcotics Anonymous following her Percodan abuse, she would not have developed anxiety attacks or been abusing tranquilizers. Neither would she feel a need to drink.

Here's another scenario that doesn't include drugs or alcohol, and therefore no chemical dependencies, yet it contains the same level of misperceived added unconscious guilt lying to the self-felt side. Instead of drinking excessively, taking Percodan or abusing the tranquilizer, suppose Gretchen begins to experience chest pains that she just can't overlook. She finds herself worried about these pains and thinking the "what if s" in regard to some fatal condition. She experiences spells of uncontrollable crying yet doesn't know why she is crying. Sometimes she'll simply say she's crying "because it hurts." She feels that something terrible might happen to her physically and is afraid to do anything that involves physical exertion. She's afraid to go up any stairs and begins to refuse to go outside the house for fear of having an attack of pain. She becomes preoccupied with worries about her health. Her husband takes her to a local cardiologist who, after extensive testing, tells her he can find nothing wrong. She, however, "knows" there's something wrong and no one can tell either Gretchen or her husband that it's her "nerves" or "all in her head." Her husband then takes her to still another cardiologist who has been described by a friend as "the best damn cardiologist on the East Coast." After repeating all the cardiac tests previously done, he admits her to the hospital for an intracardiac catheterization and further testing. These all turn out to be within normal limits, yet Gretchen still has the pains in her chest which she has noticed seem to radiate down her left arm. The cardiologist tells her that there are many physical causes of just such pain and that he's going to test for each one. He begins testing for a cervicobrachial pain syndrome, a chest wall syndrome, a costochondral syndrome, a costoclavical syndrome, brachialgia statica paresthetica, a first rib syndrome, a hyperabduction syndrome, nocturnal acroparesthesia, myctalgia paresthetica, a scalenus anticus syndrome, a scapulocostal syndrome and even a tired arm syndrome. After several weeks of testing, he finally tells Gretchen her problem is postural myoneuralgia. He explains to Gretchen and her husband that he has seen many cases of this and that it is a frequently occurring condition, but often overlooked by busy cardiologists. He further explains that all her symptoms are entirely referable to this condition. His recommendation is that she take no medications at all for the pain, abstain from alcohol, and participate in regular sessions of aerobic exercises for her chest wall, arms, and shoulders. Gretchen joins an aerobic dance class that meets three times a week with thirty other women and after several months is completely pain-free. In fact, Gretchen feels better than she has for a long time. Her crying spells have ceased and she no longer worries excessively. She has begun to enjoy life and she's found many very nice people living in this new area who have a lot in common with her. Gretchen's marked improvement in all her symptoms seem to confirm that her cardiologist's "astute" diagnosis of postural myoneuraliga was unquestionably correct. We know that Gretchen's improvement is due to her subtle emotional involvement on a part-person basis within her aerobic dancing class. One could have seen the same improvement had Gretchen become involved in Alcoholics Anonymous or Narcotics Anonymous.

Let's turn the kaleidoscope to get an entirely different scenario that will illustrate this point. Suppose Gretchen goes to a family physician with her symptoms. He listens to her carefully and when she tells him that she's been drinking more than usual, he focuses upon this, asking her for details about her drinking. She finally admits that perhaps she's been drinking too much and too often. This doctor tells her that her basic problem is underlying alcoholism which he further tells her is a condition frequently unrecognized by other doctors who don't take the time to inquire about their patients' drinking habits. They don't know about alcoholism and how it seems to be genetically determined and to have a biochemical basis. Gretchen remembers that both of her grandfathers drank heavily. This doctor admits to her that he himself went through similar symptoms and that it wasn't until he recognized his basic problem and joined A.A. that his life became better. He tells her that he has been abstaining for years and now he enjoys life. He goes on to explain to Gretchen how a person can hide her alcoholism not only from herself but from others. He emphatically tells her that until she gets help in A.A. for this basic problem her life will continue to be chaotic, as his was. He explains how people who have an underlying and unrecognized alcohol problem frequently have marital problems and are often depressed. He convinces her that she has a basic or primary problem with alcoholism and that her marital problems and her depression are all secondary to this. The doctor tells her that he will call her husband about his diagnosis and his recommended treatment. George accepts the diagnosis and after considerable initial resistance to involve herself regularly (and George supports her resistance to look outside their exclusive relationship for help), Gretchen finds herself going to A.A. meetings two or three times a week. After several months of abstinence and regular attendance in A.A., Gretchen is feeling much better. And her marriage has greatly improved. She no longer feels depressed. With Gretchen's marked improvement in all her symptoms, that diagnosis of an underlying alcoholism seems confirmed as unquestionably correct—and that's a big deception.

Another slight turn of the kaleidoscope and we can get still another entirely different scenario. Gretchen might have been watching television one evening with George. Both might have become interested in a problem on social phobias. The feelings of these phobics seem to be similar to Gretchen's. The program shows how some people develop this problem because of a subtle genetic predisposition and how these people develop fears of involving themselves with others and develop a reluctance and finally an inability to go places. Gretchen knows how she has come to spend too much time alone at home and how she fears to meet people. A local psychologist's telephone number is given and Gretchen and her husband think that it may be worth it to give that number a call. So Gretchen calls the next morning. She may tell over the phone that she has worsening marital problems, deepening feelings of depression, an increasing tendency to drink, and definitely a fear of social situations. She and George are invited to see the psychologist, who runs a phobia clinic. He explains to both of them that her basic underlying problem is a hitherto unrecognized social phobia. He tells them it is not uncommon for people with an underlying social phobia to have marital problems, to have depression, and to drink excessively. He explains that he has treated many people with symptoms exactly like hers in his group therapy sessions for phobics and they have done well. Gretchen and George agree that she should join a group at the clinic. After considerable initial resistance, Gretchen attends the group two or three times a week. After several months Gretchen is feeling much better. Her marriage relationship has greatly improved. She no longer is depressed and she's even given up drinking. With Gretchen's marked improvement in all her symptoms, that "astute" diagnosis of an underlying social phobia seems confirmed as unquestionably correct—and that's a big deception.

Give the kaleidoscope still another little turn and an entirely different scenario might come into focus. This time Gretchen decides to go to a psychoanalyst. She can't talk to George because he doesn't understand, doesn't seem to care, and gets too easily angered when she brings up those marriage problems that he feels are mostly in her imagination. She yearns to talk to someone; her core feelings of inferiority, inadequacy, unacceptableness, and guilt, which she needs to hide, are intensified by increased added unconscious guilt and seem to demand confidentiality. She can't and doesn't want to confide in any would-be friend problems that she considers personal, things she feels should be kept secret. With added unconscious guilt lying to the self-felt side, she feels something is not right about herself and, with a distortion of her past, feels she's always had something wrong about her. After relating in detail to the psychoanalyst her problems in the marriage, her depression, her increased need to drink, her social phobia, and all her other symptoms, he asks about her past. He begins to draw from her a recognition that things haven't been right in her life for many years. In fact her basic problem seems to go right back to early childhood when she was sexually abused. He explains to her that until she can resolve those underlying problems of her childhood that are not now resolved, she will continue to have problems. He further explains that it is not uncommon for people with unresolved underlying childhood problems to have marriage difficulties, depression, drinking problems, and social phobias. It all makes good sense to Gretchen and she later tells George who agrees. Gretchen accepts the diagnosis of an unresolved emotional problem of childhood and after some considerable initial resistance to involve herself regularly, which again may be supported by her husband, finds herself going to her analyst two or three times a week. After several months Gretchen is feeling much better. Her marriage is greatly improved. She no longer feels depressed or in pain. She has felt no need to drink and she no longer has a social phobia. With Gretchen's marked improvement in all her symptoms, that "astute" diagnosis of an underlying unresolved emotional problem of childhood seems confirmed as unquestionably correct—and that's a big deception.

Now let's give the kaleidoscope another little turn so that still another scenario comes into focus. Suppose Gretchen's parents hear she's not herself, so they come to visit to see how they can help. They listen to her describe her depressed feelings, her symptoms of pain and fatigue, and her reluctance to leave the house. And that listening gives emotional support. Gretchen may, with swings of ambivalence that range from blaming herself to blaming her husband, begin to tell them about her feelings that she is tired of feeling that she's inadequate, that she's no good, that she's somehow unacceptable, that she's always to blame, and that anything that goes wrong is her fault. She doesn't put all the blame on her husband. If anything, she tells her parents that she blames herself. But her parents continually listen and her increased added unconscious guilt begins to lean to the projected side and to be rationalized as a marriage problem. She may then tell how she feels her husband is too busy for her and that in the list of his priorities, she's far from the top. She begins to show some resentment and may tell her parents how her husband always wants her, for instance, "perfectly groomed." "He wants me looking like a Miss America contestant and I resent it." After her parents leave, she may confront him, accusing him of "pushing my buttons" any time he feels like it, "giving me guilt trips," and "making me feel like a puppet on a string." She may tell him she's tired of being treated "as if I have AIDS." She may accuse him of not being happy unless "I'm bent over the kitchen sink doing dishes, or on my hands and knees scrubbing." In telephone calls to her parents, she may say, "He says it's not so, yet I know he still expects me always home getting the work done. If I didn't do it, I'd be getting little messages and snide remarks that I was being an inadequate wife. He's got a subtle way of putting me down. I don't think it's fair at all." And her parents don't either. They insist that she see a marriage counselor.

So Gretchen does see a marriage counselor. She tells the counselor she's been depressed, drinking more, too much alone at home, and feeling sick, tired, and unhappy. She tells the marriage counselor that she resents having to be "second to his business." Perhaps she tells him how her parents wanted her to go home with them and what happened when she told her husband. She tells her counselor, "I told him I was leaving and that I had had it with him and his subtle ways of always putting me down which he always denies. I take it for so long and then I get mad as I was last night when I wanted to talk things out. But he said I just wanted a fight, and I had imagined everything bad about the marriage. I don't know, maybe I have! But he won't fight! I need a good fight; yet he just walks away. What's wrong with him anyway? I've had to put up with a lot! I've had to move seven times in twenty-five years of marriage. I'm the one that's had to take care of all the problems in going from one area to another, and it wasn't easy with two small boys." At the close of this session in which Gretchen expresses her ambivalent feelings about the marriage, the counselor asks to see Gretchen's husband alone.

Two days later Gretchen's husband comes to see the marriage counselor. He tells the counselor how he's at a loss to explain what has happened in the marriage. He feels things are no different than they ever have been, but somehow a problem has arisen. Perhaps he tells the counselor, "I've always wanted to make her happy since I first met her because I love her very much. She always said that even though she had material things she was so unhappy before she met me. It gave me pleasure thinking that I could make her happy and give her what she never had. When the marriage first started, we both intensely loved each other. She gave me the feeling that I was everything to her, her very reason for living. But apparently I'm not making her happy any more. In fact, I seem to be making her unhappy for some unknown reason. It can't be my business; I'm actually working less lately than I used to. She seems to be blaming me for her unhappiness now, but she won't tell me any specific thing that I'm doing or not doing that she doesn't like; in fact, she doesn't seem even to know herself. She just complains that she's unhappy in the marriage. She acts as though she doesn't care about me at all. She's quit doing things for me that she used to. We haven't had sex for weeks. She says she doesn't know why she feels the way she does. I just don't know what went wrong in the marriage."

The marriage counselor explains in the next session, when he sees Gretchen and George together, how it is obvious to him that her basic problem is and has been an underlying unresolved marriage conflict. He goes on to explain that it's not uncommon at all for a person with an unrecognized underlying marriage problem to experience depression, phobias, guilt feelings, excesses of alcohol, an inability to accept oneself and one's past, and a host of other problems. He tells them both that most physicians don't take the time to inquire into the marriage relationship and that these more superficial problems often mask the underlying true problem of the marriage relationship. He recommends marriage counseling and after some considerable initial resistance to involve themselves regularly, both find themselves seeing the marriage counselor two or three times a week. After several months, the marriage relationship has greatly improved. Gretchen no longer seems to have periods of depression and no longer has a need to drink. She's no longer phobic or irritable and she seems able to accept herself and her past. And she's more involved with others. With Gretchen's marked improvement in all her symptoms, that "astute" diagnosis of a primary marriage problem is confirmed as unquestionably correct—and that's a big deception.

There's another very important possible scenario in which Gretchen might have found herself. Suppose a neighbor of a strong religious faith recognizes that Gretchen is new to the area and that she doesn't get out much. This neighbor is rather "pushy" and seems to force herself upon Gretchen, often not accepting Gretchen's attempts to avoid her. The neighbor is persistent and Gretchen tells her about her uncontrollable crying spells, her pains, her social phobias, her anxiety attacks, and her excessive worrying. Perhaps, she even tells the neighbor her concern that she's drinking a little too much and that the marriage has become unhappy. Gretchen may emphasize that she's not sure why the marriage seems unhappy and that she's not necessarily blaming her husband any more than she's blaming herself. The neighbor doesn't make an issue of the marriage as Gretchen's parents did, but detects that Gretchen is lonely and that she's more deeply unhappy. She tells Gretchen that she knows just what her basic problem is. She has seen this so many times before in people with these very same symptoms. She tells Gretchen that her problem is spiritual unfulfillment. She further explains to Gretchen that she doesn't need to see doctors, psychiatrists, psychologists, or coun-selors. She tells Gretchen to get involved in the church. She goes on to tell that she has never seen a single person who had a deep and strong faith in God ever feel the need to see a psychiatrist, a psychologist, or a marriage counselor. Gretchen does go with the neighbor to the church and eventually finds herself going two or three times a week, after some considerable initial resistance that is well supported by her husband. Gretchen discovers that she has a lot in common with the people in the church. After several months, Gretchen's depression is gone. Her mar-riage relationship is now a happy one. Her phobias and excessive wor-rying are things of the past. She isn't hypochondriacal any more and she's stopped drinking entirely. Gretchen's marked improvement seems like proof that the neighbor's "astute" diagnosis was unquestionably cor-rect—and that's a big deception.

Instead of a marriage problem, let's consider another possible scenario that can arise from the mid-line stance with a leaning toward the pro-jected side. Suppose Gretchen begins to feel that the neighbors next door don't accept her. She may feel that they shun her, are unfriendly, and even talk about her behind her back. As she experiences more of these perceptions that may be intensifying from increasing guilt, or be-coming "more noticeable" as she may put it, she in turn may react in such a way that *does* foster an alienation with her neighbors. Gretchen may tell George about these neighbors and although he'd rather not get into this because of his preoccupation with his business and his limited time at home, he does listen to her. This listening gives her emotional support, so she begins to lean even more toward the projected side. Gretchen may then become retaliatory and openly express her anger to the neighbors. A boundary dispute might develop and Gretchen, with George's support, may seek legal help, which results in a suit. Gretchen may have told her attorney how she felt victimized by these neighbors and how they have openly harassed her. That developing marriage prob-lem that Gretchen and George previously had now disappears. Both Gretchen and George have a "common enemy"—those certain neigh-bors. Both Gretchen and her husband now have something to talk about together. They listen to each other; they support each other in this guilt projection. The marriage relationship begins to go better than it has in a long time. But that's not all, if Gretchen might have previously been depressed, or alcoholic, or phobic, or hypochondriacal, or unaccepting or self-critical of herself in some way, or, more likely, a combination of all these and more in various degrees, she is now much less so, if so at all. She doesn't need any "professional treatment" and would probably respond with anger toward anyone who might think she did. She's feeling much better than she has in a long time; her marriage is going fine and she can't wait to get into court with her attorney and her husband to seek the justice she wants and feels she deserves.

There's a whole array of possible situations in Gretchen's reality that might develop with intensified mid-line feelings of the misperceived position leaning toward the projected side. If there had been any predominance of conditions or combinations of conditions on the self-felt side that might have led to diagnoses, treatment recommendations, and health professional involvements, they now disappear. Diagnoses and those involvements with health professionals, semi-professionals, charlatans, and quacks are no longer "needed." Where there might have been some involvement before, the shift to the projected side may encompass some projected guilt that angrily terminates those relationships. And Gretchen doesn't revert to being too dependent on too few, or being exclusively dependent on her husband. That high misperceived added unconscious guilt that pushed her toward the exclusivity or concentrated dependency and later toward a professional relationship has been lowered. She can now involve herself with others comfortably, which will tend to keep her free from any of the symptoms she previously experienced.

What should be most apparent by now is that Gretchen's increased and troublesome misperceived added unconscious guilt can first of all be categorized deceptively in a wide array of contrasting diagnoses. As a result of those diagnoses, it can be lowered in a great many different ways and combinations of ways. One isn't limited to that smorgasboard of mental health related therapies at all. That same amount of increased misperceived guilt that made Gretchen too dependent on too few, too emotionally immature, and too unable to talk her problems out with the friends and people of her relationship sphere, can be lowered in a variety of possibilities. Some of these may seem illogical, or may be outright quackery. An *effective* manifest content that can meet the oral dependency need and allow the support of projected guilt has less to do with scientific fact than to do with being simply *ongoing*.

We know that any manifest content whatsoever has the potential for decreasing the unmet oral dependency need and the added unconscious guilt. We know that certain manifest contents are more acceptable for certain individuals than others and some manifest contents may be quite unacceptable for some people. What might be an acceptable manifest content at one time for an individual might be at a later time unacceptable. Any ongoing manifest content between any two or more people, however, carries the more important latent transference language that is part-oriented and has the capacity for bringing about emotional

comfortableness. We have already seen that the resulting emotional comfortableness is simply because the unmet oral dependency need and
added unconscious guilt have been decreased. We know it's an *emotional*
process, but it may appear deceptively as though it's an intellectual process when, for instance, the person learns to control her temper, learns
to stand on his own two feet and not depend on others, learns to live
with pain, learns to cope with stress, learns to think better of herself or
others, learns to improve his marriage, or learns to be a better parent.
The whole process may involve a manifest content with an emphasis on
intellectual control that fosters the misconception, "you can eventually
master it *yourself* if you just learn."

If the manifest content is so relatively unimportant to that emotional
problem resolving latent content that isn't oriented to reality at all then
another big deception should be apparent. A manifest content may be
entirely devoid of facts and may be completely erroneous as far as reality
is concerned, but still may have for many people *more* of a potential to
"cure"—to change emotional uncomfortableness to comfortableness—
than a manifest content well oriented toward the facts of reality. A manifest content couched in errors in perception, misconceptions or mutually
shared delusions or hallucinations can work marvelously well, not for
just some people but for many, much of the time. We know for instance
that quackery can bring comfortableness to many people when nothing
medical or scientific can. It does so using essentially the same underlying
and hidden emotional "curing" process that is involved in all psychological therapies and involved as well in all spontaneous communication.
A group meeting three times a week to discuss the medical benefits of
hanging upside down to increase cerebral blood flow has the potential
to cure all forms and intensities of emotional uncomfortableness. The
group doesn't even have to have a health orientation to do that. A group
meeting three times a week to discuss UFOs or aliens from outer space,
or even to prove that the moon is made of green cheese has the capacity
to cure phobias, depression, pain, marriage problems, child abuse, etc.
It can lead a person to inner peace and tranquility. It can change a person
who is unable to enjoy life to one who's able to enjoy it. It's the meeting
three times a week that does it.

One can see the deception in diagnosis in psychology and psychiatry.
Many professionals in these fields have suspected it for years. They have
recognized that it is difficult to put a diagnosis on a patient when his
individual problems that create the emotional uncomfortableness seem
unique. They have to question what is primary when so many of the
different conditions that we have seen earlier are all pushing for a diagnosis. Diagnosticians may be caught up trying to decide if a person's

problem is primarily alcoholism, or primarily a marriage problem, or primarily a depression. In other words, one could be caught up in trying to decide whether the person is primarily an alcoholic, and his marriage problems and his depression are secondary to the alcoholism. It would seem logical that if the drinking were that bad, it could cause marriage problems and depression. One could be caught up in trying to decide that the person's primary problem is depression, and his alcoholism and marriage problems are understandably secondary to this depression. Or one could be caught up in trying to decide that this person's primary problem is with his marriage, and that the person's excessive drinking and his depression are secondary to the marital problem. There is no diagnosis in psychiatry for increased unmet oral dependency needs and increased added unconscious guilt in the misperceived position super-imposed upon a high personality core guilt and a reality situation where one is too dependent on too few. One might wish that there were, but there isn't. So many people are given a deceptive diagnosis and pigeon-holed into categories where they have to be stuffed, because the diagnosis doesn't quite fit the unique picture that the individual has. It becomes a deception that is sold to the patient, sold to his family, and sold to others in the medical profession, and often this bill of sale involves the biochemical explanations we've seen before.

We have come far enough in an understanding of the kaleidoscopic array that is possible in both the presentation and the treatment of in-creased unmet oral dependency need and added unconscious guilt that we shouldn't be surprised by recent psychiatric findings. Research psy-chiatrists have been surprised to learn that antidepressant medications seem to have an anti-anxiety effect and vice versa. Phobias seem to be helped by both antidepressant and anti-anxiety drugs. We aren't sur-prised, as many psychiatrists are, to learn that antidepressants can be effective in the treatment of panic disorders. We're not surprised by findings that many cases of chronic pain and hypochondriasis seem to lessen or cease with the treatment of family problems by marital coun-seling. But psychiatry has yet to acknowledge that there may be a com-monality underlying the panorama with which human emotional uncomfortableness presents itself and a commonality to the panorama with which that uncomfortableness is lowered.

Understanding the concept of added unconscious guilt makes decep-tion associated with emotional uncomfortableness and its treatment more easily discernible. We know that added unconscious guilt is a nebulous entity that is initially nonspecific as far as reality is concerned. We know it accrues in the present on a part person, part experience and part situation basis from repressed anger. Once it reaches uncomfortable proportions one's unconscious may present a reality-oriented explanation for this increased guilt and unmet oral need to one's self and others. If so, this explanation then is metaphorical for the true cause. Or one can accept the logical explanations of others that seem to make good sense particularly when those others are educated professionals. But their explanations may be metaphorical as well. The deception is now apparent when, for instance, a young man who had been sexually abused as a child but who is now depressed is referred to a psychiatric residential setting located half way across the country that specializes in sexual abuse cases. The patient and his family are told by the professional that the past sexual abuse *is* his problem and that because of this, he *requires* a specific psychiatric treatment in a *specialized* psychiatric hospital. Not only is this patient and his family duped but also the insurance company that will pay the costs.

There is a final deception that needs to be uncovered. If the reader believes the purpose of this book was to find an understanding in that chaotic array of different forms and intensities of emotional uncomfortableness and that even greater chaotic array of various means to resolve that uncomfortableness, then he or she has been deceived. If the reader believes that the purpose in writing this book might have been to make the basic motivations of all human behavior a little more recognizable, or to reveal those marvelous psychodynamics of unconscious guilt, or to show how psychotherapy works, or to present an eclectic theory, then he or she is also deceived. The real purpose of writing this book has been to make that case against reality: against that Aristotelian logic, against the intellect of man and his ability to reason and determine consciously his behavior, and against his ability to perceive the world. It has been a case therefore against medical research of a biochemical nature in regard to mental illnesses. It has been a case against the scientific. It also includes a case against that "independence" that so many other people are telling us we need in life to be contented or happy. My purpose has been to make a case for the emotional unreality—for the illogical, the unscientific, and the primary process thinking of schizophrenics and dreamers. But aside from all these purposes—and Freud did tell us that human behavior is multiply determined—the most basic purpose in my writing this book was to allow me a chance to do something other than to listen in my professional capacity. It has given me an opportunity to meet a few of my own oral needs. Most of all, it has allowed me to project, subtly or not so subtly, a *lot* of added unconscious guilt.

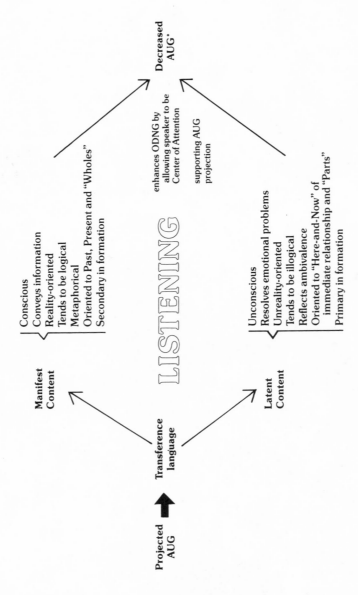

THE COMMUNICATIVE DIALYSIS OF AUG

Decreased
AUG*

Manifest
Content

Conscious
Conveys information
Reality-oriented
Tends to be logical
Metaphorical
Oriented to Past, Present and "Wholes"
Secondary in formation

LISTENING

enhances ODNG by
allowing speaker to be
Center of Attention

supporting AUG
projection

Latent
Content

Unconscious
Resolves emotional problems
Unreality-oriented
Tends to be illogical
Reflects ambivalence
Oriented to "Here-and-Now," of
immediate relationship and "Parts"
Primary in formation

Transference
language

Projected
AUG

*Lessening tendency to be
Too Dependent on Too Few
Expanding relationship sphere
Decreasing the Conditions

AUG   = Added Unconscious Guilt
ODNG = Oral Dependency Need Gratification